ARISTOPHANES AND ATHENS

Aristophanes and Athens

An Introduction to the Plays

Douglas M. MacDowell

OXFORD UNIVERSITY PRESS

Oxford University Press, Walton Street, Oxford OX2 6DP
Oxford New York
Athens Auckland Bangkok Bogota Bombay
Buenos Aires Calcutta Cape Town Dar es Salaam
Delhi Florence Hong Kong Istanbul Karachi
Kuala Lumpur Madras Madrid Melbourne
Mexico City Nairobi Paris Singapore
Taipei Tokyo Toronto
and associated companies in
Berlin Ibadan

Oxford is a trade mark of Oxford University Press

Published in the United States by
Oxford University Press Inc., New York

First published in hardback and paperback 1995
Reprinted in paperback 1996

British Library Cataloguing in Publication Data
Data available

Library of Congress Cataloging in Publication Data
Aristophanes and Athens: an introduction to the plays.
Douglas M. MacDowell.
Includes bibliographical references.
1. Aristophanes—Criticism and interpretation.   2. Greek drama
(Comedy)—History and criticism.   3. Aristophanes—Knowledge—
Greece—Athens.   4. Athens (Greece)—In literature.   I. Title.
PA3879.M23 1995 882'.01—dc20 95-3669
ISBN 0-19-872158-7 (Hbk)
ISBN 0-19-872159-5 (Pbk)

Printed in Great Britain
on acid-free paper by
Biddles Ltd., Guildford and King's Lynn

Preface

Aristophanes is the most versatile and iridescent of authors. It is hard to define his qualities at all, and quite impossible to discuss them all fully within one book of moderate length. This book is primarily an introduction for those reading him for the first time, and I concentrate mainly on the subjects of the plays in relation to the historical circumstances of Athens, because that seems to me a good way for a newcomer to approach them. I say relatively little about literary and theatrical features, although those are not entirely ignored.

Some problems about Aristophanes have aroused much scholarly controversy. I state my own views, of course, but I have tried to alert readers to the existence of alternatives, either in the text or in the footnotes. The footnotes refer, as a rule, to the more recent books and articles, in which references to earlier works can be found by anyone wanting a more exhaustive bibliography. They also give a few words in Greek, whereas the main text is written so as to be clear to readers who know only English.

I quote Aristophanes in my own translations, because I find no published translation satisfactory for my purpose. For a scholarly study, a translation must be fairly literal and accurate; but besides giving the right sense it should also convey something of the original form. In the case of Aristophanes that means it must be in verse, in rhythms which are comparable to the rhythms of the original. English verse has to be based on stress rather than quantity of syllables, and I have used the familiar English five-foot iambic line to represent the Greek trimeter, but in other respects my translations keep close to the original metres. In recent years publishers have been reluctant to publish verse translations, and consequently there are now thousands of people who think that Aristophanes' plays are in the form and language of everyday conversation. They are not; the man in the Athenian street did not speak in iambic trimeters, still less in the trochaic, anapaestic, and other forms which Aristophanes often uses. If my translations seem more formal than others now current, that does not, I believe, give a misleading impression of Aristophanes.

Douglas MacDowell

University of Glasgow
September 1994

Contents

Abbreviations and Bibliography		viii
Chronological Table of Plays		xii
1.	Intention and Interpretation	1
2.	The Audience and its Expectations	7
3.	Early Plays	27
4.	*Akharnians*	46
5.	*Horsemen*	80
6.	*Clouds*	113
7.	*Wasps*	150
8.	*Peace*	180
9.	*Birds*	199
10.	*Lysistrata*	229
11.	*Women at the Thesmophoria*	251
12.	*Frogs*	274
13.	*Women at the Assembly*	301
14.	*Wealth*	324
15.	Aristophanes and Athens	350
Index		357

Abbreviations and Bibliography

ABSA	*Annual of the British School at Athens*
AJP	*American Journal of Philology*
Ar.Femmes	*Aristophane: Les Femmes et la Cité = Les Cahiers de Fontenay* 17 (Fontenay aux Roses 1979)
Ar.Hardt	*Aristophane*, ed. J. M. Bremer and E. W. Handley = *Entretiens Hardt* 38 (Geneva 1993)
BICS	*Bulletin of the Institute of Classical Studies*
C&M	*Classica et Mediaevalia*
CA	*Classical Antiquity*
CP	*Classical Philology*
CQ	*Classical Quarterly*
CR	*Classical Review*
Crux	*Crux, essays presented to G. E. M. de Ste. Croix*, ed. P. A. Cartledge and F. D. Harvey = *History of Political Thought* 6 (1985) issue 1/2
F.Gr.Hist.	*Die Fragmente der griechischen Historiker*, ed. F. Jacoby
G&R	*Greece & Rome*
GRBS	*Greek, Roman and Byzantine Studies*
HCT	*A Historical Commentary on Thucydides* by A. W. Gomme, A. Andrewes, and K. J. Dover (Oxford 1945–81)
HSCP	*Harvard Studies in Classical Philology*
ICS	*Illinois Classical Studies*
IG	*Inscriptiones Graecae*
JHS	*Journal of Hellenic Studies*
MC	*Museum Criticum*
ML	*A Selection of Greek Historical Inscriptions*, ed. R. Meiggs and D. M. Lewis (Oxford 1969)
Nomos	*Nomos, essays in Athenian law, politics and society*, ed. P. Cartledge, P. Millett, and S. Todd (Cambridge 1990)
Noth.Dion.	*Nothing to do with Dionysos?*, ed. J. J. Winkler and F. I. Zeitlin (Princeton 1990)

P.Oxy.	Oxyrhynchus Papyri
Rh.Mus.	*Rheinisches Museum für Philologie*
TAPA	*Transactions of the American Philological Association*
Tr.Com.Pol.	*Tragedy, Comedy and the Polis*, ed. A. H. Sommerstein, S. Halliwell, J. Henderson, and B. Zimmermann (Bari 1993)
YCS	*Yale Classical Studies*
ZPE	*Zeitschrift für Papyrologie und Epigraphik*

The following list of modern books is not a complete bibliography, but gives details of some works for which I use abbreviated references. Details of other works, cited only once or twice, are given in the footnotes.

ALBINI, UMBERTO. *Interpretazioni teatrali* (Florence 1972–81).

BOWIE, A. M. *Aristophanes: Myth, Ritual and Comedy* (Cambridge 1993).

CARRIÈRE, J. C. *Le Carnaval et la politique* (Paris 1979).

CARTLEDGE, PAUL. *Aristophanes and his Theatre of the Absurd* (London 1990).

CASSIO, ALBIO C. *Commedia e partecipazione* (Naples 1985).

—— Edition of Aristophanes *Banchettanti* (Pisa 1977).

CROISET, MAURICE. *Aristophanes and the Political Parties at Athens* (trans. James Loeb, London 1909).

DAVID, E. *Aristophanes and Athenian Society of the early fourth century B. C.* (Leiden 1984).

DEARDEN, C. W. *The Stage of Aristophanes* (London 1976).

DOVER, K. J. *Aristophanic Comedy* (London 1972).

—— *Greek and the Greeks* (Oxford 1987).

—— *Greek Popular Morality* (Oxford 1974).

—— Editions of Aristophanes *Clouds* (Oxford 1968), *Frogs* (1993).

EHRENBERG, VICTOR. *The People of Aristophanes* (Oxford, 2nd edn. 1951).

FISHER, RAYMOND K. *Aristophanes' Clouds: purpose and technique* (Amsterdam 1984).

HARRIOTT, ROSEMARY M. *Aristophanes, poet and dramatist* (London 1986).

HEATH, MALCOLM. *Political Comedy in Aristophanes* (Göttingen 1987).

HENDERSON, JEFFREY. *The Maculate Muse* (New Haven 1975; repr. with addenda, New York 1991).

HENDERSON, JEFFREY. Edition of Aristophanes *Lysistrata* (Oxford 1987).

HOFMANN, HEINZ. *Mythos und Komödie* (Hildesheim 1976).

HUBBARD, THOMAS K. *The Mask of Comedy* (Ithaca, NY, 1991).

HUGILL, WILLIAM M. *Panhellenism in Aristophanes* (Chicago 1936).

KASSEL, R., and AUSTIN, C. *Poetae Comici Graeci* (Berlin 1983–   ).

KRAUS, WALTHER. *Aristophanes' politische Komödien* (Österreichische Akad. der Wiss., Phil.-hist. Klasse, Sitzungsberichte 453, 1985).

LIND, HERMANN. *Der Gerber Kleon in den 'Rittern' des Aristophanes* (Frankfurt 1990).

MACDOWELL, DOUGLAS M. *The Law in Classical Athens* (London 1978).

—— Edition of Aristophanes *Wasps* (Oxford 1971).

—— Edition of Demosthenes *Against Meidias* (Oxford 1990).

MCLEISH, KENNETH. *The Theatre of Aristophanes* (London 1980).

MARIANETTI, MARIE C. *Religion and Politics in Aristophanes' Clouds* (Hildesheim 1992).

MASTROMARCO, GIUSEPPE. *Storia di una commedia di Atene* (Florence 1974).

MOULTON, CARROLL. *Aristophanic Poetry* (Göttingen 1981).

MURRAY, GILBERT. *Aristophanes: A Study* (Oxford 1933).

NEWIGER, HANS-JOACHIM. *Metapher und Allegorie* (Munich 1957).

O'REGAN, DAPHNE E. *Rhetoric, Comedy, and the Violence of Language in Aristophanes' Clouds* (New York 1992).

OSTWALD, MARTIN. *From Popular Sovereignty to the Sovereignty of Law* (Berkeley 1986).

PADUANO, GUIDO. *Il giudice giudicato* (Bologna 1974).

PERUSINO, FRANCA. *Dalla commedia antica alla commedia di mezzo* (Urbino 1987).

PICKARD-CAMBRIDGE, ARTHUR W. *Dithyramb, Tragedy and Comedy* (2nd edn. rev. T. B. L. Webster, Oxford 1962).

—— *The Dramatic Festivals of Athens* (2nd edn. rev. John Gould and D. M. Lewis, Oxford 1968, repr. with addenda 1988).

PLATNAUER, MAURICE. Edition of Aristophanes *Peace* (Oxford 1964).

RAU, PETER. *Paratragodia* (Munich 1967).

RECKFORD, KENNETH J. *Aristophanes' Old-and-New Comedy 1: Six Essays in Perspective* (Chapel Hill 1987).

RENNIE, W. Edition of Aristophanes *Acharnians* (London 1909).

ROGERS, BENJAMIN B. Editions of Aristophanes *Acharnians* (London 1910), *Knights* (1910), *Clouds* (2nd edn. 1916), *Wasps* (2nd edn. 1915), *Peace* (2nd edn. 1913), *Birds* (1906), *Lysistrata* (1911), *Thesmophoriazusae* (1904), *Frogs* (2nd edn. 1919), *Ecclesiazusae* (1902), *Plutus* (1907).

ROTHWELL, KENNETH S. *Politics and Persuasion in Aristophanes' Ecclesiazusae* (Leiden 1990).

RUSSO, CARLO FERDINANDO. *Aristophanes, an Author for the Stage* (London 1994).

STE. CROIX, G. E. M. DE. *The Origins of the Peloponnesian War* (London 1972).

SIFAKIS, G. M. *Parabasis and Animal Choruses* (London 1971).

SOMMERSTEIN, ALAN H. Editions of Aristophanes *Acharnians* (Warminster 1980), *Knights* (1981), *Clouds* (1982), *Wasps* (1983), *Peace* (1985), *Birds* (1987), *Lysistrata* (1990), *Thesmophoriazusae* (1994).

STANFORD, W. B. Edition of Aristophanes *Frogs* (2nd edn., London 1963).

STARKIE, W. J. M. Edition of Aristophanes *Acharnians* (London 1909).

STONE, LAURA M. *Costume in Aristophanic Poetry* (Salem 1984).

TAAFFE, LAUREN K. *Aristophanes and Women* (London 1993).

TAILLARDAT, JEAN. *Les Images d'Aristophane* (2nd edn., Paris 1965).

THIERCY, PASCAL. *Aristophane: fiction et dramaturgie* (Paris 1986).

USSHER, R. G. Edition of Aristophanes *Ecclesiazusae* (Oxford 1973).

VETTA, MASSIMO. Edition of Aristophanes *Le Donne all'assemblea* (Milan 1989).

WHITMAN, CEDRIC H. *Aristophanes and the Comic Hero* (Cambridge, Mass. 1964).

WILAMOWITZ-MOELLENDORFF, ULRICH VON. Edition of Aristophanes *Lysistrate* (Berlin 1927).

ZANETTO, GIUSEPPE. Edition of Aristophanes *Gli Uccelli* (Milan 1987).

ZANNINI QUIRINI, BRUNO. *Nephelokokkygia: la prospettiva mitica degli Uccelli di Aristofane* (Rome 1987).

ZIMMERMANN, BERNHARD. *Untersuchungen zur Form und dramatischen Technik der Aristophanischen Komödien* (Königstein and Frankfurt, 1984–7).

Chronological Table of Plays

Extant plays are in capital letters.

Banqueters	427
Babylonians	426 Dionysia
AKHARNIANS	425 Lenaia
HORSEMEN	424 Lenaia
Farmers	424 Dionysia ?
Merchant-ships	423 Lenaia ?
Clouds 1	423 Dionysia
Proagon	422 Lenaia
WASPS	422 Lenaia
PEACE	421 Dionysia
CLOUDS 2	not performed
Amphiaraos	414 Lenaia
BIRDS	414 Dionysia
LYSISTRATA	411 Lenaia
WOMEN AT THE THESMOPHORIA 1	411 Dionysia
Wealth 1	408
Gerytades	407 ?
FROGS	405 Lenaia
WOMEN AT THE ASSEMBLY	391 ?
WEALTH 2	388
Kokalos	387 Dionysia
Aiolosikon 2	386 ?

The following plays are undated.

Aiolosikon 1	*Old Age*
Anagyros	*Peace* 2
Broilers	*Phoenician Women*
Daidalos	*Poetry*
Danaids	*Polyidos*
Dionysos Shipwrecked	*Seasons*
Dramas 1, or *Centaur*	*Storks*
Dramas 2, or *Niobos*	*Telemessians*
Heroes	*Triphales*
Islands	*Women at the Thesmophoria* 2
Lemnian Women	*Women Encamping*

I

Intention and Interpretation

Is it possible for us to understand an ancient comedy? The obstacles are formidable. This is not just because our copies are derived from manuscripts containing scribal errors, written in an ancient language which we know imperfectly; those are difficulties in any classical Greek text, but modern scholarship has done much to correct the errors of transmission and to improve our knowledge of the language. But a play was more than a text.

Aristophanes' primary intention was not to write a book for readers in later generations, but to provide a performance in the Athenian theatre on a particular day. The words which we now read were only one element of that performance. At least four other elements were of major importance. First, there was the speaking of the words, the tone of voice. Any actor, even an amateur, knows that the effect of a line can be drastically altered by the manner in which it is uttered: it may be made serious or comic or ironic. Second, there was the stage action. By 'business' an actor may clarify and emphasize the sense of the words, or he may divert attention from them; some action may proceed in mime with no words at all. Whereas modern plays have stage directions to help readers to imagine the action, ancient plays lack that aid. Third, there was the theatrical equipment, including costumes and scenery. Scenery may not have amounted to much in Aristophanes' time, but he certainly used comic costumes and disguises, and exploited for comic purposes certain stage equipment, notably the *ekkyklema* and the *mekhane*. Fourth, there was the music, especially the singing and dancing of the chorus. No one nowadays would think he knew all about *The Mikado* or *The Phantom of the Opera* if he had never seen a performance or heard any of the music. Can we then claim to understand *Wasps* or *Frogs*?

Even if we could be transported by some time-machine to the fifth century BC to attend a performance in the theatre of Dionysos, we should still be in difficulty, because we could not become ancient Athenians. Athenians were not just like us. They had a different way of life and different beliefs, and we should not take it for granted that they would be interested or amused or convinced by the same things as ourselves. Furthermore, they came to the theatre expecting a particular kind of performance on a particular occasion. Any modern reader can easily see that Aristophanes' plays are extremely topical; we miss many points, comic or serious, because of our ignorance of the circumstances of the time. We cannot fully appreciate the likes and dislikes, the pleasures and worries, of Aristophanes and his spectators.

Is it therefore pointless to try? Some modern critics have thought so. Taking the view that it is impossible to discover the intentions of an ancient writer and the reactions of his original audience, they consider their function to be simply to express their own reactions to the text. But this is an arid activity. Who wants to know the effect of a text on an individual modern critic? No doubt my personal reactions are interesting to myself, but your reactions may well be different, and there is no good reason for me to write, or for you to read, a book about my personal tastes. What you are interested in, if you have picked up this book, is not me, but Aristophanes. We want to know about him because he was a comic genius with an exceptional mind.

Although we can never get completely inside his mind or see every aspect of it, we can in fact see a good deal. It is not the case that we can discover nothing about his intentions. All the difficulties which I listed at the beginning of this chapter can be alleviated to some extent. For many lines in the plays it is reasonably clear what tone of voice is appropriate (the rich variety of Greek particles often helps), what stage action accompanies them, and what costumes or stage equipment are being used. The general character of the music is sometimes perceptible from the metre of the words, although we lack the tunes. Many lines or longer passages are so obviously meant to be funny that we can safely make inferences from them about the Athenian sense of humour (which actually turns out to differ less from ours than might have been expected). And we do have a fair amount of information about the political and social history of the time, enabling us to understand a substantial proportion of the topical references in the plays. So we can form an idea of what Aristophanes is getting at, at least for most of the time. We shall never understand his mind entirely, but that is no reason for not carrying our investigation as far forward as we can.

The main purpose of this book, then, is a historical one: to ascertain some of Aristophanes' purposes and intentions in writing his plays. Now, a dramatist may want his plays to appeal to the general public, or to a more limited and intellectual audience; or he may write only for a few readers or just for his own personal satisfaction, not expecting his work to be performed at all. We can safely put Aristophanes in the first category. We know that his plays were performed in competitions before a large audience, and that several of them won the first prize. One of his aims must have been to entertain and impress spectators who were not especially intelligent or learned. (The nature of the Athenian audience will be considered further in Chapter 2.) That does not preclude the possibility that he sometimes slipped in one or two jokes which would have been appreciated only by a few *cognoscenti*; and occasionally he may have overestimated the audience's intellectual interests and capacity (notably in *Clouds*; see Chapter 6). But normally his plays must have been clear and entertaining to ordinary Athenians at first sight and hearing (and that encourages us to reject some over-subtle interpretations which modern scholars have put forward from time to time).

That was presumably true also of Aristophanes' rivals, whose comedies are now lost: Kratinos, Eupolis, Pherekrates, Phrynikhos, and the rest. But we have good reason to think that Aristophanes was also trying to do something more. He was not merely hoping that the spectators would laugh more loudly at his comedies than at the others; he was attempting to do new things.[1]

Always I do something clever, bringing in some new ideas.

(*Clouds* 547)

Poets who do something new should be cherished, he claims (*Wasps* 1051–9). Some of his innovations are merely matters of dramatic technique, such as making the chorus dance its exit at the

---

[1] Cf. A. H. Sommerstein in *Antike Dramentheorien und ihre Rezeption* (= *Drama* 1, ed. B. Zimmermann, 1992) 14–33. He shows that there is some evidence from the fragments that other comic dramatists also claimed originality in various features of dramatic technique and skill, but not, like Aristophanes, in the giving of good advice to Athens.

end of the play (*Wasps* 1536–7). But there are several passages in which the chorus or a character says that the poet gives good advice or instruction to the audience. Here are some of the most explicit.

DIKAIOPOLIS. Do not resent it, men of the audience,
  If I, a beggar, speak to Athenians
  Concerning Athens in a comedy.
  For even comedy knows what is right,
  And what I'll say, though startling, will be right.

(*Akharnians* 497–501)[2]

The poet declares he deserves to receive rewards for the good that he's done you.

(*Akharnians* 633)

He says that he'll teach you a lot of good things, and so make you thoroughly happy.

(*Akharnians* 656)

        But in this case the poet deserves it,
Because he detests just the same men as we do, and ventures to say what is rightful.

(*Horsemen* 509–10)

But we've a little story with a point.

(*Wasps* 64)

And next, O ye people, pay heed to our words, if you're willing to hear some plain speaking;
For the time has arrived when the poet desires to find fault, and to blame the spectators.
He declares that they've injured him, quite unprovoked, in spite of the good that he's done them.

(*Wasps* 1015–17)

We, the sacred chorus, have a duty to the citizens:
We should offer good advice and teaching.

(*Frogs* 686–7)

Even now, you silly men, it's not too late to change your ways.

(*Frogs* 734)

---

[2] This passage, including the element of parody in it, is discussed in Ch. 4.

AESCHYLUS. First answer this question: what quality found in a poet deserves admiration?

EURIPIDES. He deserves it for skill, and for giving advice, and also because we make people

Become better in all of the cities.

(*Frogs* 1008–10)[3]

There are also other lines which, though less clearly, seem to imply a serious intent to advise the Athenians and tell them what they ought to do. But they do not occur in every play; and even where they do occur it has been argued, most strongly by Heath, that such passages are only ironic. According to Heath they display 'mock-seriousness', 'amiable banter', or 'an elaborate joke': Aristophanes, speaking through the mouth of a chorus or a character, puts on a comically solemn air, and the more he protests his seriousness, the more loudly the audience laughs.[4] Certainly it is possible for a comedian to use humour of this type, and we cannot rule out *a priori* that Aristophanes does so from time to time; but a joke used in one place is not necessarily used in another place, and we therefore have to interpret each passage individually. It is over-simple to assume that, if a play is a comedy, everything in it must be a joke. In fact even Heath allows that there is one exception, *Frogs* 686–7, in which the chorus states as a general principle that it is right for the chorus to give good advice and teaching to the city. But by admitting this exception Heath undermines his whole argument; for if we take this particular statement seriously, it means that comic choruses give good advice regularly, not in this play alone.

So, as we read the plays, it is reasonable to expect that we shall find, at least occasionally, a scene or passage in which Aristophanes

---

[3] This passage occurs in a discussion of tragedy, not of comedy; but since the poets whom Aeschylus proceeds to take as examples (Orpheus, Mousaios, Hesiod, Homer) are not authors of tragedies but of poetry of other kinds, it is likely that his question and Euripides' answer are meant to apply to all poetry, including comedy.

[4] Heath *Political Comedy* 16–21. There have been many discussions of this topic. Note especially A. W. Gomme's article 'Aristophanes and politics', *CR* 52 (1938) 97–109, reprinted in his *More Essays in Greek History and Literature* (Oxford 1962) 70–91; he stresses that Aristophanes is an artist, not a politician, but concedes that some passages in the plays have serious political intentions. For short surveys of recent views see Cartledge *Ar. and his Theatre of the Absurd*, J. M. Bremer in *Ar. Hardt* 127–34. Discussions of this aspect of particular plays are mentioned in the footnotes to the appropriate chapter.

is not just trying to make the Athenians laugh but is making some serious point which is intended to influence them. This may well be one of the things which he claims to be new in comedy (though, since we have no comedies by his predecessors, we cannot be quite sure that they never gave serious advice). But we need not expect to find this feature in every play. Some modern discussions of Aristophanes suffer from a desire to fit all his plays into a single pattern: his comic aim or method, or his political or intellectual attitude, is assumed to have been always the same. Really there is no special reason why he should have held the same views throughout a dramatic career of about forty years, or have written the same kind of play again and again.

In this book, therefore, there is not much generalization. My purpose is to take each play individually and to ascertain, as far as is practicable, what Aristophanes is getting at and what influence or effect he wishes that particular play to have on his Athenian audience. I must begin by considering what sort of an audience it was, and what sort of performance it expected.

2

The Audience and its Expectations

THE DRAMATIC FESTIVALS

For the Athenians, a play was a special occasion. Now we are accustomed to seeing plays at any time, but in the fifth century BC plays were performed within the town[1] of Athens at only two periods of the year. Both were festivals of Dionysos: the town Dionysia, which took six days in the month Elaphebolion (which roughly corresponded to our month of March), and the Lenaia, lasting four days in Gamelion (approximately January).[2] These festivals were celebrations in honour of the god, and they included religious ceremonies, processions, and choral performances as well as plays. There were plays also at local festivals (the rural Dionysia), for example at Peiraieus and Eleusis, but little is known about those. It is possible that new plays were always performed first in the town, and the rural Dionysia saw only revivals.[3]

In the time of Aristophanes the plays for the town Dionysia were certainly performed in the theatre of Dionysos beside the Akropolis, but it has been questioned whether the Lenaia plays were performed there too. In earlier times that festival had been celebrated at a precinct called the Lenaion, of which the location is uncertain.[4] Most scholars assume that, once the theatre of Dionysos was established, it was used for the Lenaia plays also; but Russo, adapting an earlier

---

[1] Throughout this book I use 'town' to mean the urban area (ἄστυ), 'city' to mean the political entity of the city-state (πόλις).

[2] For details of the festivals see Pickard-Cambridge *Festivals*.

[3] Aelian *Varia Historia* 2.13 suggests that some new tragedies by Euripides were performed at Peiraieus, but the wording is not quite explicit, and anyway this is not contemporary evidence.

[4] Cf. R. E. Wycherley *Hesperia* 34 (1965) 72–6, Pickard-Cambridge *Festivals* 37–9.

theory of Anti, has maintained that this transfer did not take place until later, so that Aristophanes' Lenaia plays were performed not in the theatre of Dionysos but in the different and less elaborate surroundings of the Lenaion.[5] Russo's general arguments from the texts of the plays are inconclusive,[6] but he has one stronger argument to which his critics have given too little weight: in Aristophanes and other texts of the fifth and fourth centuries referring to the dramatic contests at the Lenaia festival the phrase 'at the Lenaion' is regularly found.[7] The Lenaion has been identified with the precinct of 'Dionysos in the marshes' by Slater, who argues that that was the place where plays were performed at the Lenaia festival.[8] Yet it seems unlikely that an open space or makeshift theatre would have continued to be used when the theatre of Dionysos was available, and it is probably better to accept that the theatre of Dionysos was used but the phrase 'at the Lenaion' had become conventional and so continued in use even when no longer true literally.

The plays were performed in competitions, in which there seems to have been keen rivalry for the honour of winning. At both the town Dionysia and the Lenaia the number of comedies was normally five, but a widely-held modern view is that the number was temporarily reduced to three during the Peloponnesian War, to save time and expense by making each festival one day shorter.[9] Since most of Aristophanes' plays were written during those years, that would mean that we should think of him as having two competitors rather than four on each occasion. But the theory is not firmly based. The only evidence for it is the fact that the *hypotheses* (ancient introductions, written probably in the Hellenistic period) to several of his plays specify only the plays which came first, second, and third in the contest. A *hypothesis* of *Peace* is an example.

[5] C. F. Russo *Aristofane, autore di teatro* (Florence 1962) 1–21, with addenda on pp. 403–4 of the reprint (1984). (This chapter is not included in the English version of Russo's book.)

[6] Cf. Pickard-Cambridge *Festivals* 39–40, Dearden *Stage* 5–8.

[7] ἐπὶ Ληναίῳ: *Akharnians* 504, Plato *Protagoras* 327d, Demosthenes 21.10, IG 2² 1496.74, 1496.105.

[8] N. W. Slater *ZPE* 66 (1986) 255–64.

[9] A. Körte *Rh.Mus.* 60 (1905) 427–8, followed by many other scholars without discussion.

The poet was victorious with the play in the arkhonship of Alkaios, in town. Eupolis was first with *Flatterers*, Aristophanes second with *Peace*, and Leukon third with *Clansmen*.

(*Peace hyp.* iii)

But this may equally well be interpreted as meaning that only the first three competitors were awarded prizes or had their names inscribed in the records, an interpretation that may be supported by the way in which, in this particular case, Aristophanes is said to have been victorious (that is, won an award) with the play which came only second.[10] On the other hand, there is evidence that the comic dramatist Platon came fourth in a comic contest around this time,[11] and it has been argued by Luppe that the total number of comedies known to have been performed during the Peloponnesian War is too large to have been fitted into the programme if only three were put on at each festival.[12] The evidence on both sides of this argument is tenuous, but on balance it is preferable to accept that there were always five comedies at each of the two festivals.

If more than five poets, then, wanted to present comedies at the same festival, a choice among them had to be made by the magistrate in charge (the Arkhon for the town Dionysia, the Basileus for the Lenaia). Some time beforehand each poet would 'ask for a chorus',[13] and the magistrate would select five. The criteria of selection are not known; perhaps none were laid down and each magistrate chose in any way he liked. He is unlikely to have read complete scripts; he may have been guided by the previous successes and reputations of the various authors. The town Dionysia were regarded as more important than the Lenaia, and may have been more difficult to get into. The same papyrus fragment which tells us that Platon came fourth on one occasion goes on to say that in consequence he had to go back to the Lenaia; this may mean that the Arkhon would not accept the next play that he offered for the Dionysia.[14]

The two festivals also differed in the order of the plays. At the

[10] A similar phrase is used about Kratinos in *Horsemen hyp.* i.

[11] P. Oxy. 2737 col. ii lines 10–17.

[12] W. Luppe *Philologus* 116 (1972) 53–75. Some objections made by G. Mastromarco *Belfagor* 30 (1975) 469–73 and N. W. Slater *ZPE* 74 (1988) 43–57 are answered by Luppe *ZPE* 46 (1982) 157–9, 77 (1989) 18–20.

[13] *Horsemen* 513. On the distinction between asking on his own account and 'through' someone else, see pp. 34–6.

[14] P. Oxy. 2737 col. ii lines 10–17; cf. R. M. Rosen *ZPE* 76 (1989) 223–8.

Dionysia there were more tragedies (three tragedians each presented three tragedies, with a satyr-play) and they formed the climax of the festival, whereas at the Lenaia there were fewer tragedies (two tragedians each presented two) and they were preliminary to the five comedies. The different sequences of events are given by a law regulating conduct at festivals, passed probably in the first half of the fourth century.[15]

When the procession takes place for Dionysos in Peiraieus and the comedies and the tragedies, and the procession at the Lenaion and the tragedies and the comedies, and at the Dionysia in town the procession and the boys and the revel[16] and the comedies and the tragedies, and at the procession and the contest of the Thargelia . . .

(Law of Euegoros, quoted by Demosthenes 21.10)

This law apparently observes chronological order, both of festivals within the year (Dionysia at Peiraieus, Lenaia, Dionysia in town, Thargelia) and of events within each festival, and it shows that the tragedies came last at the town Dionysia (and at the Dionysia at Peiraieus) but the comedies came last at the Lenaia. But one passage of Aristophanes has been thought to provide contrary evidence. The chorus of Birds is telling the audience that wings are a great asset.

Nothing can be better, nothing pleasanter than growing wings!
If, for instance, one of you spectators were equipped with wings
And you then felt pangs of hunger at the tragic choruses,
You'd just fly away, go home and have some lunch, and afterwards,
When you'd had your fill of eating, you'd fly back to us again.

(Birds 785–9)

Birds is a Dionysia play, and the passage has been interpreted as meaning that a spectator who was bored with the tragedies might leave the theatre and return in time for a comedy, which would mean that a comedy followed some tragedies on the same day of the Dionysia.[17] But that is not necessarily right: 'to us' merely means 'to the theatre', and 'again' may mean that the winged spectator

[15] For the date see MacDowell *Meidias* 230.
[16] 'The boys and the revel' seems to cover the choral performances by boys and by men, but the exact interpretation of the phrase is doubtful. For various possibilities see MacDowell *Meidias* 232–3.
[17] e.g. Pickard-Cambridge *Festivals* 64–5.

will return to the same performances as he left, the tragedies, which he will leave not because he is bored with them but because he is hungry. So no evidence contradicts the implication of the law of Euegoros that the tragedies followed the comedies at the Dionysia; and, if it is right to regard the final event as being the culmination and most important part of the festival, it is worth noticing that this position was occupied by the tragedies at the Dionysia, but by the comedies at the Lenaia.

THE JUDGES

The method of appointing judges for the contests at the town Dionysia is fairly well attested; the method at the Lenaia, in the absence of evidence to the contrary, can be presumed to have been the same. They were picked by lot out of a larger number of citizens previously selected by the Council. Before each contest began, the Arkhon drew one name from each of ten urns, each containing the names of the candidates previously selected from one of the ten tribes. The names were called out, and the ten men came forward from wherever they were sitting in the audience. Before taking the seats at the front reserved for them, they swore an oath to vote for the best performers.[18] So an Aristophanic chorus can jocularly tell the judges, near the end of a play which happened (by the drawing of lots) to be the first one performed in its contest, not to break their oath.[19]

I'll give the judges first a little hint.
If you're clever, bear in mind the clever bits, and vote for me!
If you're glad to laugh, remember how you laughed, and vote for me!
Nearly all of you in fact, it's obvious, should vote for me!
Though I got the first position when the lottery was drawn,
Don't you let that count against me, but remember all you've heard.
Don't infringe your oath, but always judge the choruses aright.
Don't be like the girls who are no better than they ought to be,
Who can't think back any further than the latest thing they had!

(*Women at the Assembly* 1154–62)

---

[18] Isokrates 17.33–4, Demosthenes 21.17, 21.65, Plutarch *Kimon* 8.8; cf. Pickard-Cambridge *Festivals* 95–7, MacDowell *Meidias* 241.
[19] Much the same joke had been made in a comedy by Pherekrates (fr. 102).

At the end of the performances each judge wrote his verdict on a tablet, but it seems that not all ten votes were counted; perhaps five were picked out by lot and decided the contest, or perhaps counting stopped as soon as five votes for the same competitor had been announced.[20]

It would be of interest to know whether the judges were in effect a random choice of ordinary citizens, or whether the method of selection tended to produce judges of a particular class or type. One text seems to mean that a chorus-producer got the Council to include a friend of his in the preliminary selection;[21] that may have been possible because he happened to be a member of the Council himself that year, and it was not necessarily a normal occurrence. The passage of *Women at the Assembly* just quoted ('If you're clever . . .') may imply that men of all sorts are among the judges. Perhaps the best guess is that the Council would exclude from the preliminary selection anyone who was obviously incompetent to judge, or who was not expected to attend the festival, but did not otherwise restrict its choice to any particular type of citizen. At any rate there seems to be no evidence that the judges' verdict was likely to differ from the opinion of the audience in general, and Aristophanes himself implies that it did not. After the disappointing failure of his *Clouds* at the Dionysia in 423, he makes his chorus blame the audience for its defeat: 'you betrayed him' *Wasps* (1044), 'I blame you' (*Clouds* 525, in the revised version). He regards the audience as responsible for the verdict. That means either that the judges could be assumed to be representative of the audience as a whole, or that the judges normally cast their votes in accordance with the applause or boos of the audience,[22] or (most likely) both. We may conclude that, for Aristophanes, winning the favour of the judges did not require any different strategy from winning the favour of the audience.

---

[20] The fragmentary P.Oxy. 1611.30–7 seems to give several possible numbers. Five is the number in schol. *Birds* 445, Hesykhios πέντε κριταί (and Zenobios 3.64, but that probably refers to Sicily, not Athens). Cf. G. Arrighetti *Dioniso* 45 (1971–4) 302–8, M. Pope *CQ* 36 (1986) 322–6.

[21] Lysias 4.4.

[22] When Plato says that the true judge ought not to be influenced by the noise of the many (*Laws* 659a), that may imply that in practice most judges were so influenced.

THE COMPOSITION OF THE AUDIENCE

The audience for Aristophanes' plays must usually have numbered several thousand, but it is not possible to give any precise figure. Aristophanes calls it 10,000 (*Frogs* 677) and Plato 30,000 (*Symposium* 175e), but those are just round numbers; the latter at least must surely be an exaggeration. Even if we knew the number of seats in the theatre, that would not answer the question, because the theatre may not have been full for every play. Since a play was normally performed only once, we can presume that the number wishing to attend was not normally too large for them all to be able to get into the theatre at the same time. So it is obvious that the plays were not attended by the whole population of Attica. What kinds of person are more likely to have been present? There are several factors which may have restricted the audience.

1. *Place of residence*. Those who lived in or near the town could get to the theatre easily. But the remotest parts of Attica are up to thirty miles from Athens. Many country people must have found it inconvenient to walk to Athens and stay there for the period of the festival.[23] They may have had opportunities to see some of the same plays later at their local Dionysia, but at the performances in the town it is likely that town-dwellers outnumbered country-dwellers. However, this balance may have been altered in the early years of the Peloponnesian War, when many country-dwellers took refuge in the town (see p. 46).

2. *Cost*. In the fourth century there was certainly a charge for admission; Demosthenes (18.28) mentions some seats which cost two obols, but does not say whether all seats were the same price. A commentator on Demosthenes, who must have been writing some centuries later and gives no authority for his statements, offers information about theoric payments, grants from public funds to enable poor citizens to attend the festivals. He says that each citizen received two obols, one for his own maintenance and one to pay to the contractor who provided the seating, and he adds later that Perikles originated theoric payments; Plutarch also states that Per-

---

[23] Cf. Isokrates 7.52: 'many of the citizens did not come into town even for the festivals, but preferred enjoyment of their own possessions to the public entertainments.'

ikles introduced them.[24] Even if we accept this late information, the
details remain uncertain: perhaps the better seats cost two obols
and the worse one obol; or perhaps all seats cost one obol in the
fifth century but the price was increased to two obols in the fourth;
and it is not clear whether the amounts mentioned are for a whole
festival or for each day. But anyway it does seem clear that attendance
at the plays involved some expense, which poor citizens may have
preferred to avoid. Presumably a man could save money by claiming
the grant and then staying away from the theatre.

3. *Status and age.* Theoric grants were given only to citizens.
Metics (non-citizens resident in Athens) must have paid for themselves, and so probably attended in smaller numbers than citizens.
Slaves would have been unable to attend unless their masters paid
for them. Likewise boys would have to be paid for by their fathers,
if theoric payments were made only to citizens on the deme-regis-
ters.[25] References in Aristophanes show that some boys did attend
his plays.[26] In the fourth century Theophrastos mentions a man
taking his sons to the theatre with their *paidagogos*, who was presumably a slave.[27] But it is likely that adult citizens predominated in
the audience.

4. *Sex.* Whether women attended the plays is a disputed question.[28] Probably a distinction ought to be drawn between tragedies
and comedies. In Aristophanes one female character refers specifically to seeing plays of Euripides, and other evidence also implies
that women attended the performances of tragedies.[29] For comedies, however, the evidence is less clear. Two Aristophanic passages
which have sometimes been thought to prove the presence of women
do not in fact do so: in *Peace* 966 the reason why women do not get
any of the barley-corns thrown out into the audience is not necessarily that they are sitting far back in the theatre, but may be simply
that they are at home; and *Lysistrata* 1050 does not mean that women

[24] Schol. Demosthenes 1.1 (p.15 lines 27–31 and p.16 lines 8–13 in Dilts's
edition), Plutarch *Perikles* 9.3.

[25] Theoric payments for the Panathenaia were made to those registered as
members of a deme (Demosthenes 44.37), and probably the same procedure was
used for other festivals.

[26] *Clouds* 539, *Peace* 50, 766.

[27] Theophrastos *Characters* 9.5; cf. Plato *Gorgias* 502d.

[28] Cf. Pickard-Cambridge *Festivals* 264–5.

[29] *Women at the Thesmophoria* 386; cf. *Frogs* 1050–1, Plato *Laws* 658d, 817a–c.

are to ask for loans here and now in the theatre, but that they may apply later to members of the chorus at their homes, where the money is (1053).[30] On the other hand, the absence of women seems to be implied by *Birds* 793–6, which is about a man who wants to seduce a married woman: when he sees her husband sitting in the Councillors' seats in the theatre, he takes for granted that the wife is at home, not elsewhere in the theatre.[31] Likewise in *Women at the Thesmophoria* 395–7 husbands returning from the theatre expect to find their wives at home, and suspiciously search the house to see if there is a lover hidden away. But this kind of joke cannot be treated as conclusive evidence on either side of the question. More important, there are numerous places in Aristophanes where a character turns to the spectators and addresses them as 'men'.[32] Why are they never addressed as 'men and women' or 'ladies and gentlemen'? In *Peace* 50–3 the audience is analysed into its components, all male. In *Women at the Thesmophoria* 789–807 the chorus of women, when addressing the audience as 'you', clearly means men only.[33] There are only two possible explanations for this. The simpler, which I prefer, is that women were not present: even if they were present at the tragedies, it may have been thought appropriate for them to stay away from the comedies, which were probably performed on different days. The other is that they were present but were ignored: they were expected to stay in the background while the actors and chorus performed to entertain the men.[34] This latter explanation cannot be excluded, although there is no real evidence to support it. But even if it is true, it remains the case that Aristophanes addresses his plays to the male spectators.

5. *Travel from overseas.* One passage affirms that there is an important difference between the audience at the town Dionysia and the audience at the Lenaia. *Akharnians* was performed at the Lenaia in 425, and in it Aristophanes makes Dikaiopolis refer to events resulting from his play at the Dionysia the year before.

---

[30] Henderson *Lysistrata* ad loc. is right here, against Sommerstein *Lysistrata* ad loc. and Henderson *TAPA* 121 (1991) 139 n. 33.

[31] Cf. H. Box *CR* 14 (1964) 241, N. G. Wilson *GRBS* 23 (1982) 158–9.

[32] ἄνδρες: *Akharnians* 497, *Peace* 13, 244, 276, *Birds* 30, 685, *Lysistrata* 1044, *Wealth* 802.

[33] On the humour of *Women at the Thesmophoria*, addressed to men, see pp. 265–6.

[34] This explanation is ably maintained by Dover *Ar. Comedy* 16–17, J. Henderson *TAPA* 121 (1991) 133–47.

For this time Kleon won't accuse me of
Abusing Athens when foreigners are here.
We're by ourselves; it's the Lenaion contest;
No foreigners are here yet, for the tribute
And allies from the cities have not come.
But we are by ourselves, clean-winnowed now—
The metics I regard as citizens' bran.

(Akharnians 502–8)

In the spring, at the Dionysia, envoys from the cities in the Athenian Empire arrived in Athens to hand over the annual tribute, and naturally took the opportunity to see the plays at the festival. The Lenaia, on the other hand, were held in the winter, when travel was more difficult and few foreigners would be in Athens (except metics, residing in Athens permanently). Thus Kleon could complain that a comedy at the Dionysia denigrated Athens in the presence of foreigners, but the same complaint could not (Aristophanes claims) be made about a comedy at the Lenaia. However, the foreign visitors will not have formed a large proportion of the audience even at the Dionysia, and are unlikely to have affected its general character substantially.

THE AUDIENCE'S EXPECTATIONS

Aristophanes, then, was writing a script for a single performance in Athens on a particular date. He wanted to win the competition, and to get the judges' votes he needed to please and impress the audience. The audience was a big crowd of people, much larger than a modern theatre audience; but it was not by any means the entire population of Attica, nor even a fair cross-section of it. It consisted predominantly of adult male citizens, among whom poor people and country-dwellers, though not excluded, may well have been under-represented.

What were the demands or expectations of this audience? Of course the people who came to the plays expected to find them entertaining, in a broad sense; otherwise they would not have gone to the trouble and expense of attending. But different individuals find different things entertaining. Some like ribald humour, others are strait-laced. Some have political, others intellectual interests.

Some are musical, others are tone-deaf. No doubt there were some Athenians who disliked most of what the comedies offered them, and therefore stayed at home. But Aristophanes must still have had to please a wide variety of people, if he was to win the contest.[35]

Some recent writers have made much of the idea that Athenian festivals were like the carnivals common in medieval Europe and still held in some countries: general holidays on which ordinary people relax and enjoy themselves by watching or taking part in various traditional activities.[36] The comparison may have been overstated: ancient plays were certainly more varied and complex than carnivals. Nevertheless it is useful to be reminded that tradition was an important element in them. When an Athenian went once more to the theatre to see the comedies, he went because he had enjoyed last year's comedies and hoped to have the same kind of entertainment again. The following features can safely be assumed to be parts of the comic tradition, which the audience would be expecting and which Aristophanes probably felt more or less obliged to provide, at least in his earliest plays; in his later plays they become less prominent, and some of them disappear altogether.

1. *Religion*. In performances at religious festivals there are naturally some religious elements. From time to time Aristophanes introduces a hymn, a genuine invocation of a god, but usually with some comic twist to it. For example, his chorus of Horsemen naturally sings in praise of Poseidon, god of horses and of the sea, but the short line at the end of each period (marked here with a dash)[37] introduces a slightly cynical slant on horse-racing or on the exigencies of imperial administration and naval warfare.

> Lord of the horse, Poseidon, thou
> Lovest the brazen sound of hooves
> Mingled with horses' whinnying;
> Lovest the dark-prowed trireme-ships

---

[35] P. Walcot *G&R* 18 (1971) 35–50 stresses the 'popular' character of the audience.

[36] Carrière *Carnaval* 29–32, S. Halliwell *Yearbook of English Studies* 14 (1984) 7, Reckford *Old-and-New* 3–52, S. Goldhill *The Poet's Voice* (Cambridge 1991) 176–88, D. F. Sutton *The Catharsis of Comedy* (Lanham 1994) 105–18. Note the earlier and more cautious approach of Murray *Aristophanes* 1–2.

[37] My translation reproduces the original metre approximately, but cannot be exact. In the original the short lines (555, 558, 564) are in each case a catalectic form of the lines which precede, bringing the rhythm to a pause.

> —Swiftly conveying money;
> Lovest the young men's races too,
> Winning renown in chariots
>   —Or having ill success there:
> Come to our chorus, thou of the golden trident,
> Ruler of dolphins, prayed to at Sounion,
>   God of Geraistos, Kronos' son,
>   Dearest to Phormion[38] among
> Gods, and to all Athenians
>   —In present circumstances!
>
> (*Horsemen* 551–64)

More conspicuously, Aristophanes sometimes brings gods on-stage[39] as characters, and moreover as characters to be laughed at: Herakles is greedy and stupid (in *Birds* and *Frogs*), Dionysos is pretentious and cowardly (in *Frogs*), and so on. This has worried some modern critics, who have wondered whether Aristophanes was irreligious or blasphemous. But that is a misunderstanding. To the Greeks, gods were part of the world, just as much as women, birds, slaves, Akharnians, frogs, politicians, and all the other creatures who appear in Aristophanes' plays. They were powerful, but not omnipotent, and not necessarily good, and so it was quite reasonable, in appropriate cases, to make fun of them, as of anyone else, in a comedy. The Athenian audience would expect some religion at a religious festival, but in the comic part of the festival they would expect religion to be treated comically.

2. *Form and structure.* It has long been observed that certain features of form and structure are common to many of Aristophanes' plays. Typically there are: the prologue, in which the characters, in dialogue or monologue, make clear to the audience the initial situation from which the action of the play will develop; the entrance-song of the chorus (parodos); a scene in which the main character seeks help by knocking at someone else's door; a dispute leading to a debate (agon), in which two characters speak in a relatively formal metre (tetrameters); a passage known as the parabasis, delivered by the chorus alone, sometimes on subjects

---

[38] The most successful Athenian naval commander in the early years of the Peloponnesian War.

[39] Throughout this book I use 'on-stage' (or 'off-stage') to refer to what is visible (or invisible) to the audience. This does not necessarily mean that the performers were on a raised platform.

which have little or nothing to do with the story of the play;[40] further scenes showing the results of whatever conclusion was reached in the debate, often including unsuccessful attempts by new characters to interfere with those results, and alternating with songs which may include a second parabasis (taking the same form as the second half of the main parabasis); and a concluding scene (exodos) of revelry or festivity, ending with another short song. Traces of most of these features can be found also in the fragments of other comic dramatists of the fifth century, and it is clear that they were customary in comedy at that time and not peculiar to Aristophanes.

Attempts have been made to reconstruct out of these features a kind of primitive ritual or proto-comedy out of which Aristophanic comedy as we know it may be supposed to have grown.[41] Such speculations cannot be confirmed from the evidence we have, and we do not really know which of these features were old. And even if it is true that tradition had at one time required dramatists to include them in every comedy, that was no longer the case in Aristophanes' time; for he does not in fact include them in all his plays. The only play in which he uses virtually all is *Wasps*.[42] Of the other plays, *Peace* has no agon, *Clouds* has no concluding festivity, *Frogs* has no parabasis but only a 'second parabasis', and so on; in the last two plays, *Women at the Assembly* and *Wealth*, nearly all of them have disappeared. We may conclude that the tradition, whatever it was, was not so strong that Aristophanes was compelled to retain these features. Nevertheless the audience may well have looked forward to seeing and hearing them, or some of them, with the pleasure of recognition; and so Aristophanes, especially in his earlier years, brings them in whenever he finds it convenient and useful to do so.

3. *Music and dancing.* Every play had a chorus; to apply for permission to put on a play was to 'ask for a chorus' (*Horsemen* 513),

[40] The parabasis regularly consists of: a short introductory song (kommation) and a long speech in (usually) anapaestic tetrameters, ending in a continuous run of anapaests (pnigos); and then two short songs and two speeches, corresponding in length and metre, in the order song, speech, song, speech (ode, epirrhema, antode, antepirrhema).

[41] See especially F. M. Cornford *The Origin of Attic Comedy* (London 1914).

[42] Actually *Wasps* has no scene in which a character knocks at someone else's door, but the passage in which Philokleon knocks at his own door when trying to get out (152) may be regarded as a variant of this feature.

and it is clear that in Aristophanes' time a play without a chorus was inconceivable. Sometimes the chorus represented animals, such as frogs or birds. It sang and danced, usually accompanied by the aulos (a kind of pipe or oboe). Individual characters sometimes sang and danced too. We now have only the words of the songs, although the metre sometimes enables us to make guesses about the music. We know even less about the dances, but occasionally a text makes reference to a particular type of dance or movement. They might be comic (especially when danced by a chorus representing animals), or they might be impressive in other ways. For example, *Wasps* ends with a scene which evidently included different kinds of dance. First old Philokleon provides a comic parody of the old-fashioned style of dancing used by Thespis and Phrynikhos, tragedians of earlier generations.[43]

XANTHIAS. It's so long since the old man drank and heard
   The pipe, and he's enjoying it so much,
   That now he won't stop dancing. All night long
   He's been performing Thespis's old dances.
   He says he'll dance in competition with
   Modern tragedians, and prove them fogeys!

PHILOKLEON. Who sitteth and guardeth the doors of the court?
XANTHIAS. There! What did I say? Here comes trouble, you'll see!
PHILOKLEON. Let the bars of these portals be loosed! For anon
   The figure beginneth—
XANTHIAS. Or rather it's madness beginning, perhaps!
PHILOKLEON. —Of a dancer who bendeth his torso with strength.
   What a snort from my snout! What a crack from my back!
XANTHIAS. You should drink hellebore![44]
PHILOKLEON. Now Phrynikhos cowers to spring like a cock—
XANTHIAS. They'll throw stones at you soon!
PHILOKLEON. —And he then kicks his leg out as high as the sky.
   My buttocks are parted—
XANTHIAS.   Look out for yourself!

---

[43] For details of this passage see MacDowell *Wasps* ad loc. For different interpretations see E. Roos *Die tragische Orchestik im Zerrbild der altattischen Komödie* (Lund 1951), E. K. Borthwick *CQ* 18 (1968) 44–51, J. Vaio *GRBS* 12 (1971) 344–51, W. T. MacCary *TAPA* 109 (1979) 137–47, M. V. Molitor *Hermes* 112 (1984) 252–4.

[44] Hellebore was supposed to be a cure for insanity.

PHILOKLEON. —For my joints now move supply in each of my limbs.

Good, wasn't it?

XANTHIAS.   Zeus, no! Sheer lunacy!

(*Wasps* 1476—96)

Philokleon then challenges all comers. Three sons of Karkinos come forward; these were real men (not fictional characters), who evidently were expert dancers and seem to have appeared in person in the play. The chorus sings a song, which includes references to high kicks, pirouettes, and other movements, and finally joins in too (1518—37). We cannot reconstruct the dance, but clearly it was intended to provide a spectacular end to the play.

So, although the music and dancing are the aspects of the plays which are least evident to us as we read the texts, we must bear in mind that they were far more evident to the Athenian spectators. Some indeed, like spectators of modern opera, may have considered the music the most important part of the performance.

4. *Obscenity.* Aristotle asserts that comedy originated 'from the leaders of the phallic events which to this day still remain customary in many of the cities'.[45] Presumably 'the phallic events' were rituals related to human fertility, intended to encourage the gods to make the race fertile or to celebrate the fact that they had done so. We do not know what evidence Aristotle had for his assertion, but it is supported by the phallic costume and sexual jokes of Old Comedy.

The basic costume of the actors was a close-fitting leotard, padded to look comically fat, and attached to this (for male characters) was a leather phallus. Clothes worn over it would conceal the phallus from view, but in comedy characters sometimes appear undressed or not fully dressed, and then the phallus would be visible. How often this happened is a question which has been much disputed.[46] There are also numerous references in the dialogue to sexual organs (female as well as male) and excretion. Some, especially in *Lysistrata*, obviously arise from the plot of the play; but others are gratuitous, in the sense that they are not called for by the context but come as a comic surprise.

[45] Aristotle *Poetics* 1449a 11—13. Murray *Aristophanes* 3—11 emphasizes the phallic ritual behind Old Comedy.

[46] Stone *Costume* 72—126 provides a full discussion and references to earlier work.

SOCRATES. Now let me look and see first what he's doing.
   Hey you, are you asleep?
STREPSIADES.   By Apollo I'm not!
SOCRATES. Have you got hold of anything?
STREPSIADES.   No, I haven't.
SOCRATES. Nothing at all?
STREPSIADES.   No, nothing but my cock!
                              (*Clouds* 731–4)

BDELYKLEON. And indeed I'll maintain him. I'll see that he has
   What an old man requires. He'll have gruel to drink,
   And a soft cloak to wear, and a sheepskin as well,
   And a whore, who will give him a good rubbing up
   On his cock and his arse!

                                     (*Wasps* 736–40)

These are jokes, not primitive ritual. Probably an early connection between comedy and phallic ritual made it possible and
customary for comedy to use phallic costumes and language, but
Aristophanes exploits that custom for his own purposes. By mentioning explicitly what was not normally mentioned in public he
could raise laughs, and probably many men in the audience had a
special liking for this kind of humour and looked forward to it every
year. It also went naturally with personal ridicule.[47]

   5. *Personal ridicule.* Old Comedy had a tradition of making rude
comments on individuals who had become prominent, whether as
political leaders or in some other way. This tradition may well have
been connected originally with religious rituals intended to avert
the gods' envy, or with satire in iambic poetry, or with both;[48] but
in Aristophanes it is not confined to religious contexts or to iambic
passages. No doubt ordinary Athenians enjoyed the chance to feel
superior, once or twice a year, to powerful men whom they had to
treat with deference most of the time.[49] But the persons ridiculed
were not necessarily powerful. When the spectators laughed at
Pantakles, an otherwise unknown man who did not know how to
fix the crest on the helmet which he was to wear in a procession

---

[47] The abusive function of obscenity is emphasized by Henderson *The Maculate
Muse* 1–29. Cf. also A. T. Edwards *TAPA* 121 (1991) 157–79.
[48] Cf. R. M. Rosen *Old Comedy and the Iambographic Tradition* (Atlanta 1988),
E. Degani in *Ar. Hardt* 1–49.
[49] Cf. Dover *Ar. Comedy* 31–41.

(*Frogs* 1036–8), they were not asserting themselves against restraint; they were just amused at the recollection of a ludicrous incident which had occurred on a recent public occasion. Thus the tone may vary from bitter satire in one case to friendly fun in another. Each case must be assessed separately, and sweeping statements about the purpose of personal ridicule must be avoided.[50]

In some plays an actor is brought on to impersonate a real man, who may even become a major character in the play, such as Lamakhos in *Akharnians* and Socrates in *Clouds*. Such characters will be discussed later in this book in the appropriate chapters. More often a real person is just mentioned verbally, for the sake of a brief joke which may be quite incidental to the action. A particularly striking example is the standing joke about Kleonymos, a fat politician who was said to have discarded his shield; in a battle it was a serious offence to drop one's shield to run away. Aristophanes trots out this joke in play after play for over ten years.[51]

DEMOCRACY. Next, any man put on a list of hoplites
    Shan't be transferred through influence or pull,
    But stay where he was registered at first.
SAUSAGE-SELLER. That's hurt the shield-band of Kleonymos![52]

                  (*Horsemen* 1369–72)

SOCRATES. Have you ever looked up in the sky and caught sight of a
    cloud that looked like a centaur,
    Or that looked like a leopard, a wolf, or a bull?
STREPSIADES.   Yes, I have, by Zeus. What about it?
SOCRATES. They turn themselves into whatever they wish . . .
STREPSIADES. So yesterday, seeing Kleonymos passing, the thrower-
    away of his shield,

[50] For discussion of this topic see S. Halliwell *Yearbook of English Studies* 14 (1984) 6–20, J. Henderson in *Noth.Dion.* 293–307; but both tend to define the purposes of ridicule too narrowly.

[51] Besides the passages quoted, see *Wasps* 15–27, 822–3, *Peace* 673–8, 1295–1304, *Birds* 290. The joke is discussed by I. C. Storey *Rh. Mus.* 132 (1989) 247–61.

[52] Sommerstein *Knights* ad loc. considers that this passage refers to a different incident from the others. But 'it is uneconomical to assume that Cleonymus' shield became funny twice' (Heath *Political Comedy* 28 n. 51). I take the joke here to be that, if Kleonymos cannot evade service by being transferred to a different list, his shield is sure to suffer for it by being thrown away again.

Because they had seen that great coward of a man, they turned into
deer for that reason!

(*Clouds* 346–54)

PHILOKLEON. And then there's Euathlos, and that great big
Flatter-onymos, shield-discarder . . .

(*Wasps* 592)

CHORUS. Many, new, and wonderful the
            Places we have flown to are,
            And the strange things we have seen.
        An amazing tree is growing
            Farther off than Kardia,[53]
            And it's named Kleonymos.
        Though it serves no useful purpose,
            It's a great big cowardly thing.
        Every year it sprouts in springtime,
            Flourishing and prosecuting,
        But when winter comes again you'll
            Find that it's deshielduous!

(*Birds* 1470–81)

Did Kleonymos really throw away his shield in a battle? It seems
improbable, because that was an offence for which a man could be
prosecuted, and the penalty was disfranchisement.[54] Kleonymos
was a politician, and some political opponent would have been sure
to get him convicted and disfranchised if it had been possible to
convince a jury that he was guilty; yet he seems not to have been
disfranchised, for he continued to take part in public affairs. So it is
unlikely that he was really guilty of cowardice. Yet there must
have been some well-known incident which gave rise to the joke;
otherwise it would not have been funny to say that Kleonymos,
rather than any other man, had thrown away his shield. For instance,
perhaps he accidentally dropped his shield with a loud clatter in
front of a big crowd of spectators at a procession (similar to the
occasion when Pantakles had trouble with his helmet). Or perhaps
he did discard his shield in a battle, but escaped conviction by

---

[53] Kardia was a town in Khersonesos, but here there is a pun on καρδία
meaning 'heart' or 'courage'.

[54] Cf. MacDowell *Law* 160.

claiming that he did so for a good purpose, such as helping to carry a wounded comrade to safety. We can be sure that *some* fact lies behind the ridicule, but we cannot know what the fact was; and the same is true of a great many other passages of personal ridicule in Aristophanes.[55]

Did the tradition of personal ridicule leave Aristophanes free to say absolutely anything he liked about anybody, or were there any limits? The only evidence for legal restrictions comes from the scholia, and is open to the suspicion that it may be based on nothing but false inferences from jokes in comedies.[56] One scholiast (on *Akharnians* 67) says that 'the decree about not satirizing' was passed in the year 440/39 and repealed in 437/6; even if that is true, the nature of the ban is obscure, and anyway it belongs to a period before Aristophanes began writing. Another scholiast (on *Birds* 1297) thinks that a man named Syrakosios got a decree passed 'that no one was to be satirized by name'; but it is obvious from Aristophanes' plays that they were never subject to a total ban on jokes about named individuals, and modern attempts to interpret the ban as some more specific kind of restriction have not been very successful.[57] The Athenians had a law about slander; but what it forbade was not defamation in general, but certain specified allegations, if they were false. Among these, it was forbidden to say that a man had thrown away his shield. Now, Aristophanes does say that Kleonymos had thrown away his shield (most directly in *Clouds* 353) and, as we have seen, this assertion was probably false, or at least exaggerated. It seems, then, that Aristophanes did not need to obey the law about slander, at least in his earlier plays. Either comedy was formally exempt, or it was just an accepted custom that no prosecutions were brought for what was said in a comedy. I have wondered

---

[55] Some scholars have thought that allegation of foreign origin was one type of ridicule which was often made with no foundation at all, but for argument against that view see MacDowell in *Tr.Com.Pol.* 359–71.

[56] Cf. S. Halliwell *CQ* 34 (1984) 83–8.

[57] Carrière *Carnaval* 45–6 suggests that the decree banned comedies named after a real person; but he has then to assume that it was soon repealed, because several such comedies are known to have been produced a few years later, including Platon's *Kleophon* and Strattis' *Kinesias*. A. H. Sommerstein *CQ* 36 (1986) 101–8, following a suggestion by Droysen, interprets the decree as a ban on reference to the men found guilty of impiety in 415 (for mutilation of the Hermai or profanation of the Mysteries); but this does not carry conviction, because immunity from satire would have been a privilege, not a penalty.

whether what Syrakosios did in his decree was to insist that comic dramatists should conform to that law;[58] but that is not what the scholiast on *Birds* says, and it is probably better to admit that we do not know what, if anything, was prevented by the decree of Syrakosios. Whatever it was, it does not seem to have hampered Aristophanes very much.[59]

The conclusion of this chapter is that Aristophanes was writing scripts for performance on particular occasions before a large audience which consisted predominantly of male citizens living in or near the town of Athens. They had come to the theatre to enjoy themselves on a festive occasion, but not merely to hear a string of jokes. They expected a performance in a traditional form, including religious and musical elements, and also ribald humour and ridicule of members of their own community. The rest of this book is about some of the ways in which Aristophanes used and developed this traditional form of entertainment.

[58] MacDowell *Law* 128–9. When I wrote that book, I was regrettably unaware that almost the same interpretation had been proposed by M. Radin *AJP* 48 (1927) 215–30. There seems to be no clear infringement of the law of slander in *Birds* or in any later play; *Birds* 1470–81 is innuendo, not plain statement.

[59] For further discussion of this topic see S. Halliwell *JHS* 111 (1991) 48–70, J. E. Atkinson *CQ* 42 (1992) 61–4.

3

Early Plays

Aristophanes' first play was *Banqueters*. It was performed in 427 BC and came second in the contest (at which festival is not known).[1] No copy of it has survived, but we have a few quotations,[2] and also a reference to it by Aristophanes himself in the revised version of his *Clouds*.

> Ever since, in this place, some men—and I'm glad to mention them—
> Spoke so favourably of the virtuous and the vicious boy,
> And, as I was still a maid and shouldn't yet have given birth,
> I exposed them, and another girl received and took them up,
> After which you reared and educated them so well yourselves—
> Ever since that time, I've had a pledge of your goodwill to me.
>
> *(Clouds 528–33)*

The metaphor 'I was still a maid . . .' is most easily interpreted as meaning simply that he had no previous experience of writing and directing plays. In what way someone else 'received and took them up' is a problem which will be considered later in this chapter. For the moment we are concerned with the subject of the play, which involved a father with two sons, 'the virtuous and the vicious boy'. The longest fragment is nine lines of dialogue between the father and the bad son. The son is rude and abusive to his father, whom he regards as having one foot in the grave and as being far inferior to himself and his friends. The father, instead of replying

---

[1] Cf. D. Gilula *ZPE* 81 (1990) 102.

[2] For detailed commentary on the fragments see Cassio's edition, *Aristofane: Banchettanti*. However, the text and numbering I use here are not Cassio's but, as for other comic fragments, those of *Poetae Comici Graeci*, ed. Kassel and Austin.

directly, comments like a pedantic scholar on the son's affected vocabulary, attributing various words to the influence of various popular speakers.[3]

BAD SON. You're just a coffinette, scent, mourning bands.
FATHER. 'A coffinette'? That's from Lysistratos.
BAD SON. I think you'll get a stumbledown from time.
FATHER. That 'stumbledown' comes from the orators.
BAD SON. Some consequence will follow from your words.
FATHER. That's Alkibiades', that 'consequence'.
BAD SON. Why do you suspicate and criticize
   Gentlemanizing men?
FATHER.   Thrasymakhos!
   Which advocate's monstrosity is that?

                              (*Banqueters* fr. 205)

From other fragments it appears that the father was a country-man who sent his two sons to a teacher in the town. The good son ran back home, presumably in disgust at the kind of education offered, but the bad son stayed to learn all the latest tricks of the town, which were not at all what his father had expected, before returning to the farm. He became self-indulgent and effete.

FATHER. He didn't learn those lessons when I sent him, but instead he
   Learned drinking, vulgar singing, and a Syracusan diet,
   And Sybaritic feastings, Khian wine from Spartan goblets.

                              (*Banqueters* fr. 225)

And he's as smooth as any eel, with hair in golden ringlets.

                              (*Banqueters* fr. 229)

BAD SON. Now I'm really quite exhausted, what with playing pipes and
   lyres,
   And you order me to dig!

                              (*Banqueters* fr. 232)

FATHER. And next please explain some Homeric expressions: first, what
   do they mean by *korymba*?
      . . . what do they mean by *amenena karena*?

---

[3] The strange Greek words in this passage are discussed by V. Tammaro *MC* 15–17 (1980–2) 101–6. In translating I have substituted similar English coinages.

BAD SON. No, let this man instead, your son and my brother, explain
     what they mean by *idyoi*.
               . . . and what is *opyein*?

(*Banqueters* fr. 233)

Idyoi (if the text here is right; the word is an emendation) was an
obscure legal term for witnesses, and *opyein* for marriage. The bad
son prides himself above all on having learned the language of the
rhetoricians and the lawcourts.[4] That is what has made him, in his
opinion, superior to his father and brother. Presumably he is speaking to his brother when he says:

BAD SON. Have you the sophistries which I acquired?
     You ran off from the teacher, didn't you?

(*Banqueters* fr. 206)

We cannot reconstruct the story of the whole play from the
fragments, and we do not know whether the father or the bad son
came out on top in the end. Another puzzle is the nature of the
banqueters after whom the play is named. Apparently they were
men who had attended a banquet in honour of Herakles, and formed
the chorus of the play;[5] but their connection with the father and his
sons is not known.

Despite these obscurities, the fragments of *Banqueters* are important because they show that in his very first play Aristophanes was
already concerned with the difference between traditional education, based on Homer and other poetry, and the newly fashionable
study of rhetoric and sophistic argument as practised in the lawcourts, which some people considered bad for morality. This was a
theme which he took up again in *Clouds* four years later.

[4] Cf. Cassio *Banchettanti* 32–6.
[5] Test. *m* Cassio (p. 40) = test. iii Kassel and Austin (p. 122).

BABYLONIANS

Babylonians was performed at the Dionysia in 426, and may have come first in the contest.[6] The surviving fragments are scanty and uninformative.[7] The chorus is said to have consisted of Babylonians who were tattooed or branded as slaves and worked in a mill.[8] A little information about the story emerges from a comment by Athenaios on the word *oxybaphon*, which generally means a saucer.

So in the *Babylonians* of Aristophanes too we shall understand *oxybaphon* as a drinking cup, when Dionysos says about the demagogues in Athens that, when he went off to the trial, they asked him for two *oxybapha*. For it is not to be supposed that they asked for anything but cups.

(Athenaios 494d–e)

It is interesting to notice that *Frogs* was not the only play of Aristophanes in which Dionysos appeared on-stage, though why he went to a trial and what else he did in the play are quite unknown. More important, perhaps, is the reference to demagogues, because we know that one politician, Kleon, objected to this play. In Aristophanes' next play, *Akharnians*, performed at the Lenaia in 425, there are several references to *Babylonians*. First, there is a passage in which the hero of *Akharnians*, Dikaiopolis, is nervous about saying in public what he believes.

And I'm aware what Kleon did to me
Myself, because of last year's comedy.
He dragged me off into the Council-house
And slandered me and tongued me down with lies
And Kyklobor-ed[9] me and drenched me; in the end
He nearly dirty-business-ed me to death!

(*Akharnians* 377–82)

---

[6] I accept from schol. *Akharnians* 378, 503 the statement that Aristophanes' play performed at the Dionysia in 426 was *Babylonians*. The belief that this play won the first prize rests only on a questionable restoration in *IG* 2² 2325.58; cf. D. Gilula *CQ* 39 (1989) 332–8. Russo *Aristophanes* 23–4 argues that the fact that Aristophanes does not boast in *Akharnians* that *Babylonians* won the first prize implies that it did not.

[7] G. Norwood *CP* 25 (1930) 1–10 criticizes some over-confident reconstructions of the play, but his own reconstruction also goes beyond the evidence.

[8] See the evidence quoted by Kassel and Austin *PCG* under fr. 71. For speculation about the chorus see D. Welsh *GRBS* 24 (1983) 137–50.

[9] The Kykloboros was a small river which made a lot of noise.

Later he becomes more confident about speaking.

For this time Kleon won't accuse me of
Abusing Athens when foreigners are here.
We're by ourselves; it's the Lenaion contest;
No foreigners are here yet, for the tribute
And allies from the cities have not come.

(*Akharnians* 502–6)

We have already noticed the significance of this passage as evidence for the difference between the audiences at the Dionysia and at the Lenaia (see p. 16). It is clear that Kleon made a speech to the Council complaining that *Babylonians* contained material denigrating Athens in the presence of the foreigners who attended the Dionysia. A scholium on *Akharnians* 378 (quoted on p. 43) states that the play satirized officials, appointed by lot and by election, and Kleon himself. That need not be dismissed as just a conjecture by the scholiast, because he may have been able to read a copy of *Babylonians*. It is not unlikely that the play did include abusive comments on Kleon but the tradition of personal ridicule in comedy made it impossible for him to make any formal complaint about that (cf. p. 25). Whom exactly Kleon denounced to the Council and whether a trial followed are questions which will be considered later (pp. 42–4).

In the parabasis of *Akharnians* the chorus makes a further reference to Kleon's complaint, and goes on to summarize the beneficial advice which the poet has given to Athens. Although 'last year's comedy' is not specified here, the references to Athens, democracy, and the cities of the Athenian Empire make it likely that *Babylonians* is meant.

But now that he's slandered by enemies, who speak to the quickly-
   deciding Athenians
And say he makes fun of our city and treats our people with scorn and
   with insults,
He asks for permission to make a reply to the quickly-mind-changing
   Athenians.
The poet declares he deserves to receive rewards for the good that he's
   done you.
He's stopped you from being deceived too much as you listen to
   foreigners' speeches,

And from taking delight in flattering words and becoming citizen-
    gawpers.
Whenever the envoys came here from the cities before, and they wished
    to deceive you,
They would first of all call you 'violet-crowned'; and every time anyone
    said that,
Immediately on account of the 'crowns' you sat on the tips of your
    bottoms!
And if anyone wanting to wheedle you round should mention 'glistening
    Athens',
He'd get anything, just for that 'glistening' word—a compliment fit
    for a herring![10]
That's one of the ways in which he's produced a great many advantages
    for you.
He's also revealed how democracy rules those peoples who live in the
    cities.
So now for that reason the men from the cities, when coming to bring
    you the tribute,
Will arrive with a mighty desire to set eyes on this most excellent poet,
A man who has ventured to say what is right when speaking before the
    Athenians.

                                             (Akharnians 630–45)

Two topics of *Babylonians* are being mentioned here. One is the deceptive character of speeches made to the Assembly by envoys coming to Athens from cities in the Athenian Empire (the regular sense of 'the cities' in Aristophanes), who get what they want by paying a few flattering compliments to Athens. The second is the character of the governments within those cities; 'how democracy rules those peoples' is an ambivalent phrase, but probably it means that the governments were not as democratic as they professed to be. The meaning will, of course, have been clear to the members of the audience at *Akharnians* who remembered *Babylonians* from the previous year.

We do not know how these topics were presented in the play. Did *Babylonians* include a scene in which a meeting of the Assembly was shown on-stage, as in *Akharnians*, but with the difference that the speakers addressing it were envoys from allied cities rather than Athenian envoys returning from abroad? And was it the gullibility

---

[10] Pindar had called Athens 'glistening and violet-crowned' (fr.76), and the quotation had apparently become popular.

of the Assembly in this scene that Kleon declared to be a denigration of Athens? Those are only guesses, and may be quite wrong. And it is hard to guess how these topics could have been related to the chorus of Babylonians and the character of Dionysos. But at least one conclusion can clearly be drawn from the meagre evidence about this play: it dealt with important political topics in a manner which provoked a violent reaction from the leading politician of the day.

The parabasis of *Akharnians* is not entirely serious. When the poet declares that he deserves rewards for his services (633), and that the allies' envoys are longing to set eyes on the man who says what is right (643–5), that is already comic overstatement, and the hyperbole then rises even higher.

> The fame of his boldness has spread far and wide. The news has reached Persia already:
> When the envoys from Sparta went up to the King and he started his interrogation,
> The first thing he asked was which side in the war possessed the superior navy;
> And this poet was what he enquired about next, and which side he was roundly abusing,
> 'Because it's those men are the fellows' he said 'who have got so very much better,
> And they'll be the victors by far in the war when they have that man to advise them!'
> So that is the reason why offers of peace have been made to you now by the Spartans
> And they ask you to give back Aigina to them. They don't care a scrap for that island:
> The thing that they're really attempting to do is somehow to get hold of this poet.[11]
> But don't you let go of him ever; he'll put in his comedies all that is rightful.
> He says that he'll teach you a lot of good things, and so make you thoroughly happy,

[11] Apparently the poet had some connection with Aigina; he may have obtained land there when the Athenians took over the island in 431 (Thucydides 2.27.1). T. J. Figueira *Athens and Aigina in the Age of Imperial Colonization* (Baltimore 1991) 79–93 discusses the evidence connecting Aristophanes with Aigina, but places too much trust in scholia which may well be merely conjectures based on *Akharnians* 653–4. On the identity of 'this poet' see p. 39.

Not flattering, nor making offers of pay, nor fobbing you off with a
     swindle,
Nor playing the villain, nor swamping with praise, but teaching you all
     the best lessons.

(Akharnians 646–58)

Even the Spartans and the King of Persia have heard of our poet,
and are sure that his good advice will lead to victory! This is not
meant to be taken literally; Aristophanes has put it in to raise a
laugh. Yet it is followed immediately by lines which (especially the
last two, 657–8) seem impossible to interpret as jokes, and have to
be taken seriously: the comedies include what is right and what is
instructive, not flattery or deception. The whole passage (630–58)
makes a serious claim for the importance of his comedies, develops
that claim in a humorous manner, and then reiterates it firmly at the
end. He asserts that he combines fun with truth, and he includes
both fun and truth in the making of the assertion. The ability to do
this is the outstanding feature of Aristophanes' genius. We cannot
know quite how he displayed it in *Babylonians*; its manifestation in
subsequent plays will appear in the later chapters of this book.

THE MAKERS OF COMEDY

The learned men of the Hellenistic age who compiled the *hypotheses*
(introductions) and some of the scholia, though they may not have
entirely understood the conditions of theatrical performance in
fifth-century Athens, were aware that for some of his plays, including
the earliest ones, Aristophanes did not have full responsibility, and
they express this by saying that a play was presented 'through'
another man. *Babylonians, Akharnians, Birds*, and *Lysistrata* are said to
have been produced 'through Kallistratos', and *Wasps*,[12] *Amphiaraos*,
and *Frogs* 'through Philonides'. His first play, *Banqueters*, is said by

[12] The assignment of *Wasps* to Philonides, however, is probably a mistake by
the author of the *hypothesis*. At that festival (the Lenaia in 422) Philonides presented another play named *Proagon*, and it is unlikely that one man would have
been allowed to present two comedies at the same festival. Lines 1017–22 imply
that Aristophanes is responsible for *Wasps*. Other sources tell us that Aristophanes
wrote a *Proagon*, not that Philonides did. So it appears that Aristophanes wrote
two plays for the same festival; he himself presented one and Philonides the other.

one source to have been produced 'through Kallistratos' and by another 'through Philonides'; the latter is more probably correct.[13] His last two plays, *Kokalos* and *Aiolosikon*, are said to have been put on through his son, Araros. On the other hand *Horsemen*, performed at the Lenaia in 424, was the first play produced 'through Aristophanes himself'. The reason for this is explained in the parabasis, where the chorus has been praising 'the poet'.

> But the thing he says many of you have approached him and asked him
>   about in amazement,
> That he didn't put in a request by himself for a chorus a long time
>   before this,
> He told us to give you an answer to that. It wasn't because he was
>   stupid
> That he put up so long with that state of affairs. He did it because he
>   considered
> That the art of directing a comedy was the most difficult task in
>   existence.
>
> (*Horsemen* 512–16)

Some of the difficulties encountered by earlier comic dramatists, Magnes, Kratinos, and Krates, are described, and then the chorus goes on:

> It was fear of that fate made our poet delay for so long. And he said in
>   addition
> A man ought to become a plain oarsman at first, before putting his
>   hand on the tiller,
> And after that take up a post in the bow and look out for the winds and
>   the weather,
> And only then captain a ship for himself.
>
> (*Horsemen* 541–4)

These lines make clear that *Horsemen* was the first play for which Aristophanes applied for a chorus on his own, and that this new departure was not a mere formality. When a play was produced 'through Kallistratos', the function of Kallistratos was not just to give his name to a production for which all or most of the work was

---

[13] Anon. *On Comedy* (in *Prolegomena de comoedia* ed. W. J. W. Koster) p. 9 line 38, schol. *Clouds* 531; cf. D. Welsh *CQ* 33 (1983) 52–3. I now agree with Welsh that this explanation of 'other poets' in *Wasps* 1018 is preferable to the other possibilities considered in MacDowell *Wasps* ad loc.

in practice done by Aristophanes; it was to do 'the most difficult
task in existence' (516). Kallistratos was what we call the director.[14]
In Athens it was usual for the author of a play to direct the production
himself, but in the cases which we are now considering this work was
undertaken by Kallistratos or Philonides, and it is a striking fact that
Aristophanes regards directing a play as a harder task than writing it.

The nautical metaphor, with its progression from oarsman to
captain, shows that he did not take over this task all at once, but by
stages. What were the stages? This is a controversial question.
According to the usual view, with which I agree, the meaning is
simply that he gradually took a larger share in directing successive
plays. For *Banqueters*, perhaps, he did nothing but watch and learn
from the rehearsals conducted by Philonides, but for *Babylonians* he
gave a little assistance to Kallistratos, and for *Akharnians* rather
more, so that by 425/4 he felt sufficiently experienced to take
on the entire responsibility for directing *Horsemen*. But a different
interpretation has been put forward by Mastromarco and by Halliwell.[15] In their view there was also an earlier stage: first, in the
years before 427, Aristophanes contributed comic material to plays
by other authors; then, from 427 to 425, he wrote whole plays but
still did not undertake their direction, though he may have assisted
the director; finally in 424 he both wrote and directed *Horsemen*
himself. It is of course possible for one man to suggest jokes or contribute lines for another man's play;[16] but the parabasis of *Horsemen*
does not actually say that Aristophanes did so; lines 512–16 show
that it is a passage about directing, not about writing.[17] The main
support for Mastromarco's and Halliwell's view comes from the

---

[14] I use 'director' to translate διδάσκαλος, 'chorus-producer' for χορηγός,
and 'chorister' for χορευτής.

[15] G. Mastromarco *Quaderni di Storia* 10 (1979) 153–96, S. Halliwell *CQ* 30
(1980) 33–45. I gave my reasons for disagreeing with them in *CQ* 32 (1982) 21–
6, an article which is partly repeated here. See also Perusino *Dalla commedia antica*
37–57 (but her acceptance of a part of each of the two interpretations is an
unconvincing compromise which fails to reconcile *Akharnians* 628 with *Wasps*
1018) and Hubbard *Mask* 227–30. The only substantial point on which I have
changed my mind since 1982 is that I now think that *Banqueters* was more probably
directed by Philonides than by Kallistratos; see p. 35 n. 13.

[16] Halliwell *GRBS* 30 (1989) 515–28 gives other possible instances.

[17] Mastromarco *Quad. Stor.* 10 (1979) 172 considers that the nautical metaphor
supports his view by distinguishing three stages of a naval career, corresponding
to the postulated three stages of Aristophanes' dramatic career. But D. Gilula *CQ*

parabasis of *Wasps*, two years later, when the chorus refers again to Aristophanes' earlier career.

> And next, O ye people, pay heed to our words, if you're willing to hear some plain speaking;
> For the time has arrived when the poet desires to find fault, and to blame the spectators.
> He declares that they've injured him, quite unprovoked, in spite of the good that he's done them.
> Some of this was not openly done, but he secretly gave other poets assistance,
> And he used just the same trick that Eurykles does, that very ingenious prophet;[18]
> He got inside other men's bellies, from where he poured comedy forth in abundance.
> And he next after that went on openly, now taking risks on his own account also,
> And he drove his own chariot, reining the mouths of his own and not other men's muses.

> (*Wasps* 1015–22)

This passage distinguishes two stages of Aristophanes' career, a 'secret' period and an 'open' period. In my view these are the same two periods as those distinguished in the parabasis of *Horsemen*: the 'secret' period is the years 427–5, and the 'open' period begins with *Horsemen* in 424. But Mastromarco and Halliwell regard the 'secret' period as being the years before 427, while the 'open' period covers all the years from 427 onwards, when Aristophanes was writing complete plays, whether those plays were directed by himself or not. In their view *Wasps* 1018–20 is evidence that, before he started writing complete plays, Aristophanes contributed comic material to plays by other authors. Their interpretation depends above all on the word 'secretly' in *Wasps* 1018, which they insist on taking strictly. They maintain that Aristophanes' authorship of *Banqueters*, *Babylonians*, and *Akharnians* was not secret, so that this line must refer to an earlier period. I believe that this interpretation

---

39 (1989) 259–61 shows that it actually distinguishes four stages: rower, tiller man, bow officer, captain. It is just a metaphor for a gradual process, and the naval functions are not to be correlated precisely with the dramatic ones.

[18] Eurykles was probably a spirit who was supposed to speak through mediums, rather than a human ventriloquist; cf. Sommerstein *Wasps* ad loc., correcting MacDowell *Wasps* ad loc.

is too narrow; 'secretly' does not refer to deliberate concealment, but just means that Aristophanes' authorship of the early plays was not publicly announced or generally known, because they were presented not by him but by Philonides or Kallistratos.[19]

There are in fact two reasons why the view of Mastromarco and Halliwell should be rejected. The first is the correspondence between the ship metaphor of *Horsemen* 541–4 and the chariot metaphor of *Wasps* 1022. For metaphorical purposes, captaining a ship[20] and driving a chariot are identical activities. The man who does either of these things is the man who controls the vehicle. In the *Horsemen* passage it is clear that the occasion when Aristophanes became captain of the ship was the production of *Horsemen*; before that he had been in a subordinate position, like a rower, a tiller man, or a bow officer. Therefore in the *Wasps* passage the occasion when he took the reins of his chariot must have been the production of *Horsemen*; before that he was an assistant. The view of Mastromarco and Halliwell involves the inconsistency of saying that for *Banqueters*, *Babylonians*, and *Akharnians* Aristophanes was in charge (according to *Wasps*) and not in charge (according to *Horsemen*).[21] The second reason emerges from consideration of the parabasis of *Akharnians*.

> Ever since our director has been in command of comical choruses, so far
> He has never come forth[22] in the theatre before to tell the spectators he's clever.
> But now that he's slandered by enemies, who speak to the quickly-deciding Athenians
> And say he makes fun of our city and treats our people with scorn and with insults,
> He asks for permission to make a reply to the quickly-mind-changing Athenians.

---

[19] Gilula *ZPE* 81 (1990) 101–2 offers another interpretation of 'secretly'. She suggests that Aristophanes' authorship of *Banqueters* and *Babylonians* had to be kept secret because, as a new dramatist, he was permitted by law to present plays only at the Lenaia, not at the Dionysia. But that suggestion fails to explain why *Akharnians*, a Lenaia play, falls within the 'secret' period.

[20] Not 'holding the tiller'; Gilula *CQ* 39 (1989) 261 n. 9 rightly corrects me here.

[21] The same phrase καθ' ἑαυτόν, meaning 'on his own', 'independently', is used both in *Horsemen* 513 and in *Wasps* 1021.

[22] The verb used here (παρέβη) is the appropriate one for the parabasis, but its exact meaning is uncertain. It may be 'digressed'; cf. Sifakis *Parabasis* 64–6.

The poet declares he deserves to receive rewards for the good that he's
done you.

(Akharnians 628–33)

The first line of this passage makes clear that the man in question
is in charge of the chorus, and has had charge of several comic
choruses before; he is the director. Since Aristophanes at this date
had not yet had charge of a chorus (as the parabasis of *Horsemen*
shows), this man must be Kallistratos, and it is Kallistratos who is
here being given credit for the good advice given to the Athenians
in *Babylonians*.[23] This shows that the plays of the years 427–5 belong
to the 'secret' period when Aristophanes was in a subordinate
position (*Wasps* 1018–20) and not, as Mastromarco and Halliwell
would have it, to the 'open' period.

But the same man is also 'the poet' (633).[24] How could Kallistratos be called the poet when Aristophanes had written the play?
I believe that the solution lies in a correct understanding of the word
which we translate as 'poet'.[25] The Greek word originally means
'maker'. A comedy consisted of words, music, dancing, costume,
and clowning; and, before Aristophanes came along, it is by no
means clear that the words were considered the most important of
these ingredients. Earlier comedies may have contained a great deal
of cavorting by a comically dressed chorus, alternating with actors'
slapstick. The maker of a comedy was a man who devised all these
things, not the words alone. But a problem of nomenclature arose
when Kallistratos or Philonides shared the tasks with Aristophanes
(since, for all we know, such sharing was unprecedented): was the
writer of the words or the deviser of the action now to be called
the maker of the comedy? The latter may, at first, have seemed more
appropriate, especially if Philonides or Kallistratos was the senior

---

[23] It is therefore Kallistratos, not Aristophanes, who had some connection
with Aigina; cf. p. 33 n. 11.

[24] Figueira *Athens and Aigina* 101–3, if I understand him correctly, considers
that 'the director' (628) means Kallistratos and yet 'the poet' (633) means
Aristophanes. But the coherence of the passage does not permit this distinction.

[25] ποιητής. This part of my argument, originally published in *CQ* 32 (1982)
25, has been received by some readers with disbelief, even with shock (e.g.
Perusino *Dalla commedia antica* 55–7). This seems to arise from an inability
(perhaps natural in classical scholars) to conceive that anything in a comedy could
ever have been considered more important than the text. My argument still
seems to me correct, and I therefore repeat it here.

man, the one who was in charge. Only gradually, as comedy became more literary, would it become established custom to restrict the term 'maker' to the author of the script.[26]

The following account of Aristophanes' early career is to some extent speculative, but I believe it fits such evidence as we have. The first steps were those to which he alludes in *Clouds* 528–33 (quoted on p. 27). When quite a young man, with no experience of the theatre except as a member of the audience, he set about writing a play. The outcome was the script of *Banqueters*. He showed it to two or three intelligent older men of his acquaintance (the men mentioned in *Clouds* 528) and they were very favourably impressed by it: here was a comedy which rose above the usual farcical level to include coherent characterization and a moral theme. They wanted to encourage the young man; but how could they help him to get his play performed? He was without experience ('a maid' in *Clouds* 530) of organizing performances, and the Arkhon or the Basileus might be reluctant to award a chorus to a young man for a play so different from the kind of comedy which was then customary. The solution which they found was to get Philonides to take it on (*Clouds* 531). Philonides no doubt already had some experience in the theatre as an author and actor.[27] He was able to get a chorus from the Arkhon or the Basileus and to put on a performance using Aristophanes' script.[28] The performance was a success (*Clouds* 532), and so a similar arrangement was made in the next two years for *Babylonians* and *Akharnians* with Kallistratos instead of Philonides; Philonides may have been unavailable for some reason, or he may have been presenting a comedy written by himself. Kallistratos

---

[26] In the modern cinema a man who 'makes' a film does not always, or even usually, write the script. 'Hitchcock's films' are films directed by Hitchcock, not written by him. The gradual narrowing of the sense of ποιητής is paralleled by the Scots word 'makar', which originally meant 'maker' but now always means 'poet'.

[27] Philonides was both an actor (schol. *Clouds* 531, *Prolegomena de comoedia* Xc (p. 21 in Koster's edition)) and an author of whose comedies a few fragments survive. though it is not known which of them are earlier in date than 427.

[28] N. W. Slater *GRBS* 30 (1989) 68 n. 4, objecting to my account in its earlier publication, wishes to know whether the Arkhon knew that Aristophanes was actually the author, but he seems to me to have missed the point. The Arkhon may or may not have been told this, but in either case his reason for awarding a chorus to Philonides (not to Aristophanes) was that he was confident that Philonides would put on a good show.

was another experienced director (*Akharnians* 628). Aristophanes assisted him with the rehearsals for both plays, but Kallistratos was in charge. It was Kallistratos' show. It was he who was announced as the maker of each comedy and received the prize. The general public neither knew nor cared about Aristophanes—not because his contribution was kept secret deliberately, but simply because it was treated as a matter of minor importance and was not publicly announced. No one, except his friends, was interested in Kallistratos' young assistant.

But this state of affairs could not last. By the time of *Akharnians* it must have become clear that the play's success was due more to the script than to other aspects of the production. A new kind of comedy had come into existence, more articulate and literary than any that had existed before. Probably copies of the script were made for reading after the performance was over, on which the name of the author of the script would naturally appear. At any rate word somehow got around that these brilliant plays were scripted not by Kallistratos himself but by a young man named Aristophanes. A number of people ('many' in *Horsemen* 512) encouraged Aristophanes to undertake a production on his own, not merely assisting Kallistratos; and when he did so, in 424, he was able to assume, in the parabasis of *Horsemen*, that most of the audience knew that he had written the scripts for previous plays.

In later years he sometimes collaborated with Kallistratos or Philonides again, and his example was followed by Eupolis, Platon, and other writers. On those occasions, when the authors were already well-known dramatists, there is no need to suppose that the audience was unaware of the collaboration. The man who applied for a chorus (Kallistratos or whoever it was) was probably still formally regarded as the maker ('poet') of the comedy, at least for a while; there appears to be no fifth-century text in which that word is used of the writer of a comic script who was not also the director. But eventually, at any rate in the fourth century, when the music and clowning had dwindled and the words were the dominating element in a comedy, it became customary to call the writer rather than the director (when they were different men) 'the poet'; and the compilers of the didascalic inscriptions in the third century may have considered it more appropriate to put down Aristophanes than Kallistratos as the victorious poet of *Babylonians*.

THE QUARREL WITH KLEON

How then are we to understand the action taken by Kleon after the performance of *Babylonians*? In *Akharnians* 377–82 and 502–6 (quoted on pp. 30–1) Dikaiopolis says that Kleon dragged him to the Council and slandered him, complaining that he abused Athens in the presence of foreigners. This must refer to some real incident; it would have no point as merely a fictional event in the life of the countryman Dikaiopolis.[29] In 628–31 (quoted on p. 38) the chorus says that the director is slandered by enemies who accuse him of insulting Athens. It is highly improbable that this refers to a different incident;[30] we can combine the passages and say that Kleon denounced the director, Kallistratos, to the Council.

Many readers have found it puzzling that Dikaiopolis asserts that Kleon denounced 'me', rather than 'our director' or 'our poet', and various explanations have been proposed. Some consider that the part of Dikaiopolis was played by Kallistratos or by Aristophanes, and the actor steps out of his role and speaks as himself in these two passages.[31] This cannot be refuted, but there is no positive evidence for it. Another view is that Dikaiopolis is speaking as a type of comic hero who appears annually and got into trouble last year.[32] But it can hardly be the case that Kleon demanded that the comic hero appear before the Council. I think it preferable to consider these speeches by Dikaiopolis alongside four passages in which the chorus, or more likely the chorus-leader alone, speaks for the poet in the first-person singular: *Akharnians* 659–64, *Clouds* 518–62, *Wasps* 1284–91, *Peace* 754–74. If in the earliest comic performances the poet normally led the chorus himself, or took the only solo part, perhaps it later remained an accepted convention that either the chorus-leader or the leading character could speak as the poet to the audience, even when the poet was not actually performing the

---

[29] This is rightly reaffirmed by Mastromarco in *Tr.Com.Pol.* 344.

[30] E. L. Bowie *JHS* 108 (1988) 183–5 argues that there was also a separate denunciation of Eupolis, whom he thinks Dikaiopolis represents; but that is convincingly refuted by L. P. E. Parker *JHS* 111 (1991) 203–8 and I. C. Storey in *Tr.Com.Pol.* 388–92.

[31] S. D. Olson *Liverpool Classical Monthly* 15 (1990) 31–2 shows that this view has a long history.

[32] Dover *Greek and the Greeks* 296. See also S. Goldhill *The Poet's Voice* (Cambridge 1991) 190–2.

part. That cannot be proved; but anyway I see no reason to doubt that Dikaiopolis refers to a denunciation of Kallistratos by Kleon.

Kleon evidently spoke in strong terms. He may have been angry because *Babylonians* had contained comic abuse of himself, but the accusation he made openly was that Kallistratos had insulted Athens on an occasion when foreigners were present. But it is doubtful whether his speech led to any further action. Many scholars have believed that there was a formal prosecution and trial, but that view is based solely on a scholium, which had better be quoted in full.

Because of last year's comedy: he means *Babylonians*. Aristophanes directed that play before *Akharnians*, and abused many men in it. He ridiculed the officials, appointed by lot and by election, and Kleon, when the foreigners were present. He put on a play, *Babylonians*, at the festival of the Dionysia, which is performed in the spring, when the allies used to bring the tribute. Angered by this, Kleon prosecuted him for wrongdoing towards the citizens, on the ground that he had done these things to insult the people and the Council, and he also prosecuted him for being a foreigner and brought him into a trial. The Lenaia were held in the autumn, at which the foreigners were not present, when this play, *Akharnians*, was being directed.

(Scholium on *Akharnians* 378)

It is obvious immediately that this scholiast is not completely trustworthy: he has got the season of the Lenaia wrong, and he may have made other mistakes. We have to consider where he may have got his information. The references to foreigners' attendance at the Dionysia and not at the Lenaia are doubtless based on *Akharnians* 502–6. The information about the content of *Babylonians* may be based on a text of that play, of which the scholiast may have had a copy; but it cannot have provided information about what happened after its performance was over. The assumption that it was Aristophanes who directed the plays and was accused by Kleon shows that the scholiast knew nothing about the involvement of Kallistratos, but just knew that Aristophanes was the author. The sentence about the prosecution is questionable at several points.[33] The verb used for 'prosecuted' implies the legal procedure of *graphe*, but in fact a case initiated by denunciation to the Council was not

[33] The questionable Greek words are ὁ Κλέων ἐγράψατο αὐτὸν ἀδικίας εἰς τοὺς πολίτας . . . καὶ ξενίας δὲ αὐτὸν ἐγράψατο.

graphe but *eisangelia*.[34] 'Wrongdoing' is too vague to have been a formal charge in itself. 'Being a foreigner', on the other hand, is a specific charge of exercising the rights of an Athenian citizen when not entitled to them; that seems hardly relevant to Kleon's complaint as described in *Akharnians* 502–6. I think it likely that the scholiast misunderstood the reference to foreigners there, and made a poor attempt to reconstruct what happened on that basis, without actually having any evidence other than the text of *Akharnians*.[35] In fact *Akharnians* 377–82 is no more than a vivid description of a denunciatory speech by Kleon. If the denunciation had led to a trial by jury or any other consequence, surely Aristophanes would have made Dikaiopolis mention that too. So probably there was no such trial; the Council, despite Kleon's indignation, decided to take no action.[36]

In the following winter Aristophanes insists on the merits of *Babylonians* in the lines of *Akharnians* already quoted (pp. 31–4), and rounds them off with a passage in which the chorus-leader expresses defiance. Here it hardly matters whether the audience takes 'I' as meaning the chorus or Kallistratos or Aristophanes; the defiant attitude may be common to them all.[37]

So let Kleon use every cunning device
And contrivance against me, whatever he can.
For on my side I have what is good and what's right,
Which will be my defence; and never shall I
Be found guilty, like him, where the city's concerned,
Of being a coward and a bugger!

(*Akharnians* 659–64)

Actually there are few references to Kleon in *Akharnians*, but Aristophanes' resentment at the attack did not evaporate: in the

---

[34] On *eisangelia* to the Council see MacDowell *Law* 183.

[35] Another scholium on *Akharnians* 378, preserved in fragmentary form in P.Oxy. 856.25–7, follows the same interpretation but in less detail. The words ὑ]πὸ Κλέωνος δίκην ἔφυ[γε probably mean 'was prosecuted by Kleon'; Slater *GRBS* 30 (1989) 73 n. 11 may not be correct in translating them as 'escaped Cleon's charge'.

[36] J. E. Atkinson *CQ* 42 (1992) 56–61 reaches a similar conclusion, but does not distinguish the denunciation to the Council from the trial by a jury to whom the Council could have referred it. *Wasps* 1284–91 does not refer to this dispute, but to a later one, following *Horsemen*; cf. p. 176.

[37] Cf. Hubbard *Mask* 53.

following year, when for the first time he obtained a chorus for himself, he launched a fierce attack on Kleon in *Horsemen*. Meanwhile in *Akharnians* he directed his fire at other public figures, especially Lamakhos.

4

Akharnians

THE EFFECTS OF WAR

Akharnians was performed at the Lenaia in 425 BC, and won the first prize. It is a play about war and peace. The Peloponnesian War between Athens and Sparta was already in its sixth year and there was no prospect of an early end to it. The chief character of the play, Dikaiopolis, hates the war, but he fails to persuade the other Athenians to consider how peace can be made. He therefore, by fantastic means, makes a separate peace treaty for himself and his family, to the horror of the warlike old men of Akharnai who form the chorus.

The main reason why Dikaiopolis hates the war is that he has been compelled to leave his home in the country and live in the town. This was a consequence of Athenian strategy in the war's early years. The Spartans' method of conducting the war was to invade Attica with their army. Perikles realized that the Athenians, whose power was primarily naval, could not defeat the Spartans and their allies by land, and so he persuaded the Athenians not to attempt a land battle, but to take refuge within the town walls and rely on their navy to obtain subsistence from overseas.

On hearing this the Athenians did as he said, and brought in from the country their children and women, and also the property which they had at home, even taking down the woodwork of their houses too. Farm-animals they sent across to Euboia and the neighbouring islands. The removal was irksome to them, because most of them had always been accustomed to living in the country.

(Thucydides 2.14)

In *Akharnians* Dikaiopolis is one of these Athenians who have had to move into the town, and at the beginning of the play he tells the audience how he dislikes the town and longs for peace to be made so that he may return to his rural home. What does he miss about the country? A modern reader might expect him to praise the beauty of the landscape, or the more leisurely pace of rural life, but in fact he does not. The reason he gives is economic:[1] in the country he can get for nothing (by producing or gathering them) various items which have to be paid for in the town.

> I look towards the country, longing for peace,
> Hating the town and yearning for my deme,
> Which never said 'Buy coal! Buy vinegar!
> Buy olive oil!' It didn't know the word.
> It gave us everything; no buy-man there!

> (*Akharnians* 32–6)

The Spartans and their allies invaded Attica in the years 431, 430, 428, and 427. On each occasion they ravaged part of the countryside. The most serious destruction was of the vines and olive trees, which would take years to grow again; the cutting down, trampling, and burning of vines is mentioned repeatedly in *Akharnians*. But in no year did the Spartans remain for more than forty days, and in 429 and 426 they did not enter Attica at all. One might have expected countryfolk like Dikaiopolis to return to their homes between invasions, but the clear implication of *Akharnians* 32–6 and 266–7 is that they did not.[2] When they had dismantled their houses and shipped their animals to the islands, presumably they thought it not worthwhile to restore them as long as the threat of invasions remained; for they never *knew* that the Spartans were not about to invade again. Yet almost the opposite seems to be implied by a scene later in the play, where Derketes of Phyle laments that Boiotian raiders have snatched his two oxen (1018–36). Clearly his cattle either had not been shipped to an island or had already been brought back. Perhaps the explanation is that the evacuation of the countryfolk was not as complete as Thucydides makes it sound, and it was really only the farmers of the plains in western and central Attica who moved into the town, those being the areas most vulnerable to incursions from the Peloponnese. The Boiotians coming from the north, though allied to the Peloponnesians, may have made only

---

[1] Cf. S. D. Olson *JHS* 111 (1991) 200–3.
[2] These passages make my view slightly different from that of M. M. Markle *Ancient Society* 21 (1990) 156–7.

brief raids without undertaking systematic destruction.

When the first invasion occurred in 431, the enemy army advanced as far as Akharnai; and it was the Akharnians, shut up in the town and knowing that their own land was being ravaged, who were particularly clamorous that the Athenians should march out and fight, though Perikles still adhered to his policy of not doing so.[3] That may be the main reason why Aristophanes chose Akharnians to be the bellicose chorus of his play, though there is also a little evidence that the Akharnians had a reputation as brave warriors even before 431.[4] Akharnai was a small town about eight miles from Athens; from the Akropolis it must have been possible for the Akharnians actually to see the Peloponnesian army on their land. It was an important centre for producing charcoal from the woods of Mount Parnes, and that fact gives rise to several jokes and humorous metaphors about coal, wood, and fire in the course of the play. But the old men who form the chorus also have their patches of ground for agriculture, and their purpose in wanting the war to go on is to punish the Spartans for their invasions, 'to teach them not to trample on my vines' (232–3).

Dikaiopolis too hates the Spartans because his vines have been cut down (509–12). There is no difference between his and the Akharnians' suffering; the difference lies in what they want to do about it. The Akharnians want to fight back, and, although we must make some allowance for comic exaggeration, essentially that may have been the attitude of the majority of Athenians in 425. Dikaiopolis, on the other hand, regards peace as more important than revenge. This conflict of opinion, on the most serious question facing Athens at that time, is the theme of the play.

THE ASSEMBLY AND ITS ENVOYS

In democratic Athens all major decisions were taken by the Assembly (*ekklesia*); to the Assembly, therefore, Dikaiopolis must go if he wants to persuade the Athenians to make peace. The Assembly was,

---

[3] Thucydides 2.21–2.

[4] Pindar *Nemean* 2.16–17; cf. R. Osborne *Demos: the discovery of classical Attika* (Cambridge 1985) 188–9, D. Whitehead *The Demes of Attica* (Princeton 1986) 399–400, Bowie *Aristophanes* 39–42.

in theory, a meeting of all Athenian citizens (adult males of Athenian parentage), held normally on the Pnyx, a hillside west of the Akropolis. But at the beginning of the play Dikaiopolis has arrived on the Pnyx for a meeting, due as usual to begin at dawn, and no one else is there, not even the Prytaneis who have the duty of presiding.

> The main Assembly's due today
> At dawn, and yet the Pnyx here is deserted!
> They're chattering in the Agora; up and down
> They run, avoiding the red-painted rope.
> Even the Prytaneis haven't yet arrived;
> They'll get here late, then jostle one another
> Like anything, to get to the front bench,
> All streaming down together. They don't care
> A scrap for making peace. Oh city, city!
>
> (*Akharnians* 19–27)

Classical Athens is often praised for its democracy, but these lines show that there was some difficulty in making the system work. Attendance at the Assembly was sometimes so bad that a rope covered with red paint was stretched out and carried across the Agora towards the Pnyx, to round up citizens who were loitering for shopping or gossip; anyone found to be smeared with red paint was fined.[5] It sounds a desperate method of obtaining a quorum. Here the emphasis is on lateness rather than absenteeism, but another passage in which Lamakhos is said to have been elected by 'three cuckoos' (598) certainly implies a low attendance. Of course Aristophanes is satirically exaggerating the dilatoriness and apathy. Nevertheless the audience would have thought these passages pointless, rather than funny, if there had not been at least a small degree of truth in them, and so they are important historical evidence for the unwillingness of some Athenians to participate actively in their democracy.

Eventually the Prytaneis and other citizens do arrive, and the meeting begins. Most of it is taken up by the reports of envoys. The usual translation 'ambassadors' may mislead a modern reader. Greek envoys did not reside abroad on a long-term basis. They were sent to a foreign state to conduct particular negotiations, and as soon as those negotiations were finished they returned home and their

---

[5] Platon com. 82, schol. *Akharnians* 22, Polydeukes 8.104.

appointment as envoys ended. In many cases this would take only a few days. Often three men would be sent together on a mission, sometimes a larger number. They were appointed by vote in the Assembly; and they received pay, which was intended not as salary but simply to cover the cost of their transport and subsistence on the journey.

In *Akharnians* the Athenian envoys who are reporting on their return from foreign parts consist of one group (probably three men, though the number is not specified in the text) who have been to the King of Persia, and one man, Theoros, who has been to the King of Thrace. Both have been enjoying a thoroughly luxurious time, although they try to make out that it was full of hardship.

ENVOY. You sent us to His Majesty the King
　　Drawing two drachmas' stipend every day,
　　When Euthymenes was Arkhon.
DIKAIOPOLIS. 　　　　　　　　　Oh, those drachmas!
ENVOY. And we were quite worn out with travelling
　　Across Kaystrian plains, as under awnings
　　We lay on cushions in the carriages;
　　It was killing.
DIKAIOPOLIS. I meanwhile was safe and sound:
　　I lay in rubbish by the battlements![6]
ENVOY. And then our hosts kept forcing us to drink
　　From crystal glasses and from golden cups
　　Sweet undiluted wine.
DIKAIOPOLIS. 　　　　　　Oh rugged Athens,
　　Look how these envoys are deriding you!

(*Akharnians* 65–76)

Euthymenes was Arkhon in 437/6, so that (if anyone in the audience bothers to calculate) these envoys have been away from Athens for eleven years. That is a ridiculous notion, but it is clear that Aristophanes thinks that some recent envoys are vulnerable to the gibe that they have been spinning out an enjoyable jaunt at public

---

[6] Some country people taking refuge in the town during the war could find no accommodation except in the guard-towers of the town walls (*Horsemen* 792–3, Thucydides 2.17.3). They would also have to perform sentry-duty against possible enemy attacks (Thucydides 2.13.6).

expense.[7] He is exaggerating, but no doubt it was true that some envoys were well entertained by the potentates to whom they were sent, and enjoyed the opportunity to see foreign parts without having to pay the cost of travel themselves.

Theoros, who is shown reporting back from Thrace, was a real person, and is the object of jokes in later plays. So perhaps it is true that in 426 BC Theoros did go as an envoy to Thrace, and some other men to Persia, even though there is no other evidence of Athenian envoys going to Thrace or Persia in that year. But the reports which they make to the Assembly in the play cannot be more than comic distortions of their real reports: in historical fact the envoys to Persia certainly did not take eleven years, but merely a longer time than Aristophanes thought necessary; they did not bring with them the Persian official called the King's Eye,[8] but probably mentioned him in their report; and likewise Theoros may have spoken about, but not actually brought, some Odomantian soldiers.

Both missions are represented in the play as being (and may well have been in historical fact) attempts to obtain support for Athens in the war, in the form of gold from Persia and troops from Thrace. But both attempts are futile: the gold is not forthcoming, and the troops will do more eating than fighting. So the Assembly's time is wasted, and it never gets around to considering how peace can be made, which is what Dikaiopolis wants it to do. Throughout this scene Dikaiopolis represents the sensible point of view, pointing out what is wrong with the envoys and their reports. He is patriotic: his concern is not only for himself, but for the city of Athens, which he apostrophizes twice (27, 75), and for the sailors who preserve it (162–3). What he wants is a peace treaty for Athens, and the Prytaneis, when they arrest 'a man who wished to make a treaty for us and hang up our shields', are wronging the Assembly, not just Dikaiopolis (56–8).

This man, Dikaiopolis' only ally, is a character named Amphi-

---

[7] I cannot agree with Heath *Political Comedy* 37 n. 78 that the scene is pure fantasy. There is nothing entertaining (beyond fairy-story level) in a tale that some men rode in cushioned carriages and drank wine from golden cups. It becomes amusing satire only if it refers to real men who did something of this sort but would prefer to conceal it.

[8] In the play the envoys do produce this official (not an Athenian in disguise). Cf. Dover *Greek and the Greeks* 293, C. C. Chiasson *CP* 79 (1984) 131–6.

theos. His status is not adequately explained; it may involve some joke which was clear to the Athenian audience but is obscure to us. He claims to be not human but immortal, descended from another Amphitheos who was a son of Demeter. The gods have entrusted to him the task of making a treaty with Sparta, but he cannot do so because the Prytaneis have given him no money for travel expenses. Obviously part of the joke is that a god is hampered by the same kinds of problem as a human envoy. But we never hear elsewhere of a god called Amphitheos; one would expect the gods' messenger to be Hermes or Iris (both of whom appear in other plays of Aristophanes). There was, however, at least one Athenian man named Amphitheos, which probably means 'descended on both sides from gods'; it has even been argued that he and Aristophanes belonged to the same circle of friends, although the evidence for that does not amount to much.[9] It seems that Aristophanes has invented a god, and as a joke has named him after a contemporary Athenian who happened to have a divine-sounding name. There may have been some further point to the joke, but it has not been convincingly identified.[10]

Dikaiopolis, despairing of getting the Assembly to make peace, provides money for Amphitheos to become his own personal envoy. He is to travel to Sparta and make a separate treaty just for Dikaiopolis and his family. At this point the play moves from a real problem to a fantastic solution. In real life it would be impossible for one family to make peace while the rest of Athens remained at war. But in the play Amphitheos goes off and returns in about five minutes (the distance between Athens and Sparta is over a hundred miles) bringing three sample treaties for Dikaiopolis to try. The treaties (the Greek word means more literally 'libations') are in the form of wine. Dikaiopolis tastes the five-year one and the ten-year one, but likes the thirty-year one best. He takes it, drinks it, and is immediately at peace; and off he goes to hold his own private celebration of the rural Dionysia.

---

[9] *IG* 2[2] 2343; cf. S. Dow *American Journal of Archaeology* 73 (1969) 234–5. The inscription is twenty or thirty years later in date than *Akharnians*, and does not actually mention Aristophanes.

[10] For a survey of different views see Lind *Der Gerber Kleon* 136–8.

EURIPIDES AND TELEPHOS

But his celebration is rudely interrupted by the chorus of Akharnians, who threaten to stone him to death for the crime of making peace with the Spartans. Amphitheos has already fled, and Dikaiopolis is now totally isolated. He has to defend himself, but his methods of doing so are surprising. First he threatens to kill a hostage belonging to the Akharnians; the hostage turns out to be some charcoal (produce of Akharnai). Next he undertakes to speak in his defence with his head on a chopping-block, so that he may be executed immediately if the defence is unconvincing; and he brings out a block for this purpose. Finally he dresses as a beggar to evoke pity; but the ragged clothes he dons are those worn by the tragic hero Telephos, which he procures from Euripides. It will have been clear to the more intelligent spectators from the start, and to the stupidest by the end, that all three devices are tragic ones, taken from Euripides' *Telephos* and given a comic twist.

Quotation and parody of tragedy are common in Aristophanes' plays.[11] Earlier dramatists had presented comic versions of traditional myths, probably drawing them from Homer and other narrative poetry; but Aristophanes is doing something different. He is making comic use of tragedy because tragedy is part of Athenian life. Any contemporary tragedian is considered good for a laugh; in his very first speech Dikaiopolis makes a sarcastic comment on a tragedian named Theognis, to whom he prefers Aeschylus (who had died thirty years before). But the most mockable tragedian of all is Euripides.

Euripides was now in his fifties and had been writing plays for thirty years. Most of his plays which now survive were written in the later part of his life, but evidently by the time of *Akharnians* he was already regarded as the leading innovator in the tragic genre. Aristophanes brings him into the play as one of the characters, but it is his style of tragedy, not his personality, which is the comic target. Although, for some reason which we do not know, it was considered funny to refer to his mother as a greengrocer,[12] there is

---

[11] On this subject in general see Rau *Paratragodia*, M. S. Silk in *Tr.Com.Pol.* 477–504.

[12] For an interpretation of this joke in sexual terms see E. K. Borthwick *Phoenix* 48 (1994) 37–41.

no other indication that Aristophanes had any knowledge of him as a person. He simply gives to his character 'Euripides' the personality and life-style which he considers comically appropriate for the author of tragedies like *Oineus*, *Phoinix*, and *Telephos*.

Telephos had been performed in 438 BC. No complete text survives, but it is possible to reconstruct some of its action from various sources of information: there are some fragments of papyrus copies of the play, and later writers sometimes refer to the story or quote individual lines.[13] To these sources we can add Aristophanes' parodies, not only in *Akharnians* but also in *Women at the Thesmophoria*, and at several points a scholiast, who no doubt had a copy of *Telephos* before him, tells us that a particular line of *Akharnians* is a quotation from *Telephos*, or that it is a parody of a line of *Telephos* (and he gives us the original line). There is some risk of circularity, if one reconstructs the tragedy from the comic parody and then remarks that the comic parody keeps very close to the tragedy, and some modern scholars have treated more of *Akharnians* as parody than the evidence justifies. But with due caution it is possible to summarize the play.[14]

Telephos was a son of Herakles by a woman named Auge. He was born on Mount Parthenion in Arkadia; but, after being exposed to die and subsequently rescued, he somehow reached Mysia in Asia Minor, where he was reunited with his mother, was brought up, and eventually became king. Some time afterwards a Greek army invaded Mysia, and Telephos, leading the resistance, was wounded by Achilles before the Greeks withdrew. The wound failed to heal, and when Telephos consulted an oracle he was told 'The wounder will heal it'. So he travelled to Greece, disguised as a beggar, to seek a cure. This was the point at which Euripides' play began: one of the longest of the papyrus fragments contains the opening lines, in which Telephos, just arrived at Argos, hails the Peloponnese, in which he was born, at the start of what must have been a typical Euripidean prologue, reeling off information about earlier events for the benefit of the audience.

TELEPHOS. O fatherland, which Pelops marked as his,
　　Hail! and thou, Pan, who tread'st Arkadia's

---

[13] All the fragments are assembled by C. Austin *Nova Fragmenta Euripidea* (Berlin 1968), and I use the numbering of that edition.

[14] Cf. E. W. Handley and J. Rea *The Telephus of Euripides* (*BICS* Supplement 5, 1957), Rau *Paratragodia* 19–42, M. Heath *CQ* 37 (1987) 272–80.

Storm-battered crag, from whence I claim descent.
For Auge, child of Aleos, bore me
In secret to Tirynthian Herakles;
I know Parthenion mount, where Eileithyia
Ended my mother's pangs and I was born.
I suffered much, but I'll cut short my tale.
I reached the Mysian plain, and there I found
My mother, and I settled. Power was given
To me by Mysian Teuthras. I was named
Telephos by the Mysian citizens,
Because my life was stablished far away.[15]
Though Greek, I ruled barbarians, labouring
With many soldiers, till Akhaian troops
Came ranging over all the Mysian plains . . .

(*Telephos* fr. 102)

There the papyrus breaks off, but Telephos must have gone on to tell the audience about his wound and the oracle, explaining that he had now come in disguise to enemy territory to seek a cure, and including somewhere the two lines which Aristophanes borrows for *Akharnians* 440–1. The contrast between appearance and fact makes them characteristic of Euripides.

I have to seem a beggar . . .,
Be who I am, but not appear to be.

(*Telephos* fr. 104)

In due course Agamemnon and other Greeks arrived and a discussion began, perhaps on a proposal to invade Mysia again and avenge the defeat inflicted on the Greeks by Telephos. Telephos, in his disguise, intervened, and we have a quotation of three lines in which he insists on speaking.

Agamemnon, even if someone held an axe
And were about to wield it on my neck,
I'll not be silent, but reply what's right.

(*Telephos* fr. 113)

Probably at this point he uttered a deliberately ambiguous wish,

---

[15] The name Telephos is supposed to be derived from τηλοῦ, 'far away'.

intending to convince the Greeks that he was no friend of Telephos, while not actually wishing himself any harm.[16]

> Success to me; to Telephos—what I wish!
> (*Telephos* fr. 114)

Permitted to speak, he delivered a lengthy justification of Telephos (that is, of himself), who after all had only been fighting in defence of his own people of Mysia. It began with these words:

> Do not resent it, topmost men of Greece,
> If I, a beggar, speak to noblemen.
> (*Telephos* fr. 109)

Also from *Telephos*, the scholiast tells us, and probably from the same speech, came words which we find in *Akharnians* 540 and 543, and finally those in 555–6.

> And do we think
> That Telephos would not?
> (*Telephos* fr. 118)

After that speech the Greeks somehow discovered that the beggar was Telephos himself in disguise. In danger of being killed on the spot as an enemy, Telephos seized Agamemnon's infant son Orestes and rushed to the altar holding him as a hostage; he threatened to kill the baby if the sanctuary was infringed. The upshot was negotiation and agreement. The Greeks agreed to allow Telephos' wound to be healed, in accordance with the oracle, and 'the wounder' having power to do this was found to be not Achilles himself but his spear: it inflicted the wound, and filings from it, applied to the wound, healed it. In return Telephos agreed to guide the Greek forces to Troy, with which he was familiar, in their expedition to recover Helen. The longest papyrus fragment of the play, which must belong near the end, contains part of a choral song about Telephos' forthcoming guidance of the Greek fleet, and some dialogue between Achilles and Odysseus about preparations for the expedition. Although formally a tragedy, the play seems to have had a happy ending.

It is obvious that the principal point of similarity between the situation in *Telephos* and the situation in *Akharnians* is that in both

---

[16] I do not follow those editors who emend the text of schol. *Akharnians* 446 to convert the wish into a statement of fact.

plays the hero has to make a speech arguing against the continuation of a war, and maintaining that not all the wrong is on the enemy's side. Dikaiopolis urging the Akharnians, and the Athenians in general, that the war against Sparta is not justified can be compared to Telephos urging the Greeks that the war against Telephos and the Mysians is not justified. No doubt this is what first gave Aristophanes the idea of introducing Telephos into his play; and the speech in which Dikaiopolis makes his plea (497–556) is logically fundamental to the parody, since without it there would be no reason for making him imitate Telephos rather than any other character. That speech will be discussed later; but before it is reached Aristophanes prepares for it by the earlier allusions to *Telephos*. As early as line 8 there is a short quotation from *Telephos*, 'a fitting deed for Greece'.[17] Then there is the passage where Dikaiopolis protects himself against the Akharnians' attack by threatening to kill a hostage who turns out to be charcoal, a grotesque parody of Telephos' seizure of the baby Orestes. That is followed by his offer to speak with his head on a block. Presumably this is a reminiscence of Telephos' insistence on saying what is right even if threatened with execution; but whereas Telephos' remark appears to have been just an effective piece of rhetoric, in Dikaiopolis' case the Akharnians take up his offer and tell him to bring out a block, and so he does (358–67). Here Aristophanes is making fun of tragic speech by carrying out literally what in the tragedy is only rhetorical or metaphorical.

Dikaiopolis' next step in imitation of Telephos is to dress himself in ragged clothes.[18] Evidently the miserable dress of some of Euripides' characters, especially Telephos, was notorious. We can infer that in earlier tragedy it had been customary for the actors to be formally or even grandly dressed, and when Euripides took a step towards realism by putting wretched clothes on a character who was in a wretched situation, that was a startling innovation. Therefore dressing in rags makes Dikaiopolis look like a Euripidean hero, and a Mysian cup and other accessories make him look like Telephos specifically. But this is only a superficial resemblance between the two characters, since Dikaiopolis does not have the same motive as Telephos for wearing rags. Telephos needed to disguise himself in

[17] But possibly this phrase was already in general use and is not intended as parody here; cf. Dover *Greek and the Greeks* 229.
[18] This probably means one tattered piece of cloth used as a cloak. Cf. R. M. Harriott *G&R* 29 (1982) 40 n. 7.

order to avoid recognition by the Greek commanders; a beggar's
dress was a good disguise because it was normal for a beggar to
wander from place to place and a stranger so dressed would be less
likely to provoke questions about who he was and where he came
from. But Dikaiopolis, though he does speak of taking in the chorus
at one point (443), never seriously pretends to be anyone but himself. So for him the rags are not a disguise. They are a device for
arousing the Akharnians' pity. They are also a means of acquiring skill
at speaking, for it is comically assumed that when he is dressed like a
Euripidean character he becomes able to speak like one (444–7).

To get the rags, Aristophanes has had the brilliant idea of making
Dikaiopolis go to visit Euripides in person. This episode is not essential for the story (Dikaiopolis might just have put on any rags he happened to have), but it makes an excellent comic scene. Euripides
is brought on wearing rags himself, and he has a vast stock of rags
belonging to different characters, who are named one after another
until he reaches the particular one, Telephos, whose rags Dikaiopolis
desires. The notion that each character has distinctive rags, stored
separately in Euripides' house, is absurd, and is an effective comic
device for mocking the use of miserable dress in his tragedies.

Did Aristophanes expect the audience to recognize all his
allusions to tragedy? When the hostage and the block are introduced,
neither Euripides nor Telephos has yet been mentioned. It was
thirteen years since *Telephos* was performed; indeed Dikaiopolis
later calls it 'that old play' (415). Aristophanes himself may have
had access to a written copy of it, so that he could check the details,
but that was certainly not true of most of the spectators. It is improbable that many of them could have taken all the points of parody,
without even being told initially which play was being parodied, if
they had not in some way had their memories of *Telephos* refreshed in
the years between 438 and 425. Possibly it had been performed at
local festivals at Peiraieus or Eleusis or elsewhere; possibly the most
distinctive parts of it had been held up to ridicule in other comedies
and so had already become familiar material for jokes. But another
possibility is that most of the audience just laughed at the comic
presentation of tragic style in a broad sense, and only a minority
was familiar enough with *Telephos* to appreciate all the details.[19]

[19] Cf. R. M. Harriott *BICS* 9 (1962) 1–8. In general, on the reception of a
parody by a reader or listener unfamiliar with the original work, see M. A. Rose
Parody: Ancient, Modern, and Post-Modern (Cambridge 1993) 36–45.

THE CAUSES OF THE WAR

Now Dikaiopolis is ready to make his speech in defence of the Spartans and of his decision to make peace with them. He has brought out the chopping-block over which he offered to speak. He has procured and donned the tragic rags which will arouse pity and inspire him with tragic language. At line 496 the chorus calls on him to speak—and immediately most of the preparations are forgotten. His speech is addressed not to the chorus, but to the audience; he makes no attempt to conceal his identity; though still wearing the rags, he does not ask for pity;[20] there are a few quotations from *Telephos*, but most of the speech is not in tragic language; and the block is never mentioned again. It is characteristic of Aristophanes to abandon a joke without ceremony as soon as it has served its turn.[21] Now the tone is suddenly changed.

DIKAIOPOLIS. Do not resent it, men of the audience,
    If I, a beggar, speak to Athenians
    Concerning Athens in a comedy.[22]
    For even comedy knows what is right,
    And what I'll say, though startling, will be right.
    For this time Kleon won't accuse me of
    Abusing Athens when foreigners are here.
    We're by ourselves; it's the Lenaion contest;
    No foreigners are here yet, for the tribute
    And allies from the cities have not come.

(*Akharnians* 497–506)

Here Dikaiopolis states very clearly that this speech is going to

---

[20] In the next scene the rags evoke Lamakhos' contempt rather than pity, and so Dikaiopolis probably discards them at 595.

[21] Recent critics have, to my mind, overstated the connections between Dikaiopolis' comic visit to Euripides and his largely serious speech about the causes of the war. See R. M. Harriott *G&R* 29 (1982) 35–41, H. P. Foley *JHS* 108 (1988) 33–47, N. R. E. Fisher *G&R* 40 (1993) 35–7.

[22] The word used for comedy in lines 499–500 is not the usual κωμῳδία but the rarer τρυγῳδία, 'trygedy'. This may be intended to suggest a resemblance to tragedy; cf. O. Taplin *CQ* 33 (1983) 331–3, A. T. Edwards *TAPA* 121 (1991) 157–63.

be different from most comic speeches.[23] He is going to criticize Athens, and his criticisms, though they may arouse resentment, will be justified. He alludes for the second time to the fuss made by Kleon about *Babylonians* last year, and asserts that this time criticism of Athens should be accepted because there are no foreigners in the audience at the Lenaia.[24] Aristophanes has made it as plain as he can that the rest of this speech will have some serious content. However frivolous comedy may be, there are some occasions when it says something serious and true, and this speech is going to be one of them. And it goes on to give an account of how the war began: trivial disputes concerning the small city of Megara were allowed to escalate, and the Athenians took up an unduly stubborn attitude to a reasonable Spartan request.

Although it has such a careful and explicit introduction, some modern critics have refused to accept that the speech has any serious content, and insist that it is no more than a joke. It has been maintained that 'the speech is parody from start to finish. We cannot with confidence take it seriously.'[25] This dichotomy is unsound, because it is of course possible for serious points to be made by means of a parody. But in the present instance it is not true that the speech is parody from start to finish. It is true, of course, that the spectators are expected to recollect Euripides' scene in which Telephos, disguised as a beggar, argued that the Mysians were not responsible for the war against the Greeks. To emphasize the similarity Aristophanes has made Dikaiopolis put on rags like Telephos and then begin his speech with almost the same words.

> Do not resent it, topmost men of Greece,
> If I, a beggar, speak to noblemen . . .

> (*Telephos* fr. 109)

---

[23] I have discussed this speech in *G&R* 30 (1983) 148–55, and I repeat here some parts of that article. Some of my arguments have been criticized by C. Carey *Rh.Mus.* 136 (1993) 245–62; on the whole I am unconvinced by his objections, but I have modified my view in some details.

[24] On the quarrel with Kleon see pp. 42–5; on the audience at the Lenaia see pp. 15–16.

[25] W. G. Forrest *Phoenix* 17 (1963) 8–9. Much of Forrest's article is effectively demolished by de Ste. Croix *Origins* 369–70, but not the statement that the speech is parody, which is reiterated by N.R.E. Fisher *G&R* 40 (1993) 38.

Do not resent it, men of the audience,
If I, a beggar, speak to Athenians . . .

(*Akharnians* 497–8)

But how much more of Dikaiopolis' speech is taken from Euripides? I believe that the extent of the borrowing has been overestimated. The evidence is of three kinds.

1. The scholia on *Akharnians* tell us that certain lines are taken
from Euripides, either exactly or with only slight alteration. These
are (besides 497–8): the first half of 540 ('You'll say "It should not
have." '), the second half of 543 ('Far from that!'), and part of 555–
6 ('And do we think that Telephos would not?'). The scholia do not
say that any other part of the speech is a quotation. The scholiast,
whoever he was (probably a Hellenistic commentator), obviously
had a copy of Euripides' play in front of him, and if he checked
through the speeches of Telephos and Dikaiopolis carefully enough
to notice that such an ordinary phrase as 'Far from that!' was
common to both of them, it is unlikely that he missed any other
quotations. However, one must acknowledge the possibility that
not all his notes have got copied out into the surviving medieval
manuscripts.

2. A few words used in the early part of the speech are used also
in the early part of *Women at the Thesmophoria* 466–519, the speech
in defence of Euripides made by his Relative disguised as a woman.
These are: the first half of 504 ('We're by ourselves'), the verb of
509 ('I hate'), and part of 514 ('Why do we blame . . . for this?').
Perhaps the reason is that in both places Aristophanes is quoting
from *Telephos*.[26] But it is not certainly so; the words are all common,
and the similarity of the situations and arguments in the two speeches
(urging the abandonment of hostility towards an old enemy) could
have led Aristophanes to use similar wording in both places without
even realizing that he was doing so.

3. The word used for a ship in 541 is poetic, and since the phrase
('voyaging in his bark') seems out of place in the logic of Dikaiopolis'
argument, it has been inferred that it is quoted from *Telephos*.[27]

These quotations do not amount to a great deal. It is misleading
to say that the whole of Dikaiopolis' speech is a parody of Euripides.

---

[26] Cf. Starkie *Acharnians* 106–8 (on lines 504 and 514).
[27] σκάφος: Rennie *Acharnians* ad loc., Sommerstein *Acharnians* ad loc.

What Aristophanes has done is to put the speech into the setting of Telephos' speech by dressing Dikaiopolis in Telephos' costume, and by putting a few words from Telephos' speech at the beginning, at the end, and in one sentence or so in between. That is enough to suggest the general similarity between the two, in that each is arguing against war before a hostile audience. But the specific arguments used in the central part of the speech are not the same. Although we do not know what Telephos' arguments were, obviously he cannot have talked about sycophants denouncing Megarian shawls, and a prostitute named Simaitha, and Perikles' decree, and so on. It is not plausible to say that those things have been put in for the sake of imitating Euripides.

But some people say that they have been put in for the sake of imitating Herodotos. At the beginning of Book 1, Herodotos says that according to the Persians it was the Phoenicians who were responsible for the origin of the conflict between the Greeks and the barbarians, because they kidnapped Io, daughter of the King of Argos; then some Greeks kidnapped Europa, daughter of the King of Tyre, and others kidnapped Medea, daughter of the King of Kolkhis; and in a later generation Paris carried off Helen, which led to the Trojan War. It has frequently been said that this part of Herodotos is parodied by Aristophanes in lines 524–9.[28] But I cannot find any good reason for believing that. I do not know whether Herodotos' book was published before or after the performance of *Akharnians*; opinions differ about its date. But even if it was before, it is most unlikely that many Athenians were familiar enough with it to be able to recognize a parody of one particular part of it unless Aristophanes had given very obvious signals indeed to warn them that a parody of Herodotos was coming. But in fact there are no such signals. Dikaiopolis does not mention the name of Herodotos; nor does he mention the Persians or the Phoenicians or the Trojans or any of the other people who occur in Herodotos' opening pages. He mentions three prostitutes, but that would hardly have made the Athenians think of all those daughters of kings. Above all, Dikaiopolis does not use any Herodotean vocabulary or turns of phrase.[29]

[28] Herodotos 1.1–5; cf. Forrest *Phoenix* 17 (1963) 8, Rau *Paratragodia* 40, Dover *Ar. Comedy* 87, de Ste. Croix *Origins* 240, L. Edmunds *YCS* 26 (1980) 13, H.-J. Newiger *YCS* 26 (1980) 222.
[29] D. Sansone *ICS* 10 (1985) 5–7 demurs at this statement, and observes that μὲν δή is very common in Herodotos. His observation is correct, but the phrase

Whereas the beginning and end of the speech do quote a few words from Euripides, the middle does not quote any words from Herodotos. There is really nothing in the speech which bears any resemblance to Herodotos at all.

So it is not plausible to maintain that the material in this speech has been put there by Aristophanes just for the sake of making amusing parodies. Although he uses a light touch for most of the speech, deliberately mentioning homely or vulgar items such as cucumbers and prostitutes, nevertheless he does expect his audience to accept that the Peloponnesian War resulted from the series of events which he recounts. It has been claimed that 'his account of the war's origins, so elaborately prepared for, turns out to be utterly preposterous'.[30] But this is not so. We should compare it with Thucydides' account of the events which led to the war. Here are two extracts from Thucydides.

Among others who came forward and made various complaints of their own were the Megarians; they pointed out a considerable number of disagreements, and in particular that they were excluded from harbours in the Athenian Empire and from the Athenian Agora, in contravention of the treaty.

(Thucydides 1.67.4)

On a later visit to the Athenians, [the Spartans] told them to withdraw from Poteidaia and to let Aigina be independent; and most emphatically and plainly they declared that there would not be war if the Athenians annulled the decree about the Megarians, in which they were forbidden to use the harbours in the Athenian Empire and the Athenian Agora. But the Athenians neither accepted the other demands nor annulled the decree, accusing the Megarians of cultivating sacred and unowned land and of receiving runaway slaves.

(Thucydides 1.139.1–2)

Dikaiopolis' account is more detailed.

Some men of ours—and I don't say the city;
Remember this, that I don't say the city,
But just some johnny-rascals, mis-struck coins,
Disfranchised, and mis-minted, and mis-foreign,

occurs elsewhere too and hardly seems distinctive enough to alert an audience to a parody.

[30] Heath *Political Comedy* 17, followed by Carey *Rh.Mus.* 136 (1993) 257.

Were sycophants: 'From Megara, those shawls!'
Wherever they saw a cucumber or hare
Or piglet or garlic or some lumps of salt,
Those were 'Megarian' and were sold that day.
Now that was just a little local matter;
But a prostitute, Simaitha, was stolen away
From Megara by some young men, kottabos-drunk.[31]
So the Megarians, garlic-puffed[32] with pain,
Stole two of Aspasia's prostitutes instead.
From that beginning, then, the war broke out
All over Greece, because of those three strumpets.
Then in anger Perikles the Olympian
Lightened and thundered and confounded Greece
And made laws in the style of drinking-songs:
'Megarians banned on land, in the Agora,
And on the sea and on the continent.'
Then the Megarians, starving step by step,
Entreated the Spartans to get the decree reversed,
The one resulting from the strumpet-girls;
But we refused, though they asked us many times;
And after that arose the clatter of shields.

(*Akharnians* 515–39)

The sequence of events which Dikaiopolis presents may be trans-
posed into more pedestrian language as follows. First, some disreputable Athenians hampered the sale of Megarian goods in Attica
by constant accusations that some law or regulation was being
infringed (515–22). It is unlikely that there was an otherwise
unknown decree, passed earlier than the well-known one, that
excluded Megarian goods specifically. More probably customs duties
were payable by law on all goods imported to Attica from any
source, and Megarian farmers and weavers, who lived so near that
they could easily slip into Attica by land, had been in the habit of
bringing their products across the frontier and selling them without
paying the duties. Suddenly some people started trying to enforce

[31] Kottabos was a game played at drinking-parties: each drinker, as he finished
a cupful of wine, aimed the last drops from his cup at a target in the middle of
the room. Here the meaning is that the young men had got through many cupfuls.
R. Scaife *GRBS* 33 (1992) 25–35 argues that the game was associated with both
love and war.

[32] Fighting cocks were fed on garlic to make them pugnacious. The symbolic
significance of garlic is discussed by E. Csapo *Phoenix* 47 (1993) 115–20.

the law; but Dikaiopolis regards the accusers as unreasonable and disreputable, and therefore calls them sycophants and not proper citizens.[33]

Next, according to Dikaiopolis, some young Athenians, when drunk, carried off from Megara a girl called Simaitha. The Megarians were annoyed, and in retaliation some of them carried off from Attica two girls in whom Aspasia (mistress of Perikles) was interested. Presumably all three girls were slaves. Dikaiopolis makes the incidents sound like kidnapping. But in affairs of love 'steal' does not have to imply the use of physical force, and if the two girls belonging to Aspasia were merely inveigled away, it may be possible to identify this incident with 'receiving runaway slaves' in Thucydides 1.139.2. In any case it may be included among the 'considerable number of disagreements' mentioned in Thucydides 1.67.4; that is a perfectly good phrase for what Dikaiopolis describes in 515–27.

Then Perikles, indignant on Aspasia's behalf, proposed the decree excluding Megarians from the Agora and from harbours in the Athenian Empire; the Megarians and the Spartans several times asked the Athenians to rescind the decree, but the Athenians refused, and so the war began (530–9). 'Perikles the Olympian lightened and thundered' means that he behaved as if he were Zeus, controlling the whole universe,[34] and 'in the style of drinking-songs' is a reference to songs that list numerous items; the implication is that the decree was very sweeping and comprehensive. The 'many times' that the Megarians and the Spartans asked the Athenians to rescind the decree cannot all be identified exactly, but there need not have been more than three occasions: perhaps one direct approach by the Megarians to the Athenians, the Spartan request recorded in Thucydides 1.139.1, and the final one mentioned in Thucydides 1.139.3. So nothing in this part of Dikaiopolis' speech conflicts significantly with Thucydides' summary of the events concerning the Megarian decree.

Dikaiopolis clearly means to say that the Athenians' refusal to annul the decree was the thing which caused the Spartans to declare

---

[33] Cf. de Ste. Croix *Origins* 383–6. On sycophants see pp. 74–5.

[34] Whether the phrase refers also to Perikles' style of oratory is disputed. Cf. Dover *Greek and the Greeks* 297, N. O'Sullivan *Alcidamas, Aristophanes and the Beginnings of Greek Stylistic Theory* (Stuttgart 1992) 107–15.

war. Thucydides too makes clear that this was what the Spartans said: 'they declared that there would not be war if the Athenians annulled the decree about the Megarians' (1.139.1). Now, it is well known that Thucydides considered that 'the truest cause' of the war was not the Megarian decree, but Spartan fear of the growth of Athenian power; in his view the decree was merely the catalyst which precipitated the real cause. But Dikaiopolis too says something which is not very different from that. In 540 he points out that the incidents which he has been describing may be thought an inadequate reason for fighting; but he goes on to say that if the Athenians had had similar provocation, if some Spartan had taken not some slaves, nor all the produce imported from some ally, but merely one little dog from Seriphos (one of the least important places in the Athenian Empire), the Athenians would have reacted with even more military and naval fuss. That is as much as to say that the reason for the Spartans' declaration of war was really that they were sensitive to Athenian encroachment on their own sphere of influence.

So Dikaiopolis' account of the outbreak of war, though expressed in a manner suitable to comedy, is not inconsistent with the account given by Thucydides;[35] it is not illogical or incredible; and I see no reason why it should not be essentially true. Of course it does not tell us everything. In particular, Aspasia's loss of her two girls may not have been the only reason why Perikles proposed the Megarian decree; he may have had a strategic or political reason too. Nevertheless it must be admitted that modern scholars have had great difficulty in discovering a strategic or political reason, and have not succeeded in reaching general agreement about what it was.[36] Aristophanes' suggestion, that Perikles was induced by a personal motive to take an action for which the strategic and political justification was weak, therefore deserves serious consideration.

That all this is meant to be taken seriously, as a convincing argument, is confirmed by what happens afterwards. Neither the

[35] Fisher *G&R* 40 (1993) 38 illogically asserts that it is not reconcilable with Thucydides' account because it omits some things which Thucydides mentions. Carey *Rh.Mus.* 136 (1993) 252–3 commits a similar error, failing to see that Dikaiopolis' and Thucydides' accounts are both likely to be incomplete, and that Perikles may have had more than one motive.

[36] Cf. B. R. MacDonald *Historia* 32 (1983) 385–410, giving references to many other discussions.

chorus of Akharnians nor any other character contradicts what Dikaiopolis has said. In other plays we find a debate, in which two speakers present opposite sides of a case, one refuting the other; but in this play Aristophanes does not present any opposite view for consideration. What happens is that the chorus splits into two halves, one half accepting what Dikaiopolis has said, the other half annoyed at it.

SEMICHORUS A. Do you, a beggar, dare speak so of us
   And blame us for some wretched sycophant?
SEMICHORUS B. Yes, by Poseidon! Every single thing
   He says is right, and none of it's untrue.
SEMICHORUS A. And if it's right, was he the man to say it?

(*Akharnians* 558–62)

Line 562 is clearly an admission that what Dikaiopolis said was in fact right. Subsequently, after the scene with Lamakhos, the whole chorus gives a verdict at the beginning of the parabasis: 'This man is victorious with what he has said, and he's now winning over the people concerning his treaty' (626–7). That is an assertion that Dikaiopolis convinces not just other characters in the play, but the people—that is, the people of Athens who are the audience in the theatre. It is the kind of pronouncement which is intended to assist its own fulfilment. Aristophanes in effect says 'You all believe now that the war is a mistake and it is right to make peace', and he hopes that will help to make the spectators think they do believe it.

LAMAKHOS

Those members of the chorus who still favour war call for Lama-khos, who immediately appears fully armed, having a helmet with a big crest of feathers and a shield bearing a terrifying portrayal of a Gorgon. Lamakhos, like Theoros earlier in the play, was a real man, not fictional, and held military office in the tribe to which Akharnai belonged. His career cannot be fully reconstructed, but we have some information about it. We first hear of him on a naval expedition led by Perikles to the Black Sea around 436 BC, when he was put in command of thirteen ships.[37] He may then have been only in his twenties, for in *Akharnians*, about ten years later, it is still possible for Dikaiopolis to call him young (601) and make a sexual joke which implies that he is young and good-looking (592). In 424 he again commanded a naval force in the Black Sea.[38] Later he was one of the commanders of the great expedition to Sicily, where he was killed fighting in 414, and after his death he was remembered as a brave soldier.[39]

What position he held at the time of *Akharnians* is not quite clear. In 593 he calls himself a general (*strategos*). But in 1073 he receives orders from the generals, which implies that he is not a general himself but holds a subordinate rank, probably as a taxiarch. Attempts to explain away the inconsistency are not altogether successful. 593 may not be dismissed as a quotation from tragedy which need not be taken literally.[40] Nor is it satisfactory to say that in 1073 Lamakhos is a general receiving a request from his fellow-generals;[41] for in 1079–83 he makes no protest that his colleagues have taken a decision in his absence to give him an unpleasant task without consulting him, but accepts without question that he must obey the orders of his superiors. So it seems better to adopt the suggestion that he was a taxiarch when *Akharnians* was written, but was elected a general shortly before the performance, either at a by-election or at the regular election of generals for the next year; Aristophanes then, for the sake of topicality, made a last-minute alteration in the script to introduce the word 'general' in 593, but found it impracticable to rewrite 1073–83 at that late stage.[42]

In any case, whether Lamakhos was a general or a taxiarch, it does not seem that he can have made a financial profit from his military office. There is in fact no clear evidence that generals or

---

[37] Plutarch *Perikles* 20. This does not necessarily mean that he was a general (and therefore over thirty years old) at that date.

[38] Thucydides 4.75.

[39] Cf. *Women at the Thesmophoria* 841, *Frogs* 1039.

[40] So Rennie *Acharnians* ad loc.; but the line contains the colloquial form ταυτί, and the metre infringes Porson's law.

[41] So N. V. Dunbar *CR* 20 (1970) 269–70.

[42] Cf. D. M. Lewis *JHS* 81 (1961) 120, M. V. Molitor *CR* 19 (1969) 141. The change in 593 need not have been anything more than the substitution of τὸν στρατηγὸν for ταξίαρχον. 598 refers to Lamakhos' election as an envoy on a previous occasion, not to his election as general; see below.

taxiarchs were paid at all in this period.[43] Yet Dikaiopolis proceeds
to accuse Lamakhos of making money from office, contrasting him
with himself and the old Akharnians of the chorus.

LAMAKHOS. Do you, a beggar, speak so of the general?
DIKAIOPOLIS. Am I a beggar?
LAMAKHOS.   Well, what are you, then?
DIKAIOPOLIS. True citizen, not a keen-on-office-ite,
    But, since the war began, a soldier-ite.
    You're, since the war began, a salary-ite.
LAMAKHOS. I was elected—
DIKAIOPOLIS.   By three cuckoos, yes!
    That's why I got so sick and made a treaty,
    Seeing grey-haired men serving in the ranks,
    While young men such as you had scuttled off:
    Some towards Thrace, drawing three drachmas' pay . . .

    .   .   .   .
LAMAKHOS. They were elected.
DIKAIOPOLIS.   What's the reason, then,
    That you somehow all keep on drawing pay,
    While none of these men do? Marilades,
    Have you served as an envoy, though you're grey?
    He nodded 'no'; yet he's a sober worker.
    Drakyllos? Prinides? Euphorides?
    Have you seen Ekbatana or Khaonia?
    They answer 'no'. But Koisyra's son has,
    And Lamakhos.[44]

(*Akharnians* 593–602, 607–14)

This passage is not about Lamakhos' election to the generalship
or to any military office. The point is that, whereas Dikaiopolis and
other grey-haired men performed military service, younger men
such as Lamakhos got away to places where no fighting was going
on, by being elected as envoys to Thrace or Ekbatana (in Persia) or
Khaonia (in Epirus).

[43] The Old Oligarch ([Xenophon] *Ath. Pol.* 1.3) draws a contrast between the
generalship and offices held for profit.
[44] 'Koisyra's son' was Megakles, an aristocrat of the famous Alkmeonid family.
(On problems in the historical genealogy see B. M. Lavelle *GRBS* 30 (1989)
503–13; on his reconstruction this Megakles was really the grandson of Koisyra.)
Since he and Lamakhos are named after the mention of Ekbatana and Khaonia, I
wonder if Megakles was one of the envoys who went to Persia in 426 (see p. 51)
and Lamakhos went as an envoy to Khaonia in the same year.

We should therefore draw a distinction between two topics which
Aristophanes includes in his satirical presentation of Lamakhos. One
is the accusation that Lamakhos, like Theoros and others, has made
financial gains and avoided campaigns by getting himself appointments as an envoy. Although he invokes democracy (618) and justifies himself by claiming to have been elected (598), Dikaiopolis
brushes the claim aside with scorn: 'By three cuckoos'. Envoys were
elected by voting in the Assembly, and here once again, as at the
beginning of the play, Aristophanes is suggesting that the Assembly's
decisions do not represent the true interests and wishes of the
Athenian people, because many of them do not attend it. Consequently lucrative and enjoyable appointments as envoys go to
unscrupulous office-seekers, and not to other men who are deserving, such as an old man in the chorus who is 'a sober worker'
(611). The whole passage is scornful, not jocular, and no doubt
Aristophanes means it to be taken seriously. Yet it is not really very
convincing. Citizens who did not bother to attend the Assembly had
only themselves to blame if they did not like its decisions. And it
was to the advantage of the Athenian people that important posts
should not be held by nonentities, on the system of Buggins's turn,
but by capable men. Aristophanes has made the mistake of thinking
that the job of an envoy is as easy as it looks, so that anyone could
do it.

The other charge against Lamakhos, which we should keep separate, is that as a military officer he behaves in a conceited and
pompous manner. We have no means of knowing how far Aristophanes has exaggerated this, and how far Lamakhos actually did
boom and swagger in real life; perhaps he did boom and swagger a
little, and Aristophanes has made the most of it. But this, unlike the
accusation of exploiting appointment as an envoy, is not a serious
political criticism, but is due rather to dramatic requirement. The
play needed to have a character, and not merely the chorus, standing
for war, in opposition to Dikaiopolis; and that character had to be
made to look foolish. For this dramatic purpose, three things made
Lamakhos particularly suitable. First, his name happened actually
to mean 'great fighter' and could be used to make a comic jingle
with the word for 'fight' (269–70, 1071). Secondly, he was the
general or taxiarch of the particular tribe (Oineis) to which the
deme of Akharnai belonged. And thirdly, there was his Gorgon
shield. Aristophanes has a good deal of fun with the fact that Lama-

khos' shield is decorated with a terrifying picture of a Gorgon's face, and his helmet with large plumes. These must have been well-known features of Lamakhos' armour in real life. Plumes and Gorgons were in fact common, but presumably Lamakhos' were bigger and fiercer-looking than anyone else's. Aristophanes has combined these facts and a bombastic manner to produce a personification of militarism.

TRADERS AND SYCOPHANTS

Lamakhos declares his determination to carry on the war, and Dikaiopolis proclaims that all Peloponnesians, Megarians, and Boiotians may trade with him, but not with Lamakhos. After the parabasis[45] Dikaiopolis marks out his own Agora for this purpose, and soon two traders arrive. Both come from enemy states, but neither is presented as unfavourably as Lamakhos or the Athenian envoys earlier in the play.

The first to arrive is a man from Megara with his two little daughters.[46] In real life, we must remember, the Megarians not only were on the enemy side but were widely regarded as being responsible for starting the war. In an Athenian play we might expect a Megarian to be treated in a thoroughly hostile manner; we might expect the Athenian audience to laugh gleefully at his starvation and other sufferings. But what we find is just the opposite: the audience is encouraged to sympathize with the Megarian and regard him as a friend. When he appears, his first words are a greeting to the Agora.

MEGARIAN. Hail, Athens' Agora, that Megarians love!
  By the god of friendship, I missed you like a mother!

(*Akharnians* 729–30)

Is this just cupboard love, and does the Megarian love the Athenian market because he can exploit Athenian customers and make a profit out of them? No, that is not the right interpretation, because Aristophanes has not put in any words to hint at that. He could very

---

[45] On the parabasis see pp. 31–4. It is largely a digression from the main theme of the play. A. M. Bowie *CQ* 32 (1982) 27–40 tries to find connections, but they are not all convincing. See also Hubbard *Mask* 47–56.

[46] I repeat here, with minor changes, a discussion of the Megarian which originally appeared in *G&R* 30 (1983) 156–8. A different view is taken by Carey *Rh.Mus.* 136 (1993) 248–9.

easily have done so. He does in fact do something like that in *Birds* 37–8, for example, where a character comments that Athens is 'great and prosperous, open to everyone—for paying fines'. Aristophanes could have given *Akharnians* 730 a similar twist in its tail, but he has not. The Megarian does not say 'I missed you, a place open to everyone—for making profits'; he says 'By the god of friendship, I missed you', which puts his motive in a favourable light.

The Megarian and his daughters are starving after six years of war;[47] and because he has nothing else to offer in the market, he decides to sell the two little girls disguised as pigs, and they willingly agree.

MEGARIAN. Which would you rather do, be sold or starve?
GIRLS. Be sold, be sold!
MEGARIAN. I say so too. But who'd be such a fool
  As to buy you, an obvious waste of money?
  But still, I've got a Megarian device:
  I'll dress you up and say I've brought some pigs.

(*Akharnians* 734–9)

When Dikaiopolis reappears, he at first thinks that the 'pigs' look quite human (774), but eventually accepts that they really are pigs and agrees to buy them (811–12).[48] The humour of this scene comes partly from the comic dressing-up, and partly from elaboration of a sexual pun on the word for 'pig'.[49] But there is also a serious element in it, which comes to the fore when the plight of people in Megara is described.

DIKAIOPOLIS. What else are you doing in Megara?
MEGARIAN.   What we do.
  When I was starting on my journey here,
  The Probouloi were trying hard to find
  The quickest way to get our city—ruined!

[47] This scene shows the effect of the war, including the frequent Athenian invasions of the Megarid. It has nothing to do with the pre-war Megarian decree. Cf. de Ste. Croix *Origins* 237–9.

[48] It is part of the joke that Dikaiopolis is taken in by the disguise. Bowie *Aristophanes* 33 takes it too seriously when he writes of 'enslavement of Greeks by Greeks'.

[49] For detailed exposition of the pun see Dover *Ar. Comedy* 63–5, L. Edmunds *YCS* 26 (1980) 17–18.

DIKAIOPOLIS. Your troubles will soon be ended then.

MEGARIAN.   That's right.

DIKAIOPOLIS. What else at Megara? What's the price of grain?

MEGARIAN. With us it's like the dear gods—very dear!

DIKAIOPOLIS. You've brought salt?

MEGARIAN.   You yourselves control it, don't you?

DIKAIOPOLIS. Or garlic, then?

MEGARIAN.   What garlic! You yourselves,
    Whenever you invade, are like field-mice:
    You dig out every clove of it with sticks.

                                        (*Akharnians* 753–63)

Salt and garlic were the two best-known products of Megara, but Athenian invasions have caused so much destruction that not even those are now being produced. The Megarian therefore has nothing; but Dikaiopolis is not gloating, nor is the Athenian audience encouraged to do so. The jokes here are sardonic comments made *by* the Megarian, not at him: 'the quickest way to get our city—ruined!', 'like the dear gods—very dear!' He blames not only the Athenians but also the Megarian government. In the first half of the play, especially in the opening speech, we heard about the troubles Dikaiopolis and other Athenians were having because of the war, and much of the blame for them was put on officials, the Prytaneis. Now in the second half of the play, in the opening scene after the parabasis, we hear about the troubles the Megarians are having because of the war, and the blame for them is put on Megarian officials, the Probouloi. There is a clear parallelism here, suggesting that countrymen on both sides should make common cause against incompetent leaders. It is quite unconvincing to suggest (as some have) that the audience is expected to sympathize with Dikaiopolis but laugh at the plight of the Megarian. Their hardships are presented as being essentially similar, though the lines about the Athenians taking the Megarians' salt and garlic do suggest that the Megarians are even worse off than the Athenians, and that the Athenians ought not to be so hard on them. Dikaiopolis does in fact agree to buy the 'pigs', and defends the Megarian when a sycophant tries to accuse him.[50]

[50] The statement of Dover *Ar. Comedy* 81 that Dikaiopolis drives the sycophant away 'for interference with *his* well-being, not with the Megarian's' is incorrect. Lines 819–20, 823–4, and 827 all show that the sycophant is accusing the Megarian, not Dikaiopolis. In 830 Dikaiopolis consoles and encourages the Megarian.

The second trader is a Boiotian from Thebes. He too is from an enemy state, but his situation is just the opposite of the Megarian's. Boiotia has more good agricultural land, and consequently the Boiotian brings with him a wide range of foodstuffs, with delicacies such as eels from Lake Kopais which were not available in Athens in wartime. Dikaiopolis is delighted with them; his only problem is to find anything to offer in exchange which the Boiotian does not already have. The comic solution to the problem is a sycophant: that is a thing produced in Athens and nowhere else!

It is convenient to use 'sycophant' to translate *sykophantes*, but the meaning differs from the usual sense of 'sycophant' in modern English. The Greek word is a disparaging term for a prosecutor.[51] In Athens, for most kinds of offence against the state or the community, there was no publicly appointed prosecutor. Instead anyone who wished (or, for some offences, any Athenian citizen who wished) could prosecute in a public case. Some men no doubt brought such cases simply from public spirit, wishing to see justice done; some to improve their own reputation as orators or politicians; some as a means of injuring a personal or political opponent. And for some kinds of prosecution, perhaps because they concerned offences which were more liable than others to be ignored, an extra incentive was provided by giving a financial reward to the prosecutor if he won the case. One of these kinds of prosecution was *phasis* (literally 'showing' or 'revealing'),[52] which could be used against goods wrongfully imported, because they came from an enemy state or had been brought in without payment of customs duty. Anyone who wished could point out the offending goods to bystanders in the market and to the appropriate officials. If the accused trader was found guilty, the goods were confiscated and sold; half the proceeds was retained by the state and half was given to the successful prosecutor. That was his incentive to take action.

But perhaps the incentives given to volunteer prosecutors were too great. At any rate the system gave rise to a notorious nuisance. This was the man who made a practice of prosecuting without justification, either because he hoped to get the payment which fell

---

[51] For recent discussion of sycophants in Athens see MacDowell *Law* 62–6, R. Osborne and D. Harvey in *Nomos* 83–121, S. C. Todd *The Shape of Athenian Law* (Oxford 1993) 92–4.

[52] On *phasis* and the Aristophanic evidence for it, see MacDowell in *Symposion 1990* (ed. M. Gagarin, Cologne 1991) 187–98.

due to a successful prosecutor, or because he hoped to blackmail the accused man into bribing him to drop the accusation. It was this kind of man who was called a sycophant, and sycophants are among Aristophanes' favourite targets. They appear on-stage in *Akharnians*, *Birds*, and *Wealth*, and are mentioned in other plays; the play performed at the Lenaia in 423, which may have been *Merchant-ships*, had an attack on sycophants as its main theme (according to *Wasps* 1037–42). Aristophanes presents sycophancy as if it were a regular, though disgraceful, profession, rather like prostitution. Probably the true situation was not so clear-cut. The term is subjective and opprobrious, not just factual. Many a defendant, even if guilty, would angrily call his accuser a sycophant, but no prosecutor would ever use the word of himself, and perhaps no prosecutor made a regular living by prosecution; how many found it a useful source of supplementary income, we cannot say.

THE PLEASURES OF PEACE

The delicious food which Dikaiopolis buys from the Boiotian is the first real advantage that he gets from making peace (for his celebration of the rural Dionysia was cut short by the Akharnians), but from this point on everything goes his way. He starts making preparations for a scrumptious feast. Presently a herald proclaims a drinking competition,[53] and a messenger invites Dikaiopolis to dine with the priest of Dionysos. While Lamakhos is called out for a military expedition, from which he later returns comically wailing about his injuries, Dikaiopolis wins the drinking contest and returns with two pretty girls. Thus he ends the play triumphant, in an orgy of food, drink, and sex.

Some critics have considered that Dikaiopolis here is totally selfish,[54] but this seems to be a false interpretation. Certainly he

[53] On the Anthesteria see pp. 280–1. The drinking competition had presumably been in abeyance during the war because the destruction of vines had diminished the supply of wine.

[54] Dover *Ar. Comedy* 87–8, H.-J. Newiger *YCS* 26 (1980) 223–4, A. M. Bowie *CQ* 32 (1982) 40, H. P. Foley *JHS* 108 (1988) 45–6, N. R. E. Fisher *G&R* 40 (1993) 39–41. A contrary view is rightly taken by L. P. E. Parker *JHS* 111 (1991) 204–6; C. Carey *Rh.Mus.* 136 (1993) 250, with some reason, considers that Aristophanes is deliberately vague on the matter.

enjoys himself, but he does not wish to prevent other people from enjoying themselves too. In the early part of the play it is made quite clear that he wants the Assembly to make peace for Athens as a whole, and it is not until that has been found impossible that he takes steps to make a private peace. When he has his treaty, it is not he who refuses to share it with the Akharnians; it is the Akharnians who furiously condemn it. He does share it with the Peloponnesians, Megarians, and Boiotians, in the sense that he is willing to trade with them; he bans Lamakhos from his market, but does not explicitly ban other Athenians (623–5, 720–2). The question is: do other Athenians want peace? Gradually it begins to seem that they do. Already at the beginning of the parabasis the chorus says that he is winning over the people (626). After seeing the market in operation, the chorus declares 'I shall never receive War into my home' (979) and looks forward to life with Reconciliation. Then comes the herald proclaiming the drinking competition; the proclamation is addressed to people in general, not just to Dikaiopolis (1000–2).

Yet there are some individuals who are excluded. Besides Lamakhos, whose request to buy some food is rejected (959–70), there is a man named Derketes of Phyle, who wants peace because the Boiotians have raided his farm and taken his pair of oxen. Derketes must have been a real man, not a fictional character, but we know nothing else about him. Possibly he was a man who had spoken in favour of war, until he himself suffered some loss by it, and Aristophanes therefore considered that he deserved no sympathy.[55] In the play Derketes asks Dikaiopolis to anoint his eyes with peace, or to give him a drop of peace to take away (1028–34). (In the first half of the play peace is represented on-stage as wine, in the second half as ointment, probably olive-oil, reflecting the fact that the Spartan invasions destroyed vines and olive-trees.) Dikaiopolis refuses and sends Derketes away, and the chorus comments that it seems he will not share with anyone the pleasant thing which he has obtained by his treaty (1037–9). The point is that anyone wanting the advantages of peace must himself make the appropriate effort. The same point is immediately made again with another example: a bridegroom asks for a spoonful of peace, so that he may avoid military service and stay at home with his bride (1051–3). Again Dikaiopolis refuses, because the bridegroom merely displays lazi-

---

[55] Cf. MacDowell *G&R* 30 (1983) 158–60.

ness and lechery instead of taking active steps to bring the war to an end. But he relents when he gets a request from the bride; she does not deserve[56] to suffer from the war, because it is not within the power of a woman to make a peace treaty.

DIKAIOPOLIS AND ATHENS

Who is Dikaiopolis? It is easy to say that he is the chief character in the story, an old countryman who makes a private peace. But this answer is inadequate. He is indeed a character in the story, but before all else he is a comedian in the theatre.[57] When the play begins, he is an actor who comes and talks to the audience. He has no name (until 406, when a third of the play is already past), and for the first minute or two he says nothing about the story or his own part in it. Instead he chats about theatrical matters, giving his comments on some recent performances; he has been in the audience to watch them.[58] Even when he begins to describe the basic situation of the story, he continues talking to the audience until 42. After that the action of the play goes forward, but Dikaiopolis is in the theatre still: his longest speech of all is addressed to the audience (497–556), and even when speaking to another character he can imply that he and the audience should side together against the chorus.

> I have to seem a beggar for today,
> Be who I am, but not appear to be.
> The audience must realize who I am,
> Whereas the chorus must stand by like fools
> For me to cock a snook with phrasicles.

(Akharnians 440–4)

He is not merely an actor; he is the narrator or compère. In his first speech he tells the spectators that the scene is on the Pnyx; they do not know that until he tells them. Later he says that he is

---

[56] I retain the manuscripts' reading ἀξία in 1062; cf. Dover *Greek and the Greeks* 302 n. 41.

[57] Reckford *Old-and-New* 63–9 gives a similar analysis, but with more emphasis on Dikaiopolis as a clown.

[58] On the question whether the incident concerning Kleon (5–8) was part of a play, see pp. 95–7.

going into his house in the country (202), and then that he is going
to the house of Euripides (394); in each case that forthwith becomes
the scene. Wherever he goes, the play goes; and if he does not say
where he is, the scene is nowhere—or rather, it is back in the
theatre.

The meeting of the Assembly provides an interesting illustration
of the ambivalence of his role.[59] In this scene it seems clear that the
Prytancis are played by non-speaking actors who appear at 40, but
there can hardly be a further crowd of actors to represent the
ordinary citizens attending the meeting. Instead the speakers simply
address the audience in the theatre, so that the citizens attending
the play find that they are virtually playing the part of themselves
attending the Assembly. Dikaiopolis then, as an ordinary citizen,
must take a seat in or near the audience. He watches and listens to
the speakers, but he soon begins to find the proceedings unsatisfactory, and when he grumbles loudly to his neighbours or jumps
up to protest, the dramatic effect is that of a protest emanating from
the audience. At 110 he becomes so discontented that he stands
up, dismisses the envoy, and himself takes over the questioning of
Pseudartabas. The proceedings in the real Assembly could not be
taken over by one of the citizens in that manner. But this is not the
real Assembly; it is a comedy, and Dikaiopolis is intervening on
behalf of the audience in his capacity as compère. In fact he virtually
is the comedy.

> For even comedy knows what is right,
> And what I'll say, though startling, will be right.

> (*Akharnians* 500–1)

What comedy knows, Dikaiopolis says. Dikaiopolis and comedy
are here regarded as identical, and with one voice they say what is
right. At this point we should also consider Dikaiopolis' name. The
audience is not expected to discover his character from his name;
by the time his name is given (406) his character is already well
established. Nevertheless, there his name is, and it is repeated at
intervals through the play. Aristophanes will not have invented a
name which was unsuitable for the character or inconsistent with
it. What does the name mean, then? It is a compound of words
meaning 'just' and 'city', but the form of the compound does not

[59] Cf. N. W. Slater in *Tr.Com.Pol.* 397–401.

make clear the relationship between the two parts. It might mean 'just towards the city' or 'having a just city' or 'making the city just', and other similar compounds in Greek poetry do not enable us to make a confident choice among these possibilities.[60] Perhaps Aristophanes did not intend the audience to get a precise sense out of the name; it just gives a general impression that the man has something to do with right behaviour in public affairs.

Dikaiopolis, then, is closely identified with the citizens in the theatre and with doing what is right. Fundamental to the effectiveness of *Akharnians* is the contrast between his exceptional reality and the unreality of what he achieves. An actual Athenian takes off into fantasy. The point at which the fantasy begins is the appearance of Amphitheos. Amphitheos is a god who is ready to make a peace treaty with the Spartans, if only his travelling expenses are paid, but Dikaiopolis alone is willing to pay them. Peace is obtained as if by magic. Peace is wine; peace is olive-oil; peace enables Dikaiopolis to return home to the country, and to trade with anyone he wishes. Peace leads to pleasures of every kind—but only for the man who has made the effort to obtain it. Aristophanes is saying to each Athenian: 'Suppose there were a heaven-sent opportunity to make peace at this moment, with just a little effort on your part. Would you be ready to forget the past and make the effort? See what the result would be if you did!'

[60] Cf. MacDowell *G&R* 30 (1983) 162 n. 37.

5

Horsemen

THE TITLE

The title of Aristophanes' play performed at the Lenaia of 424 BC has usually been translated into English as *Knights*. That is a misleading name. In modern Britain a knight is a gentleman, usually over fifty years of age, who has been rewarded with the appellation 'Sir' in recognition of his services to administration, business, the arts, or some other field of public endeavour. Most knights have probably never ridden a horse in their lives. The title of Aristophanes' play, by contrast, refers to the men, probably all young, who rode horses for their service in the Athenian army. *Cavalry* might be a suitable translation, but even that is not entirely satisfactory, since cavalry now generally use motor vehicles rather than horses. It is better, following the example of Bugh's book *The Horsemen of Athens*, to use the name *Horsemen*, which translates the Greek word more literally and less misleadingly.

KLEON

The play is a virulent attack on Kleon. Kleon was the leading politician in Athens at this time, and yet we do not know a great deal about what he did. Thucydides relates his activities on only four occasions: the debate about Mytilene in 427 BC, the Pylos campaign in 425, the proposal of a decree about Skione in 423, and the Amphipolis campaign in which he met his death in 422. Later sources add very little by way of hard facts. But it is clear that he differed from earlier politicians in significant respects.[1]

---

[1] See especially W. R. Connor *The New Politicians of Fifth-Century Athens* (Princeton 1971).

One important difference was his social origin. Earlier politicians had generally come from prominent Athenian families, affluent enough to give them a gentlemanly education and then sufficient leisure to devote to public affairs. Kleon did not come from a leading family, but was associated with the making and selling of leather. Aristophanes simply calls him a tanner, and uses this as the basis for jokes and sarcasm about Kleon and leather.[2] Whether that means that he came from a background of poverty is not clear. It cannot be true that he spent every day tanning leather with his own hands or selling it in the Agora, or he would have had no time for politics; he must have owned slaves who did those things for him. Indeed it has been argued that his family, though not aristocratic, was wealthy,[3] but the evidence for that is tenuous, consisting of only two items of doubtful significance. First, Kleon's father was named Kleainetos and belonged to Kydathenaion, a town deme of the Pandionis tribe, and one Kleainetos was the chorus-producer for the victorious dithyrambic chorus of men from Pandionis at the Dionysia in 459;[4] if that was Kleon's father, he must have been quite well off to afford the expense of being a chorus-producer. But perhaps it was not Kleon's father, who was not necessarily the only man in Pandionis named Kleainetos. Second, a scholium on *Horsemen* 44 says: 'His father Kleonymos (*sic*) had a workshop of slave tanners.' But that does not prove that Kleon inherited wealth, since the workshop may have been small and the slaves few. In addition, attempts have been made to trace connections by marriage between Kleon and well-to-do families; but even if such connections were certain they would tell us nothing about the wealth of his own family, for many Athenians would probably be willing to form an alliance by marriage with the family of a leading politician after his rise to power, even if he was not wealthy.[5] So the belief that Kleon's family was wealthy, though it could be true, does not rest on firm foundations.

[2] This aspect of *Horsemen* is discussed in detail by Lind *Der Gerber Kleon* 33–85.

[3] Connor *The New Politicians of Fifth-Century Athens* 151–2, Kraus *Ar. pol. Kom.* 170–1.

[4] *IG* 2² 2318.34; cf. Pickard-Cambridge *Festivals* 104.

[5] J. K. Davies *Athenian Propertied Families* (Oxford 1971) 318–20 attempts to trace connections, but his conclusions are reasonably questioned by F. Bourriot *Historia* 31 (1982) 404–35. For evidence that later a family might be proud of a connection with Kleon see Demosthenes 40.25.

Another important difference between Kleon and earlier politicians lay in his style of oratory. Thucydides, on mentioning him for the first time, says: 'Besides being the most violent of the citizens in other respects, he was also by far the most capable of persuading the democracy at that time' (3.36.6). That implies that his manner of addressing the Assembly was violent, without explaining exactly what that means; but it probably means shouting and rudeness. Those two features are mentioned explicitly in the *Athenaion Politeia* attributed to Aristotle: 'He was the first to shout and utter abuse on the platform, and he delivered a public speech girt around when the other men spoke in an orderly manner' (28.3). Plutarch expands this further: 'He put an end to orderly conduct on the platform, and in public speaking he was the first to shout and pull his cloak away and strike his thigh and stride around while he was speaking' (*Nikias* 8.6). Earlier orators had kept their hands inside their cloaks,[6] but Kleon evidently slipped his cloak off one or both shoulders, having it secured by a belt, to enable him to gesticulate with his hands so as to hold the attention of a crowd. It is reasonable to relate this to the nature of Kleon's political support: whereas other politicians were supported by the influence of prominent families and groups of friends, Kleon's support came more from a mass of ordinary citizens, and his oratory had to be of a kind that would arouse and attract large numbers of people.

Perikles and other political leaders before him had mostly held the elected military office of general (*strategos*), but Kleon, as far as we know, was never a general until he was unexpectedly elected in 425. The events are narrated by Thucydides in Book 4; here they can only be summarized. An Athenian force under the command of the general Demosthenes had occupied the small peninsula of Pylos in the south-west Peloponnese, and was besieging some Spartan troops, including a number of Spartiates (full Spartan citizens), on the nearby island of Sphakteria. The Spartan authorities, anxious for the safety of the Spartiates, sent envoys to Athens offering a peace treaty, but Kleon persuaded the Athenians to demand concessions which were unacceptable to the Spartans, and the negotiations collapsed. The siege of Sphakteria therefore continued, but it took longer than the Athenians had expected; news reached Athens that their force was in difficulties from lack of provisions, while the

---

[6] Aiskhines 1.25, Plutarch *Ethika* 800c.

Spartans were succeeding in smuggling food through to their men on the island. The Athenians began to regret not having accepted the offer of a peace treaty.

This is the point at which the conduct of Kleon emerges most vividly in the pages of Thucydides (4.27–39). Realizing that he was incurring blame for obstructing the making of peace, he declared that the messengers were not telling the truth about the situation at Pylos. The messengers told the Athenians, if they did not believe it, to send other men to see, and so Kleon and Theagenes were appointed to go as observers. Kleon now realized that if he went he would be forced to admit he had been wrong about the facts. So he said it was no use sending observers; they should send a force. He pointed at Nikias, one of the generals, and said that, if the generals were really men, they could easily sail and capture the Spartans on the island, and that, if he himself had been in office, he would have done it. So Nikias offered to hand over the generalship to him. At first Kleon professed readiness to accept, but when he found that the offer was serious he became nervous and tried to withdraw; yet the more he tried to back out, the more the crowd in the Assembly clamoured that he should accept. In the end he undertook the generalship, and declared that within twenty days he would either bring the Spartans to Athens alive or kill them on the spot. The Athenians laughed at the absurd promise. But when Kleon reached Pylos, he and Demosthenes commanded an assault on Sphakteria and overcame the Spartan resistance. Some of the Spartans were killed, but 292, including about 120 Spartiates, were brought to Athens within twenty days, so that Kleon's rash promise was fulfilled. The story, as related by Thucydides, who is notoriously hostile to Kleon, makes him appear unscrupulous and boastful. He got enormous credit for his achievement; but ought the credit to have been given rather to Demosthenes, who had nearly completed the campaign before Kleon arrived?

THE SERVANTS OF DEMOCRACY

Horsemen presents a story about the slaves of a householder named Demos. As a matter of fact there was a real man named Demos living in Athens at this period (mentioned in *Wasps* 98 for the purpose of a quite different joke), but it was not a normal Athenian

name and the real man is completely irrelevant to *Horsemen*. What
we have here is a personification of what the Greeks called *demos*. In
some ways it is comparable to the personification of Peace and War
in *Peace*, and of Wealth and Poverty in *Wealth*, but Demos differs
from those in being much more human.[7]

The word *demos* has more than one use, and it is not easy to
decide how to translate it. However, we can clearly exclude here
the sense of a political district or 'deme'. The translation commonly
given is 'people', but in modern English that is hardly adequate.
'People' was formerly a singular noun, but now it is normally used
as the plural of 'person' and refers to a number of individuals. That
is not what Aristophanes means by *demos*. He is referring to the
political community of Athens, manifested in the meetings of the
Assembly on the Pnyx. Though made up of individuals, it acts and
reacts as a unit, and it is this collective political unity which is
personified in the character Demos. No English word exists that
will translate it quite satisfactorily, for the simple reason that the
phenomenon does not exist in the English-speaking world. Yet we
ought to translate it somehow; if we evade translation and just
speak of Demos, it is too easy to forget that the character is a
personification. The least unsatisfactory solution, I think, is to call
him Democracy. Although this English word is often more abstract
than *demos*, it can mean 'the populace in power' (as when we say,
for example, that certain measures taken by the oligarchy in 411
were annulled by the democracy in 410), and that is probably as
near as we can get in English to the notion personified in this play.

The character does not appear on-stage until half-way through
the play, but early on he is described by one of his slaves.

> The master we two have
> Is country-tempered, bean-eating and prickly—
> Democracy of Pnyx, a cross old boy,
> And hard of hearing.

> (*Horsemen* 40–3)

It was normal for an Athenian to be formally named with the
name of his deme; so here, to make him sound like an Athenian
citizen, the Pnyx (which was not a deme, but the place where the
Assembly usually met) is named as if it were Democracy's deme.

---

[7] For a detailed study of this personification see Newiger *Metapher* 11–49.

But how are we to interpret the rest of the description? It is obviously not true that all Athenian citizens attending meetings of the Assembly were old and came from the country. It is true that several Aristophanic heroes share these features (Dikaiopolis, Strepsiades, Trygaios), but that seems an insufficient reason for portraying Democracy in this way. Rather, this is Aristophanes' attempt to characterize the manner in which the Assembly received speeches and events. Although many individual Athenians might be young and urbane, if you wanted to win over the Assembly *as a whole* you had to speak as you would to a crotchety old countryman, explaining your points loudly and clearly and taking care not to give offence.

As the play begins, two of Democracy's slaves come on-stage yelling with pain because they have just been beaten. (This is a comic opening, not a sad one; audiences enjoy comic violence.) They complain about a newly-bought slave named Paphlagon who keeps getting the other slaves beaten, and presently one of them turns to the audience to explain the situation more fully. He begins with the description of their master, already quoted, and then goes on:

> At the last New Moon[8]
> He bought a slave, a tanner, Paphlagon,
> Very villainous and very slanderous.
> This tanner-Paphlagon, when he'd seen through
> The old man's ways, bowed down before the master
> And fawned and cringed and flattered and deceived him
> With odds and ends, and said this sort of thing:
> 'Democracy, just try one case; then take
> A bath, tuck in, sup, eat, accept three obols!
> Shall I serve you supper?' Then he snatches up
> Something that one of us got for the master,
> And Paphlagon gets the thanks! The other day
> I made a cake, a Spartan one, at Pylos;
> That pesky perpetrator popped in, pinched it,
> And served it up himself, the cake I made!
> He keeps us away, and won't let someone else
> Attend on the master; standing with a strap
> At dinner, he whisks away—the politicians.
> He makes the old man mad as any Sibyl
> With oracles, and seeing him stupefied,
> He's got a system: he tells outright lies

[8] New Moon (the first day of the month) was market day.

About the household, and then *we* get whipped,
While Paphlagon runs round to all the slaves,
Asks, harasses, gets bribes, by saying this:
'You see how Hylas is whipped because of me?
Unless you bribe me, you shall die today!'

(*Horsemen* 43–68)

It is obvious that the slaves of Democracy are an allegorical representation of the politicians serving the Athenian state, and that Paphlagon represents Kleon. That is made plain by calling him a tanner at the start of the description; no normal household slave would be a tanner. The references to trying a case for a fee of three obols (a juror's daily pay), to Pylos, and to whisking away the politicians (instead of flies) show how the allegory is to be applied to real-life Athens. The rest of this passage keeps within the allegory, but its implications are clear: Kleon has secured the trust and favour of the Assembly by flattery and by proposing small benefits for the citizens, such as an increase in the pay of jurors (cf. p. 163); he claims credit for services to Athens which have really been performed by others, notably at Pylos; he prevents other politicians from serving Athens, and gets them punished unfairly, unless they submit to his blackmail; and he deludes the Assembly by quoting oracles. These are themes which will be developed later in the action of the play.

The name Paphlagon should refer to a slave brought from Paphlagonia, in the north of Asia Minor. It was common for Athenian masters to name their slaves after their countries of origin, such as Thratta from Thrace (*Akharnians* 273) and Phryx from Phrygia (*Wasps* 433). These were immediately recognizable as slaves' names (much as we recognize Rover and Fido as dogs' names). Probably Paphlagon was a name in this category; it may be just accidental that we do not find it elsewhere in surviving Athenian texts, and Aristophanes may have picked it almost at random as a typical slave's name, not implying that Kleon actually has any connection with Paphlagonia.[9] However, there is one passage in the play where he exploits the name by saying that the man is boiling (919, *paphlazei*),

---

[9] The use of this servile name in the allegory should not be interpreted as an allegation that Kleon was actually of foreign birth. Neither in this play nor elsewhere is there any assertion that Kleon was of non-Athenian origin.

and it is possible that he already had this pun in mind when he chose the name.[10]

The identity of the two slaves who appear at the start of the play has been considered more problematical. Clearly the allegory requires that they represent other Athenian politicians or generals, and some of the manuscripts in fact identify them as Demosthenes and Nikias. However, that evidence is not conclusive, because the attributions of lines to speakers in medieval manuscripts are largely due to scholiasts and editors, and probably few or none of them were written in by Aristophanes himself. Demosthenes and Nikias are not named in the actual text; and it has been argued by Dover that no passage in the opening dialogue required for the appreciation of its humour any knowledge of the character of any real person, and that we do not know whether it was practicable to identify Demosthenes and Nikias for the audience by portrait-masks or other visual means.[11]

Nevertheless it cannot be denied that in 54–7 one of the slaves claims that he made the cake at Pylos which Paphlagon stole and served up as his own. Demosthenes was the only man from whom Kleon could be accused of stealing the credit for the victory at Pylos, and since it is already clear by this point that the slaves of Democracy represent politicians or generals and Paphlagon represents Kleon, the spectators are bound to identify the speaker of 54–7 as Demosthenes, whether or not they have so identified him earlier. In these lines, at least, it is not true that the humour can be appreciated by someone who knows nothing of Demosthenes and Kleon. As for the other slave, no Athenian in 424 could have been in any doubt that Nikias was the other leading figure who had recently been upstaged by Kleon, because it was Nikias' generalship that Kleon took over when he went to Pylos. Besides, whereas most slaves in Aristophanes are fond of wine, this particular slave refuses to drink any and is ridiculed by his fellow as a water-drinker (87–9); and Nikias is the one public figure of this period who is specifically

---

[10] D. M. Lewis *Sparta and Persia* (Leiden 1977) 21 suggests that Aristophanes has in mind a Paphlagonian eunuch named Artoxares, who was powerful at the court of the King of Persia at this time. However, the allegory in *Horsemen* takes the form not of an oriental court but of an Athenian household.

[11] Dover *Greek and the Greeks* 274–5. See also V. Tammaro *Eikasmos* 2 (1991) 143–50.

stated to have avoided parties and social occasions.[12] The timidity
and religiosity of this slave are also characteristic of Nikias.[13]

I therefore believe that the two slaves do represent Nikias and
Demosthenes. What remains uncertain is whether their identity
was obvious to the audience from the moment they came on-stage,
from their masks or from something else in their appearance, or
only emerged later from the spoken lines. Dover's discussion has
shown that it would not generally have been easy to produce recognizable portrait-masks in ancient Athens, and we do not know
whether there was any distinctive feature of either Demosthenes or
Nikias which would have made it easy in their particular cases. As
it happens, we do know that Kleon had such a feature: his fearsome
eyebrows.[14] Yet Paphlagon, it seems, was not given a mask which
realistically portrayed Kleon, for just before his first appearance
Demosthenes says:

> Don't be afraid, he isn't true to life,
> Because the costume-makers were afraid
> To make a likeness. All the same, he will
> Be recognized; the audience is clever!

> (*Horsemen* 230–3)

That seems to imply that some characters in Athenian comedy,
including perhaps Demosthenes and Nikias in this play, *are* dressed
and masked so as to look like the real men they represent, but
Paphlagon is not, because the costume-makers were afraid of
Kleon.[15] The character will still be recognizable as Kleon in some
way, but Demosthenes does not reveal how. The spectators will
have seen for themselves a moment later, but now it is impossible
for us to know what Paphlagon looked like.

---

[12] Plutarch *Nikias* 5.1; cf. A. H. Sommerstein *CQ* 30 (1980) 46–7.

[13] Cf. Sommerstein *Knights* 3.

[14] Kratinos 228; cf. D. Welsh *CQ* 29 (1979) 214–15. A Corinthian cup,
showing a male Sphinx with wild hair and beetling eyebrows, is discussed by E.
L. Brown *JHS* 94 (1974) 166–70 and I. Worthington *Eranos* 88 (1990) 1–8; they
argue that this is a caricature of Kleon. Whether it actually is so or not, at any
rate it indicates how a caricature of Kleon would have been possible.

[15] Dover *Greek and the Greeks* 273–4 suggests that the costume-makers were
afraid that the mask, if they made it, would be so frightening that they would be
frightened of it themselves. But that interpretation seems to me too complex to
be intelligible from Demosthenes' words. See also V. Tammaro *Eikasmos* 2 (1991)
152.

THE SAUSAGE-SELLER

At the beginning of the play the two slaves representing Demosthenes and Nikias, having just suffered a beating, want to find some
way to save themselves. They consider the possibility of running
away, but reject it because Paphlagon is everywhere and sees everything, so that they would certainly be caught. (In real life it was
common at this period for slaves to run away if they were badly
treated. Compare *Clouds* 7: 'a time when I can't even beat my
slaves!') Nikias next suggests that they should commit suicide by
drinking bull's blood; it was popularly believed that bull's blood was
poisonous, and that the great Themistokles had killed himself by
this method. Demosthenes thinks a drink of wine would be nicer,
and might cause him to have a good idea; and, in true comic fashion,
as soon as he takes a drink he does have a good idea. His plan is to
steal Paphlagon's oracles from him while he is asleep. Conveniently,
again in true comic fashion, he is asleep now, and Nikias immediately
steals an oracle, which Demosthenes reads.[16]

DEMOSTHENES. So that's what you were guarding, Paphlagon:
　You feared the oracle about yourself!
NIKIAS. What?
DEMOSTHENES. This says how the man will meet his end.
NIKIAS. How will he?
DEMOSTHENES.　　　How? The oracle declares
　That first of all there is a hemp-seller
　Who'll be the first to rule the state's affairs.
NIKIAS. Well, that's one seller. Tell me what comes next.
DEMOSTHENES. And second after him a sheep-seller.
NIKIAS. Two sellers now. And what must this one do?
DEMOSTHENES. Rule, just until another man shall come,
　More loathsome still; and that's the end of him.
　Next comes a leather-seller, Paphlagon,
　A thief, a brawler, with Kykloboros' voice.[17]
NIKIAS. And so the sheep-seller must meet his end
　Then from a leather-seller?
DEMOSTHENES.　　　　　　　Yes.

---

[16] Since some modern writers assert that the ancients always read aloud, not
silently, it should be noticed that this passage (like Euripides *Hippolytos* 864–80)
attests silent reading.
[17] A loud voice; cf. p. 30 n. 9.

NIKIAS.   Oh dear!
If only there could be one seller more!
DEMOSTHENES. There is just one more, with a monstrous trade.
NIKIAS. Who's that? Please tell me!
DEMOSTHENES.   Shall I tell you?
NIKIAS.   Yes.
DEMOSTHENES. A sausage-seller will drive this one out.
NIKIAS. A sausage-seller? Poseidon, what a trade!

                                   (*Horsemen* 1 25–44)

Why does the slave Paphlagon have an oracle? Demosthenes has
already told us 'He makes the old man mad as any Sibyl with oracles'
(61), and it seems a safe inference, even though there is no evidence
for it outside this play, that Kleon actually did read out oracles in
the Assembly,[18] and that at least one of them was interpreted by him
as supporting his own position as a political leader. But the oracle
in the play is intended to be funny, and must differ from the real
oracle.

It gives a sequence of political leaders. These are not holders of
any official position: Athens had no elected president or prime
minister. Yet it does seem to have been usual to regard one man as
'leader of the people', not because of any formal power but simply
because popular opinion regarded him as the dominant figure; and
in the fourth century it became common to make a list of such
leaders, each one succeeded by the next in chronological order.[19]
But no other such list survives as early as this one in *Horsemen*, and
no other list names any leader between Perikles and Kleon. This list
is therefore important historical evidence for Athenian politics in
the short period between the death of Perikles and the ascendancy
of Kleon; for it would be pointless unless the hemp-seller and the
sheep-seller were real leaders, even though they may have been less
important than Aristophanes makes them sound. According to the
scholia, they were in fact respectively Eukrates and Lysikles, both
of whom are also mentioned later in the play (254, 765). Lysikles
is known to have been a general in 428/7, when he was killed in
Karia;[20] but nothing is known about the political activities of either

---

[18] Cf. Rogers *Knights* xxxvii, T. Gargiulo *Eikasmos* 3 (1992) 153–64.
[19] προστάτης τοῦ δήμου: cf. P. J. Rhodes *A Commentary on the Aristotelian
Athenaion Politeia* (Oxford 1981) 345–6.
[20] Thucydides 3.19.

of them. Presumably it is true that they were somehow involved in trading in hemp (for making ropes) and in sheep.

Those may have been fairly respectable trades. Sausage-selling, on the other hand, was clearly a low-class activity. That is implied unmistakably by its position in the list. In the cases of Eukrates, Lysikles, and Kleon, Aristophanes was constrained by the facts to name hemp, sheep, and leather, if those were the trades with which those men were really connected; but in the case of his own fictional character he could have chosen any trade, and he has decided that a suitable trade for a character who is to be presented as the lowest of the low is sausage-selling. There were probably few sausage-sellers in Athens. No real ones are known, and the comments of Demosthenes and Nikias (141, 144) imply that they were unusual. We must bear in mind that generally cattle were not killed for food except as sacrifices on religious occasions. From references in the play it appears that a sausage-seller procured the intestines or tripes of sacrificed animals from the priests,[21] fashioned them into sausages, and sold them in the Agora or beside the town gates (1245–7).[22] As a profession, dealing in the inner parts of animals must have been messy and distasteful, and may not have been very profitable either. No one would take it up who could find a better way of earning a living.

This, then, is the comic plot: Paphlagon (Kleon) can be ousted only by a man even more disgusting than himself. It is an absurd comic idea, not a serious cynical one.[23] Aristophanes is not putting forward a serious argument that a man who has attained power by the methods used by Kleon can be ousted only by the same methods; for this passage does not mention Kleon's methods of attaining power. Aristophanes has simply observed that three recent politicians have been 'sellers', each of a lower type of goods than the one before, and by false comic logic has deduced that the next will be a seller of an even lower type. Once again the author of the comedy immediately produces just what the characters want:

[21] Lines 301–2 imply that he should make some payment for 'the gods' sacred tripe'. Cf. J. Wilkins in *Tria Lustra, essays and notes presented to John Pinsent* (ed. H. D. Jocelyn, Liverpool 1993) 119–26.

[22] The gates meant are probably the Sacred Gate and the Dipylon, in Kerameikos on the north-west side of Athens; cf. Lind *Der Gerber Kleon* 173–84. This may have been a less reputable place for trade than the Agora.

[23] Here I disagree with Kraus *Ar. pol. Kom.* 127.

Demosthenes and Nikias meet a sausage-seller, and Demosthenes tells him that he is to be the saviour of Athens and governor of everyone, controlling the seas from Karia to Carthage. (At this point the household of Democracy and his slaves has been forgotten; the Sausage-seller is to be the new leader of Athens, not merely the dominant slave in the household. The household will re-emerge later in the play.) At first, not surprisingly, he can hardly believe it, and Demosthenes has to reassure him that he possesses just the qualities that a political leader requires.

SAUSAGE-SELLER.   But how can I
   Become a great man? I'm a sausage-seller.
DEMOSTHENES. That's just the reason you're becoming great:
   You're bad, and brash, and from the Agora.
SAUSAGE-SELLER. I don't think I deserve to have great power.
DEMOSTHENES. Whatever makes you think you don't deserve it?
   Perhaps you have some good deed on your conscience.
   Your parents weren't respectable?
SAUSAGE-SELLER.   God, no!
   I'm of bad family.
DEMOSTHENES.   That's a piece of luck.
   How well you're qualified for politics!
SAUSAGE-SELLER. I've got no education either, squire.
   My reading and my writing's very poor.
DEMOSTHENES. You've reached 'poor' standard? That's one point
      against you.
   For education and good character
   Don't fit a man to be a demagogue;
   He must be ignorant and loathsome now.

         .   .   .   .   .

SAUSAGE-SELLER. I'm tickled by that prophecy. Still, I wonder
   If I can govern the democracy.
DEMOSTHENES. A simple job; do just what you do now.
   Stir up the business, mince it all together,
   And always get the people on your side
   By the cook's trick of adding sweetened—phraselets!
   The other things a demagogue requires,
   A raucous voice, low birth, and Agora ways,
   All that a politician needs, you have.

                              (*Horsemen* 178–93, 211–19)

From this passage we can list the qualities which Demosthenes perceives in the Sausage-seller. These are, by implication, the qualities which Aristophanes perceives in Kleon and other contemporary politicians. The joke is that qualities normally regarded as undesirable are the very ones needed for success in politics.

First and foremost, the Sausage-seller is 'bad', and comes of a 'bad' family. This word, *poneros*, is not easy to interpret. It is derived from a word meaning 'work' or 'labour'; thus Hesiod uses it to describe the labouring Herakles.[24] So at first sight it is tempting to take it here as signifying that the Sausage-seller belongs to the working class. If taken in that way, it is not a comment on his character but on his status in society, and implies that Kleon and other politicians are of a lower social class than politicians of earlier times. But I do not believe it is correct to interpret the word in that way here, because in Aristophanes and his contemporaries it seems always to mean 'bad', either morally or in the practical sense of 'useless'. The Sausage-seller is not useless, and the meaning must rather be that he is a scoundrel, from a family of scoundrels.

Secondly, he is ignorant. He has not had the cultural education which well-to-do Athenians gave their sons. He has learned reading and writing, but is not good even at them.

Thirdly, he is 'from the Agora'. This can mean both that he was born and resided in that area, as was probably true of Kleon,[25] and that he has made a living from selling goods in the market. The Agora was a place of talk and bustle, and a man who spent most of his time there would be sharp, brash, and pushy, unlike a slow countryman or a gentlemanly aristocrat. From crying his wares he would also develop a loud, penetrating voice; and a loud voice was a notorious feature of Kleon.

Fourthly, there is his method of working, which involves stirring things up. Two verbs having this sense, which may also be translated 'disturb', 'harass', or 'confuse', are used frequently in this play.[26] Aristophanes considered these suitable words to describe Kleon's political style. But just as the Sausage-seller adds sweeteners to his mixture when making sausages, so Kleon makes his policies acceptable to the Assembly by his alluring style of oratory.

[24] Hesiod fr. 248–9 (Merkelbach and West).

[25] Kleon's deme was Kydathenaion, which bordered on the Agora and may indeed have included part of it. The leather-sellers' area (*Horsemen* 852–4) is likely to have been in that deme. Cf. Lind *Der Gerber Kleon* 94–131.

[26] ταράττειν and κυκᾶν. This image is studied in detail by L. Edmunds *Cleon, Knights, and Aristophanes' Politics* (Lanham 1987) 1–37.

THE HORSEMEN

The Sausage-seller, still doubtful about confronting Paphlagon, wonders who will be his allies. Demosthenes replies:

> There are a thousand Horsemen, valiant men;
> They hate him, and they'll come to your support.
> The best class of the citizens will come,
> The brightest of the audience will come,
> And I'll come! And the god will lend his aid.

(Horsemen 225–9)

These persons are the cream of Athenian society. (When Demosthenes unexpectedly includes himself among them, that is a joke.) They are not the kind of people one would expect to find supporting someone even worse than Kleon, but they are so hostile to Kleon that they will support anyone at all who has some chance of ousting him. And first and foremost among them are the Horsemen.

The Horsemen were those Athenian citizens who performed their military service on horseback, rather than on foot as hoplites.[27] As Demosthenes says, at this period they numbered one thousand.[28] They were rich young men: rich, because each had to provide his own horse; young, because stirrups were not in use, and they had to be athletic enough to mount and ride without them. They evidently regarded themselves as an élite part of the army and of society, and they affected a distinctive appearance: they wore long hair (like the Spartans) and probably gilded leather circlets round their heads.[29] They participated in various operations in the early years of the Peloponnesian War, and at the time of *Horsemen* the most recent was an incursion into Corinthian territory in the summer of 425, when they earned much of the credit for the Athenian victory

---

[27] For recent detailed studies of the Horsemen see G. R. Bugh *The Horsemen of Athens* (Princeton 1988), I. G. Spence *The Cavalry of Classical Greece* (Oxford 1993), L. J. Worley *Hippeis* (Boulder 1994).

[28] This figure does not include a separate force of 200 mounted archers, making a total of 1200 mounted soldiers (Thucydides 2.13.8).

[29] This interpretation of *Horsemen* 580 is not certain. It depends on the sense of στλεγγίς. This word commonly means an athlete's scraper; but Polydeukes 7.179 says that it can alternatively mean gilded leather worn round the head, and this interpretation may be supported by the Horsemen wearing circlets in the Parthenon frieze.

at the battle of Solygeia.[30] In the parabasis (595–610) the Horsemen
pay a humorous tribute to their horses with special reference to that
expedition, on which they endured a sea voyage: the horses even
helped to row the ships, and hunted crabs for their dinner! In
another passage Paphlagon claims that he had been intending to
propose the erection of a monument on the Akropolis to com-
memorate the Horsemen's courage, but they deride this claim as
humbug (266–70).

Apparently there had been hostility between the Horsemen and
Kleon for some time, but it is difficult to make out what had actually
happened between them. Evidence comes mainly from the scholia,
and some of it may be no more than guesses based on the text
of the plays. One scholium says, according to two of the later
manuscripts, that Kleon did the Horsemen some harm when he was
one of them.[31] It could be true that Kleon was a Horseman when
he was a young man, if it is true that his family was wealthy; but, as
we have seen, the evidence that his family was wealthy is weak, and
this scholium does not make it much stronger, because the words
in question do not appear in the earlier manuscripts. Most of the
manuscripts at this point say that Kleon was abused and provoked
by the Horsemen, and then follows a phrase of doubtful meaning:
perhaps 'he applied himself to politics',[32] which would mean that it
was this dispute which originally prompted him to become a politician; but an ingenious alternative interpretation, which may be
correct, is 'he attacked their allowance (*katastasis*)', meaning that
he put forward a proposal to reduce the financial payments made to
them.[33] The scholiast adds that he accused them of failing to perform
their military service; on what occasion, he does not say, but since
he attributes the information to the fourth-century historian Theopompos, we must not dismiss it as being merely a figment of the
scholiast's imagination.

There is also the passage at the beginning of *Akharnians* in which
Dikaiopolis remembers a recent event which he enjoyed.

I know what cheered my spirit when I saw it:

[30] Thucydides 4.44.1.
[31] Schol. *Horsemen* 226b, only in manuscripts Vat and Lh.
[32] W. R. Connor *Theopompus and Fifth-Century Athens* (Cambridge Mass. 1968) 50–3.
[33] C. W. Fornara *CQ* 23 (1973) 24.

It was the five talents vomited up by Kleon.
That brightened me up; and I just love the Horsemen
For doing that, 'a fitting deed for Greece'!

(Akharnians 5—8)

How did the Horsemen make Kleon vomit up the sum of five talents? This question has been much discussed and there is no agreed answer.[34] The context suggests an incident in the theatre: the other events which Dikaiopolis mentions here are all theatrical or musical ones, including one concerning a tragedy which dismayed him, and it would seem to fit the context perfectly if this event which he enjoyed was a scene in a comedy in which Kleon and the Horsemen appeared as characters, possibly but not necessarily Aristophanes' own *Babylonians,* performed in the previous year. However, a scholium on the passage says: 'Kleon was made to pay five talents because he insulted the Horsemen. For Kleon received five talents from the islanders, to persuade the Athenians to relieve their contributions.[35] When the Horsemen noticed it, they spoke against him and demanded the money from him. Theopompos mentions it.' This means that Kleon received a bribe from some cities in the Athenian Empire to persuade him to propose a reduction in the amount of the tribute payable by them, or a less steep increase than they would otherwise suffer; but the Horsemen somehow discovered it and, to get their own back on him for some previous insult, denounced him, so that he had to hand over the money (to whom, the scholiast does not make clear). Again, we may wonder whether all this is merely a conjecture by the scholiast, until, again, the reference to Theopompos gives us pause. Theopompos presumably had some evidence for what he wrote; but how much of what the scholiast says really came from Theopompos? Theopompos could have referred to or quoted from a comedy as evidence of the hostility between the Horsemen and Kleon; but if so, was the comic statement fact or fiction? From the information which we have, I do not think it possible to be sure whether the vomiting up of five talents was an incident in a comedy or in real life, but in either

[34] See especially Connor *Theopompus and Fifth-Century Athens* 53—9 and E. M. Carawan *CQ* 40 (1990) 137—47, giving references to many earlier discussions.
[35] The exact text of this phrase is doubtful, but it must refer to the tribute. See the *apparatus criticus* in N. G. Wilson's edition of the scholia on *Akharnians*.

case it does show that there was hostility between Kleon and the Horsemen before the date of *Akharnians*.

Other causes may also have contributed to the dispute. According to a hypothesis proposed by Lind,[36] there may have been friction at a local level within the deme Kydathenaion between Kleon, owning a tannery which created an unpleasant smell in the neighbourhood, and a nearby *thiasos* of Herakles (a religious and social group) which numbered Simon and other Horsemen among its members. This hypothesis has some evidence to support it, but it depends on the identification of Simon the commander of the Horsemen at the time of this play (*Horsemen* 242) with Simon the priest of a *thiasos* twenty or thirty years later.[37] It remains uncertain; but it usefully reminds us that the hostility between Kleon and the Horsemen may have had various origins, not necessarily political.

THE CONTEST

The contest between Paphlagon and the Sausage-seller is in three main parts. First they simply dispute with each other, each claiming superiority in personal qualities and abusing his opponent. Next each harangues the Council in an attempt to win its support; this takes place off-stage during the parabasis, and is reported in a long speech by the Sausage-seller (624–82). In the third and longest part, occupying nearly half the play, they compete for the favour of Democracy. This part, with Democracy on-stage as judge, is itself in three sections: first Paphlagon and the Sausage-seller argue verbally, each claiming to serve Democracy better than the other; secondly each produces oracles which he claims support him; and finally each brings Democracy gifts. At every stage of the contest it is the Sausage-seller who emerges victorious.

The personal qualities in which each claims to surpass the other in the first part of the contest are primarily impudence (*anaideia*) and boldness (*thrasos*), besides general wickedness. These qualities have been acquired by an upbringing in the Agora. The main ways in which the qualities are manifested are loud shouting, and theft which is denied and brazened out. For a while this is little more

---

[36] Lind *Der Gerber Kleon* 87–164.
[37] *IG* 2^2 2343.

than assertion by Paphlagon and counter-assertion by the Sausage-
seller in a tit-for-tat manner.

PAPHLAGON. Both of you will die this minute!
SAUSAGE-SELLER. I'll out-bawl you three times over!
PAPHLAGON. I shall shout you down with shouting!
SAUSAGE-SELLER. I shall bawl you down with bawling!

                . . . .

PAPHLAGON. Look me in the eye, not blinking!
SAUSAGE-SELLER. I, like you, am Agora-nurtured!

                . . . .

PAPHLAGON. I admit I thieve, but you don't!
SAUSAGE-SELLER. Yes I do, by Agora's Hermes!
PAPHLAGON. And, if seen, I swear I didn't!
SAUSAGE-SELLER. That's a trick you've learned from me, then![38]

                    (*Horsemen* 284–7, 292–3, 296–9)

As the scene develops from this slanging-match into a slightly
more orderly debate, the Sausage-seller relates an anecdote to dem-
onstrate the superiority of his upbringing as a thief.

SAUSAGE-SELLER. And, yes, there are some other pranks that I played
   in my boyhood.
   I used to say this sort of thing, and so deceive the butchers:
   'Look, look, boys! Don't you see? Up there! It must be spring! A
      swallow!'
   And they would look, and I would steal a chop while they were looking.
DEMOSTHENES. Oh, what a clever chop you are! You planned that very
   neatly:
   You stole before the swallows came, like people eating nettles![39]
SAUSAGE-SELLER. I did it, and I wasn't seen. If one of them did see me,
   I'd hide the meat between my legs and swear I didn't do it.
   And once a politician said, when he'd just seen me do that,
   'That boy is certain to go far; he's bound for public office!'

                          (*Horsemen* 417–26)

The comic basis of the competition is that it is praiseworthy to

---

[38]   Line by line, Paphlagon boasts of a 'skill' and then the Sausage-seller claims
that he also possesses it; in 299 he not only claims that he knows the trick but
goes one better by claiming that he knew it before Paphlagon did. Recent editors
(Sommerstein, Mastromarco) are wrong to break the stichomythia by attributing
298 to the Sausage-seller and 299 to Paphlagon.
[39]   Nettles are best eaten in early spring, when they are too tender to sting.

be bad: the worse one is, the better. But Aristophanes has difficulty in keeping up this logical inversion, as is clear especially in the interventions by the Horsemen. They denounce Paphlagon as a villainous and loathsome bawler, whose boldness pervades every-thing (303–5), but they are delighted at the appearance of an even bigger scoundrel who will surpass him in villainy and boldness (328–32). For this apparent contradiction it might be possible to devise a logical explanation: perhaps they think that Paphlagon can be defeated only by his own weapons, but that once he has been defeated the Sausage-seller will become a reformed character or will simply go away. But in fact Aristophanes has not provided any such explanation; he has left untied the loose ends of the Horsemen's logic, and indeed he has let the same kind of inconsistency get into the lines of Paphlagon and the Sausage-seller too. For example, the Sausage-seller accuses Paphlagon, the leather-seller, of selling poor-quality leather to country people 'wickedly' (316–18); yet, in a contest of impudence and theft, that ought to be a point in favour of Paphlagon, not against him. At the end of this part of the contest each accuses the other of trickery or wickedness (450), two of the very qualities in which each was supposed to be showing his own superiority (331–2); and the Sausage-seller actually defeats Paphla-gon not by showing himself to be better in those ways but by hitting him (451–6).

It seems, then, that presenting a comic inversion of conventional public morality was not Aristophanes' primary concern in this scene. That was just a joke which he was willing to abandon when-ever it got in the way of a more important purpose. The more important purpose is to vilify Kleon. Paphlagon's charges against the Sausage-seller are absurdly inconsequential: for example, he catches sight of a cup of Khalkidian design, and takes it as evidence that the Sausage-seller and Demosthenes are inciting Khalkis to revolt against the Athenian Empire (237–8). But the Sausage-seller's charges against Paphlagon are much more realistic. Paphlagon, he says, has reaped what another man sowed, and now wants to sell off the ears of corn (392–4); that is obviously an allegorical reference to Kleon's getting credit for the success at Pylos after Demosthenes had done most of the work, and it implies that he hopes to get money for releasing the Spartan prisoners. Paphlagon, says the Sausage-seller, while ostensibly getting support for Athens from Argos, is actually meeting Spartans there to do a deal with them on his own account (465–7).[40] The allegation that Kleon hoped to be paid by the Spartans for arranging the release of their prisoners may be false; we have no other evidence either to confirm or to refute it. But it is clearly a serious allegation, which some Athenians in Aristophanes' audience may have believed to be true. And it is clearly inconsistent with the comic situation in which the Sausage-seller should be trying to prove that Paphlagon is *less* bold, impudent, and avaricious than himself.

Paphlagon rushes away to denounce the Sausage-seller to the Council. The Sausage-seller runs after him, and in the next scene after the parabasis he returns to describe his victory. Paphlagon was thundering out a speech accusing the Horsemen of conspiring against Athens. The Councillors were very alarmed, but then the Sausage-seller barged in and bawled out that sprats were on sale very cheap in the Agora; he advised them in confidence to seize all available bowls, so that no one but themselves would be able to buy sprats (for lack of a receptacle to put them in) and the price would fall even lower. The Councillors were delighted with his news and his advice, so that he immediately became far more popular than Paphlagon. Paphlagon tried to regain the lead by proposing a sacrifice of a hundred cows as a thank-offering (which would mean a meat meal for everyone at public expense), but the Sausage-seller outbid him by proposing two hundred cows, and a thousand goats as well. Now, in a final effort, Paphlagon held out what he thought would be an even more tempting bait—peace.

> But he entreated them to wait a bit,
> 'Until you hear the Spartan herald speak,'
> He said; 'he's come for peace negotiations.'
> But with one voice the Councillors all cried
> 'Now? Peace negotiations? Yes, of course,
> When they've just heard that sprats are cheap in Athens!
> We don't require peace; let the war go on!'
> They shouted for adjournment of the meeting,
> And started jumping over all the railings.
> I slipped out, bought up all the coriander
> And all the onions in the Agora,
> And gave them as a favour, free of charge,
> To people needing seasoning for their sprats,
> And they all cheered and praised me to the skies.

[40] ἰδίᾳ (467) does not mean 'in secret', but 'for his personal advantage'.

So with an obol's worth of coriander
I've won the Council over, and here I am!

(*Horsemen* 667–82)

This is the fullest comic description of a meeting of the Council. (Whereas the Assembly meets in the first scene of *Akharnians*, no extant play shows a meeting of the Council on-stage.) The Councillors were ordinary citizens selected by lot. The passage implies that they were more concerned for their own dinners than for public policy, and were easily taken in by any politician who offered the prospect of a good meal. This is a rather unfavourable view of the democratic Council, but the satire is directed primarily at the rival politicians who try to outbid each other in attracting the citizens' support.

So the Sausage-seller has won that part of the contest. Paphlagon returns too, and after another exchange of threats he appeals to Democracy to punish the Sausage-seller. Now Democracy, personified as an old man in accordance with the description given earlier, at last appears. But we have still not got back to the allegory in which the politicians are presented as slaves in Democracy's house. Instead the two rivals now call themselves Democracy's lovers (732–40); and as the scene develops once again into something like a formal debate, the services which Paphlagon claims to have performed are not things which a slave or even a lover would do, but the real political acts of Kleon. The Sausage-seller, being a fictional character, cannot point to any real political acts of his own; so, apart from providing the old man Democracy with a cushion and a pair of shoes, his main contribution in this scene is to argue that Paphlagon's services are not as beneficial as he claims. This scene in fact is the nearest that the play ever gets to a serious critique of Kleon's policies. The criticisms will be considered in the last part of this chapter.

Next Paphlagon and the Sausage-seller each present oracles to Democracy. This scene develops more fully a theme introduced earlier (see p. 90): Kleon must in fact have read out to the Assembly oracles which he claimed supported him. Here Aristophanes has fun parodying the oracular style, and we need not assume that his parodies reproduce Kleon's actual oracles. The first pair is the most significant. Paphlagon reads out an oracle telling the Athenian to keep safe 'the holy jagged-toothed dog' who barks for him and provides him with—pay; and he asserts that the dog is himself. The Sausage-seller reads out another oracle telling the Athenian to take heed of the dog Kerberos, who wags his tail, eats up the dinner when the Athenian is not looking, and licks out the plates and the—islands (1015–34). Evidently Kleon had compared himself to a watch-dog, defending Athens. Aristophanes, through the mouth of the Sausage-seller, turns Kleon's own simile against him, identifying the dog as the hell-hound Kerberos, and using the image of a greedy dog to suggest that Kleon eats up the profits from the Athenian Empire. This image will be used against Kleon again, to greater comic effect, in *Wasps*.

The final scene of the contest turns to farce. Paphlagon and the Sausage-seller run to and fro, each producing from his box or hamper delicious items of food for Democracy. Although they are not actually called slaves in this scene, and political allusions appear now and then, essentially we are now back in the allegory of the servants in Democracy's household which was established at the beginning and then forgotten for a considerable part of the play. A climax is reached when Paphlagon produces some hare's meat, highly regarded as a delicacy, and the Sausage-seller has nothing comparable to offer.

PAPHLAGON [*to the Sausage-seller*]. You've no hare's meat to give him; I have, though!
SAUSAGE-SELLER [*aside*]. Oh blast! Where can I get some hare's meat from?
    Now then, my soul, think up some saucy trick!
    [*Paphlagon brings out a dish of hare's meat.*]
PAPHLAGON [*to the Sausage-seller*]. See this, you poor old fool?
SAUSAGE-SELLER.   I don't care now,
    Because I see some envoys over there
    Coming to me with purses full of money.
PAPHLAGON [*putting down the dish*]. Where?
SAUSAGE-SELLER.   Can't you leave the foreigners alone?
    [*Picking up the dish*] Democracy, you see this hare I've brought you?
PAPHLAGON. My god, you've just sneaked in and stolen mine!
SAUSAGE-SELLER. Yes, that's what *you* did with the men from Pylos.
DEMOCRACY [*to the Sausage-seller*]. Tell me, what made you think of filching it?
SAUSAGE-SELLER. 'The thought's Athena's, but the theft is mine.'[41]

---

[41] This line is apparently a quotation or parody, but its source is not known.

DEMOSTHENES. I ran the risk, though.
PAPHLAGON.   And I did the cooking.[42]
DEMOCRACY. Be off! The man who served it gets the thanks.
PAPHLAGON. Oh misery! I'm being outimpudenced!

(*Horsemen* 1192–1206)

Here Paphlagon is beaten at his own game. Previously he filched the Spartan cake which Demosthenes had made at Pylos and got the credit for serving it up (54–7); now, with the image changed from a cake to a hare, Demosthenes hunted it, Paphlagon cooked it, but the Sausage-seller served it up and got the credit for it. Thus the Sausage-seller has surpassed Paphlagon in impudence. And yet this does not conclude the contest. As a final test, to enable him to reach a wise verdict, Democracy looks inside both their hampers: the Sausage-seller's hamper is empty, because he has given Democracy everything he had, but Paphlagon's contains far more good food that he has kept for himself than he gave to Democracy. So the Sausage-seller is declared the winner. The basis of the final verdict is quite different from the original basis of the contest: the Sausage-seller has won not by impudence, but by being a self-sacrificing servant of Democracy.

THE REHABILITATION OF DEMOCRACY

It is curious that it is not until the contest is over that the name of the Sausage-seller is revealed as being Agorakritos, meaning 'disputing in the market-place' (1257–8). It is almost as if Aristophanes suddenly realized that he had forgotten to give the character a name, and so produced one here although it had no dramatic function in the remainder of the play. For there is no more disputing now, and the tricks of the Agora are replaced by a kind of magic. Democracy entrusts himself to the care of the Sausage-seller, and after the second parabasis the Sausage-seller reports to the chorus that he has boiled down Democracy to make him beautiful. (This was a kind of sorcery at which, according to myth, Medea was skilled.) Forthwith Democracy appears, restored to the form which

---

[42] On the interpretation of this line see MacDowell *CQ* 44 (1994) 328–9.

he had in years gone by; he wears dress of a kind that was customary in the days of the Persian Wars, complete with the cicada brooch that was fashionable then.[43] The reason for this transformation is not stated by the Sausage-seller, but it is evidently a consequence of getting rid of Paphlagon. Aristophanes means that, without Kleon, Athenian politics will revert to an older and better style, and he makes the point visually by giving a more old-fashioned and splendid appearance to his allegorical figure Democracy.

Democracy has gone back half a century not only in appearance but also in mental attitude. There are two faults in particular from which he is now freed. One is his gullibility. Until now, he used to be taken in by an orator in the Assembly who said he loved and cherished him, and by an advocate in a lawcourt who told the jurors that, unless they imposed a fine in his case, they would starve because the state would have no money to pay them (1340–9, 1358–61). The other fault is that he used to vote in favour of spending public money on pay (presumably for jurors) in preference to building warships (1350–3). Now, since his transformation, Democracy is ashamed of those faults, though the Sausage-seller reassures him that the politicians were really to blame (1354–7).

What will his policies be in future, then? We might have expected the Sausage-seller, who has taken over from Paphlagon, to say what must be done, but he does not. Democracy has his own ideas, and they are surprisingly specific. First, the oarsmen on the warships will get their pay in full when they come back into port. Second, no influence will enable a hoplite to be transferred from one list to another (when the one list is called up for service and the other is not). And third, the young men, not yet adult, who chatter pretentiously in the Agora are to be banned from it. This third policy is no doubt a joke, but the first two look like remedies for genuine grievances. We may infer that there had been at least one or two recent occasions when sailors had not received their pay in full on time, and when some individuals had evaded service as

---

[43] The emphasis is on his attire and his mentality. It is not stated that he has become physically young, and 'rejuvenation' is the wrong word to use here. (In 1349, γέρων must be translated 'senile'. The question there is about his former mental condition, not about his date of birth.) Probably the actor still wore the same mask as in earlier scenes, but different clothes; if he had changed his mask as well as his clothes, he would hardly have been recognizable as the same character. For a different view see S. D. Olson *Eranos* 88 (1990) 60–3.

hoplites by getting themselves transferred from one list to another.

The implication is that these changes of policy are a reversion to the old Athens of half a century ago. In one case we can confirm this: there had been a famous occasion when the Athenians, on the proposal of Themistokles, had voted to spend a windfall of silver on building warships, instead of distributing it among themselves.[44] We cannot be so sure about the others, but it is at least plausible that in earlier times there had been less disingenuous rhetoric in the Assembly, and that the navy had been paid more promptly before the Peloponnesian War placed a strain on the revenue. No doubt this final scene of the play contains an element of nostalgia for the good old days which may not have been as good in reality as Aristophanes imagined, but there may be some truth in the picture too.

The play ends with the rehabilitated Democracy enjoying a thirty-year peace treaty, which is personified by attractive girls, and a life in the country instead of the town (1388–95); this is virtually the same result as Dikaiopolis attains at the end of *Akharnians*. Paphlagon is reduced to being a sausage-seller at the town gates, as an apt penalty for his misdeeds. Agorakritos apparently has power to ordain these things, but he says nothing at all about what he himself will be doing in future. (He will have meals at the Prytaneion and a front seat at the theatre, replacing Paphlagon (1404–5), but those are not full-time activities.) At the end he has become something like a *deus ex machina* organizing human affairs but himself remaining outside them.

Judged by its dramatic coherence, *Horsemen* is not one of Aristophanes' best plays. It begins as a conflict between the good slaves and the bad slave in Democracy's household, but before long the household recedes from the centre of attention and it becomes a conflict in which the winner will be the ruler of Athens. This is supposed to be a contest in impudence; by a comic inversion of logic, the worse man will win. At some points the Sausage-seller is indeed the more impudent; yet this is not kept up, and in the end he wins because he is *not* an impudent thief like Paphlagon but a better servant of Democracy. We might then expect the play to end with the triumphant Sausage-seller receiving his reward. But in fact it is Democracy, called on to judge the contest, who in the end

---

[44] Herodotos 7.144.1.

receives the prizes as if he were the hero of the play.

One may analyse this formally in terms of a 'double plot',[45] or one may say more informally that Aristophanes seems to have changed his mind as he went along, but anyway it is evident that dramatic coherence was not his main aim. He was more concerned to present a comic picture of Athenian politics. It is ultimately a favourable and optimistic picture. Government by the democratic Assembly admittedly has many weaknesses and makes many mistakes. In particular the Assembly does not always understand the issues before it, and can be misled by the rhetoric of dishonest politicians. Yet its honesty and common sense will win through in the end. Despite the inconsistencies in the plot, that portrayal of Democracy is consistently implied throughout the play, and it is made explicit in a choral interlude towards the end of the contest.

CHORUS.   Democracy, you exert
              A glorious rule indeed,
              When all are afraid of you
                  As if of a tyrant.
              And yet you are gullible;
              You like being flattered and
              You're easily led astray.
              You gape in amazement at
              Each speaker; your mind, though here,
                  Is gone on its travels!

DEMOCRACY.   That hair on your head has no
              Intelligence underneath
              If you believe I'm a fool:
                  I do it on purpose!
              I'm really enjoying all
              This nannying every day.
              I like to maintain a man
              As leader in thievery,
              Until, when he's full right up,
                  I hoist him and thrash him!

                          (*Horsemen* 1111–30)

The later part of the song makes clear that 'I hoist him and thrash him' is a metaphor referring to condemnation in a lawcourt for

---

[45] R. W. Brock *GRBS* 27 (1986) 15–27, criticizing the interpretation by M. Landfester *Die Ritter des Aristophanes* (Amsterdam 1967).

theft (1147–50). What Aristophanes is saying here is that under democratic rule politicians who defraud the state are eventually caught and punished. This is not a joke; there is nothing particularly funny about it. It might, however, be wishful thinking, attractive to a complacent audience; or it might be intended to encourage the audience to live up to it. Did the Athenians really catch and punish fraudulent politicians? In particular, did they punish Kleon? The answer seems to be: no, there is no evidence that Kleon was ever convicted of theft.[46] Has Aristophanes then missed his target?

THE FAULTS OF KLEON

Kleon was indeed the target, of that there can be no doubt. The play is not an attack on politicians in general. Other politicians are objects of satire only in short passages (mainly in the second parabasis, 1264–1315). In the early part of the play Demosthenes and Nikias, though presented on-stage, can hardly be said to be satirized; perhaps a few lines can be interpreted as mild ridicule, such as those implying that Demosthenes likes wine and Nikias does not, but on the whole these two are shown as good characters, contrasted with Kleon. Kleon alone is pilloried from the beginning to the end of the play.

Some of the invective against Kleon may be regarded as conventional, perhaps taken over from the tradition of abuse in iambic verse, and therefore not to be taken literally.[47] This applies particularly to the first part of the contest, when Paphlagon and the Sausage-seller are slanging each other, and it applies above all to the obscenities. But other parts of it, such as the numerous references to Pylos, are obviously not conventional but are specific to Kleon. These are not to be dismissed as fantasy.[48] The play would indeed be pointless if the character Paphlagon had nothing in common with the real Kleon. Some specific assertions about Kleon may be true, and others lies. It is not easy for us to distinguish the truth from the

[46] *Clouds* 591–4 implies that Kleon had not yet been convicted of theft when that play was performed in 423.

[47] Cf. R. M. Rosen *Old Comedy and the Iambographic Tradition* (Atlanta 1988) 59–82.

[48] Heath *Political Comedy* 37 wrongly says that Aristophanes' portrayal of Kleon 'is, and is meant to be recognised as, fantasy'.

fiction, but we can catalogue the main activities attributed to Kleon in the play, and consider in which cases criticism may have been justified.

1. *Kleon favours continuation of the war and obstructs efforts to make peace.* In view of Aristophanes' support for peace in *Akharnians* and later plays, it is perhaps surprising that he does not give it more attention in *Horsemen*, but there are at least two passages in which the point is clear.[49] In 794–7 Paphlagon concedes that he opposed an offer of a treaty, but claims that he did so in order to make Athens the ruler of Greece. The Sausage-seller derides this claim, declaring that Paphlagon's real purpose is to get profits for himself from other parts of Greece; once peace is made and Democracy can go back to the country to live, he will find that rural life is much better than living on jury pay in the town (801–9). The point is made again at the end of the play, when Democracy is presented with thirty-year peace terms which Paphlagon had hidden away, and is going to return to the country with them (1388–95). The accusation that Kleon prevented peace is undoubtedly true: his opposition to the making of a treaty in the summer of 425 is recorded by Thucydides (4.21). But this was a controversial policy, on which many Athenians must have thought Kleon was right.

2. *The victory at Pylos.* Kleon claimed and received credit for the victory; we can safely infer from this play, although it is not mentioned in other texts, that he was rewarded with the two privileges of free meals at the Prytaneion (280–1, 709, 766, 1404) and a front seat at the theatre (702, 1405). But Aristophanes repeatedly says or implies that it was Demosthenes who really deserved the credit (54–7, 392, 742–5, 1200–1). How much of the credit was actually due to each, it is hardly possible for us to judge, but it is clear that Thucydides at least thought that Demosthenes, not Kleon, made the plan which led to victory (4.32.4).

3. *Taxation of the rich and distribution to the poor.* Paphlagon claims that when he was a member of the Council he procured a large amount of money for the public treasury by extorting it from individual citizens (774–6). This probably means that Kleon proposed the imposition of a capital levy (*eisphora*) on the richest class

[49] Cf. de Ste. Croix *Origins* 367. I. Worthington *L'Antiquité Classique* 56 (1987) 56–67 rightly points out the paucity of the references to making peace in this play, but goes too far in arguing that Kleon is not criticized on this ground at all.

of citizens, for soon afterwards Paphlagon threatens to make the Sausage-seller pay such levies by getting him registered in that class (923–6). He also claims that he supports the ordinary people by enabling them to receive three obols as daily pay for jury service (51, 255–6, 799–800, 904–5). These policies may be interpreted as two sides of the same coin. Although there is not much other evidence for it, it is quite likely that taxing the rich to support the poor really was a policy of Kleon's. The rich would naturally complain about it, and Aristophanes makes the Sausage-seller comment to the effect that it is easy to give money away if you get it by stealing it from somebody else (777–8), but many Athenians must have thought it a good policy.

4. *Raising the tribute*. Tribute is mentioned in 313, and bribes from allied cities in 438–9, 802, 834–5, 930–3. These passages are best interpreted as meaning that Paphlagon blackmails the cities of the Athenian Empire, and they pay him money to avoid increases in the amounts of tribute payable by them. There are also more general references to Paphlagon's oppression of 'the islands' or 'the foreigners' (1319, 1408). These are broadly in accord with the known fact that Kleon was the proposer of severe treatment for the people of Mytilene after their rebellion against Athens, and with the imperialistic sentiments which Thucydides attributes to him on that occasion (3.36–40). The amounts of tribute were in fact increased sharply in the year when *Horsemen* was performed, 425/4, and modern historians have generally considered that Kleon was responsible for the increase.[50] We can cautiously accept that this was indeed Kleon's policy. But the allegations of blackmail in this connection are not supported by other evidence and may be mere slander.

5. *Prosecutions*. References to Paphlagon's 'slanders' begin at line 7 and are numerous throughout the play. It is also alleged that he blackmails people by threatening to accuse them (65–70). Paphlagon himself claims credit for a case in which he put a stop to buggery, getting a man named Gryttos[51] deleted from a list (877). The incident is otherwise unknown, but presumably Kleon prosecuted the man on a charge of prostitution and so got him disfranchised.

[50] For a summary of discussion of this question see ML pp. 194–7.
[51] The name is uncertain: perhaps Grypos or 'the hook-nosed man'. Cf. V. Tammaro *MC* 25–8 (1990–3) 149–50.

Paphlagon also claims that single-handed he put a stop to 'the conspirators' (861–3). This too must refer to some real incident, not known to us but recognizable by the Athenian audience, and it may well have been a prosecution by Kleon. The Sausage-seller replies that Paphlagon stirs up the city deliberately, like eel-fishers stirring up mud at the bottom of a lake, in order to produce an advantage for himself (864–7), and there are many other references in the play to 'stirring up' or 'harassing' (cf. p. 93). It must be true that Kleon sometimes prosecuted people, since otherwise these references would have seemed pointless to the audience. But we cannot know whether any of those whom he prosecuted were actually innocent.

6. *Theft of public funds.* Besides explicit statements about theft (258, 826–7, 1224–6) there is a passage about eating monstrous amounts which can be interpreted as a metaphor for the same thing (353–62).[52] But we should regard this accusation as comic slander. If Kleon had really stolen public money, surely someone would have prosecuted him for it, and Aristophanes would not have missed the chance of mentioning that.

7. *The leather trade.* The play contains many jokes about Paphlagon making leather and selling it in the Agora. Kleon's social background has already been considered (see p. 81). No doubt it was true that he was connected in some way with the manufacture and sale of leather, but we have no firm evidence that he carried it on in person. At one point it is alleged that he has a gang of young leather-sellers, and of honey-sellers and cheese-sellers who live near them, who are ready to seize power if he is threatened with ostracism (852–7). If Kleon really had a private force of this kind, it was obviously a serious matter; but we do not hear of it elsewhere, and it is probably just a comic invention by Aristophanes, based on the fact that those trades were carried on in the same area in or near the Agora.[53]

8. *Loud and overbearing speeches.* There are many references to Paphlagon's shouting, and in the performance no doubt the actor imitated Kleon's voice. Paphlagon also tries to prevent other people from speaking by interrupting them (58–60, 336–42). The evidence of Thucydides and later writers about Kleon's oratory has already

[52] It may also imply a desire for power; cf. J. Davidson *CQ* 43 (1993) 57–9.
[53] On the topography see Lind *Der Gerber Kleon* 94–117.

been mentioned (see p. 82), and it is clear that Aristophanes' portrayal of it is at least partly true, though it may well be exaggerated.[54]

9. *Cajoling the Assembly.* Flattering the Athenian people and gaining their support by offering them small advantages or treats provide one of the main themes of Aristophanes' satire. It reaches a climax in the last part of the contest, when Paphlagon and the Sausage-seller compete in presenting Democracy with nice items of food (1151–1226). We have no other evidence that Kleon actually promised trivial profits to the Athenians (apart from the jurors' pay). But politicians often try to gratify their electorate, and it would not be at all surprising if Kleon did so.

10. *Oracles.* This is another prominent theme, especially in the part of the contest in which Paphlagon and the Sausage-seller produce rival oracles, each claiming that the prophecies support himself (997–1097). There is no other evidence that Kleon did exploit oracles. But this is not a feature of Aristophanes' satire of other politicians in other plays, and the likeliest explanation of its inclusion in *Horsemen* is that Kleon had in fact read out oracles to the Assembly on at least one or two occasions.

Thus some of Aristophanes' charges against Kleon are certainly or probably true, while others may be only half true or completely false. At least two (nos. 1 and 3) are deliberate policies which must have had the approval of many Athenians. Aristophanes may have disagreed with those policies, but we cannot regard him as an objective critic launching an attack purely on grounds of political principle; he had suffered an attack by Kleon on his own work, *Babylonians*, two years before, and *Horsemen* is part of an ongoing vendetta. This play must be regarded as a mixture of fair criticism, exaggeration, and lies, motivated not only by a desire to entertain the audience and win the contest of comedies, but also by political disagreement and personal resentment. Aristophanes' aim was not to present an amusing fiction, nor on the other hand objective history. It was to expose Kleon to ridicule and scorn.

Horsemen came first in the contest at the Lenaia, and afterwards Aristophanes regarded it as a great triumph.

[54] Cf. N. O'Sullivan *Alcidamas, Aristophanes and the Beginnings of Greek Stylistic Theory* (Stuttgart 1992) 115–24.

> I hit Kleon in the belly when he was a powerful man,
> But refrained from jumping on him afterwards when he was down.
>
> > (*Clouds* 549–50)

> And even if Kleon's had a lucky break,
> We shan't make mincemeat of him yet again.
>
> > (*Wasps* 62–3)

In *Horsemen* he struck Kleon down and made mincemeat of him—or so he says. Consequently some scholars have found it paradoxical that the Athenians elected Kleon to be a general again for the year 424/3. The date of the election is not known, but it may well have been quite soon after the Lenaia.[55] So the references in *Clouds* and *Wasps* do not mean that Kleon was removed from office. But the activities for which he was satirized in *Horsemen* were not (except for the Pylos campaign) ones which depended on holding office, but rather on the power of his oratory in the Assembly. So the success which Aristophanes claimed for his play was most probably that it diminished Kleon's ability to sway the Assembly by his speeches. This claim may, for all we know, have been justified.

---

[55] In the fourth century generals were normally elected in the seventh prytany (February or March), but there is no evidence of the date of the election in the fifth century.

6

Clouds

STREPSIADES AND HIS DEBTS

In *Clouds* Aristophanes moves away from the political topics of *Akharnians* and *Horsemen* to a theme much closer to that of his first play, *Banqueters*: the education offered by sophists, especially in rhetoric. As in *Banqueters*, he uses a father–son relationship to dramatize it, but this time in a subtler way. Whereas *Banqueters*, as far as we can tell from the fragments, simply presented an old-fashioned father with two sons, of whom one learned the new rhetoric and the other did not, in *Clouds* the father urges his only son to take lessons from the sophists; when the son refuses, the father tries to take lessons instead, and then, when the father has failed, the son learns rhetoric in the end. This makes a more complex and varied plot.[1] Except in one scene near the end, the play does not present a conflict between an old man representing what is old and a young man representing what is new, and modern interpretations in terms of 'the generation gap'[2] are wide of the mark.

The play was originally performed at the Dionysia in 423 BC, but the text we now have is a version which has been partly revised at a later date. The extent and purpose of the alterations will be considered later in this chapter; but this problem need not affect our reading of the earlier scenes, in which there is no reason to think that any substantial change has been made.

At the start we see the old man and his son in bed.[3] The son is fast asleep, but the old man, whose name will be given later as Strepsiades, is tossing and turning, and then sits up and explains to

---

[1] Cf. Harriott *Aristophanes* 165–70.
[2] On this concept in general see E. W. Handley in *Tr. Com. Pol.* 417–30.
[3] His wife is not present; presumably she sleeps in the women's part of the house. Cf. R. D. Griffith *Prometheus* 19 (1993) 135–40.

the audience that he cannot sleep because he is worried about his debts.

> It's killing me,
> Seeing the moon now going through the twenties—
> Interest is coming on!
>
> (*Clouds* 16–18)

The significance of the moon is that Athenian months were lunar (29 or 30 days each) and money-lending was arranged by the month. Interest was normally reckoned by the month, not by the year, and had to be paid by the end of each month. A creditor wishing to prosecute a debtor, either for not paying the interest or for not repaying the whole loan when it was due, initiated the prosecution on the last day of the month; this was the day called Old and New,[4] because it was transitional between the old moon and the new moon. On this day the magistrates in charge of such cases[5] sat to receive applications; the prosecutor had not only to deliver his charge but also to pay a court fee, which, if he won the case, the debtor would have to refund to him.[6] The old man knows he cannot pay what he owes, and so is dreading the approaching Old and New day.

He blames his son for the debts. The son is an enthusiast for horse-riding and chariot-racing; he is dreaming of horses, and talks in his sleep about racing, while the father lies awake worrying about the cost of the horses. (In English, losing money on horses generally means losing bets. That is not the point here; the young man is a rider, not a gambler.) A horse was a conspicuously expensive possession (rather like a fast car in modern society): how has the son acquired this extravagant taste? The old man says it was his wife's fault. Still talking to the audience, he begins to reminisce: as a young country yokel he married an aristocratic girl from the town, 'a niece

---

[4] ἕνη τε καὶ νέα: *Clouds* 1134, 1178–9, etc. The first day of the month was called New Moon, νουμηνία: *Clouds* 1191, 1195–6.

[5] The magistrates are not specified in *Clouds*, but they would presumably have been the thirty deme-judges, who formerly travelled around the demes of Attica to receive private actions (Aristotle *Ath. Pol.* 26.3). I conjecture that during the Peloponnesian War they no longer travelled around the countryside but sat in the town. Details of their proceedings are not known; probably they had authority to decide summarily claims up to a certain figure, but took claims for larger sums to trial by jury.

[6] πρυτανεῖα: *Clouds* 1136, 1180, etc.; cf. MacDowell *Law* 239.

of Megakles son of Megakles', accustomed to luxury.[7] It was she who encouraged their son to take an interest in horses. As soon as he was born, she wanted to give him a name including -ipp- (from *hippos* meaning 'horse') such as Xanthippos or Kallippides, which would sound aristocratic, while her husband wanted to follow the Athenian custom of naming the boy after his grandfather, Pheidonides (from *pheido* meaning 'thrift'). In the end they compromised on Pheidippides. This is not in itself an absurd name, for it was borne by some real Greeks;[8] but Aristophanes expects the audience to laugh at the reasons for choosing it. It is only for the sake of this joke that he has called the character Pheidippides; the name has no further significance for the story of the play.

So the situation is that Pheidippides' love of horses has landed his father deep in debt. As often in Aristophanes, the initial exposition of the basic situation is followed almost at once by the hero's fantastic plan for setting it right. His son shall go to have lessons.

STREPSIADES. Please change your ways as quickly as you can,
    And go and learn the lessons I advise.
PHEIDIPPIDES. Say what you want.
STREPSIADES.   You'll do it?
PHEIDIPPIDES.   Yes, I will,
    By Dionysos!
STREPSIADES. Then look over here.
    Now can you see that little door and house?
PHEIDIPPIDES. I see it, father. Tell me what it is.
STREPSIADES. That is the Thinkery of clever souls.
    That's where men live who talk about the sky
    And argue that it is a baking cover,
    And it encloses us, and we're the coals.
    They teach a person, if he pays them money,
    To win at speaking, whether right or wrong.

    .   .   .   .   .   .

    Do, please, I beg you, please, my dearest boy,
    Go and be taught!

[7] On Megakles see p. 69 n. 44; on Strepsiades' wife, C. G. Brown *Prometheus* 17 (1991) 29–33; on the characterization of Strepsiades as a countryman, Fisher *Clouds* 47–50. The view of D. Ambrosino *MC* 21–2 (1986–7) 95–127 is that the marriage is an allegory of the relationship between the whole lower and upper classes in Athens; but that is unconvincing.

[8] On the origin of the name see O. Panagl in *Festschrift für Robert Muth* (ed. P. Händel and W. Meid, Innsbruck 1983) 297–306.

PHEIDIPPIDES.   And what am I to learn?
STREPSIADES.   It's said that they have both the arguments,
The one which is the better, and the worse.
They say that one of these two arguments,
The worse one, wins by saying what is wrong.
If you learn that wrong argument for me,
Of all these debts I owe because of you
I shan't pay anyone a single obol!

(*Clouds* 88–99, 110–18)

Strepsiades' plan is that Pheidippides should take lessons in speech-making, and in particular that he should learn the argument which 'wins by saying what is wrong'. He is to learn how to argue cleverly in favour of what is not true, so that those who hear him are convinced. Then, when Strepsiades is prosecuted for not paying the money he owes, Pheidippides will speak in court in his support and persuade the jury that Strepsiades owes nothing. The scheme is essentially dishonest. When the old man reveals his name a few moments later (134) as being Strepsiades (from *strepsai* meaning 'to turn'), which might be translated as MacTwister, that will seem to the audience to be quite appropriate. We have here a new comic hero, not a repetition of a character from an earlier play. Whereas Dikaiopolis in *Akharnians* is concerned for the city of Athens and for what is just and right, and his name reflects those concerns (see pp. 78–9), Strepsiades shows no patriotism and openly desires what is unjust and wrong. The Sausage-seller in *Horsemen* may seem rather more like Strepsiades, inasmuch as he excels in dishonesty and badness, but is not really much like him; for the Sausage-seller wins by means of his own cleverness and ingenuity, but Strepsiades is old, forgetful, and slow (129) and turns out to be incapable of learning to make clever speeches or of understanding abstract topics.[9] We seem, then, to be presented with a hero who has no heroic quality at all; he is admirable neither morally nor intellectually. Yet this is not quite a fair description; for his troubles are blamed on his son and his wife, while he himself does at least show commendable resolution in trying to do something about them (126–32).[10]

[9] Cf. P. Green *GRBS* 20 (1979) 15–25.
[10] Cf. K. J. Reckford *ICS* 16 (1991) 125: 'his engaging simple-mindedness, his openness to experience, his resilience, and what we might call his sheer survivability'.

The audience will hardly admire him, but they will sympathize more with him than with the other characters in this play.

SCIENCE

Pheidippides disgustedly refuses to go and take lessons, and so Strepsiades makes up his mind to go himself, and knocks at the door of a building called *phrontisterion*. This is a comically grand noun invented by Aristophanes, which we can translate Thinkery or Reflectory.[11] The building is a college headed by Socrates and Khairephon. The door is opened by a rather patronizing student, who condescends to tell Strepsiades what Socrates and Khairephon have been doing today.

STUDENT. This morning Socrates asked Khairephon
    How many feet of its own a flea could jump,
    Because one bit the brow of Khairephon
    And jumped off on to Socrates's head.
STREPSIADES. How did he measure it?
STUDENT.   Very cleverly.
    He melted wax, and then he took the flea
    And dipped the feet of it into the wax;
    On cooling, Persian boots[12] were formed on it.
    He took them off, and measured up the distance.
STREPSIADES. Oh Zeus the king, what subtlety of mind!
STUDENT. What about this, another cogitation
    Of Socrates's?
STREPSIADES. What? Do tell me, please.
STUDENT. He had been asked by Khairephon of Sphettos
    His view about the humming sound of gnats:
    Does it come through the mouth or through the rump?
STREPSIADES. What answer did he give about the gnat?
STUDENT. He said that the intestine of the gnat
    Is narrow, and because it is so thin
    The breath is forced straight through towards the rump;
    The narrow pipe leads to a cavity,
    The arse, which, from the force of breath, resounds.
STREPSIADES. And so the gnats' arse is their trumpet, then!
    What a felicitous intestination!

(*Clouds* 144–66)

---

[11] Cf. S. M. Goldberg *CP* 71 (1976) 254–6.
[12] A type of footwear generally worn by women. Cf. Stone *Costume* 227–9.

Aristophanes is making fun of serious activities. Normally we should not think it unreasonable for a specialist in zoology or natural history to wish to ascertain how far a flea can jump or the method by which a gnat's hum is produced. But Aristophanes uses various devices to make this science appear absurd: the objects of investigation are small insects, which most Athenians would regard as trivial pests not worthy of study; the investigation begins when a flea jumps from Khairephon's head to Socrates', which implies that both investigators are dirty and flea-ridden; instead of measuring the jump in normal feet, they follow comic logic in using the flea's foot as the unit of measurement, and employ a ridiculously elaborate method of ascertaining the size of it; and the explanation of the gnat's hum, in superficially convincing scientific language, leads to a vulgar conclusion.

Not only entomology is studied in the Thinkery. When the student lets Strepsiades see inside, he finds other students engaged in various absurd activities which turn out to be geology, astronomy, geometry, and geography. Then he catches sight of a man suspended in mid-air on a basket or drying-rack.[13] This turns out to be Socrates himself, who replies to Strepsiades in a very pompous manner.

STREPSIADES. Hey, Socrates!
   Socratikins!
SOCRATES. Why do you call me, mortal?
STREPSIADES. Would you first tell me what you're doing, please?
SOCRATES. I levitate and contemplate the sun.
STREPSIADES. Contempt,[14] for gods? But then why do it from
   A basket, not from earth?
SOCRATES.   I never could
   Have rightly found out matters in the sky
   Without suspending my judgement and my thought,
   Combining it with air as fine as itself.

---

[13] ταρρός (226): a flat wicker shelf normally used for maturing cheeses; cf. D. Ambrosino *MC* 19–20 (1984–5) 51–69. The text implies that here it is suspended by ropes from the theatre's *mekhane* (crane), rather than placed (as Ambrosino prefers) on the roof of the scene-building. Cf. Russo *Aristophanes* 117–18.

[14] Strepsiades mishears or misunderstands Socrates' word περιφρονῶ, 'think about', as ὑπερφρονῶ, 'despise'. Ordinary Greeks considered the sun to be a god.

If I had looked up from the ground below,
I'd have discovered nothing; for the earth
Is sure to draw thought's moisture to itself.
The same thing happens in the case of cress.

(*Clouds* 222–34)

Cress was a very ordinary vegetable; once again Aristophanes is using anticlimax to make fun of a scientific notion. Hanging oneself up so as to suspend judgement is obviously another joke. But is the whole theory just a piece of Aristophanic absurdity? We too must suspend judgement for the moment and see what follows. Strepsiades persuades Socrates to come down to the ground, and says he wants to learn the argument, the one that does not pay money back. He is willing to give Socrates any fee he asks, and to swear by the gods that he will pay it. 'You'll swear by gods!' says Socrates contemptuously, and explains that gods like Zeus do not exist. The divinities that he and the other thinkers honour are Clouds and Air. He invokes the Clouds, and they appear, forming the chorus of the play. Strepsiades is mightily impressed with them, and this leads on to a disquisition by Socrates on meteorology: rain is produced by clouds, and so is thunder, which is caused by clouds filled with water and whirled around in the sky so that they fall against one another. No doubt the audience is expected to laugh at his pompous and complicated exposition, and may perhaps not stop to think whether the things he is saying are actually true or not. But at least one of the points which he makes is one which all of us now would accept as true: rain is produced by clouds, not by Zeus, and the observable fact that it does not rain when there are no clouds is a perfectly sound piece of supporting evidence.

The other scientific theories which Aristophanes attributes to Socrates are ones which we are not likely to believe. But at least some of them were believed by some people at that time. In fact it was at this period that scientific theories had started to make an impression in Athens. Although the Ionian philosophers, beginning with Thales of Miletos, had commenced a century or more previously to propound their theories about the nature of matter and the origin of the world, Miletos was a long way from Athens, and it is unlikely that ordinary Athenians heard much of these new ideas until the middle of the fifth century. That was when Anaxagoras came to Athens.

Anaxagoras came from Klazomenai in Asia Minor. No doubt he had visited Miletos and heard all about the theories of the earlier Ionian philosophers. He settled in Athens and became a friend of Perikles. He held a complicated theory about matter and mind, which need not be discussed here; he also put forward a new account of the heavenly bodies. The sun, the moon, and the stars, he said, are fiery stones, shining because of their heat, and the reason why they move is that they are carried round by the rotation of the sky (*aither*). They look small just because they are a long way off from us; really the sun is bigger in size than the Peloponnese. He also gave explanations of eclipses, earthquakes, winds, and other phenomena, including thunder, which (according to one account) he said was a collision of clouds.[15] So this is where some of the ideas which Aristophanes attributes to Socrates came from: the notions that thunder is produced by clouds bumping against one another, and that the whirl of the sky makes them move, are crude summaries of theories of Anaxagoras.

Another scientist of this period was Hippon, who believed that all matter was derived ultimately from water and fire. The theory which we find in *Clouds* 95–7 (quoted on p. 115) is attributed to him by a scholium there. Evidently he tried to explain the sky that we see above us by comparing it to a baking-cover. A common method of baking was to light a fire on a stone floor and cover it with a hemispherical cover; when the floor and the cover were thoroughly hot, one would lift the cover, rake away the coals and ashes, put the dough on the hot floor in their place, and put the cover over it so that it would be baked by the accumulated heat. So the theory must have been that the sky was a solid hemispherical cover above the earth. Whether or not the attribution to Hippon is correct, there is no reason to doubt that such a theory had been put forward seriously by someone, although the statement that we are the coals under the cover may well be Aristophanes' own comic addition.

But perhaps the main source of the scientific ideas satirized in *Clouds* was Diogenes—generally called Diogenes of Apollonia to distinguish him from other philosophers of the same name, although it is not known for certain which of the several cities named Apollonia was his place of origin. He lived in the middle of the fifth

[15] Diogenes Laertios 2.9.

century and held views which blended those of several earlier thinkers, mainly Anaximenes, Herakleitos, Anaxagoras, and Leukippos. Most significant is the importance which he attached to air. It is obvious that air is essential to life, because when we cease breathing we cease living, but Diogenes considered that air was the instrument not only of life but also of thought. This part of his theory is recounted by Theophrastos.

As has been mentioned, he says that one thinks with air, pure and dry; for moisture impedes intelligence. That is why one thinks less in sleep, inebriation, and surfeit. The fact that dampness removes intelligence is shown by the fact that other living beings are inferior in intellect; for they breathe the air from the earth and they take wetter food.

(Theophrastos *On Perception* 44)

This bears a strong resemblance to *Clouds* 227–33 (quoted on pp. 118–19), in which Socrates claims that he thinks more clearly when raised up off the ground. It is not identical: Socrates there speaks of thought's moisture being attracted by the earth, whereas Diogenes, according to Theophrastos, seems to have believed that it was the earth's moisture which was injurious to thought. But the two accounts are obviously versions of the same theory. Probably Aristophanes (or possibly Theophrastos) has reproduced the doctrine inaccurately, but we need not doubt that it was indeed Diogenes' doctrine on air that he meant to satirize.

Thus the scientific doctrines of the Thinkery are not purely Aristophanes' comic inventions. They include, albeit in garbled form, some theories which we can ascribe confidently to Anaxagoras or Hippon or Diogenes. Others whose authors we cannot identify, such as the theory about lightning (404–7), could also be based on ideas circulating in Athens in Aristophanes' time, even though we have no other record of them.

RELIGION

Science impinges on religion. Ordinary Greeks believed that the weather, especially thunder, lightning, and rain, was produced by Zeus. When Socrates tells Strepsiades that the Clouds are responsible, he is not just talking meteorology; he is saying that the Clouds are the only true goddesses.

STREPSIADES. But Zeus the Olympian—surely, by Earth, at least you think him a god, don't you?

SOCRATES. What, Zeus! Don't be so absurd. Zeus doesn't exist.

STREPSIADES.   But I don't understand you.
Who is it who rains? Because that's the first thing, I think, that needs some explaining.

SOCRATES. The Clouds do, of course. I'll soon show you that: there is very strong evidence for it.
Tell me, where have you ever before now observed, without Clouds, there was any rain falling?
You'd expect Zeus to rain when the weather was clear, while the Clouds were away from the country.

STREPSIADES. By Apollo, that's good; you fitted it in very well with what you were saying.
I always imagined that Zeus had a sieve, through which he was passing his water!
But explain to me next who the thunderer is; that's the thing which gives me the jitters.

SOCRATES. The Clouds make the thunder, by rolling around.

STREPSIADES.   In what way?—you stopper at nothing!

SOCRATES. They're filled up with plenty of water, and then, whenever they're forced into motion,
Hanging down in the sky and full up with the rain, because of necessity, heavy
And falling against one another up there, they are bursting, and that makes a rumble.

STREPSIADES. But who is the person who forces them so into motion? That must be Zeus, surely?

SOCRATES. Not at all; a celestial whirl.

STREPSIADES.   What? Whirl? Well, that's something I never noticed:
Zeus doesn't exist, and Whirl is the king who has taken his place as the ruler!

(*Clouds* 366–81)

Strepsiades of course has misunderstood: he takes Whirl to be another divine personage like Zeus. Socrates does not really mean that, but he does speak of Clouds and Air as gods. Here again Aristophanes is constructing comedy out of seriously held beliefs. Diogenes of Apollonia apparently called air God, or a god.[16] So

---

[16] Diogenes fr. 5 (Diels-Kranz); cf. Cicero *De natura deorum* 1.29.

Aristophanes makes Socrates address a prayer to Air, in the same way as other people pray to Zeus or Apollo (264), and swear 'By Air!' when he gets cross (627). And he mischievously adds more gods by analogy: if Air is a god, why should not Sky (*aither*), Space (*khaos*), Breath, and Talk[17] be gods too (265, 424, 627)? Above all he adds Clouds as Socrates' goddesses.[18] Clouds are air, but they are thick air which one cannot see through. They are like smoke, obscuring the view. 'Smoke' seems to have been a colloquial term for a lot of talk with no action, rather like 'hot air' in English,[19] and in this play Aristophanes uses clouds similarly to represent empty talk and waffle. It is as if the play had a chorus of 'hot air'. Yet clouds, being in the sky, were traditionally associated with the Olympian gods, especially Zeus, who in Homer is often 'Zeus the cloud-gatherer'; and Aristophanes curiously allows them to retain that character in the lyrics of the parodos and the parabasis, where they sing of Zeus and other Olympians, even though in the dialogue they and their airy companions are invoked as the *only* divinities (365, 423–4). Probably those lyrics, which are very conventional in expression,[20] are to be regarded as hymns not closely integrated with the action of the play (cf. p. 17).

It is not known whether Anaxagoras and other scientists of his time denied the existence of the traditional gods explicitly. Protagoras professed agnosticism rather than atheism: 'Concerning gods, I have no knowledge either that they exist or that they do not exist or what form they take; for there are many obstacles to knowledge, including the obscurity of the subject and the brevity of human life.'[21] But there is no doubt that Anaxagoras and others were believed to reject the gods at least by implication: if the sun was a fiery stone, it was evidently not a god. There is a fair amount

[17] In line 424 'tongue' must mean the activity of talking, not the physical organ in the mouth.

[18] Lines 265, 316, 329, 365, 423–4 are quite explicit and refute the view of O'Regan *Rhetoric* 44 (with n. 51) that Socrates does not regard the clouds as goddesses. For a survey of other interpretations of the chorus, some of them very far-fetched, see O'Regan *Rhetoric* 52–5.

[19] καπνός: cf. MacDowell *Wasps* 177 (on line 324). In *Clouds* 330 this word is applied to clouds.

[20] Cf. M. S. Silk *YCS* 26 (1980) 107: 'triteness, inflation, and pervasive lack of point'.

[21] Protagoras fr. 4 (Diels–Kranz).

of evidence that atheism was a legal offence in Athens at this time. We are told that a decree, proposed by Diopeithes sometime in the 430s, laid down that those who did not recognize the gods or taught theories about 'the things up above' (astronomy and meteorology) should be prosecuted by *eisangelia*, a procedure generally used for treason, and that this decree was aimed at Anaxagoras (and through him at Perikles).[22] There are various accounts of the trial of Anaxagoras: according to one, he was prosecuted by Kleon and defended by Perikles, and was condemned to exile from Athens and a fine of five talents; in another, he was prosecuted by Thoukydides, fled from Athens to avoid trial, and was condemned to death in his absence; in another, he was present when condemned to death, and while he was being held in prison awaiting execution Perikles persuaded the Athenians to let him off.[23] Protagoras too, it is said, was condemned to exile and his books were burned.[24] These trials are not mentioned by any fifth-century author, and there is some doubt whether they really took place.[25] But even if they did not, it is known that 'not recognizing the gods whom the city recognizes' was part of the charge against Socrates at his trial in 399, and there can be no doubt that ordinary Athenians regarded with suspicion intellectuals who seemed to be atheists. At the very end of *Clouds* Strepsiades picks out one reason above all for attacking the sophists.

> Pursue them, hit them, pelt them, for many reasons,
> But most of all because they wronged the gods!

> (*Clouds* 1508–9)

We can safely interpret this, not as an eccentric opinion of

---

[22] Plutarch *Perikles* 32.2.

[23] Diogenes Laertios 2.12–14.

[24] Aristotle fr. 67 (Rose), Plutarch *Nikias* 23.4, Diogenes Laertios 9.52.

[25] K. J. Dover *The Greeks and their Legacy* (Oxford 1988) 135–58, in an article maintaining that before the prosecution of Socrates intellectuals were free to express their beliefs, suggests that all the evidence about these trials originated either from misinterpretation of comedies or from a lost work by Demetrios of Phaleron written at the end of the fourth century, which may have exaggerated the antagonism between the Athenians and philosophers. This hypothesis cannot be definitely refuted, but the positive evidence for it is not strong, and it is probably too sceptical about the information which survived into Hellenistic and Roman times. Cf. G. B. Kerferd *The Sophistic Movement* (Cambridge 1981) 21.

Strepsiades or of Aristophanes, but as an expression of a widely held view that atheism was sinful.

RHETORIC

Strepsiades is so impressed by his first meeting with the Clouds that he becomes even keener to enter the Thinkery as a student. He is ready to face an austere life of hunger, thirst, dirt, cold, and beating, and he lists the qualities that he hopes to acquire. Although the precise meaning of a few of the colloquial terms is doubtful, the general sense of tricky eloquence is clear.

> So now let them do whatsoever they wish
> To this body of mine; I consign it to them
> Prepared for a beating, for hunger, for thirst,
> To be dirty, to freeze, to be flayed to hold wine,
> If only I get clear away from my debts
> And am able to make people think that I am
> Audacious, glib-tongued, energetic and brash,
> Disgusting, a gluer-together of lies,
> A coiner of phrases, a dab-hand at trials,
> A law-stone, a rattle, a reynard, a drill,
> A slyboots, a humbug, a sticker, a swank,
> A goadster, a villain, a twister, a pest,
> A greedy consumer of finicky scraps.
> If those are the names that I'm called in the street,
> They are welcome to treat me however they like;
> In fact, if they wish,
> They can pull out my guts, by Demeter, and serve
>   Them up to the thinkers for dinner!

(Clouds 439–56)

Entering the Thinkery is treated much like initiation into religious mysteries, and as Strepsiades is led inside he feels as if he were entering the cave of an oracle (507–8).[26] The parabasis (to be discussed later) follows, and when he reappears his education has already begun, and his stupidity and forgetfulness are already exasperating Socrates. The first lessons are about grammar and metre,

---

[26] Cf. Marianetti *Religion* 41–75 and *Symbolae Osloenses* 68 (1993) 5–31, Bowie *Aristophanes* 112–24.

which are regarded as preparatory for the study of rhetoric. (Ancient orators attached importance to the rhythm of their sentences.) These provide Aristophanes with material for some fairly obvious jokes: puns on *metron*, meaning either 'metre' or 'measure', and on *daktylos*, meaning either 'dactyl' or 'finger'; and confusion of masculine and feminine nouns, which leads to some prominent Athenian men being ludicrously spoken of as feminine. Next Socrates, with a superficial resemblance to a modern psychiatrist, tells Strepsiades to recline on a couch and think about his problems. But Strepsiades' thoughts are all vulgar or absurd, he cannot remember anything he has been taught, and Socrates refuses to teach him any more.

Strepsiades, in despair, tries once again to persuade his son to take lessons, and this time succeeds. He leads Pheidippides to the Thinkery and begs Socrates to teach him.

> Please see that he learns those two arguments,
> The one which is the better, and the worse,
> Which says what's wrong and overturns the better.
> At any rate make sure he learns the wrong one!

> (*Clouds* 882—5)

After a scene in which the two arguments appear in personified form and debate their respective merits (which presents some problems and will be discussed later) Pheidippides enters the Thinkery and eventually reappears, having learned 'the worse argument'. Now we hear the kind of rhetoric taught in the Thinkery. Strepsiades is afraid that his creditors will initiate a prosecution by paying court fees on the next Old and New day; Pheidippides declares this impossible, on the ground that a day cannot be both old and new. That is, he takes the conventional name of the last day of the month, and by literal interpretation reduces it to absurdity. Strepsiades is triumphant for a while, and exuberantly chases away two creditors who come seeking repayment of their money. But then comes his downfall. He and Pheidippides have a dispute about the merits of old and modern poetry. (This is the one part of the play in which the father defends what is old and the son defends what is new.) As a result Pheidippides not only hits his father but proceeds to prove, by means of the type of argument he has learned, that father-beating is quite right and proper. To the Greeks, attacking one's own parents was the quintessentially wicked crime, and the point here is that

Pheidippides is now so good at rhetoric that he can defend even the worst possible action.

PHEIDIPPIDES. First tell me this: when I was a boy, did you not give me beatings?
STREPSIADES. I did, to do you good, because I cared for you.
PHEIDIPPIDES.   Then tell me,
    Should I not do you good as well, in just the way that you did,
    And beat you, since you say that that's what doing good is, beating?

(*Clouds* 1409–12)

Pheidippides is exploiting what modern philosophers have called the naturalistic fallacy, identifying the commendatory term 'good' with a specific activity, beating. Strepsiades of course is not enough of a philosopher to know how to refute it. Instead he appeals to custom and law.

STREPSIADES. But nowhere is it the rule to give this treatment to a father!
PHEIDIPPIDES. But wasn't it a man who set this law up in the first place,
    Like you and me, who made a speech and so convinced the ancients?
    And for the future, then, am I not just as much entitled
    To set a new law up for sons, that they should beat their fathers?
    But all the blows that we've received before the law's enactment
    We shall remit; we freely give those thrashings away for nothing!
    You only have to look at cocks and all those other creatures,
    How they attack their fathers. Yet they're just the same as we are—
    Except of course for one thing: *they* don't put decrees in writing.
STREPSIADES. Well, why in that case, since you copy everything that cocks do,
    Why don't you feed on dung as well, and use a perch to sleep on?
PHEIDIPPIDES. That's not the same, and Socrates would certainly not think so.

(*Clouds* 1420–32)

Thus Pheidippides answers Strepsiades' appeal to custom and law by pointing out that laws are made by men and can be altered by men. He regards the natural behaviour of animals as a more acceptable precedent. But then Aristophanes significantly allows Strepsiades to perceive the weakness of this argument: no one would regard the natural behaviour of animals as a satisfactory model for men to follow in every respect. Pheidippides turns out to be incapable of rebutting this: he can only refer to Socrates as a superior authority. Here Aristophanes implies that Strepsiades is right and Pheidippides' clever argument unsound.

As with the science and the religion of the Thinkery, so also with its rhetoric: we can identify some at least of the real men whose beliefs and activities Aristophanes is satirizing.[27] The most important is Protagoras. Protagoras came from Abdera in Thrace, and in the time of Perikles he visited Athens at least twice and probably oftener. He was interested in words, and was apparently the first person to distinguish the genders of nouns as masculine, feminine, and neuter;[28] this distinction provides the basis of the jokes in *Clouds* 658–92. Above all he was the person who claimed to be able 'to make the worse argument the better'.

Many real Athenians, like Strepsiades, had weak cases which they wanted to win in the lawcourts. In earlier, simpler times no doubt it was assumed that a case would be won by the litigant who had the stronger evidence on his side, but by the fifth century, if not before, it had been realized that a man with weak evidence might still win if he presented it cleverly. Aristotle comments on this kind of argument, giving an example from Korax of Syracuse: a man accused of assault, if he is physically weak, can argue that he is unlikely to have committed a crime of that sort; but if he is physically strong, he can argue that he is unlikely to have committed it because he would have known that everyone would suspect him.

So both appear probable; but in fact the former is probable, whereas the latter is not probable straightforwardly but only in the way that has been described. And this is what making the worse argument the better is. This was why people rightly objected to Protagoras' prospectus; for it is a lie, and not truly but apparently probable. It does not form part of any art except rhetoric and eristic.

(Aristotle *Rhetoric* 1402a. 22–8)

Aristotle is anxious to make clear that rhetorical ingenuity does not make a bad argument really better. His account shows that this kind of ingenuity was older than Protagoras, for Korax is supposed to have been the very first teacher of rhetoric. But it also shows that it was Protagoras who was particularly associated with the claim to

[27] For a fuller discussion of this topic see O'Regan *Rhetoric* 9–21.
[28] Aristotle *Rhetoric* 1407b 6–8, *Sophistical Refutations* 173b 19–22.

teach people how to make the worse argument the better, by finding ways of supporting the side of a case which *prima facie* is the less likely to be right.

This kind of argument is also associated with Antiphon. Antiphon was a distinguished Athenian orator who eventually was executed for his share in the oligarchic revolution of the Four Hundred in 411 BC. We possess three speeches written by him for delivery by various litigants in actual homicide cases, and also three 'tetralogies', each of which is a set of four short speeches (two for the prosecution and two for the defence) in an imaginary homicide case. The attribution of the tetralogies to Antiphon has sometimes been questioned,[29] but anyway it seems probable that all these texts, both the speeches for real cases and the tetralogies, were distributed in writing as models of how unusual or difficult cases might be presented. Much use is made, especially in the tetralogies, of arguments from probability. Here is an example from the *First Tetralogy*.

PROSECUTOR. ... Who is more likely to have attacked him than the man who had already been seriously harmed by him and was expecting to be harmed even more? That man is the defendant. He had long been his enemy ...; so naturally he plotted against him, naturally he defended himself against his enemy by killing him ...

DEFENDANT. ... If the seriousness of our enmity makes it natural for you to suspect me now, it was more natural for me, before committing the crime, to foresee the suspicion now falling upon me, and to stop anyone else I knew plotting against him, rather than commit it myself and deliberately come under obvious suspicion.

(Antiphon 2a.5–6, 2b.3)

The defendant's argument here, 'I am not likely to have committed the crime, because I would have known that everyone would think it likely that I committed it', is just like the one which Aristotle attributes to Korax as an example of 'making the worse argument the better'. The date of the tetralogies is unknown, and we cannot be sure whether Antiphon was already teaching the use of such arguments before Aristophanes wrote *Clouds*, but instruction of this general type is undoubtedly what Aristophanes was satirizing.

Antiphon is associated also with arguments about 'nature' and 'law'—if this is the same man. Reasons for regarding 'Antiphon the orator' and 'Antiphon the sophist' as two distinct persons are

[29] Cf. E. M. Carawan *AJP* 114 (1993) 235–70.

inconclusive;[30] but even if they were distinct, Aristophanes' satire involves them both. Fragments of a work entitled *Truth*, attributed to Antiphon the sophist, are important evidence for fifth-century discussion of the conflict between *physis*, meaning 'nature', and *nomos*, generally translated 'law' but also covering unwritten customs and norms of behaviour required in a community. Interpretation of the fragments is difficult and at some points controversial, but Antiphon seems to regard life according to nature as preferable; laws are attempts to restrict nature.[31] Evidently this is the view which is being satirized in *Clouds* 1420–32. Strepsiades complains that father-beating is not in accordance with law or custom, and Pheidippides regards nature, exemplified in this case by the behaviour of cockerels, as a better guide for human conduct.

SOCRATES

So *Clouds* contains more or less clear allusions to theories and activities which we can attribute to several real individuals, especially Anaxagoras, Protagoras, Diogenes, and Antiphon. But none of those men is named in the play. Sometimes there are general references to 'thinkers' or 'sophists', but for the most part Aristophanes makes Socrates responsible for all the intellectual activities and theories that are mentioned. Now, we possess extensive accounts of Socrates, his way of life, talk, and beliefs, in the works of Plato and Xenophon. To be sure, those two writers were his admirers and undoubtedly present favourable rather than objective portraits, and Plato in his later works is certainly not giving us Socrates' philosophy but his own philosophy through Socrates' mouth. Aristophanes, on the other hand, is a comedian and a satirist. We should therefore not expect his picture of Socrates to be identical with Plato's or Xenophon's. Nevertheless it has seemed to most modern readers that the discrepancies are too great to be explained as being due merely to the difference of genre. Aristophanes appears to be not merely observing from a different viewpoint but describing

---

[30] For a summary of the controversy see G. B. Kerferd *The Sophistic Movement* (Cambridge 1981) 49–51.

[31] P. Oxy. 1364, 1797, 3647 = *Corpus dei Papiri Filosofici Greci e Latini* 17.1–2. For discussion with bibliography see Kerferd *The Sophistic Movement* 111–17.

different facts. The disagreements have been carefully catalogued and discussed by Dover,[32] and here they will be treated only briefly. Essentially they are of two kinds.

1. *Subjects of study.* In *Clouds*, as we have seen, Socrates devotes attention to astronomy, meteorology, natural history, and other scientific subjects; he disbelieves in the traditional gods and sets up a new religion; and he is expert in rhetoric, especially in making weak arguments convincing. Plato makes Socrates reject all this, most strikingly in a passage of the *Apology*, which purports to be a record of what he said at his trial in 399 BC.

Many men have made accusations against me to you for many years now, none of them true. . . . that there was a clever man called Socrates, who was a thinker about the things up above, investigated everything that was underground, and made the worse argument the better. . . . And the most unreasonable thing of all is that it's impossible to discover and reveal their names—except in the case of a comic poet.

(Plato *Apology* 18b–d)

The comic poet meant is Aristophanes, who is named a few lines later, and Plato is here putting into the mouth of Socrates an explicit denial of the beliefs and subjects of study attributed to him in *Clouds*. (Whether memories of Aristophanes' play did influence the jurors who voted against Socrates, as Plato evidently believed, is another question, which cannot now be answered.)

2. *Personal activities.* In *Clouds* Socrates is the head of the Thinkery, a school for the instruction of students, who reside in the building; he possesses knowledge which is revealed only to those who pay him fees. But according to Plato and Xenophon he did not keep a school or charge fees, and did not profess to have any expert knowledge or to be able to teach anyone; he just conversed with those, mainly young men, whom he met in public places or in other people's houses. Plato sharply distinguishes between Socrates and the sophists. This distinction depends on defining sophists rather narrowly. Some writers, from Herodotos onwards, in fact use the term 'sophist' in a general sense to refer to any wise man, and in this sense it was certainly reasonable to call Socrates a sophist. But more narrowly the word was used for a man who gave instruction in advanced studies in return for fees. According to Aristophanes

[32] Dover *Clouds* xxxii–lvii.

Socrates was a sophist in this sense too, but not according to Plato.

The discrepancies between Aristophanes' portrayal of Socrates and Plato's have long puzzled modern readers, but the explanation now generally accepted is the one which has been admirably expounded by Dover. Essentially it is this: Aristophanes wanted to write a play ridiculing intellectuals and their pretensions; for practical dramatic reasons he needed to have one character representing the intellectuals; most of the leading intellectuals were not suitable for this purpose because they were foreigners not well known to the Athenian public (Anaxagoras and Protagoras had almost certainly left Athens for good some years before *Clouds* was performed); Socrates on the other hand was familiar to most Athenians because he had lived in Athens all his life, his appearance was noticeable and mildly comic (snub nose, prominent eyes, thick lips), and he frequently engaged people in conversation in public; Aristophanes therefore chose Socrates to be a character in his play and simply assigned to that character all the intellectual theories and activities which he wished to ridicule.[33] The fact that some of them really belonged to other men, not to Socrates, was, to Aristophanes, of no importance.

Against this view Nussbaum has maintained that Aristophanes' portrayal of Socrates is less inconsistent with Plato's than has generally been supposed, and that it is largely correct.[34] Some of her points are far-fetched, and she tends to treat the play as if it were a philosophical document rather than a comedy,[35] but it does seem right to modify Dover's account in a few respects. First, Socrates' interest in natural science may well have been greater at the time of *Clouds* than Plato allows him to admit twenty-four years later in the *Apology*, for Plato himself elsewhere makes Socrates say that when he was young he was very interested in scientific questions and investigated 'what happens concerning the sky and the earth'.[36] To

[33] Cf. Cartledge *Aristophanes* 26: 'For his incarnation of the evils of Sophistry Aristophanes needed some instantly recognisable public figure, and Socrates (then aged 46) must have seemed heaven-sent.'

[34] M. Nussbaum *YCS* 26 (1980) 43–97. Cf. also Marianetti *Religion* 108–32.

[35] Cf. Fisher *Clouds* 243–8.

[36] Plato *Phaidon* 96a–c. This passage implies a quite lengthy investigation, and is not compatible with the suggestion that 'Socrates rejected mechanistic theories of causation as soon as he came up against them' (Dover *Ar. Comedy* 118). For a summary of different views of it see R. Hackforth *Plato's Phaedo* (Cambridge 1955) 127–31.

dismiss this as being really autobiography of Plato, not of Socrates, is less plausible than to accept it as a genuine fact about a period of Socrates' life which had not necessarily ended before *Clouds* was written.

Second, though Socrates did not organize a school or charge fees, it is obvious from Plato that he was an educator. A group of young men gathered around him and could be regarded as his followers. They did not pay him fees, but they probably gave him presents and shared meals and drinking-parties with him, so that he did obtain some material benefits.[37] His method of teaching was not to give lengthy lectures and rhetorical displays, as some sophists did; instead he put questions to one interlocutor at a time, and criticized the answers he received, causing people to examine their own ideas critically. Aristophanes makes him use this method in *Clouds* too, when he tries to teach Strepsiades, though most of Strepsiades' answers are so stupid or wrong-headed that they do not lead to any extensive analysis.[38]

And finally there is the matter of 'making the worse argument the better', which is after all the main purpose of Strepsiades and Pheidippides in going to the Thinkery. We may accept that the real Socrates aimed at discovering the truth, and disapproved of rhetoric which aimed at defeating an opponent regardless of truth. Nevertheless it is plain from all the early works of Plato that Socrates' most characteristic activity was to take a proposition or definition which was widely held to be true and prove it false. That is just what Strepsiades wants himself or his son to learn to be able to do. The difference (an all-important difference, though Strepsiades does not see it) is that the Platonic Socrates refutes statements which are *apparently* true, whereas the Aristophanic Socrates refutes statements which are *actually* true. Skill at arguing is common to both.

Thus the right conclusion is that Aristophanes' portrayal of Socrates, though inaccurate and unfair in many ways, is not wholly false. It is a comic reflection of the man in a distorting mirror, not a picture of a quite different man.

---

[37] Diogenes Laertios 2.74.
[38] Cf. E. A. Havelock *YCS* 22 (1972) 1–18.

THE REVISION OF THE PLAY

We must now revert to the parabasis, which occupies the time between Strepsiades' admission to the Thinkery and his failure to learn what Socrates tries to teach him.[39] The main speech (518–62) is unusual in several ways. It is not in anapaestic tetrameters, but in a metre known as eupolidean, uniquely among the surviving plays (although there is some evidence that this metre was used also in the parabases of some comedies now lost).[40] It uses the first-person singular 'I' to mean Aristophanes himself, not the chorus (cf. p. 42). But its most remarkable feature is that it refers to the play's lack of success in the contest of comedies (which may mean that it came either fourth or fifth, if there were five plays in the contest; cf. pp. 8–9).

> Now, spectators, I intend to speak quite freely to you all
> And to tell the truth—by Dionysos who has nurtured me!
> I declare—and if I'm not sincere, then may I fail to win,
> And not be considered clever—I thought you intelligent,
> And I thought this play the cleverest of all my comedies;
> That was why I wanted you to taste it first, the one that gave
> Me the greatest trouble. I was worsted, though, by vulgar men,
> And retreated; that was not what I deserved. I blame you, then,
> Clever men, since all this effort that I put in was for you.

> (*Clouds* 518–26)

Aristophanes here is complaining that he was defeated (524–5) and yet is looking forward to the possibility of winning (520). Clearly this passage was composed after the original performance of the play, and was inserted in place of a speech in (presumably) anapaestic tetrameters,[41] with a view to a second performance in another contest. Further evidence for the date of this speech occurs a few lines later (551–9) when Aristophanes refers to the attacks made by other comic dramatists on the politician Hyperbolos. First he mentions Eupolis' *Marikas*, which cannot have been performed

[39] On the problems of this parabasis cf. Hubbard *Mask* 88–112.

[40] It is almost impossible to represent the intricacies of the eupolidean metre in an English translation, and instead my version imitates the similar but simpler trochaic tetrameter.

[41] A scholium on 520 says that this passage is not in the same metre as 'the one in the first *Clouds*'.

earlier than the Lenaia of 421, since it alluded to Kleon as being dead and Kleon died in the autumn of 422.[42] Then he mentions a play by Hermippos, which was subsequent, and therefore not performed earlier than the Dionysia of 421; 'and now all the others' follow suit, with plays which therefore cannot be earlier than 420. So this speech (518–62) was written no earlier than 420.[43] However, another part of the parabasis (the epirrhema, 575–94) refers to the recent election of Kleon as general, and looks forward to the possibility of his being convicted of accepting bribes and stealing from public funds. This must belong to the original version of the play. It cannot have been written when Kleon was already dead, and indeed Aristophanes would surely not have retained it in the script for a performance after the death of Kleon in 422.[44] It is reasonable to conclude that he rewrote parts of the play but did not complete the task of revision, and thus that the proposed second performance never took place.

The scholia refer several times to 'the first *Clouds*' and 'the second *Clouds*' and to differences between them. Evidently the commentator (or commentators) who wrote these notes, probably in the Hellenistic period, possessed copies of both versions and was able to compare them. Perhaps the same man, or else a contemporary, wrote this comment which we find among the *hypotheses* to the surviving version.

This is the same play as the previous one, but it has been partly[45] revised, as if in fact the poet wanted to produce it again but in the end for whatever reason did not do so. Altogether correction has been carried out in almost

---

[42] Schol. *Clouds* 549b, 553 (Eupolis fr. 211).

[43] It is unlikely that 'all the others' continued writing plays attacking Hyperbolos after he was ostracized. So this speech was probably written before that ostracism, which occurred not later than 415. The contrary view, that *Clouds* was revised after the ostracism of Hyperbolos, is maintained by S. Bianchetti *Studi Italiani di Filologia Classica* 51 (1979) 221–48 and E. C. Kopff *AJP* 111 (1990) 318–29, but rightly rejected by I. C. Storey *AJP* 114 (1993) 71–84 and J. Henderson in *Nomodeiktes, Greek Studies in Honor of Martin Ostwald* (ed. R. M. Rosen and J. Farrell, Ann Arbor 1993) 591–601.

[44] O'Regan *Rhetoric* 77 believes that Aristophanes did deliberately retain this passage when revising the play, and that it is 'hilariously futile'. It seems to me that after Kleon's death it would have been futile without being hilarious.

[45] The sense of ἐπὶ μέρους must be 'in part', not 'in details', because the writer goes on to mention substantial passages which have been revised in their entirety. Cf. Fisher *Clouds* 23 n. 16.

every part. Some things have been removed, and some have been worked in and remodelled in the arrangement and in the interaction[46] of the characters, and some, such as the following, have undergone the revision in their entirety: for example, the parabasis[47] of the chorus has been replaced, and where the right argument talks to the wrong one, and finally where the school of Socrates is burned.

(*Clouds hyp.* vii Coulon = i Dover)

Modern critics have made innumerable suggestions about how the first *Clouds* may have differed from the second.[48] Most of them are quite unverifiable, but the *hypothesis* just quoted does specify three parts of the play where the revised version which we have differs completely from the original version, and our speculations will have a firmer basis if we concentrate on those. One is the parabasis; we have already seen that the main speech of the parabasis belongs to the revision. The other two are the contest between the Better and Worse Arguments, and the final scene of the play. These must now be considered in turn.

THE TWO ARGUMENTS

When Strepsiades asks that Pheidippides should be taught 'the better and the worse argument', Socrates replies that he will learn from the arguments in person (886). He himself goes off-stage, and immediately the two Arguments appear. Henceforth I call them Arguments with a capital letter, because they are characters in the play. But this is a strange personification, and its strangeness is not much diminished by the observation that Hesiod included Arguments among the children of Strife,[49] for Hesiod was not presenting

---

[46] The word here translated 'interaction' ($\delta\iota\alpha\lambda\lambda\alpha\gamma\dot{\eta}$) could also mean 'succession', the order in which the various characters appear, or 'exchange', the substitution of one character for another.

[47] 'Parabasis' here, as often, must refer to the main speech only, not including the system of ode, epirrhema, antode, antepirrhema.

[48] For recent discussion of this question see Dover *Clouds* lxxx–xcviii, P. Fabrini *Annali della Scuola Normale Superiore di Pisa, Classe di Lettere e Filologia* 5 (1975) 1–16, T. K. Hubbard *CA* 5 (1986) 182–97, O'Regan *Rhetoric* 133–9.

[49] Hesiod *Theogony* 229, adduced by Newiger *Metapher* 142–3, Dover *Clouds* lviii. Epikharmos wrote a comedy entitled $\Lambda\dot{o}\gamma o\varsigma$ $\kappa a\grave{\iota}$ $\lambda o\gamma\acute{\iota}\nu a$, which may mean *Masculine and Feminine Arguments*, but it is unknown whether it included Arguments appearing on-stage as characters.

visible performers in a theatre. What does an Argument look like when played by an actor? A scholium on 889 declares 'The Arguments are present on-stage in wicker hutches fighting like birds', which seems to mean that the dispute was presented in the guise of a cock-fight. But nothing in the text of the play as we have it confirms this description. On the contrary, 889 itself, in which one Argument tells the other to 'come along', seems to preclude the possibility that they were cocks carried or wheeled on-stage in wicker cages. Later one Argument is explicitly called a man (1033–5) and says 'Please take my cloak' (1103). So there can be no doubt that they appear in human form; the scholium is mistaken.[50]

The names are difficult too. *Logos* is a general word for speaking, also having a wide variety of special senses, but in this play Strepsiades is mainly concerned with speaking in a lawcourt and in particular with arguing to win his case, and so it seems fair in this context to use the translation Argument rather than merely Speech. The Greek comparative adjectives used to distinguish the two Arguments basically mean 'stronger' and 'weaker', but are often used more vaguely to mean 'better' and 'worse'.[51] Consequently they are ambiguous in the present context: is each Argument being called logically strong or weak, or is he being called morally good or bad? Conveniently, the English words 'good' and 'bad' have a similar ambiguity, because we call an argument 'good' if it is logically strong, not necessarily meaning that it supports a morally praiseworthy conclusion. So we may call the two characters Better Argument and Worse Argument. When Strepsiades wants the worse argument which can defeat the better argument (112–15, 882–4),

[50] Cf. Russo *Aristophanes* 109. In an attempt to explain the scholium Dover *Clouds* xc-xciii suggests that the Arguments appeared as birds in the first version of the play, and this suggestion is supported by O. Taplin *Proceedings of the Cambridge Philological Society* 213 (1987) 93–6 (modified in his *Comic Angels* (Oxford 1993) 103), D. Fowler *CQ* 39 (1989) 257–9, E. Csapo *Phoenix* 47 (1993) 1–28, 115–24. But there is no actual evidence for it; cf. Hubbard *Mask* 93 n. 15. As will be seen below, it is questionable whether the Arguments appeared in the first *Clouds* at all.

[51] κρείττων and ἥττων. Strepsiades also calls the Worse Argument ἄδικος, but the expression δίκαιος λόγος does not occur within the text of the play; cf. Dover *Clouds* lvii–lviii. But Dover is curiously inconsistent here: he does not believe that Aristophanes named the characters δίκαιος and ἄδικος, and yet he adopts the English names Right and Wrong, which translate δίκαιος and ἄδικος rather than κρείττων and ἥττων. See also Newiger *Metaphor* 134–43.

Aristophanes is exploiting the ambiguity to create a comic paradox: a logically bad argument cannot refute a logically good one, but what Strepsiades really desires is a morally bad argument (defending dishonesty) which seems good enough logically to defeat a morally good principle.

As often in an Aristophanic agon, the characters begin by abusing each other and then proceed to a formal debate, in which Better Argument speaks first. But the subject of his speech is unexpected. One might have thought that he would expound the reasons why Strepsiades should pay his debts, or defend honesty in general. But in fact that topic is never mentioned in this part of the play. Instead Better Argument describes what he calls 'the old education' of boys. Boys went to the music teacher, who taught them traditional songs, and to the physical trainer. They had to walk along the street in an orderly manner, not wrapped up in warm cloaks; they had to keep quiet and defer to their elders. A young man who has been educated in this way does not spend his time chattering in the Agora and the lawcourts, nor frequent the bath-house and the brothel, but devotes himself to athletics and develops a handsome physique. All this may be a fair description of the aims and ideals of conventional Athenian education, even if in practice they were often not achieved. But modern readers are apt to be startled by the emphasis on the boys' bodies.

BETTER ARGUMENT. At the physical trainer's the boys were required to extend their thighs forward when sitting,
To ensure that the onlookers wouldn't catch sight of anything leading to anguish.
And afterwards each of them when he stood up had to smooth the sand over behind him,
And see that his youthfulness didn't leave any impression for lovers to look at.
In those days no boy would have ever put on any oil lower down than his navel,
And the consequence was that his genitals bloomed, like dewy and velvety peaches.[52]

(*Clouds* 973–8)

The best modern editor of *Clouds* goes so far as to criticize Better

[52] Pubescent hair, if unoiled, dries fluffily, following bathing after exercise. Cf. P. T. Eden *CQ* 34 (1984) 233–4.

Argument for 'his obsession with boys' genitals'.[53] But perhaps the Athenian audience would have considered this interest normal rather than obsessive. We must remember that in antiquity and in a warm country boys and young men were often scantily dressed, so that their bodies were far more visible than in our own society; Greeks of the classical period were strongly aware of human beauty, as their art shows; and homosexual admiration of young men and boys was regarded as quite normal. But physical copulation was a different matter. Better Argument praises the virtue of *sophrosyne* (962, 1006, 1060), which means self-control in general but in the present context certainly refers to abstention from sexual misconduct. He likes the boys to be handsome to look at but not to misbehave themselves, and this view was probably shared by a large proportion of the Athenian audience. Dover has argued that this passage is a caricature of an earlier generation's uninhibited expression of homosexual zest,[54] but that seems not to be a correct assessment. Better Argument's language does not display as much uninhibited obscenity as that of some other Aristophanic characters, such as Paphlagon and the Sausage-seller in *Horsemen*, and he disapproves of sexual activity (994–6, 1014).[55] For him, homosexual desire is normal but ought to be inhibited. Most Athenians would probably have agreed that this was the right principle, even if they did not live up to it in practice.[56]

The account of boys' schooling seems inappropriate to its context in the play. Pheidippides is already a young man. Presumably he has undergone the traditional boys' education already; if he has not, it is too late now for him to join in with the ten-year-olds. The question now is what kind of speech or argument he should learn. But Better Argument has not described any kind of speech. On the contrary, he emphasizes the desirability of *not* speaking.

[53] Dover *Clouds* lxiv. A similar view is taken by Fisher *Clouds* 198.

[54] Dover *Clouds* lxiv–lxvi.

[55] Note the verb of 994–5, 'to *do* nothing shameful'; thought is free. This expression must surely cover homosexual activity, after which heterosexual activity is added in 996. If so, the assertion of Henderson *The Maculate Muse* 76 that 'Just Logic does not prohibit pederasty' is misleading.

[56] According to Henderson *The Maculate Muse* 76–7, 217–18, 'Unjust Logic at once perceives his rival's unhealthy sexual inhibitions' and argues that it is 'much healthier' not to repress desires. But that is a post-Freudian American view, not an ancient Greek one. Worse Argument does not in fact argue that indulging desires is healthy, but that it is pleasurable.

BETTER ARGUMENT. But still you'll be glistening, fully in bloom, and
   devote all your time to gymnastics,
   Not to prickliperversative babble and chat in the Agora, like the men
   now do.
   You won't trail into court for some trivial perishing argutenacious
   proceedings.

(*Clouds* 1002–4)

Thus the character's programme is inconsistent with his name;
he will not in fact teach Pheidippides to speak or argue better, either
logically or morally. He will teach him to avoid speaking and arguing.
   Worse Argument, when it is his turn, speaks rather more to the
point. He declares that he will defeat his opponent by using worse
arguments. Whether he means that his arguments will be bad logically or morally, he does not say; in fact they turn out to be morally
bad, and logically—not good, but superficially convincing. He
begins by picking up Better Argument's disapproval of hot baths.

WORSE ARGUMENT. Now watch how I'll refute the education he relies
   on.
   He first says that he won't allow you bathing in hot water.
   And yet why criticize hot baths? What reason have you for it?
BETTER ARGUMENT. Because it's very bad; because it makes a man a
   coward.
WORSE ARGUMENT. Stop! Now I've got you by the waist, a grip you
   can't escape from!
   Just tell me this: which one of Zeus's sons do you consider
   The best in spirit? Which of them performed so many labours?
BETTER ARGUMENT. There was no better man than Herakles, in my
   opinion.
WORSE ARGUMENT. Have you seen any baths of Herakles, then, which
   were cold ones?
   And yet was any man more brave?
BETTER ARGUMENT.   That's it! That's just the nonsense
   They're talking all the time! All day you hear the young lads chatter,
   And that's what fills the bath; meanwhile the wrestling-grounds are
   empty.

(*Clouds* 1043–54)

Better Argument believes that hot baths make a man less hardy and less likely to stand up to the rigours and dangers of war; this may or may not be true, but it has at any rate been widely believed at other times and places besides ancient Athens. To refute it, Worse Argument refers to 'baths of Herakles', a name given to various warm springs. The syllogism is supposed to be: Herakles had hot baths; Herakles was not a coward; therefore hot baths do not make a man a coward. The internal logic is sound; if one accepts the premisses, the conclusion follows. But the premisses are 'facts' drawn from mythology. Worse Argument proceeds to draw further conclusions from mythical 'facts', culminating in a defence of fornication and adultery.

WORSE ARGUMENT. Suppose you've erred: you fell in love, seduced,
    and then they caught you.
  You're done for, since you cannot speak. If you consort with me,
    though,
  Do what comes naturally: prance, laugh, consider nothing shameful!
  If you're convicted of seduction, make the man this answer:
  Say you've committed no offence. Give Zeus as your example:
  Zeus also is too weak, you'll say, to withstand love and women,
  And how can you, a mortal man, be stronger than a god is?

(*Clouds* 1076–82)

As everyone knows, Greek gods were not necessarily good. Greek mythology, much of it very old, did not conform to the moral rules which were conventional in the classical period. Worse Argument exploits this inconsistency, drawing from mythology logical instances which conflict with classical morality. This rhetorical trick may be one which many speakers had recently been exploiting at the time of *Clouds*; at any rate Better Argument seems to recognize it as a familiar enemy (906, 1052). Yet he has no defence against it, because he believes in the myths himself. He can only try to find other mythical examples pointing to morally better conclusions (1063, 1067), and does not realize that he ought to reject this method of arguing altogether.[57] Better Argument, in short, is not good at arguing; it is his moral beliefs that are better. Worse Argument, by contrast, is a clever arguer in favour of what is morally bad. He completes his speech and wins the contest by

---

[57] Cf. Fisher *Clouds* 202: 'Worse Argument's powers of persuasion appear to be strong because his opponent is easily led into weak positions'.

maintaining that chastity is a bad thing. ('Wide-arsed' or 'open-arsed' refers literally to habitual submission to buggery.)

WORSE ARGUMENT. What does it matter if he's open-arsed?
BETTER ARGUMENT. Why, it's the worst thing that could happen to him!
WORSE ARGUMENT. What will you say if I defeat you there?
BETTER ARGUMENT. Nothing. What could I say?
WORSE ARGUMENT.   Well, tell me, then:
       What class provides the advocates?
BETTER ARGUMENT. The open-arsed men.
WORSE ARGUMENT.   I agree.
       What class provides tragedians?
BETTER ARGUMENT. The open-arsed men.
WORSE ARGUMENT.   That's quite right.
       What class are politicians from?
BETTER ARGUMENT. The open-arsed men.
WORSE ARGUMENT.   Do you see
       What nonsense you were talking now?
       Look which there's more of in the audience.
BETTER ARGUMENT. All right, I'll look.
WORSE ARGUMENT.   And can you see?
BETTER ARGUMENT.   Yes, far the most
       Are open-arsed men, by the gods!
       There's one I know, and him as well,
       And that long-haired man over there—
WORSE ARGUMENT. How is it, then?
BETTER ARGUMENT.   I'm beaten! Oh,
       You buggered men, here, by the gods,
       Please take my cloak and let me run
       And join you—I'm deserting!

                          (*Clouds* 1085–1104)

This 'proof' is a comically outrageous exaggeration of the facts, including a joke at the expense of the audience. Better Argument is convinced by it, but Aristophanes does not expect the audience to be convinced, but to laugh, and at the same time to realize that logical-sounding arguments do not necessarily lead to true conclusions. The point of the scene is that Better Argument, who is right, is defeated by Worse Argument, who is wrong, because Worse Argument is a clever speaker. That point is certainly relevant to the theme of *Clouds* as a whole, and yet in other respects the contest between the Arguments does not fit well into the play. Several discrepancies can be listed.

1. In this scene (beginning from 886) the Arguments are teachers, competing for the opportunity to teach Pheidippides. In the rest of the play the better and worse arguments are things which may be learned (e.g. 116, 882, 1148); Socrates is the teacher (e.g. 244, 877, 1147).

2. In this scene the main point made by Worse Argument is that he makes unbridled sexual indulgence possible. In the rest of the play there is no suggestion that Socrates and the sophists indulge in sex or encourage others to do so.

3. Worse Argument also favours luxuries such as hot baths, whereas Better Argument champions a life of austerity. In the rest of the play it is Socrates and his pupils who live an austere life, with no warm clothes or shoes, abstaining from wine and baths (e.g. 103, 416–17, 439–42, 835–7).

Nor does the rest of the play make any reference to this scene.[58] If 886–1106 (or 886–1110) were absent from the text, we should not be aware that anything was missing. This is how it would run.

STREPSIADES. Please see that he learns those two arguments,
The one which is the better, and the worse,
Which says what's wrong and overturns the better.
At any rate make sure he learns the wrong one!
Teach him! And punish him! Make sure you give
His mouth a good edge for me, suitable
For cutting little trials up, on one side;
Sharpen the other side for bigger business.
SOCRATES.[59] Don't worry! You'll get him back a clever sophist.
PHEIDIPPIDES. A pale and wretched one, I rather think!

(*Clouds* 882–5, 1107–12)

The *hypothesis* (quoted on pp. 135–6) says that the scene 'where the right argument talks to the wrong one' is one of those which 'have undergone the revision in their entirety', and we should interpret that as meaning that lines 886–1106 (or 886–1110) were not in the first *Clouds* but were added in the second. Whether

---

[58] I take 1149, literally 'whom you just led in', to mean 'my son, whom you took into the Thinkery', not 'that Argument, whom you put on-stage'. In Greek to bring on-stage is normally 'lead out', not 'lead in', and Socrates put two Arguments on-stage (if he put any), not one.

[59] Line 1111 is attributed to Socrates in the manuscripts. Recent editors transfer it to Worse Argument, as is necessary when 886–1106 are included in the play.

anything else was cut out to make room for them, we cannot say
for certain, but there is no particular reason to think that it was
so.[60] The new passage takes in some respects a different line from
the rest of the play, and this has produced some inconsistencies
which Aristophanes failed to remove, perhaps because he never
completed the revision. His reasons for inserting the new scene are
connected, I shall suggest, with his reasons for altering the ending.

THE ENDING

Other plays of Aristophanes end in triumph. In the last scene the
hero, having carried out his plan or accomplished his aim, becomes
able to indulge in such pleasures as eating and drinking, singing and
dancing, the exercise of power and sex. Even Philokleon in *Wasps*,
though he does not carry out a clever plan, enjoys himself dancing
at the end of the play; and *Women at the Thesmophoria*, though it has
no celebration, does end with a successful escape. Only the revised
version of *Clouds* ends in failure. Strepsiades' cunning scheme seems
at first to be succeeding, his son has learned the worse argument,
and he has got rid of two creditors; but then he unexpectedly gets
beaten by his son, realizes that his scheme was a dreadful mistake,
sets fire to the Thinkery, and chases Socrates and the students away.[61]
He does succeed in taking his revenge on Socrates, but his plan to
evade his debts has failed, and he is not happy at the end.

This is the revised ending. We are told by the *hypothesis* (quoted
on pp. 135–6) that this is one of the parts which were entirely
changed in the revision, and a scholium on 543 confirms that 'the
school of Socrates being burned' was not in the first *Clouds*. Naturally
we wonder what the original ending was. Of course it is easy

---

[60] The play need not have had originally any formal agon; *Akharnians*, for
example, has none. Russo *Aristophanes* 102–4 suggests that Khairephon was a
prominent character in the first *Clouds*, and was cut out in the second to make
room for the Arguments.

[61] For the stage action at 1508 see Dover *Clouds* ad loc. An alternative
interpretation, maintained by E. C. Kopff *GRBS* 18 (1977) 113–22, is that
Socrates is burned to death inside the Thinkery. But that is inconsistent with the
text at 1508, and is rightly rejected by F. D. Harvey *GRBS* 22 (1981) 339–43,
M. Davies *Hermes* 118 (1990) 237–42.

enough to make guesses about what may have been in a lost work of literature. The difficult thing is to control the guesses and find reasons for believing one to be more likely than the others to be right. But in the case of *Clouds* we do have one kind of guidance, and that is the characteristic pattern of Aristophanic plays. Strepsiades, like many Aristophanic heroes, devises a cunning scheme; if the first *Clouds* resembled the other plays, his scheme must surely have succeeded. It is reasonable to presume that, after seeing off his creditors with the help of Pheidippides, he ended in triumph and finally indulged in some kind of festivity. That would be the characteristic conclusion for an Aristophanic comedy.

But the first *Clouds* failed in the contest in 423: why? Again many guesses are possible. Perhaps the other plays in the competition were exceptionally good. Perhaps the actors and choristers in *Clouds* performed inadequately. But here we can invoke Aristophanes' own comments on the failure of the play, and he does not attribute it either to the excellence of his rivals or to the weakness of his performers. In the revised parabasis he disparages his rivals as vulgar, and says nothing of the performers,[62] but blames the audience for failing to appreciate the cleverness of his play (518–26, quoted on p. 134). He makes the same point again in the parabasis of *Wasps* (where 'he' is Aristophanes), after alluding to the achievements of his earlier plays.

> So that was the kind of defender you had, who was cleansing the country from evils.
> But then, when last year he was sowing a crop of the newest ideas, you betrayed him
> And rendered them sterile, unable to grow, through not understanding them clearly.
> However, with many and many libations he swears by the god Dionysos
> That nobody ever had heard in their lives any comedy better than that one.
> So that's a disgrace and discredit to you, that you didn't at first understand it,
> But there isn't a single intelligent man who thinks any the worse of our poet,
> If he overtook all of his rivals and then came a cropper and crashed his conception!
>
> (*Wasps* 1043–50)

---

[62] Contrast *Peace* 781–90, which does seem to be a criticism of some of the performers of the previous year's *Wasps*; cf. MacDowell *Wasps* 327 (on line 1501).

So Aristophanes' own opinion was that *Clouds* contained clever new ideas, but the audience failed to understand what he was getting at. Presumably the novelty lay in the presentation of the ideas and activities of Socrates and the sophists, a more intellectual subject than that of any previous comedy. In what way, then, can the audience have failed to understand? Here I offer another guess, more speculative than my previous guesses, but I believe it is at least consistent with what we know of Athens at that period.[63] I suggest that, when the Athenians saw Strepsiades triumphing as a result of his adherence to the sophists, they thought that the play implied approval of sophistry, in the same way as *Akharnians* implies approval of peace because Dikaiopolis is triumphant when he has made peace. Aristophanes seemed to them to be recommending dishonesty, false rhetoric, and—worst of all—atheism.[64] Atheism always alarmed them, because they feared that the gods would punish not just individual atheists but Athens as a whole if atheism were allowed to flourish unchecked. That was why they had condemned Anaxagoras and Protagoras, and it was one of the reasons why they would later condemn Socrates.

If that is correct, we can now see why Aristophanes made the alterations that he did make in the text.[65] He had not really intended to imply approval of sophistry and atheism, but to satirize them; but apparently his satire had been mistaken for approval. So, besides altering the parabasis to include comments on the play's failure, he wrote new scenes for two parts of the play.

First, he decided that the opposition to sophistic education should also have a spokesman. This could be arranged by inserting an agon, with speeches both for and against; and he hit on the idea (not used in the first *Clouds*, as far as we know) of making the better and worse arguments mentioned elsewhere in the play into two characters

---

[63] Murray *Aristophanes* 87–8 takes a similar view, but on slightly different grounds.

[64] A. W. H. Adkins *Antichthon* 4 (1970) 13–24 considers that the Athenians may have been shocked especially by the use of mystic terminology for initiation into the Thinkery. But he may have overestimated the degree to which this would have been regarded as blasphemous; cf. G. J. de Vries *Mnemosyne* 26 (1973) 1–8.

[65] I concentrate here on the main theme of the play, but I do not exclude the probability that Aristophanes tried at the same time 'to broaden the play's humorous and theatrical appeal' (Hubbard *Mask* 105). However, Hubbard's argument that lines 537–44 refer to this change is questionable; cf. S. D. Olson *Philologus* 138 (1994) 32–7.

speaking in the debate. Worse Argument naturally defends the kind of rhetoric taught by the sophists, and uses some obviously false arguments to do so; but what was Aristophanes to make Better Argument say? That was a problem; if Better Argument refuted Worse Argument at this point, the play would come to an end too soon. Instead, Aristophanes has made Better Argument speak about the traditional education of boys, which is barely relevant to the play but would be likely to receive the audience's approval, and has let Worse Argument win the debate by an argument so obviously and outrageously false that it leaves the impression that Better Argument is really in the right.

But the most important alteration is at the end of the play. Strepsiades now discovers that sophistic education is a bad thing, and turns against the sophists. I presume that the new ending begins at 1303. Up to this point Strepsiades has been successfully chasing his creditors away, but now the chorus hints that his success will be short-lived.

CHORUS. How bad behaviour lures men on!
    For this old man desires it:
  He wants to misappropriate
    The money that he borrowed.
  And something will today, for sure,
  Befall this sophist, so that he
  Will suddenly get something bad[66]
    From these misdeeds he's started.

  I think that he will shortly find
    What he has long been seeking:
  His son will be so skilful at
    Expressing contradictions
  To what is right, that he will win
  Against all rivals that he meets,
  However villainous his case.
  Perhaps, perhaps he'll soon begin
    To wish his son were voiceless!

(*Clouds* 1303–20)

This leads into the scene in which Pheidippides argues that it is right to beat his father, and so to Strepsiades' change of heart and

---

[66] The reading 'get something bad' is doubtful; cf. Dover *Clouds* ad loc., Sommerstein *Clouds* ad loc.

the burning of the Thinkery. All this hangs together and so is probably all new. Nothing earlier in the play seems to be related to the new ending[67] except a single sentence in 1113–14, where the chorus says to Strepsiades 'But I think you will regret this'. As it stands this sentence is oddly isolated, but a scholium on 1115, though obscurely worded, seems to say that five verses of the first *Clouds* are omitted at this point;[68] so perhaps Aristophanes inserted 1113–14 in the course of his revision, to foreshadow the new ending.

But the patchwork remains all too visible. It is not only that the insertion of the agon of the Better and Worse Arguments has produced inconsistencies with the rest of the play (see pp. 143–4). The awkwardness caused by the new ending is worse. It is especially noticeable in the role of the chorus.[69] The Clouds in the earlier part of the play are introduced as the goddesses of Socrates and the other thinkers (252–3); it is Socrates himself who calls upon them to appear (264–74). They tell Strepsiades that, because he desires to obtain wisdom from them, they will grant him good fortune if he makes victory in 'making war with his tongue' his supreme aim (412–19), and they assure him that, if he follows this course of action, he will live a most enviable life (463–5). Later, when he specifically and sincerely asks them to give him good advice, they advise him that the best thing is to send his son to take lessons (793–6). At the end all this turns out to have been misleading and false, and Strepsiades turns on the Clouds to blame them in a rather solemn manner.[70]

[67] I cannot agree with Fisher *Clouds* 183 that the Clouds 'describe their own unpredictability themselves in 812–13', foreshadowing their change of attitude at the end of the play. The words τὰ τοιαῦτα do not mean 'ourselves', but 'such circumstances', referring here to Strepsiades' availability for exploitation by Socrates. Cf. Dover *Clouds* 198 (on line 813).

[68] Cf. D. Holwerda *Mnemosyne* 11 (1958) 38–41, Sommerstein *Clouds* 215 (on lines 1113–30).

[69] Cf. Whitman *Aristophanes* 128–9. Against this C. Segal *Arethusa* 2 (1969) 143–61 makes a valiant but to my mind unsuccessful attempt to defend the chorus in terms of 'multiplicity of meaning'; similarly Marianetti *Religion* 76–107 argues that it 'accentuates the confusion and misunderstanding that dominated Athens'. Bowie *Aristophanes* 124–30 gives evidence that the Clouds are regarded as divine powers, but that does not prove (as he seems to think) that they are presented from the start as opponents of Socrates: Socrates too regards them as goddesses.

[70] Cf. M. S. Silk in *Tr.Com.Pol.* 498–504 on the 'tragic coloration' of this passage.

STREPSIADES. I've suffered this, O Clouds, because of you;
    I trusted you with all of my affairs.
CHORUS. No, it's yourself that you must blame for this;
    You turned yourself to wicked practices.
STREPSIADES. Then why did you not tell me at the time,
    But urged me on, a poor old countryman?
CHORUS. We regularly do that to a man
    We see in love with wicked practices,
    Till finally we cast him into trouble,
    Just so that he may learn to fear the gods.
STREPSIADES. Alas! That's hard to bear, Clouds, but it's just.
    It wasn't right to cheat my creditors
    And keep their money. Come with me, my boy,
    And we'll destroy that scoundrel Khairephon
    And Socrates; they were deceiving us!

                      (*Clouds* 1452–66)

The Clouds' change of attitude is too unexpected, and the attribution of responsibility is muddled. If Strepsiades must blame himself for what has happened, and his punishment is just, why should he attack Khairephon and Socrates? If the Clouds are opponents of Socrates, why did Socrates himself invoke them? Strepsiades tried to argue, against Socrates, for belief in the power of Zeus: why then should he be punished 'so that he may learn to fear the gods'? The old beginning of the play simply does not prepare the way adequately for the new ending. Probably Aristophanes realized, when he had partly revised the text, that his attempt to rewrite bits of it was resulting in a botched job, and that was why he abandoned his plan for a second performance.[71]

[71] Cf. Whitman *Aristophanes* 137: 'The poet seems to have recognized that he could not moralize his play without ruining it, and given up the attempt.'

7

Wasps

A STRANGE DISEASE

Two slaves are on watch in front of a house. The door is barred and nets cover the windows. A man, who turns out to be the master of the house, is sleeping on the flat roof. The slaves, whose names are Xanthias and Sosias, are inclined to doze off, but one wakes the other, and each recounts the dream he has just had. The dreams are comic allegories about Athenian politicians: Kleonymos and Kleon, Theoros and Alkibiades. These political jokes serve to 'warm up' the audience before the main story of the play begins, and also imply that political themes will be prominent in it.[1] Soon Xanthias turns and speaks directly to the audience to explain the situation.

> The man that you can see there is our master,
> Asleep up there, the big man on the roof.
> He's shut his father up indoors; we've got
> To guard him and prevent him going out.
> His father's suffering from a strange disease:
> No one would ever make out what it was
> Unless we told him. Go on, have a guess!
>
> (*Wasps* 67–73)

This leads to a striking passage of 'audience participation' (pretended, not actual), in which the slaves pretend to hear guesses from several prominent men in the audience. Of course the guesses are all wrong, and are actually jokes against the individuals who are supposed to have made them. Eventually Xanthias reveals the nature of the old man's illness: he has a passion for sitting on a jury, for trying cases and condemning people. 'Such is his frenzy' (111). It

---

[1] For a detailed analysis of the humour of this passage see Paduano *Il giudice* 49–70.

is obviously a comic notion to regard enthusiasm for the law as a kind of mental illness, but a modern reader naturally wonders how it could have been possible for a man to spend all his time on a jury. No one, however enthusiastic, could do this in a modern society.

The explanation lies in the organization of the lawcourts. The Athenians by Aristophanes' time had established a system for deciding disputes and accusations which was more democratic than perhaps any other nation has ever had. Instead of letting verdicts be given by an official or an expert, they had hit on the idea of trial by jury, by which a verdict given by a number of ordinary citizens is regarded as being equivalent to a verdict given by the whole community. This was one of their greatest contributions to democratic civilization.[2]

In 422 BC, when *Wasps* was performed, the system worked like this. At the beginning of each year volunteers were called for, and a list of 6,000 jurors was drawn up. Volunteers had to be citizens over thirty years of age. For each case requiring trial the jury was drawn from this list. The size of the jury varied according to the type of case but was always, by modern standards, very large: never less than 200, often 500, and for a few serious cases 1,000 or more. Several buildings were used as courts, not all of which had been built for that purpose: in *Wasps* there is mention of the Odeion (1109), which was originally erected for musical performances, and of the New Court (120), which presumably was purpose-built. Each magistrate, or board of magistrates, held trials always in the same court: thus we hear of the court of the Arkhon and the court of the Eleven (1108). At the time of *Wasps* each juror was allocated to one court for the whole year: the jurors in the play are all going together to the same court in which they sat on the previous day to try another case (242–4).[3]

Each trial was convened by an Arkhon or other magistrate. But he was not a legal expert; in most cases he was an ordinary citizen selected by lot for the year. Thus he was not like a modern judge and did not give rulings or advice on legal questions; he was simply a chairman who called for the speeches and other proceedings in

[2] For a fuller summary of the stages of development see MacDowell *Law* 24–40.

[3] *Women at the Assembly* 681–8 shows that this was changed in the fourth century. By then jurors were being assigned to courts by lot each day to make bribery more difficult.

the proper order. The prosecutor or plaintiff spoke first, and the accused or defendant afterwards. Each spoke for himself, and litigants were not represented by lawyers as in a modern court; but each could also call witnesses or friends to speak in his support, provided that he kept within his time-limit. The time-limit was the same for both sides, measured by a water-clock (*klepsydra*). This was a large pot or pail, having at the bottom a small hole which could be plugged. It was filled with water, and when a speech began the plug was removed; the speaker had to stop when all the water had run out. The pot was then refilled for the opposing speaker.

At the end of the speeches the jury voted. There was no summing-up or advice from a judge, and no discussion among the jurors; each juror had to make up his own mind on any question of law as well as on the facts of the case. He voted by placing a pebble or sea-shell in an urn; there was one urn for conviction and one for acquittal. When all had voted, the votes were counted and the majority decided the verdict; a tie counted as acquittal. For some offences the penalty was fixed by law, but in other cases, if the verdict went against the defendant, the jury had to decide the penalty or the amount of compensation to be paid. The prosecutor proposed a penalty or amount of compensation, the defendant proposed another (naturally more lenient), each made a speech in support of his proposal, and then the jury voted again to choose between them. This time a different method of voting was used, for which *Wasps* provides the only contemporary evidence: each juror had a small wooden tablet with a thin covering of wax, on which he drew a long line to vote for the prosecutor's proposal or a short line to vote for the defendant's. After the result was declared, the court proceeded to the next case. A court could try several cases on one day (unless it was adjourned early, a possibility mentioned in *Wasps* 594–5). At the end of the day each juror was paid a fee of three obols.

So the old man in *Wasps* is one who volunteers for jury service every year because he enjoys all the court proceedings. Especially he enjoys voting defendants down: he is comically sadistic. Xanthias proceeds to describe the symptoms of the strange disease, with allusions to various features of the court.

> I'll tell you what our master's illness is:
> It's jurophilia, the world's worst case!

He loves this judging business; it upsets him
If he's not sitting on the court's front bench.
He doesn't get a wink of sleep at night;
Or if he does drop off, still all night long
His mind goes fluttering round the water-clock.
Because he's used to holding voting-pebbles,
He gets up with three fingers pressed together,
Like putting incense on, on New Moon day.

   .   .   .   .   .

He's so bad-tempered, he awards them all
Long lines, and like a bee or bumble-bee
He comes in with his nails stuffed up with wax.
And just in case he might run out of pebbles
For judging with, he keeps a beach at home!

(*Wasps* 87–96, 106–10)

The dramatic function of this speech is not to satirize the court, but to describe a comic character. There is no indication here that Aristophanes saw anything wrong with the voting procedures, the water-clock, and so on; but the old man is obsessed with them. Xanthias goes on to explain that his grown-up son, who has now taken charge of the household, is worried about his father's illness. He has tried verbal persuasion and religious cures, but those have had no effect; so now he and the slaves have shut the old man up in the house to prevent him physically from going to the court. At the end of the speech the father's name is given as Philokleon, meaning 'Love-Kleon', and the son's as Bdelykleon, meaning 'Loathe-Kleon'. These comic names are another indication that the play is going to have a political aspect.

After the long descriptive speech we see the characters in action. Philokleon makes farcical attempts to escape from the house: he climbs out of the chimney, pretending to be smoke; he pushes at the door and tries to climb out of the window; he hangs on to the underside of the donkey being led out to market, like Odysseus clinging to a sheep to escape from the Cyclops; he tries to creep out under the eaves of the roof. Bdelykleon and the slaves rush around, making frantic efforts to keep him in. This is one of Aristophanes' liveliest scenes of slapstick, in which the antics convey visually what Xanthias has already described in words: Philokleon wants to get out of the house and Bdelykleon wants to keep him in.

The passage is of major importance in the history of farce,[4] but it has no political or satirical implication.

JURORS AND WASPS

The chorus consists of old men who serve on a jury, colleagues of Philokleon, but very different from him in character.[5] Whereas he is lively, they are decrepit. On their first appearance Aristophanes emphasizes their extreme age: they reminisce about their military service at Byzantion half a century ago, but many of the friends who served with them then are dead now (235–7). Now they are stumbling along in the dark to reach the court early, and are frightened of tripping over stones in the road (245–7). Some boys, their sons, carry lamps to light the way, and a duet between the chorus-leader and his son shows their poverty.

BOY.   Will you give me something, father,
           If I ask you for a present?
CHORUS.   Yes, of course, boy. Just you tell me
           What's the nice thing that you're wanting
           Me to buy you? Knucklebones, eh?[6]
           I suppose that's what you'll say, boy.
BOY.   No, dried figs, dad, 'cos it's nice—
CHORUS.   No,
           Not if you were being hanged now!
BOY.   Then I shan't guide you in future!
CHORUS.   From this pittance I must buy
               Meal and wood and fish for three,
               And you ask me now for figs!

BOY.   Tell me, father, if the Arkhon
           Doesn't now hold any sitting
           Of the lawcourt for today, what
           Can we then buy any lunch with?
           Have you something we can hope for,
           Any 'sacred way of Helle'?

---

[4] Cf. MacDowell *Themes in Drama* 10 (1988) 1–7.

[5] On the characterization of the chorus by means of music and metre see B. Zimmermann *Studi Italiani di Filologia Classica* 2 (1984) 19–23.

[6] Sheep's knucklebones were a cheap toy, used much like modern dice for various games. For a different interpretation see T. Long *ICS* 1 (1976) 16 n. 3.

CHORUS. Oh, alas, Zeus!
No, I don't know where on earth our
Dinner's then going to be got from.

(*Wasps* 291–311)

Unlike Philokleon, who has a wealthy son to support him, these jurors really do need the pay of three obols; they have nothing else to live on. But they are not without spirit. Another aspect of their character is revealed, in the most visible way, when they get angry with Bdelykleon for keeping their colleague shut up at home. They throw off their cloaks to prepare for a fight (408), and suddenly it is seen that they have the form of wasps, with fearsome stings (420, cf. 225).[7] Besides being old men, they are somehow wasps at the same time. This is a very striking piece of symbolism, by which Aristophanes is making a point about jurors in real life. Most of the time jurors seem to be just feeble old men, but when they are provoked they can be fierce and hurtful; they can sting by imposing serious penalties.

Later, in the parabasis, this allegory is worked out in more detail. The old men claim that they did Athens good service in the past, by fighting against the Persians and by building up the Athenian Empire, thus producing the tribute out of which the pay for jurors is now provided; and in the last part of the parabasis there is a clever comparison between conditions in the courts and in a wasps' nest.

If you thoroughly inspect us, you will find in all respects
That in way of life and habits we are very much like wasps.
In the first place, there's no creature, after it has been provoked,
More sharp-spirited than we are, none that's more cantankerous.
Then we manage just as wasps do all the rest of our affairs:
Gathering together in our swarms, as if in hives,
Some of us are with the Arkhon, some where the Eleven sit,
Some in the Odeion, judging, packed in tightly—just like this—
Close against the walls and stooping forward to the ground, and so
We can hardly move a muscle, like the larvae in their cells.
And to make a living also we are very well equipped,
For we just sting everybody and procure a livelihood!
But there are some drones among us, not possessing any sting,

---

[7] This costume is worn only by the chorus, not by Philokleon, who is never called a wasp. This is proved by the fact that Xanthias, after conversing with Philokleon, does not yet know that the jurors are like wasps (223–9), and sees the stings for the first time when the chorus strips for action (420).

Who just stay back here in Athens, eating up what we've produced
From the tribute, though they never do a stroke of work themselves.
This is what especially irks us, if a man eats up our pay
Never serving in the army, never for his country's sake
With an oar-spar or a spear-shaft or a blister in his hand.
But I think that for the future any citizen at all,
If he doesn't have a sting, should not receive three obols' pay!

(*Wasps* 1102–21)

Not only Aristophanes' amusement but also his sincere sympathy with the jurors is unmistakable. Most of them are old, yes, but that is not their fault. They are the men who saved Greece from the barbarians at Marathon and at Salamis, and made Athens great; now in their old age they deserve to be supported, by being allowed to earn three obols in this comparatively easy manner. The only jurors who deserve criticism are the few younger ones, who claim the pay without having earned it by service in the past. Athens had no system of old-age pensions; Aristophanes here is virtually proposing the introduction of such a system, by suggesting that the veterans, and they only, should be allowed to draw the pay of three obols.

Although there are these few younger 'drones' on the juries, Aristophanes clearly implies that most of the jurors are elderly and poor. Was this really true? The question has been much discussed, but it is not easy to find decisive evidence.[8] No citizen over thirty years old (unless disfranchised for some offence) was excluded from the juries by law, but the question is whether in practice men of certain classes or types were more ready to volunteer than others. Apart from *Wasps*, most evidence about juries is in forensic speeches of the late fifth or the fourth century, and it has been argued that the speakers sometimes imply that the jurors whom they are addressing are prosperous.[9] However, recently more careful analysis has shown that speakers find it more prudent to assume, rather, that their listeners are a range of citizens, not confined to any particular social class;[10] and since men who were actually poor may have preferred to be addressed as if they were not,[11] this evidence helps

[8] For a good survey of different views see S. C. Todd *JHS* 110 (1990) 149–63; cf. also A. Crichton *BICS* 38 (1991–3) 59–80.

[9] A. H. M. Jones *Athenian Democracy* (Oxford 1964) 36–7.

[10] M. M. Markle in *Crux* 281–9, R. K. Sinclair *Democracy and Participation in Athens* (Cambridge 1988) 124–7.

[11] Cf. Dover *Morality* 34–5.

hardly at all to establish the real character of the juries.

Discussion has therefore been based largely on more general considerations. There can be no doubt that the original purpose of introducing pay for juries was to ensure that rich men did not predominate in them; a poor man could not afford to abstain from his normal work unless he was paid to do so. Thucydides (2.37.1) makes Perikles say that no one is prevented by poverty from making his contribution to the city, and it has been argued that this purpose will have been achieved: men of moderate means would leave their regular work to perform jury service.[12] The main objection to this argument is that an able-bodied man could make considerably more than three obols a day by other work, and it seems unlikely that more than a small number would have accepted a diminution of income in order to serve on a jury.[13] Attempts have been made to get round this objection by pointing out that a large proportion of Athenians were farmers: whereas a craftsman or a labourer would lose his normal income if he spent time on a jury, a farmer could, at certain times of year, take a day off without doing any harm to his crops and his income from them.[14] Yet this fact is not sufficient to show that many able-bodied men attended for jury service. We must remember that jurors volunteered for a whole year. True, there was, as far as we know, nothing to prevent a man from volunteering for the year, taking the oath, and then attending on only a few days; but men who seldom attended will for that very reason have had less effect on the character of the juries. That character must have depended primarily on the jurors who attended regularly throughout the year; and those who could attend regularly without loss of other income will have been mostly the old men who were no longer fit for harder work. They had time on their hands, and three obols a day, though it was not much, was better than no income at all.[15]

So, despite the paucity of corroborative evidence, probability supports the implication of *Wasps* that most jurors were old men who had little or no other source of income. No doubt Aristophanes has exaggerated their age and poverty for dramatic effect. A man

---

[12] Markle in *Crux* 271–81.

[13] Cf. Jones *Athenian Democracy* 37 (with n. 86 on pp. 143–4).

[14] Todd *JHS* 110 (1990) 168–9, Markle *Ancient Society* 21 (1990) 149–65.

[15] Cf. Sinclair *Democracy and Participation in Athens* 127–30, M. H. Hansen *The Athenian Democracy in the Age of Demosthenes* (Oxford 1991) 183–6.

who had fought at Salamis would have been at least in his late seventies by 422, and one who had fought at Marathon ten years older. Probably not many of the jurors in 422 had in fact taken part in those battles, but many of them would have fought for Athens at the time when the Athenian Empire was being established. It was a fact that Athens' greatest successes in military and naval terms were achieved in the period 510–446. In *Wasps* Aristophanes is pointing out that the juries now contain many of the survivors of those days. Although there are a few brief jokes about their youthful mischief and scrounging (237–9, 354–5, 556–7), their main achievements are praised in the parabasis, not disparaged, and it is made quite clear there that, despite their weakness in old age, they deserve the gratitude and support of the younger generation.

'CONSPIRATORS' AND 'TYRANNY'

When the Jurors learn that Philokleon is being prevented from going to court by his son, who wants him to stop being a juror and is ready to support him in comfort at home, they are highly indignant. Their first thought is that Philokleon must have annoyed his son by saying 'something true about the ships' (342–3). The exact point of this is obscure, but most probably some speaker in the Assembly not long before *Wasps* was performed had complained that some Athenian triremes were in a bad state of repair; that would annoy the richer citizens because they, as trierarchs, would have to pay the cost of bringing the ships up to a proper standard. But that theme is not taken any further in this play, and the Jurors go on to abuse Bdelykleon in more general terms as a hater of the city (411), a hater of democracy (473), a conspirator (345, 483), and a tyrant or sole ruler (417, 464, 470, 474, 487).

The first two of these four terms of abuse are easily understood. The juries of ordinary citizens were regarded as an essential part of Athenian democracy. Indeed Philokleon thinks that, as a juror, he *is* the community: virtually 'l'État c'est moi' (917). The Jurors believe that the trials are ordained by the gods (378), and that Bdelykleon is trying to stop them altogether (413–14). Actually, of course, their fears are wildly exaggerated. Bdelykleon is just concerned about his own father's welfare; he is not trying to abolish the juries or the democracy.

The accusation of conspiracy is less clear, but we have met it before in *Horsemen*. Paphlagon (Kleon) several times calls his opponents conspirators, and in one place boasts that he put a stop to some conspirators.[16] The Jurors in *Wasps* are supporters of Kleon, and are following his example when they call Bdelykleon a conspirator. This is not intended to refer to a plot merely within Athens; it means conspiring with a foreign enemy. Paphlagon alleges that the Horsemen and the Sausage-seller have been conspiring with the Persians and the Boiotians (*Horsemen* 478–9), and the Jurors accuse Bdelykleon of associating with Brasidas, the Spartan general (*Wasps* 475), and say that he has his hair and beard long (466, 477). In Athens long hair was affected by rich young men, especially the Horsemen, and so Bdelykleon has his hair long to conform to that fashion; but the Spartans also wore long hair, and so Bdelykleon's hair is taken, by comic logic, as evidence that he favours the enemy of Athens. The accusation is absurd: Aristophanes is satirizing Kleon's proclivity to fling unfounded accusations of treason at his opponents.

Even more absurd is the charge of tyranny. This seems to be a new term of abuse, not found in the earlier plays; or rather it is a revival of a term current long ago, for it was now eighty-eight years since Hippias had been expelled, and his subsequent attempt to regain the tyranny with Persian support had failed. Since then there had been no challenge to the democratic constitution. But now in *Wasps* we find Aristophanes satirizing accusations of tyranny. This must mean that Kleon had recently said that someone wanted to make himself sole ruler of Athens, but who? We cannot be sure of the answer. It may have been Nikias or Demosthenes, but it is hard to imagine that the accusation would have been at all plausible in either of those cases. If it had been Lakhes, one would have expected the accusation to resurface later in the play, when the dispute between Kleon and Lakhes is satirized in the trial of the dog; but there is no mention of tyranny in that scene. The one man whom we know to have been accused by his enemies of aiming at tyranny a few years later is Alkibiades.[17] Perhaps his flamboyant behaviour had already attracted this kind of comment as early as 422. Anyway, whoever it was that Kleon had called a would-be tyrant, it is clear that Aristophanes regards such talk as ridiculous.

---

[16] *Horsemen* 257, 452, 476, 628, 862. Cf. p. 110.
[17] Thucydides 6.15.4.

BDELYKLEON. Everything is 'tyranny' for you now, and 'conspirators',
Both in serious prosecutions and in trivial ones as well!
I'd not heard a word about it, not for fifty years or more,
But it's just as cheap as kippers in the Agora today.
If you listen there, you'll hear the word keeps rolling round and round.

(*Wasps* 488–92)

Fishmongers and greengrocers, says Bdelykleon—and tarts too, adds Xanthias—accuse of aiming at tyranny anyone who wants to make any but the most ordinary purchase. This is not a purely political accusation, but a social one. It is inverted snobbery, a resentment of anyone who tries to rise above the common level. Kleon probably criticized the life-style of Alkibiades (if he was the target). The allegation will have been that Alkibiades showed by his conduct that he considered himself superior to ordinary people, and so (a non-sequitur) that he hoped to make himself ruler of Athens. But Bdelykleon sweeps all this away with ridicule, and the Jurors do not mention either tyranny or conspirators again in the rest of the play.

KLEON

What does Aristophanes think is wrong in the courts? As we have seen, he is not criticizing the formal court procedures or the appointment of old men as jurors. Serious criticisms emerge mainly when Philokleon and Bdelykleon have a debate (the agon of the play) on the question whether the life of a juror is really a good life or not.[18] Philokleon maintains that it is, and he describes his typical day. The speakers in court flatter him and do all they can to entertain him, while he remains free to give any verdict he wishes. No one can hold the jurors to account if they give a wrong decision (587). So Philokleon thinks that he is as powerful as Zeus (619), and he gets paid three obols for it too! This does imply that jurors sometimes give a wrong verdict, as Bdelykleon remarks in one line (589), but the main argument of his reply is directed differently. The beginning of his speech is significant.

[18] The rhetoric of this debate is discussed by Harriott *Aristophanes* 36–43.

BDELYKLEON. It's a difficult task for intelligent men, far above the
comedians'[19] level,
To discover a cure for an ancient disease, a congenital fault in the city.

(*Wasps* 650–1)

There is a noticeable resemblance between this opening and the
opening of Dikaiopolis' great speech in *Akharnians* (see pp. 59–60).
Both refer to the fact that the play is a comedy, but make clear that
this particular speech is going to rise above comedy's normal level.
This prepares the audience to take the speech more seriously than
usual. The reference to a disease may seem to echo the earlier
account of Philokleon's strange disease, but in fact Bdelykleon does
not go on to talk about Philokleon's personal obsession but about a
weakness in real-life Athens. He plunges straight into finance. He
estimates the total annual revenues of Athens from tribute, taxation,
and other sources to be nearly 2,000 talents, while pay for jurors
consumes no more than 150 talents. He takes for granted that most
of the money coming in from the Empire ought to be distributed to
the jurors; but in fact it is not.

PHILOKLEON.   What becomes of the rest of the money,
then? Where does it go to?
BDELYKLEON. It goes to the men who declare 'I shall never betray the
Athenian—rabble!
I shall keep up the fight in defence of the people for ever!' It's your
doing, father:
You're bamboozled by that kind of speaking, and so you choose that
kind of speaker to rule you.
And when once they're in power they begin taking bribes—fifty talents
in every instalment!
They threaten the cities to make them pay up, and they talk in this
manner to scare them:
'Pay the tribute, quick sharp, or I'll ruin your city by hurling my
thunderbolt at it!'
But if you get a nibble of just the scrag-end of your Empire, you're
perfectly happy.

.   .   .   .

Of course you're a slave! Isn't that what you are, when all of those men
are in office,

---

[19] More literally 'trygedians'; cf. p. 59 n. 22.

Not only themselves but their yes-men as well, all collecting good
    salaries from it?
While if somebody gives you three obols, you're pleased! But you
    earned them by personal service,
By rowing the ships and by fighting on land, by sieges and effort and
    hardship.
        .   .   .   .
The truth is, they want you, you see, to be poor. If you don't know the
    reason, I'll tell you.
It's to train you to know who your tamer is. Then, whenever he gives
    you a whistle
And sets you against an opponent of his, you jump out and tear them
    to pieces.
If they really desired to provide a good life for the people of Athens,
    it's simple.
Just look at the number of cities, a thousand, that bring us the tribute
    at present.
If each of those cities were ordered to feed twenty men and supply
    what they wanted,
Twenty thousand Athenian citizens then would be living surrounded
    by hare's meat
And by garlands of every conceivable kind and by new milk and cream
    and cream-cheeses,
And enjoying rewards that the country deserves, that the Marathon
    trophy has earned you!

                                    (*Wasps* 665–72, 682–5, 703–11)

Bdelykleon's allegations are complex. Some politicians (not
named, but Kleon's prominence elsewhere in the play justifies the
presumption that he is meant here) make speeches declaring their
determination to champion the Athenian populace. 'You'
(Philokleon, here regarded as representative of the jurors in general)
are taken in by this rhetoric, and therefore elect those politicians to
office. Most Athenian officials were appointed by lot, but the reference here must be to those appointed by election: military officers
such as Kleon, who was a general this year; public advocates[20] such
as 'the son of Khaireas' (mentioned in 687; his identity is uncertain);

---

[20] For the various kinds of *synegoroi* see MacDowell *Wasps* 198–9 (on line 482).
According to Aristotle *Ath. Pol.* 54.2 those who prosecuted magistrates at the
examination of their accounts were appointed by lot, but in Aristophanes
(*Akharnians* 676–718, *Horsemen* 1358–61, *Wasps* 686–94) they are evidently poli-

envoys, who are prominent in *Akharnians*, would also fall under this heading, although they are not mentioned explicitly here. These men, says Bdelykleon, receive pay at a higher rate then the jurors (one drachma, which is twice the amount for a juror, is specified in 691 for a public advocate), and they also receive hefty bribes. Public advocates get bribes from men they are prosecuting (693), but the largest bribes are those given to politicians by cities in the Empire (669–77). As in *Horsemen* (see p. 109), this must mean that the allied cities bribe Athenian politicians to refrain from proposing increases in the amounts of tribute which they have to pay to Athens. There is a weak link in the logic at 668–9,[21] since a politician could make such a proposal to the Assembly without having been elected to office; but no doubt Aristophanes is thinking of Kleon, who did in fact hold office as a general.

Bdelykleon has not a scrap of sympathy for the allied cities. He regards it as entirely right and proper that they should pay to support Athens, because Athens saved Greece from the barbarians at Marathon (711). His complaint is that the money which they pay goes to a few politicians and not to ordinary Athenians. Instead of paying bribes to avoid an increase of tribute, he wants them to devote their funds to enabling the jurors and many other Athenians to live a more luxurious life (706–10). Interwoven with this is a complaint that the politicians manipulate the jurors in the courts. They want the jurors to remain poor, so that the jurors will give verdicts against the politicians' opponents (703–5). Again the logical link is not very clear, and is to be explained by the fact that Aristophanes is really thinking of Kleon in particular. It was Kleon who had proposed the increase of the jurors' pay to three obols, and so the jurors were grateful to him for that and generally voted against anyone whom Kleon prosecuted; but if they were not so poor, they would no longer be grateful for this pittance and Kleon's influence over them would evaporate.

The real object of Bdelykleon's attack, then, is not the jurors, who he says deserve better treatment than they at present get, but

ticians who have put themselves forward for election (see especially *Akharnians* 685). Probably the method of appointment was changed from election to lot at some time after the date of *Wasps*.

[21] My translation 'when once they're in power' may be a little too emphatic, but κᾷθ' certainly implies that bribes from the cities follow election.

Kleon. Kleon not only makes profits for himself by blackmail, but also has acquired improper influence over the courts so that he can use them for defeating his political opponents. If he wants to get rid of an opponent, he simply prosecutes him (or gets one of his supporters, such as Theoros, to prosecute him), and the jurors will then convict him whether he is really guilty or not. This is similar to the attack in *Horsemen* on Kleon's prosecutions (see pp. 109–10).

Yet it must not be taken to imply that Kleon's opponents were all innocent. One kind of trial receives particular attention in *Wasps*, and that is *euthyna*, the examination of officials at the end of their term of office. The details of the procedure for this examination are not clear; although the fourth-century procedure is known, there are some grounds for thinking that it was different in the fifth century.[22] But at any rate it is certain that officials who had received public money had to render accounts of what they had received and what they had spent, and if they were accused of misappropriation they could undergo trial by jury, in which a public advocate prosecuted. This is probably the type of case which Kleon, perhaps through a supporter holding the office of advocate, most often brought against his opponents, for his opponents would be politicians who were sometimes elected to offices and thus became liable to it. Does Aristophanes then represent those men as Kleon's innocent victims? Certainly not, as we see in Philokleon's account of his typical day.

PHILOKLEON. When I first come along to the court from my bed, they're awaiting me there at the railings—
Such great big men, four cubits in height! Then as soon as he sees me arriving,
A man gives me his hand—oh, such a soft hand!—that's been stealing the treasury's money.
And they bow down low as they make their entreaties and pour out their pitiful speeches:
'Have mercy, sir, please, if you ever yourself filched money when you were in office,
Or when on your military service you went to the market for food for your messmates!'

[22] Cf. MacDowell *Law* 170–2, Ostwald *Sovereignty* 55–62. (MacDowell *Wasps* 145 (on line 102) wrongly assumes that the later procedure was already current in the fifth century.)

But he'd never have known I existed, if not from when last he was tried and acquitted!

(*Wasps* 552–8)

Philokleon is flattered and delighted that these important men are so obsequious towards him, but his words reveal that they are obviously guilty of theft, and indeed regard stealing from public funds as quite normal. The accused man recognizes Philokleon because he has been on trial for the same offence before. If we need to ask why he was acquitted last time, the answer will be that he bribed Kleon or the public advocates (as described in 692–5) to persuade the jurors to let him off. When Bdelykleon speaks in reply to Philokleon, he makes no attempt to refute this part of what Philokleon says, and Aristophanes leaves the impression that all politicians are crooks, not just Kleon and his supporters but his opponents too. This conclusion is reinforced by the trial of the dog which follows.

THE TRIAL OF THE DOG

The chorus declares that Bdelykleon has won the debate, and Philokleon too has been convinced by the reasoning; yet he is not converted emotionally. He so loves judging in the court that he cannot bear the thought of giving it up. His son therefore arranges for him to have a private court at home for trying domestic cases. Just at the right moment a domestic offence is committed: one of the dogs of the household has run into the kitchen and gobbled up a cheese, and the other dog is ready to prosecute him for theft. So equipment is arranged to set up a court, with comic improvisations for the voting-urns, the railings, and so on, and also some comforts for Philokleon which are not available in the real courts: a bowl of soup, a chamber-pot, and a cock in a cage to wake him up by crowing if he falls asleep during the speeches. He is the sole member of the jury, Bdelykleon is the presiding magistrate, the thievish dog is the accused, and the other dog is the prosecutor.

This scene is the best in the play, and it is effective at more than one level.[23] First, it carries the story forward by getting Philokleon

---

[23] Reckford *Old-and-New* 251–62 analyses this scene in detail, but overstates its resemblance to a game.

finally to give up his devotion to jury service. Second, it can hardly
fail to be effective visually, with the court setting and with two
actors dressed as man-sized dogs. The accused dog's puppies,
perhaps played by young boys, also make an appearance. So do a
cheese-grater and other kitchen utensils, which are called up as
witnesses; the cheese-grater is supposed to speak, though what it
says is not audible to the audience (963–6). If these also are played
by human actors, their appearance must add to the comic look of
the scene.[24] Third, there is the satire of courtroom procedure and
arguments, especially in the speech for the defence. When the
accused dog is called on to speak, he is tongue-tied, and Bdelykleon
speaks on his behalf in a parody of weak defence arguments, while
Philokleon as usual is determined to convict.

BDELYKLEON. It's difficult to answer on behalf
  Of a slandered dog, but still I'll try to speak,
  Because he's good, and chases wolves away.
PHILOKLEON. No, he's a thief and a conspirator!
BDELYKLEON. Oh no, he's not; he's the best dog alive.
  He's able to take charge of lots of sheep.
PHILOKLEON. What use is that, if he eats up all the cheese?
BDELYKLEON. What use? He fights for you, and guards the door.
  He's good in every way. And if he stole,
  Forgive him; he's never learned to play the lyre.

(*Wasps* 950–9)

Obviously the dog's theft is indefensible, but Bdelykleon tries to
defend him by listing his good qualities.[25] In Athenian courts, as we
know from surviving speeches, it was common for a defendant to
ask the jury to acquit him because he had fought for Athens in war,
or had performed liturgies (paying the expenses of ships, choruses,
and so on), or, more feebly, because he intended to perform such
services in future. So Bdelykleon recounts the dog's services, in

[24] It is not impossible for the cheese-grater and other utensils to be played by
mute actors appropriately costumed. One may compare modern stage-adap-
tations of *Alice in Wonderland* and *Through the Looking-Glass*, in which actors play
not only various animals, cards, and chessmen, but also an egg, a leg of mutton,
and a pudding. But the alternative possibility that an ordinary cheese-grater etc.
are carried on-stage by slaves cannot be excluded.

[25] M. Heath *Papers of the Leeds International Latin Seminar* 6 (1990) 235 wrongly
calls this speech 'utterly mendacious'. The joke is rather that Bdelykleon, unwill-
ing to lie, has difficulty in finding good things to say about Labes.

rather vague terms, and argues that he is disadvantaged by his upbringing. Only gentlemen who had had a good education learned to play the lyre. Probably some Athenian speaker not long before *Wasps* was performed had said 'I haven't learned to play the lyre' in order to contrast himself, as a man of the people, with some rich adversary, and Aristophanes mocks this plea by applying it to the dog. After the cheese-grater has been called up as a witness, the defence speech goes on to attack the prosecutor, and it reaches its crowning absurdity when Bdelykleon calls up the dog's puppies (976–8). Athenian defendants used sometimes to bring their children into court to arouse the jury's sympathy,[26] and here again Aristophanes mocks pleading which is not properly relevant to the case.

A fourth important feature of the scene is the political satire. The accused dog is named Labes, which in Greek sounds like 'taker' or 'snatcher', a suitable name for a thieving dog. But when the audience hears that it is a Sicilian cheese that he is accused of taking (838), a man with a very similar name, Lakhes, is likely to come to mind, because Lakhes had been in command of an Athenian naval expedition to Sicily and had been accused by Kleon of making money for himself out of it. At the start of the trial Bdelykleon reads out the formal charge, in which the prosecutor is called Dog—in Greek, Kyon. In case any members of the audience are slow to take the point, deme names are added in the usual manner of formal documents: Kyon of Kydathenaion has prosecuted Labes of Aixone (894–5). Everyone in the audience will have known that Kydathenaion was Kleon's deme and that Aixone was Lakhes', and will have understood from this point onwards that the accusation of one dog by the other is an allegory of the accusation of Lakhes by Kleon.

Modern scholars have wondered whether this is a representation of a trial which actually took place or a flight of Aristophanes' fancy. Lakhes' expedition to Sicily was in the years 427–5,[27] and the examination (*euthyna*) of his conduct as a general there must have taken place in 425, two and a half years before the performance of *Wasps*. If Aristophanes is satirizing an actual trial, is it that *euthyna* trial? It would be surprising if the object of his satire were not more up-to-date than that. Or is it a more recent trial? But once the

---

[26] Cf. *Wasps* 568–73 and Demosthenes 21.99 with MacDowell *Meidias* ad loc.
[27] Thucydides 3.86–115.

euthyna had been held, a man could not be prosecuted again for his actions in that term of office.[28] If Kleon prosecuted Lakhes in 423/2, it must have been on some different charge, not for embezzlement of public funds as a general in Sicily; yet *Wasps* contains no suggestion of any different charge.[29] It is also a difficulty that earlier in the play the chorus refers to the trial of Lakhes (not the trial of Labes the dog) in the future tense (240). If this is a reference to a trial which was already past when the play was performed, it implies that the play is set in the past, not in the present, which is contrary to Aristophanes' practice as we otherwise know it. All these difficulties can be avoided if we suppose not that Kleon had actually prosecuted Lakhes, but that shortly before *Wasps* he had been making speeches criticizing Lakhes, alleging that he had enriched himself out of public funds in Sicily three years before, and perhaps threatening to prosecute him on some charge not yet clearly defined. Aristophanes then has fun imagining what the trial would be like if Kleon were to prosecute Lakhes. This satirical scene may even have helped to persuade Kleon not to go ahead with a prosecution; at any rate there is no other evidence that he ever did.[30]

Lakhes seems to have been more a soldier than a politician (it is as a typical soldier that he appears in Plato's *Lakhes*), and that is the point of a contrast in the speech for the defence.

BDELYKLEON. For this dog Labes eats up all the bones
    And giblets, and he's always on the move,
    Whereas the other one——! He's just a house-guard,
    And stays at home; whatever gets brought in,
    He claims his share——or otherwise he bites.

                              (*Wasps* 968–72)

It is as if Kleon had never gone to Pylos. As far as Aristophanes is concerned, Kleon is the politician who undertakes none of the hardship and danger of fighting, but remains in Athens and still expects to profit from the war. This comes out most strongly in the

---

[28] Demosthenes 20.147, 24.54.

[29] Mastromarco *Storia di una commedia* 47–64 argues that Lakhes was accused in this year of betraying Athenian interests in Thrace. But Thrace is not mentioned in the trial of the dog, whereas Sicily is (897, 911).

[30] Cf. MacDowell *Wasps* 164 (on line 240). Ostwald *Sovereignty* 212–13 n. 59 still maintains that there was a real trial and Aristophanes was 'free with his dates'.

prosecution speech, where the allegory is a marvellous mixture of
dogs and sailors, Sicily and cheese.

DOG. Men of the jury, you have heard the charge
   I've brought against the defendant. He has done
   Terrible things to me and the yo-heave-hos.
   He ran into the corner, Sicilized
   A great big cheese, and gorged himself in the dark.
PHILOKLEON. Oh yes, it's obvious! Just now he gave
   A horrible belch of cheese right over me,
   The loathsome cur!
DOG.   He didn't give me any,
   Although I asked him. Who'll look after you,
   If no one throws out bits for me, the Dog?

     .   .   .   .   .

   So don't you let him go. Of all the dogs,
   This man's the one who eats by far alonest!
   He sailed completely round the mixing-bowl
   And then he ate up all the city's rind.

     .   .   .   .   .   .

   So punish him for this, because two thieves
   Can't be supported by a single wood.
   Then I shan't bark for nothing and in vain,
   But otherwise I won't bark any more!

(*Wasps* 907–16, 922–5, 927–30)

'One wood will not support two robins' was the proverb, but
Aristophanes makes the Dog substitute 'thieves'. The two dogs—
that is, Kleon and Lakhes—are both thieves, but Kleon is the worse
of the two, because he demands a share of the loot without himself
doing anything but bark. He claims that this is a service for which
he deserves to be rewarded. It is likely that Kleon really had claimed
that he was the watch-dog of Athens. That gives extra point to the
presentation of him as a dog in this scene, and it also explains
some other canine references to him. In particular, Aristophanes
sometimes speaks of him as Kerberos, the terrible watch-dog at the
entrance to Hades.[31] Overcoming Kerberos was one of the labours
performed in myth by Herakles, and in the parabasis, which immedi-

---

[31] *Horsemen* 1030, *Peace* 313; cf. pp. 101–2.

ately follows the trial scene, Aristophanes claims to have been as
bold as Herakles.[32]

> And when he began to direct, he declares, he didn't attack human
>   beings;
> He displayed the same spirit as Herakles did, and he tackled the greatest
>   opponents,
> And at once, from the very beginning, he boldly faced up to the jagged-
>   toothed monster.
>
> (*Wasps* 1029–31)

'The jagged-toothed monster' is Kleon, the terrible dog. The
lines refer back to *Horsemen*. In *Wasps* he said 'We shan't make
mincemeat of him yet again' (63) and it seemed that Kleon would
not appear. But in effect he is brought on-stage in the trial scene, in
a guise probably suggested by his own boastful language.

A DIFFERENT WAY OF LIFE

At the end of the trial of the dog Philokleon, who all along has been
determined to convict Labes, is tricked by Bdelykleon into casting
his vote in the acquittal urn. When he discovers what he has done,
he is horrified and decides immediately to give up judging. He
evidently regards himself as no longer competent to do it.[33] He now
agrees to adopt the new and pleasanter way of life that Bdelykleon
wants to provide for him. Here, as throughout the play, Bdelykleon

---

[32] Cf. G. Mastromarco *Rivista di Filologia e di Istruzione Classica* 117 (1989)
410–23.

[33] K. Sidwell *C&M* 41 (1990) 9–31 sees the trial and acquittal of the dog as a
ritual cure for Philokleon's disease; Bowie *Aristophanes* 88–93 sees it as a rite of
passage; M. Menu in *L'Initiation* (ed. A. Moreau, Montpellier 1992) 2.165–84
sees all the later scenes as parody of a religious initiation. The chorus's reference
to a new rite (876) would fit any of those interpretations, but the other evidence
adduced to support them is weak, and I am not convinced that Aristophanes
meant the trial and later scenes to be an imitation or parody of any religious
ritual.

is a good son who desires to give his father the best life possible.[34]

This different way of life has several aspects. First there are new clothes. Hitherto Philokleon has always worn a *tribon*, the cheapest kind of cloak, often mentioned as characteristic of poor men, including most of the citizens attending the Assembly or serving as jurors.[35] Now Bdelykleon gives him instead a *khlaina*, a heavier cloak, of a particular type called *kaunakes*, with woollen tufts or tassels hanging all over it, making it very thick and warm. It has been imported from Persia, and Philokleon has never seen such a cloak before. Aristophanes may be making a topical joke about some Athenians who had recently visited Persia as envoys, if they brought back cloaks of this type.[36] Philokleon is also made to give up his ordinary shoes and put on footwear of a type called 'Lakonian', probably a kind of boot fastened with straps.[37] The point is that the *kaunakes* and the Lakonian boots are warmer and more expensive, and this scene is important as evidence that rich Athenians, in some cases at least, dressed differently from poor ones.[38]

The second aspect of Philokleon's new way of life is going to parties in superior society. This part of the play is important evidence for the customs of the symposium or drinking-party.[39] Philokleon has never attended one before, and most of the humour of the scene arises from his ignorance of how to behave at one. Although his uncouthness is exaggerated for comic effect, this must imply that the symposium was customary only at higher levels of Athenian society, or anyway not at the lowest level.

[34] Bdelykleon's conduct towards his father is summed up by the chorus in terms of praise at the end of the play (1462–73). Hubbard *Mask* 130 n. 34 is wrong when he says that Bdelykleon's motives in giving clothes to Philokleon are less creditable than the Sausage-seller's in giving clothes to Democracy in *Horsemen*; in fact the Sausage-seller is selfish, wanting to become ruler of Athens, whereas Bdelykleon is unselfish, wanting to benefit his father at his own expense.

[35] Cf. Stone *Costume* 162–3. J. Vaio *GRBS* 12 (1971) 336 sees it as politically significant, because it would be worn by supporters of Kleon.

[36] Cf. MacDowell *Wasps* 278–9 (on line 1137), Stone *Costume* 168.

[37] Cf. MacDowell *Wasps* 281 (on line 1158), Stone *Costume* 225–7; but there is no good reason for Stone's suggestion that Lakonian boots are more appropriate for younger men.

[38] About thirty years later it appears from *Women at the Assembly* 74, 269, etc. that it had become normal for most Athenian men to wear Lakonian boots, at least in winter. Presumably they had become cheaper by then.

[39] On many aspects of the symposium see O. Murray (ed.) *Sympotica* (Oxford 1990).

The procedure is that the guests bring their own food for dinner, carried by a slave (1250–1); the host provides wine and perhaps additional items of food. They recline around the room on couches covered by rugs (1208–13), and slaves pour water over their hands to wash them (1216). Next, slaves carry small tables into the room, on which the food is placed, and the guests eat (1216–17). When they have finished eating, their hands are washed again, and the drinking is initiated by pouring libations (1217). At this stage music is provided by a female slave playing a pipe (*aulos*).

Bdelykleon tries to instruct Philokleon both about conversation and about singing at the symposium. He should not tell rude or childish stories, but should speak impressively about his own achievements. The singing consists of *skolia*, traditional songs which the guests are expected to know. One man sings the first line or two, and then another has to continue. To give his father some practice, Bdelykleon pretends to be one distinguished man after another, singing the beginning of a *skolion*, and the joke is that each time Philokleon gets the continuation wrong, converting the song into a satirical comment on the distinguished man concerned.

The guests at this imaginary symposium are Kleon and men who are known, or may be assumed, to be friends and supporters of Kleon, namely Theoros, Aiskhines, Phanos, and 'a foreigner, Akestor's son'.[40] Since Kleon is attacked elsewhere for his vulgarity, especially in *Horsemen*, it is at first sight surprising that he is used here as an example of high society, as if he were a friend of Bdelykleon, whose name means 'Loathe-Kleon'. Of course Aristophanes names Kleon and his friends here because he wants to make jokes against them, but he could not have done so convincingly if they would have been out of place at a symposium. From this we see that, although they claimed to protect the rights of ordinary Athenians, they were not themselves regarded as ordinary Athenians but as important men, not out of place in a high-class social circle. Yet they were not aristocratic; whereas in the archaic age the symposium may well have been a custom of aristocratic circles only, this passage of *Wasps* shows that that was no longer true in the late fifth century. As for Bdelykleon's name, that is now forgotten (it is not mentioned after 372). Since he won the debate in the agon, he and his father no longer hold different views about Kleon; the contrast

⁴⁰ On Akestor see MacDowell in *Tr.Com.Pol.* 365–7.

now is between a son familiar with wealthy society, such as Kleon, and a father ignorant of it.

When they actually go to a symposium, described for the audience by Xanthias, the guests turn out to be a quite different group: 'Hippyllos, Antiphon, Lykon, Lysistratos, Theophrastos, Phrynikhos' set' (1301–2).[41] The last phrase makes clear that this was a well-known social group. Eleven years later, in 411, two of the leaders of the oligarchic revolution were Phrynikhos and Antiphon, and it is probable that the same two men are meant here; Lysistratos may also have been connected with Antiphon politically.[42] But that does not mean that Phrynikhos' set was an oligarchic club.[43] It is not clear that any oligarchic revolution was being planned as early as 422, nor that the members of the group held oligarchic views at this time; Phrynikhos himself is said to have opposed oligarchy as late as 412/11.[44] So Phrynikhos' set should be regarded simply as a group of men with similar tastes and interests. It is because of their social prestige, not for any political significance, that Aristophanes has chosen this group to be the one whose symposium Philokleon has attended; they are an outstanding and well-known part of Athenian society. Aristophanes regards them as snobs, who treat too contemptuously those whom they regard as their inferiors. That is why it is funny to hear that Philokleon has discomfited them.

At this symposium, as recounted by Xanthias, the main form of entertainment was not singing *skolia* but making comparisons. In this conversational game the men would take turns to compare one another to something in a witty or funny manner. Philokleon's first venture in it was a success, with two comparisons of Lysistratos which most of the other guests applauded (1311–14). But then he became rude, making boorish jokes and insulting them all in turn. He treated them with *hybris* (1303, 1319). Eventually he became

[41] I. C. Storey *Phoenix* 39 (1985) 317–33 discusses the identity of each of these individuals.

[42] A man named Lysistratos was prosecuted at the instigation of Philinos (probably Kleophon's brother) in a case parallel to one for which Antiphon wrote the defence speech (Antiphon 6.36). But the circumstances of this affair are obscure.

[43] I repeat here a few lines from MacDowell *Wasps* 303 (on line 1302), but I no longer maintain that this Lykon is the Lykon who later accused Socrates; cf. Storey *Phoenix* 39 (1985) 322–4.

[44] Thucydides 8.48.4–7.

drunk, left the party taking the girl-piper with him, and now reappears on-stage with a blazing torch, which he uses as a weapon for hitting everyone he meets on the way home. A female bread-seller, whose basket he has upset, delivers a summons for damage to her goods (1406–8), and a man delivers a summons for *hybris* (1417–18), before Bdelykleon manages to carry him inside the house by force.

Hybris is a concept which I have discussed elsewhere.[45] Briefly, it is an exuberant and self-indulgent frame of mind, associated especially with wealth and with excessive eating and drinking, leading to behaviour which in many cases involves insulting and dishonouring other people. Philokleon certainly displays *hybris* induced by drinking, both verbally, when he speaks rudely to the guests at the symposium, and physically, when he hits people in the street. It has been inferred that this was appropriate conduct at the end of a symposium,[46] but this is a misinterpretation of Aristophanes. The joke is that Philokleon does everything wrong. Bdelykleon wanted him to go to a symposium, but is annoyed, not pleased, at the result. Xanthias regards it as outrageous, not normal, that Philokleon beat him with his stick for no reason (1292–6, 1307, 1322–5). The other guests do not accompany him on his rampage through the streets. No doubt men did sometimes in historical fact get drunk and display *hybris*, but that should not be thought of as proper behaviour, even among the wealthy, in Athens in Aristophanes' time.

The final aspect of Philokleon's new way of life is dancing. This part of the play has already been discussed briefly in Chapter 2 (pp. 20–1). Philokleon performs movements from old-fashioned tragic dances, while the sons of Karkinos give a display of dancing in the modern style. Aristophanes' main purpose here is to provide a musical finale which is both spectacular and novel (cf. 1536–7). It also completes the story of Philokleon in an artistically satisfactory way, because his frivolous activity at the end of the play is as different as possible from his severe activity of judging at the beginning of it. He has gone from one extreme to the opposite extreme. His change from an austere way of life to a prosperous one has been effected.

---

[45] MacDowell *G&R* 23 (1976) 14–31 and *Meidias* 18–23. For a much fuller discussion see N. R. E. Fisher *Hybris* (Warminster 1992).

[46] O. Murray in *Nomos* 144–5.

Although he does not yet know how to behave properly in his new circumstances, we are left to assume that he will learn that in time, as the chorus says in an optimistic song near the end.[47]

> I envy the prosperity
>> Which this old man's attained to
> In place of his austerity.
> He's learning different lessons now;
>> He'll make a transformation
> To live in soft luxurious style.
>
> But perhaps he may not want to,
> For it's always difficult to
>> Leave one's natural character.
> Many people, though, have done it:
> Taking good advice from others
>> They have changed their way of life.
>
> (*Wasps* 1450–61)

A LITTLE STORY WITH A POINT

Wasps has often been seen as a satirical criticism of the Athenian courts and juries, but that is a misinterpretation.[48] As we have seen, Aristophanes does not find fault with the courts' formal arrangements and voting procedures. He never suggests that the jury system should be abolished. His presentation of the jurors is sympathetic rather than hostile. They are simple old men, honest and well-meaning, who deserve financial support because of their great service to Athens against the Persians when they were young. The trouble is that they are misled by clever orators and unscrupulous politicians. It is not wrong in principle that elderly citizens should perform jury service, but it is wrong that they put up with low pay and patronizing treatment which is really humiliation. Aristophanes is attacking the cynical manipulation of the jurors by Kleon for his own profit. Despite the disclaimer 'We shan't make mincemeat of him yet again' (63), it is clear that he does regard

---

[47] On the significance of this song see MacDowell *Wasps* 319 (on lines 1450–73). D. Konstan *TAPA* 115 (1985) 44, dissenting from my view, overlooks the future tense in 1454.

[48] Cf. Rogers *Wasps* xvi–xvii.

criticism of Kleon as one of the topics of the play. He virtually says so in the second parabasis.

> There are some men who asserted that I'd made my peace with him.
> That was at the time when Kleon charged at me and harassed me
> And abused me and provoked me. Then, when I was being flayed,
> People not involved looked on and laughed to see me yelling out.
> They cared not a scrap for me, though. All they wanted was to know
> Whether I, when Kleon squeezed me, would emit some little joke.
> I could see the situation; so I played the ape a bit.
> In the end, though, now the vine-prop's cheated and let down the vine!
>
> (*Wasps* 1284–91)

Here the chorus speaks for Aristophanes in the first person (cf. p. 42) and refers to a dispute after the performance of *Horsemen*.[49] There is no independent evidence of a dispute at that time, but it would have been natural for Kleon to try to retaliate for Aristophanes' onslaught in that play. The course of the affair was that Kleon attacked Aristophanes by an abusive speech and perhaps in other ways, such as a prosecution or a threat of one (1285–6);[50] Aristophanes received no support from the public (1287–9); so he gave way, perhaps by making some kind of public apology (1290), which was thought by some people to be a sincere reconciliation (1284); but now, in *Wasps*, he has renewed his attack on Kleon (1291).

Yet *Wasps* is not a second *Horsemen*. Kleon is not the principal subject of the play. The purpose of the play is described at the start by Xanthias. It is the most explicit such statement in any of the plays, and yet it is almost entirely in negative terms.

XANTHIAS. Now let me tell the audience the theme,
    But first, by way of preface, these few words:

---

[49] It is not possible to make the passage refer to the dispute after the performance of *Babylonians* (cf. pp. 42–4), which would mean that 1291 referred to *Horsemen*, because 'now' in that line must refer to the present play, not to one performed two years ago. Cf. G. Mastromarco in *Tr.Com.Pol.* 348–54; however, the main target of Aristophanes' trickery (1290–1) must surely be Kleon, not other comic dramatists as Mastromarco suggests.

[50] Croiset *Ar. and Pol. Parties* 89–92, followed by Sommerstein *Acharnians* 2–3, conjectures that this was when Kleon prosecuted Aristophanes on a charge of simulating citizenship. But schol. *Akharnians* 378 is hardly adequate evidence for that; cf. pp. 43–4.

Not to expect a great ambitious work,
Nor that we've filched some laughs from Megara.
We haven't got a pair of slaves to throw
Nuts from a basket to the audience,
Or Herakles being cheated of his dinner;
We've no more insults for Euripides,
And even if Kleon's had a lucky break,
We shan't make mincemeat of him yet again.
But we've a little story with a point;
It's no more intellectual than yourselves,
But cleverer than vulgar comedy.

(*Wasps* 54–66)

He means that *Wasps* is intermediate between two kinds of comedy.[51] On one side there is vulgar comedy, which is equated with 'laughs from Megara'. We do not know much now about Megarian comedy, but the implication is that it consists of simple and perhaps childish entertainment. The examples given are the scattering of small eatables among the audience and Herakles presented as a hungry glutton roaring for food. In other plays Aristophanes does sometimes include this type of humour, or at least comes fairly near it: barley-seeds are scattered among the audience in *Peace* 962 (but barley-seeds are less appetizing, and perhaps he is only parodying the practice of scattering nuts), and Herakles is enthusiastic about food in both *Birds* and *Frogs*. On the other side, plays about Euripides or Kleon are examples of comedy that is 'great'. That certainly includes *Horsemen*. Whether it also includes *Akharnians* is less clear. Euripides appears in one scene of that play, and several other scenes allude to his *Telephos*; but some commentators on *Wasps* 61, including myself, have thought that Aristophanes could hardly speak of his own play as insulting. I am now less sure that that objection is cogent; the line may refer to *Akharnians*, or it may refer to some play not now extant. But in any case Aristophanes is contrasting *Wasps* with comedies which have a substantial political or literary theme. And his comment that it is 'no more intellectual than yourselves' is probably an oblique reference to the failure of *Clouds* in the previous year because, as he

---

[51] I now regard my earlier analysis of this passage (MacDowell *Wasps* 136–7) as not quite satisfactory. Paduano *Il giudice* 9–18 discusses it in detail and emphasizes its chiastic arrangement.

believed, the audience failed to understand that play's intellectual content (cf. pp. 145–6).

Wasps, then, is not a play having ambitious aims like those earlier comedies, but a little story which includes a point for the audience to think about (64). Kleon's use of the courts is food for thought, but primarily the play is the story of the old juror and his conversion to a different way of life. Some critics, regarding it as a satire on the courts, have complained that the last third of it is irrelevant, but that is an error. It is the character of Philokleon that unifies the play. Right from the start his son is urging him to adopt a new way of life (e.g. 115–17, 341), and the play would be incomplete if the result of this plan were not shown.[52]

The characterization of Philokleon is excellent, but its purpose is amusement, not psychological truth.[53] He is an old man, and his weaknesses due to age are often mentioned (165, 276, 809–10, etc.). Yet he is extremely active, especially when trying to escape from the house by climbing out of the chimney, hanging on to the underside of the donkey, and so on. He is quick-witted, crafty, and resourceful, and yet so simple that a very easy trick causes him to confuse the two voting-urns (990–2), and he makes the most elementary mistakes in his conduct at the symposium. All this is not consistent or realistic, but it is highly entertaining, and that is, in part, why we like the old scallywag. Logical readers have found this puzzling.[54] It is clear that Philokleon is wrong in his obsession with judging and condemning, and later he is wrong again in his drunken and rude behaviour. Bdelykleon, on the other hand, is right; his main function in the play is to present the true or sensible view of every question. He serves as a foil to Philokleon, a standard of normality by which the old man's absurdities may be measured. But that makes him a comparatively dull character, whereas we like Philokleon because he makes us laugh. His conduct, even when wrong, seems somehow forgivable.[55] Although he behaves badly when he gets drunk, the raucous woman and the two pompous men who threaten to summon him are unattractive because of their

[52] Cf. Russo *Aristophanes* 127, J. Vaio *GRBS* 12 (1971) 335–51.

[53] The main aim of Paduano's book *Il giudice giudicato* is to analyse Philokleon's psychology in Freudian terms of repression and obsession, but the attempt seems to me misguided.

[54] Cf. Dover *Ar. Comedy* 125–7.

[55] Cf. D. Konstan *TAPA* 115 (1985) 33–5.

litigiousness, and we are glad when he outfaces them. Even in court he is not as hard-hearted as he pretends to be: at the end of the trial scene he actually sheds tears of pity for the accused, though he hastily pretends they were caused by his hot soup (982–4). Most important, we are made to feel that he is not really responsible for the harm that he does in the courts. He is the dupe of Kleon and Kleon's friends. They are the villains. Philokleon is an ordinary man who has been led astray by them. When his eyes are opened, the truth comes to him as a surprise and a shock (696–7, 713–14). And it is because he evokes our sympathy as well as our laughter that he is a great comic character.

8

Peace

FLYING TO HEAVEN

The war had been in progress since 431 BC, but by the spring of 421 peace was imminent. Thucydides analyses the reasons (5.14–17). The Athenians, who had been confident of total victory after their success at Pylos in 425, then suffered defeats at Delion in 424 and at Amphipolis in 422. So they were now less sure that they could win the war and began to think it would be better to make terms with Sparta, for fear that the allied cities in their Empire might revolt and join forces with Sparta against them. The Spartans, for their part, had suffered an unexpected disaster at Pylos and were afraid of a possible revolt by the helots. They were also aware that their thirty-year treaty with Argos was about to run out, and did not relish the prospect of fighting Athens and Argos simultaneously.

Perhaps even more cogent was the loss of war leaders on both sides. Kleon and Brasidas, who commanded the Athenian and Spartan armies respectively at Amphipolis, were both killed in that battle. Thucydides remarks that they had both opposed peace, Brasidas because he derived success and honour from the war, Kleon because 'he thought that in peacetime his wickedness would be more obvious and his slanders more distrusted'. With them gone, the most influential leaders were the cautious Nikias in Athens and King Pleistoanax in Sparta, both of whom were apprehensive of being blamed for any defeats if the war continued. So negotiations began. But even now it was difficult to get both sides to agree on terms. The talks continued through the winter, and it was not until just after the town Dionysia, in the spring of 421, that the treaty, generally called the Peace of Nikias, was concluded. That was the festival at which *Peace* was performed.

The play shows a countryman who hates the war and seeks peace, just like Dikaiopolis in *Akharnians*, although the method he uses is

different. The countryman in this play is named Trygaios, which
means 'grape-harvester'. He has decided to go to see Zeus and ask
what his intentions are, since he seems to be destroying Greece. To
get up to heaven, where Zeus lives, he has procured a huge flying
dung-beetle, and he proceeds to fly to heaven on its back. This
provides a fine opening for the play, with two slaves scurrying to
and fro to fetch enough dung-cakes to feed the beetle, and then
Trygaios himself flying across the stage mounted on it, while his
children call plaintively to him from the ground. Critics have
regarded this scene as the best in the play. Certainly it must have
been striking visually. The flight of Trygaios on the beetle was shown
by means of the machine (*mekhane*), a kind of crane which could
raise an actor from the ground off-stage and swing him round into
the audience's view.[1] It was used in tragedies to show a character
flying. Here Aristophanes mocks it by making Trygaios call out to
the operator off-stage.

TRYGAIOS. I'm terrified, and I'm not joking now!
    Machinist, pay attention! I can feel
Wind getting at my guts! If you're not careful,
I'll be providing fodder for the beetle!

(Peace 173–6)

But the scene is not just visual farce. It is a parody of a particular
tragedy, Euripides' *Bellerophon*. Bellerophon was the hero who slew
the monstrous Chimera; subsequently all his children perished in
some way, and he set off for heaven on the winged horse Pegasos to
complain to Zeus, but the horse threw him and he was lamed by
the fall. Euripides' play is lost, and we do not know exactly which
parts of the myth it showed, but evidently Euripides did use the
stage machine to show Bellerophon riding to heaven on Pegasos.
Aristophanes presents a comic version of the same situation, and
the scholia tell us specifically that two lines (76, 155) are adapted
from lines of *Bellerophon*. It is difficult to trace details of the parody
beyond this, but it may well be that the structure of the whole scene
is based on Euripides, including the description of the hero by a
slave before he appears, his cry heard from within the house, his
flying appearance to the accompaniment of anapaestic verses, and
his rather formal dialogue with a character on the ground before his

---

[1] On this machine and its use see Dearden *Stage* 75–85.

flight proceeds.[2] But naturally Trygaios' flight comes to a successful comic end, not a tragic one, and he lands safely in heaven.

THE CHARACTER OF WAR

Trygaios knocks at the door of the house of Zeus, and it is opened by Hermes. Presumably the audience recognized Hermes at once by his characteristic dress (broad-brimmed hat, winged boots, caduceus), but his manner at first is not at all what a god's should be; for comic effect Aristophanes makes him talk like a bad-tempered janitor. However, when Trygaios gives him a tip (a present of meat), he becomes more affable and explains that Zeus and all the other gods have gone away, leaving him to look after their property. When Trygaios asks why, the tone becomes more serious.

TRYGAIOS. What was the reason that the gods moved out?
HERMES. Their anger with the Greeks. They settled War
    Here, where they'd lived themselves, and handed you
    Over to him to do just as he liked.
    They went to live as high up as they could,
    Because they didn't want to see you fighting
    Or hear your supplications any more.
TRYGAIOS. And why did they do that to us? Do tell me.
HERMES. Because you chose to carry on the war
    Although they often tried to make a treaty.
    The Spartans, if they gained a bit, would say
    'By the Two Gods, the Attican shall pay!'
    But if you Atticans did well and then
    The Spartans came to you to talk of peace,
    You'd say at once 'They're cheating, by Athena!'
    'By Zeus, they are! We'd better not agree.
    They'll come again, if we hold on to Pylos.'
TRYGAIOS. That's typical of our Athenian talk!

(Peace 203–20)

These lines are not exactly funny, but sarcastic. They are likely to have made the Athenian audience feel rather uncomfortable and regretful. It was true that in the last ten years there had been some

    [2] Cf. Rau *Paratragodia* 89–97.

god-sent opportunities to make peace, which had all been missed. It was not really surprising if the gods were angry.

Hermes goes on to explain that War has imprisoned Peace in a deep cave, and has procured a large mortar in which to grind down all the Greek cities. War then appears with his mortar, in which he is going to mix the ingredients for a popular dish called *myttotos*, but each ingredient turns out to be a Greek place with which a particular product is associated: the leeks are Prasiai, the garlic is Megara, the cheese is Sicily, and the honey is Attica. War is about to pound all these together, but finds he has no pestle. So he sends his servant Tumult for a pestle, first to Athens and then to Sparta; but Tumult finds that each of those cities has recently lost its pestle—Kleon and Brasidas respectively.

This passage is a striking allegory of the war.[3] We cannot be sure how novel the personification of War and Tumult was. Earlier poetry occasionally mentions them in personal terms, but does not characterize them in detail.[4] Aristophanes himself describes War as a riotous drunkard in *Akharnians* 979–87, but War does not appear on-stage there, and is not known to have done so in any other play before *Peace*. Here he appears as a brutal ogre. The people of Greece are simply his food; he intends to crush them utterly and gobble them down. This is a much more destructive characterization than the one in *Akharnians*, where War brawls and spills the wine but there is no suggestion that he will eat up his host. His implements for pounding the Greeks are, or rather were, Kleon and Brasidas. Kleon is called a pestle in *Horsemen* 984 too, but again a change is perceptible: in *Horsemen* Kleon is the principal villain, but in *Peace* Kleon was merely a tool in the hands of War, and anyway has now perished, while War seems to be an all-powerful force which even the gods no longer control.

It is the achievement of Trygaios that he defeats War. Yet curiously this is not shown in the play directly. War goes off-stage to make a new pestle and never reappears. It weakens the dramatic effect of the play that War (unlike Lamakhos in *Akharnians* and Paphlagon in *Horsemen*) is not shown on-stage being defeated and humiliated. Instead Aristophanes has chosen to move straight on to another allegory.

---

[3] Cf. Newiger *Metapher* 114, Moulton *Ar. Poetry* 85–92.
[4] e.g. *Iliad* 18.535, Pindar fr. 78 (Snell and Maehler).

RESCUING PEACE

Trygaios sees that, while War is indoors making a new pestle, this is the opportunity to rescue Peace from her imprisonment. He calls on 'farmers and merchants and carpenters and craftsmen and metics and foreigners and islanders', in fact on everyone, to come and help. The chorus immediately arrives, and its members are so delighted at the prospect of peace that they cannot help dancing for joy. Hermes reappears and tries to stop the rescue: Zeus, he says, has ordained the death penalty for anyone found bringing Peace out of the cave. But Trygaios cleverly wins Hermes over by suggesting that the Moon and the Sun (worshipped by the Persians) might take over Greece, so that they, not the gods, would receive the Greeks' sacrifices in future; on the other hand Hermes, if he agrees to help, will be given some extra festivals. Trygaios also gives Hermes a gold cup to make a libation.

So Hermes agrees to help, and after the libation and a prayer he and Trygaios organize the rescue. The members of the chorus pull on ropes to draw Peace up out of the cave. But it is hard to get everyone to pull together. First the Boiotians are not pulling properly. Then Lamakhos (who stood for war in *Akharnians*) is obstructing the effort, and the Argives are not pulling at all but just laugh at other people's trouble and distress, while making profits out of both sides. (Argos was neutral in the war.) The Spartans are pulling manfully—or some of them are.[5] The Megarians pull, but to no effect, because they are starving. Some men pull in one direction, some in another. And then, after a reference to the Megarians' involvement with the outbreak of the war, comes a comment on the Athenians.

> You men of Megara, go to the ravens,[6] won't you!
> The goddess still remembers you, and hates you:
> You were the first to smear her with your garlic.
> And you Athenians, stop holding on
> And pulling from the point that you're at now;
> You're not achieving anything but—trials!

[5] Doubt about the text of 479–80 makes it uncertain what the Spartans' difficulty is, but the most probable interpretation is that only the Spartan prisoners held in Athens are in favour of making peace, and they are prevented by their fetters from taking any action.

[6] The regular imprecation meaning 'go to hell!'

But if you really want to pull her out,
Give way a little bit towards the sea.

(*Peace* 500–7)

The reference to trials is the regular joke about Athenian litigiousness and juries (as in *Clouds* 208, for example), but the last line
is a more serious comment on Athenian policy: Athens is a sea-
power and should relinquish her ambitions to control large parts of
the mainland. Finally it is decided that the farmers will do best on
their own. Everyone else is ordered to stop pulling, and the farmers
draw Peace up into the light.

Critics have found many difficulties in the details of this scene.
One is a problem of location: Trygaios is in heaven, which he
reached only after a precarious flight, and yet when he calls for
other people to help him they arrive at once without any suggestion
of a long journey, as if the scene were on earth. Then there is the
problem of their identity: does the chorus include Greeks of all
cities and all occupations, or does it consist of Athenian farmers
only, the other Greeks being supernumerary or imaginary?[7] Again,
who is it that has imprisoned Peace: War (223) or Zeus (371–2)?
And who is the organizer of the rescue: Trygaios (305) or Hermes
(428–9)? This last question might be answered if we could be sure
which lines are spoken by Trygaios and which by Hermes here
(431–519).[8] The other questions are not clearly answered by the
text, and Aristophanes may have left them vague because he thought
them unimportant. What is important in this scene is the co-oper-
ative effort. He wants to convey to his audience that the recovery
of peace is possible only if people pull together, not if they oppose
and obstruct one another. This theme differs from the theme of the
earlier part of the play. Previously Trygaios was, in comic form, the
bold hero setting out on a lone quest, but in this scene everyone is
being urged to join in.

---

[7] Cf. Sifakis *Parabasis* 29–32, Dover *Ar. Comedy* 136–9, Zimmermann *Untersuchungen* 1.262–5, Cassio *Commedia* 69–77, Hubbard *Mask* 241–2.
[8] Cf. Cassio *Commedia* 64–6.

THE CAUSES OF THE WAR

Now that Peace has been rescued, there is a moment for reflection.
Why has she been away so long? Hermes, being a god, knows the
answer. He gives it in a speech which in some ways resembles a
speech in an agon, though no one makes a speech in opposition to
him.[9] He begins by going back to the origins of the war in the 430s,
so that his theme is much like Dikaiopolis' in *Akharnians* 497–556.

CHORUS. But wherever did she get to? She's been gone from us so long.
    Won't you please explain it to us, you most favourable of gods?
HERMES. Well, you cleverest of farmers, 'hearken then, and mark my
        speech,'[10]
    If you wish to hear about her and the way she was destroyed.
    It was Pheidias who began it, when he got in trouble first.
    Perikles then, getting frightened that he might share Pheidias' fate—
    Since he knew your character, and feared that biting way you have—
    To forestall his own disaster, set the city all ablaze,
    Striking just a tiny spark of a Megarian decree!
    Then he fanned the flame of war to such a height that from the smoke
    All the Greeks were soon in tears, both over there and here as well.[11]
    Once the crackling sound of burning came from a reluctant vine,
    And a jar got knocked and crossly kicked back at another jar,
    There was nobody to stop it. That was when Peace disappeared.
TRYGAIOS. By Apollo, that's the first time anyone has told me that!
    I'd not heard of the connection that Peace had with Pheidias.
CHORUS. Nor had I till now. So that's the reason for her lovely face—
    Since she's Pheidias' relation! Well, well, so we live and learn.

                                                    (*Peace* 601–18)

Like Dikaiopolis, Hermes regards the Megarian decree
(excluding Megarians from the Athenian Agora and from harbours
in the Athenian Empire), and the refusal by Perikles and the
Athenians to annul it, as the event which started the war, because
neither the Athenians nor the Peloponnesians would give way. But

---

[9] Cf. Cassio *Commedia* 79–85.
[10] The quotation is from Arkhilokhos. Arkhilokhos addresses 'indigent citizens', and 'indigent' is sometimes substituted for 'cleverest' in Aristophanes'
line; but see Cassio *Commedia* 84 n. 7 for arguments against this.
[11] 'There' is Megara and the Peloponnese, 'here' is Athens. Hermes is speaking
in the Athenian theatre, and the house of Zeus is forgotten in this passage.

the personal motive of Perikles which he adduces is different: Dikai-opolis attributes Perikles' attitude to indignation on behalf of his mistress Aspasia, but Hermes attributes it to fear that he might be caught up in the disgrace of his friend Pheidias. Pheidias, the sculptor of the Parthenon and of the great statue of Athena placed inside it, was accused of misappropriating some of the gold and ivory supplied for the statue, and also of including representations of himself and Perikles among the figures on Athena's shield. Perikles, Hermes means, was afraid that he himself might be accused of being an accomplice in those offences, and that if he were prosecuted he might be convicted by a vindictive jury ('he knew your character, and feared that biting way you have'), and so he provoked the war in order to divert the Athenians' attention.

This is the only fifth-century text linking the accusation of Phei-dias to the outbreak of the war, but the link was well known to later writers. We find it in Diodoros, who at this point is following the fourth-century historian Ephoros, and in Plutarch, who found more sources attributing Perikles' stand on the Megarian decree to this motive than to any other.[12] Presumably Aristophanes' audience understood the point without difficulty. We, however, have two serious problems about it.

The first problem concerns the date of the prosecution of Phei-dias. Neither Diodoros nor Plutarch dates it. The only text giving a date is a fragment of Philokhoros quoted by a scholiast, in which the readings are disputed; an emendation giving the date 438/7 is commonly accepted.[13] But if that is right, it leaves too long an interval; the prosecution of Pheidias in 438/7 cannot have been the event which prompted Perikles' proposal of the Megarian decree in (probably) 433, still less his refusal to annul it in 431. An alternative view is based on the inscription of the Parthenon accounts, which shows that surplus gold and ivory was sold in 434; if that was the year in which the statue of Athena was completed, it should also be the year of the prosecution of Pheidias in connection with it.[14] Yet neither piece of evidence is conclusive: the emendation of

---

[12] Diodoros 12.39–40 (with the reference to Ephoros in 12.41.1), Plutarch *Perikles* 31.

[13] Schol. *Peace* 605, quoting *F.Gr.Hist.* 328 F121; cf. J. Mansfeld *Mnemosyne* 33 (1980) 40–7.

[14] *IG* i³ 449.389–94 (ML 59.21–6); cf. C. Triebel-Schubert *Mitteilungen des Deutschen Archäologischen Instituts: Athenische Abteilung* 98 (1983) 101–12.

Philokhoros, though plausible, is not certain, and we cannot be sure
that the sale of gold and ivory in 434 means that the statue was
completed in that year. Thus we do not really know the date of the
prosecution of Pheidias, and the connection between it and the
outbreak of war cannot confidently be rejected on chronological
grounds.

But is that connection supposed to be a historical fact at all? This
is the other problem of the passage. Pheidias is not mentioned in
Dikaiopolis' account of the origins of the war in *Akharnians*: why
has Aristophanes inserted him into Hermes' account in *Peace*? This
explanation of the war is a new one. Trygaios and the chorus say
that they have never heard it before; that must mean that it was not
something which had been familiar to all Athenians for years. Some
scholars conclude that Aristophanes has just invented it.[15] That
seems improbable. Plutarch found it in the majority of his sources,
and it is not very likely that all of them were derived from this one
brief mention in *Peace*. Besides, Hermes does not explain his allusion
in any detail: Pheidias was 'in trouble', and Perikles was 'frightened
that he might share Pheidias' fate'. That is not enough to make the
point clear to an audience previously unacquainted with it. Again,
if it is just invented by Aristophanes, what is its purpose? Is it a
satirical attack on Pheidias and Perikles? Both had been dead for
years. Is it simply a joke? It does not seem particularly funny.

What we have to understand is that throughout the Peloponnesian
War, and perhaps especially in 421 when opinion was flowing strongly towards peace, there were many individuals who were opposed
to the war and tried to explain that it was due to misguided and
discreditable motives. No doubt they were constantly thinking of
different explanations. The war was due to Spartan jealousy of
Athens; to the dispute between Kerkyra and Corinth; to the Poteidaia affair; to the complaints by Aigina; to the encroachment of
Megara on sacred land; to disputes about runaway slaves; to the
Athenian decree against Megara; to Aspasia's influence over Perikles
... Now someone, we should assume, has suggested that Perikles
started the war to divert attention from his involvement in the
misdemeanours of Pheidias. This is a recent suggestion, which has
probably not yet reached the ears of country folk like Trygaios and
the chorus; but townsmen, who may well have formed the greater

---

[15] Cf. de Ste. Croix *Origins* 236, Sommerstein *Peace* 160 (on line 605).

part of the audience, have all heard about it, and will for that reason be interested to hear a god stating it as a fact.

If the connection of Pheidias, Perikles, and the outbreak of war was a recent talking-point in 421, that does not necessarily mean that it was true. Nor does it necessarily mean that Aristophanes himself believed it, although it is noticeable that Trygaios and the chorus do not express disbelief. Perhaps Aristophanes had not decided whether to believe it or not, but thought it anyway interesting enough to be included in his play. The Peloponnesian War had many contributory causes, and this could have been one of them. Indeed Hermes goes straight on to mention yet another which is not in Dikaiopolis' speech but is plausible enough: some leading Spartans were bribed by members of the Athenian Empire to make war on Athens.

HERMES. Then the cities in your Empire, when they realized that you
    Were enraged at one another and were giving bare-toothed snarls,
    Were afraid that you'd want tribute; so they made all kinds of schemes,
    And they bribed the most important of the Spartans to their side.
    Those men, being avaricious, also inhospitable,
    In a quite disgraceful manner turned out Peace and seized on War.
    Everything that brought them profit brought the farmers only harm:
    For the triremes sailed from here in order to retaliate,
    Eating up the fig-shoots that belonged to men who weren't to blame.
TRYGAIOS. On the contrary, it served them right: I had a black-fig tree
    Which I'd planted and I'd nurtured, and they came and chopped it
    down!
CHORUS. Yes, by Zeus, it served them right: I had a big six-bushel bin,
    And they came and threw a stone in it and broke it all to bits!

(*Peace* 619–31)

The sequence of events described by Hermes is complex but logical. The cities in the Empire (in practice this would mean a few leading men) were alarmed at the political disputes going on within Athens,[16] because they were afraid that these would lead to an increase in the amounts of tribute demanded from them. Why they thought this is not explained, but presumably it seemed that Perikles' rivals, if they succeeded in ousting him, would embark on

---

[16] Not, at this point, disputes between Athens and the Peloponnesians, because 'you' clearly means 'Athenians' in 619–21.

more expensive policies; or perhaps both Perikles and his rivals were proposing more public expenditure in bids to gain popular support.[17] But if Sparta defeated Athens and broke up the Empire, the cities would become independent and would be freed from the obligation to pay tribute. So they set about bribing some leading Spartans to make war. The Spartan leaders were happy to provoke war when bribed to do so, but this caused damage to their own farmers when the Athenians made retaliatory raids on their territory from the sea. Aristophanes naturally does not enter into details of the peculiar structure of Spartan society, but the farmers here are presumably *perioikoi*, Lakonian country folk of non-Spartan origin, as well as the farmers of other Peloponnesian cities; we know that the Athenians raided the territory of Epidauros, Troizen, Halieis, Hermione, and Prasiai in the second year of the war, at the same time as the Peloponnesian army was invading Attica.[18] Thus the mention by Hermes of Athenian raids on the Peloponnese prompts Trygaios to comment that Athenian farmers also suffered from Peloponnesian invasions, and by this skilful transition Aristophanes passes on to the situation of Athenian country folk after the war began.

HERMES. Here too, when the working people flocked in from the
          countryside,
     Just the same thing happened to them: they were sold, quite unawares.
     In the town they missed their grape-pips; they were longing for dried
          figs;
     So they looked to orators for help. The orators could see
     That the poor men were resourceless and in need of barley-groats;
     So they pitchforked out this goddess with their bawling and their
          shouts—
     Though she often reappeared, because she pined for Athens so.
     Then they shook up all the allies that they saw were fat and rich,
     Bringing forward accusations: 'That man sides with Brasidas!'
     You would then react like puppies, and you'd tear the man apart.
     For the city had grown pallid, and it just sat tight in fear;
     Any slander that was thrown it, it would gobble up with joy.
     Then the foreigners, on seeing how rich men were being hit,
     Went to those who struck the blows and tried to stop their mouths
          with gold.

[17] Cf. Sommerstein *Peace* 161 (on line 621).
[18] Thucydides 2.56.

So they made the politicians wealthy, while you failed to see
Greece would soon be desolated. And the man responsible
Was a leather-seller—

TRYGAIOS.   Stop, stop! O lord Hermes, say no more!
Let that man remain, I beg you, where he now is, down below!
We don't own him any longer; that man isn't ours, he's yours!
    Anything you say about him,
    Even if he was a villain
    When he lived, a glib accuser
    And a stirrer and disturber,
    All the names you call him now are
      Aimed at what belongs to you!

(*Peace* 632–56)

Here Hermes is no longer speaking of the origins of the war, but
of what happened when it was in progress. Country people took
refuge in the town of Athens but longed to return to their rural life,
as Dikaiopolis does at the beginning of *Akharnians*. They expected
the politicians to bring that about, but instead they were 'sold', just
like the Peloponnesian farmers. By this comparison Aristophanes is
trying to create a bond of sympathy between farmers on both sides,
being exploited by politicians on both sides, but the circumstances
were not really identical; 'sold' simply means that the politicians
sacrificed the farmers' interests to their own profits.[19] Now he is
not thinking of Perikles but of those who came to power in Athens
after Perikles' death, and the situation is the one already satirized
in *Horsemen* and *Wasps*. The politician wants the war to continue and
the farmers to be kept in town, where he can harangue them in the
Assembly and the courts. He threatens rich men from the allied
cities with prosecution, accusing them of supporting the Spartan
general Brasidas (perhaps truly in some cases, if they are the same
men from the allied cities who bribed Spartan leaders to make war);
if they come to trial, his influence over the juries secures their
conviction, but in many cases they bribe him to drop the prosecution. Thus he becomes rich. And the politician who does this
(mentioned as an individual in 647, no longer in the plural) is, of
course, Kleon.

So Hermes' account of the war, besides echoing Dikaiopolis'
concerns in *Akharnians*, comes in the end to be an attack on Kleon,

[19] Cf. Cassio *Commedia* 92–3.

recalling some of the same themes that were presented more fully in *Horsemen* and *Wasps*. The treatment of those themes is briefer here because Kleon is dead now. As Trygaios says, he belongs to Hermes (as conductor of the dead to the underworld), not to us. But even now Aristophanes cannot forget his loathing for Kleon personally and his conviction that most of the ills of Athens in the last few years were Kleon's fault. This is one of the most serious parts of *Peace*, and there is no reason to doubt that Aristophanes meant it to be believed. It is not a string of jokes; the tone is not humorous, but bitter.

The details differ considerably from Dikaiopolis' account of the origins of the war. That is partly because Hermes extends his account to include developments after the war had begun, but also because he includes the connection between Perikles and Pheidias and the allies' corruption of leading Spartans; on the other hand he omits the influence of Aspasia and says much less than Dikaiopolis about the disputes with Megara. That does not prove that either Dikaiopolis' or Hermes' account is untrue. As I have said (but it is worth repeating), the war had many contributory causes; which of them were the most significant was, and still is, a matter of opinion and judgement. Aristophanes could not give an exhaustive account in fifty lines; he had to make a selection, and if his selection in *Peace* differs from that in *Akharnians*, that means only that after four years of thought and discussion he had changed his estimation of the significance of some factors, while others had perhaps come to his attention for the first time.

ESTABLISHING PEACE

Peace, like War, is personified in early poetry,[20] but it is doubtful whether she was publicly recognized as a goddess in the time of Aristophanes. The only evidence that she was is a hesitant statement by Plutarch: 'they say' that the Athenians established an altar of Peace in celebration of the Peace of Kallias in the mid-fifth century,[21] but it is possible that Plutarch or his source has attributed the wrong date to the cult of Peace which was established in celebration of the

[20] e.g. Hesiod *Theogony* 902, *Works and Days* 228.
[21] Plutarch *Kimon* 13.5.

treaty made between Athens and Sparta in 374 BC. Nor is it certain that Peace had appeared on-stage in a play previously.[22] It may be that the visible representation of Peace in personal shape was an innovation by Aristophanes.

It is clear that Peace is represented on-stage by a statue, not by an actor. She speaks no audible words; the excuse is made that she will not speak to the spectators because she is angry at their treatment of her, and so she whispers questions to Hermes who repeats them aloud (658–705). Two other comic dramatists mocked Aristophanes' use of a statue of Peace,[23] which implies that this was a novelty. The statue is drawn into view at 519 and there is no indication in the text that it is ever removed. Presumably it remains on-stage for the rest of the play as a visible symbol that peace now prevails. Later Trygaios proceeds to establish Peace with a sacrificial ritual, and prays to her as a goddess (974–7). Of course the performance of such a ritual in a comedy was not equivalent to the inauguration of a new cult in real life, but Aristophanes may be implying that such a cult is desirable, foreshadowing its actual establishment forty-seven years later.

Peace is accompanied by two attendants, but they are characters of a very different kind.[24] They are attractive girls and are the subjects of sexual comments and jokes. Like similar non-speaking girls in other plays they are presumably played by male actors comically dressed to look like nude females.

One is named Opora. This word means the season of late summer when fruit is gathered, and also the ripe fruit itself. It is most often used of grapes or figs, and since Trygaios' name is also derived from a word used mainly in connection with grapes, that is clearly the kind of fruit which is most relevant here, and Opora is best translated into English as Vintage. During the war, as we know especially from *Akharnians*, one of the Athenian countrymen's main grievances was that their vines were cut down by the invading Spartans, so that they were short of grapes and wine. Hermes tells Trygaios ('Grape-harvester') to take Vintage as his wife; living with her in the country he will produce—bunches of grapes (706–8). In due course this

[22] A fragment of a lost play by Aeschylus (451n Radt) may contain a reference to Peace as a character on-stage, but the restoration is doubtful. Cf. C. Corbato in *Studi Triestini di Antichità in onore di L. A. Stella* (1975) 323–35.

[23] Eupolis 62, Platon 86.

[24] Cf. Newiger *Metapher* 108–11.

wedding forms the joyful concluding scene of the play.

The other girl is Theoria. This word means Sight-seeing or Festival-going, and is used especially of attending a festival at some distance from home. In wartime many festivals held in the Attic countryside had to be abandoned, and it was difficult or impossible for Athenians to travel to the great festivals held elsewhere, such as those at Olympia and Delphi.[25] This girl, beside her other qualities, smells of 'not doing military service' (526).[26] Hermes tells Trygaios to take her and deliver her to the Council, to whom she belonged before (713–14). This appears to mean that Councillors travelled at public expense to represent Athens at festivals elsewhere, a fact not otherwise clearly attested.[27] Trygaios does hand her over to the Council; the Councillors had front seats in the theatre, and this passage involves some comic by-play between Trygaios and the audience (871–908).

Vintage and Festival-going represent the pleasures of life in peacetime, whereas Peace herself is the supernatural being who makes those pleasures possible. She deserves respect and honour. Yet she is not welcomed by everyone; like other Aristophanic heroes, Trygaios in the second half of the play suffers from intruders who interfere with the fulfilment of his plan.

First comes Hierokles, an oracle-collector. Hierokles was a real person, satirized also in a comedy by Eupolis (fr. 231), where he is called 'lord of oracle-singers'. It seems right to identify him with a Hierokles mentioned in the well-known Athenian decree about Khalkis in Euboia, where he is in charge of making 'the sacrifices for Euboia in accordance with the oracles', and to date that decree in 446/5.[28] If so, that shows that twenty-four years before *Peace* he was already regarded as an authority on oracles. Now he is said to come from Oreos in Euboia (1047); that probably means that he was one of the Athenians who settled there in 446/5. From his inclusion in *Peace* we may reasonably infer that he had recently visited Athens and made a public speech quoting an oracle in support of

[25] Examples in 874 and 879 show that festivals both inside and outside Attica are relevant here.

[26] It is not necessary to emend the text to transfer this quality to Peace; cf. Rogers *Peace* 199, Sommerstein *Peace* 157 (on line 524).

[27] However, Demosthenes 19.128 refers to '*theoroi* from the Council' who normally attend the Pythia festival at Delphi.

[28] *IG* i³ 40 (ML 52) 64–6.

the opposition to making peace; for as soon as he appears in the play Trygaios knows that that will be his line (1048–9).

When he is seen approaching, Trygaios' slave asks 'Is it some seer?' and Trygaios replies 'No, it's Hierokles the oracle-collector' (1046–7). 'Oracle-collector' (*khresmologos*) has a different meaning from 'seer' (*mantis*), and is a more disparaging term. A seer was a person who, by inspiration or study, was good at interpreting divine signs provided by sacrifices and by other phenomena such as the flight of birds, dreams, eclipses, and thunderstorms. An oracle-collector collected prophecies which had been uttered by other people, either at established oracles such as Delphi and Dodona or by individual seers; he would then bring out and chant[29] those which seemed to be relevant to a particular occasion, and expect to be rewarded for doing so. Such collections might well be passed down from father to son; the name of Hierokles (meaning 'of sacred renown') was evidently bestowed by a father interested in divine matters, and it may be that Hierokles had inherited a collection of oracles.

Another oracle-collector appears in *Birds* 959–91. He reads his oracles out of a book, but Hierokles in *Peace* does not mention a book and seems to recite his oracles from memory. He attributes them to a seer named Bakis, who was inspired by the Nymphs (1070–1), and to Sibylla (1095). Both of these are also mentioned as sources of Kleon's oracles (*Horsemen* 61, 123, 1003). The name Sibylla was given to several female seers; the first may have been one who lived at Erythrai in Asia Minor in the sixth century. The original Bakis seems to have lived in Boiotia at the beginning of the fifth century, and Herodotos for one thought his prophecies trustworthy (8.77). The emphasis on Bakis in *Horsemen*, *Peace*, and *Birds* indicates that his prophecies were popular during the Peloponnesian War. Aristophanes clearly regards them as ridiculous, but his satirical attack does not mean necessarily that he considers all divination false. Rather, he is attacking frauds who produce spurious prophecies, and he thinks that most prophecies attributed to Bakis fall into that category.[30] The prophecies in *Peace*, like those in *Horsemen* and *Birds*, are parodies composed by Aristophanes of those attributed to Bakis, doubtless including some phrases quoted

[29] Oracle-collectors 'sang' oracles, e.g. Thucydides 2.8.2, 2.21.3.
[30] Cf. N. D. Smith *CA* 8 (1989) 140–58.

from them verbatim. Like many prophecies they are in hexameter verse. When Hierokles arrives to find Trygaios cooking a sacrificed sheep, he first tries to give unwanted advice about serving up the meat and then, on learning that the sacrifice is to Peace, breaks into hexameters forbidding peace-making.

HIEROKLES. 'Not yet indeed is it dear to the hearts of the blessed immortals
That ye should cease from the strife, till the wolf and the sheep shall be wedded.'

(*Peace* 1075–6)

Bakis, like other prophets, evidently has elaborate ways of saying 'never': the wolf weds the sheep, the crab walks straight (1083), the hedgehog is made smooth (1086). But Trygaios calls Hierokles a charlatan (*alazon*, 1069, 1120), a man who does not really possess the expertise which he claims:[31] he invents prophecies after the event (1085), cheats the Athenians (1087), and now wants to get a share of the meat and wine (1105). So Trygaios chases him away, after retorting in similar terms.

HIEROKLES. Will no one give me a share of the meat?
TRYGAIOS.   No, it isn't permitted
For us to give you a share, till the wolf and the sheep shall be wedded.

(*Peace* 1111–12)

The other intruders are craftsmen and dealers in manufactured goods. A maker of agricultural implements and a maker of wine-jars are delighted because peace has created a big demand for their products, but an arms-dealer, a helmet-maker, and a spear-maker are disgruntled because no one now wants to buy their goods. Is this the starting-point for some moralizing about how even the best policies do harm to someone? Not at all. Trygaios (and Aristophanes) shows no sympathy for the armourers, and mocks their products by suggesting new uses for them: a cuirass will make

---

[31] Trygaios' slave, on first catching sight of Hierokles, thinks he looks like a charlatan (cf. A. H. Sommerstein *CQ* 36 (1986) 361–2), but it is not clear what feature of his appearance gives that impression. On the meaning of *alazon* cf. MacDowell in *'Owls to Athens', Essays on Classical Subjects Presented to Sir Kenneth Dover* (ed. E. M. Craik, Oxford 1990) 287–92.

a good pot for crapping in (1224–39), a war-trumpet can be used as the target for a game of kottabos (1240–4), and so on. The audience is not encouraged to feel sorry for these men who have lost their livelihood. They ought to make their living in other ways.

THE JOYS OF PEACE

At the end the celebration of Trygaios' wedding to Vintage is in full swing. There is a brief scene in which two boys practise the songs which they are going to sing at the party; the joke here is that one boy, who knows only songs about war, turns out to be the son of Lamakhos, while the other is the son of Kleonymos and sings about throwing away his shield (cf. p. 23). Otherwise the last part of the play and also the second parabasis, which precedes the scene with the manufacturers, are taken up with dancing and singing about the pleasures of peace, contrasted with the hardships of war. The mood is much the same as at the end of *Akharnians*, but this time there is more emphasis on returning to the countryside and on extending the benefits of peace not just to all Athenians but to all Greeks.[32]

This is a celebration of the peace which Trygaios has brought about. It is not, as many scholars have supposed, a celebration of the Peace of Nikias.[33] I say this, not only because the Peace of Nikias had not yet been formally concluded when the play was performed, but because it would not make an Aristophanic comedy. It would be strange for Aristophanes to write a play in which the hero by great effort and fantastic means achieves merely something which everyone else has achieved already. On the contrary, the point must be that Trygaios accomplishes what has not been accomplished in real life.[34]

We should infer that when Aristophanes planned this play peace had not yet been attained. We do not know how long it took him to write a play. No doubt details could be added or altered right up

---

[32] Cf. Dover *Ar. Comedy* 137, Cassio *Commedia* 139–45.

[33] e.g. H.-J. Newiger *YCS* 26 (1980) 228: 'a celebration of the official conclusion of the peace treaty'.

[34] This point is rightly stressed by C. M. J. Sicking in Κωμῳδοτραγήματα, *studia Aristophanea viri Aristophanei W. J. W. Koster in honorem* (Amsterdam 1967) 115–24. However, this does not necessarily mean that, as Sicking suggests, the Peace of Nikias, when made, was not expected to bring lasting peace.

to the day of performance, but the main theme at least probably had to be settled at the time when he applied to the Arkhon to 'ask for a chorus'; it is not known at what time of year that was done, but surely it must have been at least a couple of months before the festival.[35] Whenever it was, Athens was still at war and Aristophanes did not foresee that a treaty would be concluded, or almost concluded, by the time his play was performed. So he planned a play in which the hero has a fantastic scheme for seeking peace, a play stressing the need for universal co-operation, ridiculing opponents of peace, and picturing the pastoral utopia to which peace might lead. When it turned out that by the time of the Dionysia a peace treaty was imminent, so that the play was almost out of date before it was performed, it was too late for him to substitute a different play.

Akharnians and *Peace* are more alike in theme than any other two extant plays of Aristophanes. In both an old countryman wants to end the war in order to return to the countryside, he successfully carries out an impossible plan for doing so, and in the end he achieves pleasures of eating, drinking, and sex. In both there is an important speech about the causes of the war, attributing it to a series of petty motives; satire is directed against individuals who oppose peace, especially Lamakhos and Hierokles, not against those who favour it, such as Nikias. Thus Aristophanes in both plays, besides entertaining the audience, is encouraging the Athenians to think that the reasons for continuing the war are weak, and the advantages to be gained by making peace are far greater. If it is right to regard *Peace* as the weaker of the two, 'perhaps rather a tame drama',[36] that is mainly because Trygaios faces less opposition than Dikaiopolis: the chorus is on his side from its first appearance, and Hierokles is not as powerful a figure as Lamakhos. But that is a reflection of the historical facts: there was indeed less opposition to making peace in 421 than there had been in 425.

---

[35] If authors were selected at the same time as chorus-producers, and if Aristotle *Ath. Pol.* 56.3 means by 'then' that chorus-producers were appointed immediately after the Arkhon entered office, that would be more than eight months before the Dionysia.

[36] Murray *Aristophanes* 57. On the other hand Moulton *Ar. Poetry* 107 considers that the presentation of festivity in lyrical modes gives the play 'irresistible charm'.

9

Birds

TWO FUGITIVES

Two men are wandering along in some remote spot. Most of Aristophanes' plays are set in Athens (or at least begin there), but *Birds* is in a far-off rocky place, and the travellers seem to be lost.

EUELPIDES. I don't know where on earth we've got to now.
PEISETAIROS. Could you find where your country is from here?
EUELPIDES. From here, no; nor could Exekestides!

(*Birds* 9–11)

Exekestides was apparently a man who had recently shown great ingenuity in getting himself recognized as an Athenian citizen; so these lines use a topical joke to make clear to the audience that the two speakers are Athenians who are a very long way from Athens.[1] Then a similar joke about another would-be citizen, named Akestor and nicknamed Sakas, leads into an explanation of why they have left home, given straight to the theatre audience.

You see, you men who've come to listen here,
We have the opposite disease to Sakas:
He's not a citizen, but pushes in,
While we're of honourable descent and clan
Among our fellow-citizens, we've not
Been shooed away, but flown out on both—feet.
It's not that we don't like our native city;
We don't deny it's great and prosperous,
Open to everyone—for paying fines.
Cicadas sing just for a month or two
Upon the branches, but Athenians
Sing on their lawcourt trials all their lives!

[1] On Exekestides and Akestor see MacDowell in *Tr.Com.Pol.* 364–7.

And that's the thing that's made us walk this walk,
Carrying basket, pot, and myrtle wreaths:[2]
We're wandering round to find a carefree place
Where we can settle down and spend our time.

(*Birds* 30–45)

So they are hoping to find a place where they will live more happily than in Athens. They want somewhere that is 'carefree'; the Greek word here implies particularly freedom from political and legal business,[3] and the references to trials and paying fines make clear that the long arm of the law is what they want to evade. Much the same is implied a little later, when they explain themselves to Tereus.

TEREUS. Where were you born?
PEISETAIROS.   Where the fine triremes come from!
TEREUS. Not jurors?
PEISETAIROS.   Oh no, just the other way;
    We're anti-jurors.
TEREUS.   Is that seed sown there?
PEISETAIROS. You'll find a little in the countryside.
TEREUS. And what's the business that you've come here for?
PEISETAIROS. We wanted to consult you.
TEREUS.   What about?
PEISETAIROS. Because you were a human once, like us,
    And you owed people money once, like us,
    And you preferred not paying once, like us.

(*Birds* 108–16)

Tereus knows at once that the city with the best triremes in its navy is Athens, but he also knows that in Athens there are a lot of jurors. (The audience is expected to laugh at the incongruous connection of ideas.) The two men, however, so far from being jurors themselves, want to avoid juries. Rather than Athenian townsmen, they are normal human beings: they get into debt, and like to avoid paying what they owe. (Again the audience laughs at the

---

[2] The basket, pot, and myrtles are probably for an inaugural religious ceremony, or possibly just for a symposium. Cf. R. Hamilton *GRBS* 26 (1985) 235–9, Bowie *Aristophanes* 152.

[3] ἀπράγμων: for full discussion of this term see L. B. Carter *The Quiet Athenian* (Oxford 1986).

sequence of thought.) It has been maintained that they 'are utterly sick of Athens, sick of the high prices, the burden of debt, the everlasting informers, the ferocious law-courts, and the whole cloud of anxiety'.[4] But that is too broad a description. Their concern is more specific. They are afraid of being prosecuted for debt or for minor offences, and they want to avoid paying up. Their motive is much the same as the motive of Strepsiades in *Clouds*. But it is differently treated. Whereas Strepsiades explains at some length how he got into debt, in *Birds* we hear no details of the two men's problems. This helps the individual spectator to identify himself with them; no one in the audience would think Strepsiades was just like himself, but many could assume that the more vaguely indicated problems of the two men in *Birds* were like their own, and so would sympathize with them and share their desire for a carefree place to live.

The two men give their names in 644–5. Both names are evidently invented by Aristophanes. One is Euelpides, an optimistic name: 'Hopefulson'. The other is given in the manuscripts as Peisthetairos, but scholars have objected that Peisth- is an ungrammatical form. Possibly it should be corrected to Pisthetairos, 'Trusty comrade'; more probably it should be Peithetairos or Peisetairos, 'Persuading comrades', and since Peis- is more usual than Peith- in Athenian names (such as Peisistratos and Peisandros) I follow most recent scholars in adopting that form here.

At first the two men are not clearly differentiated, and there are difficulties about the assignment of speeches to one or the other. (It is generally agreed that Aristophanes himself seldom or never wrote the name of the speaker at the beginning of each speech; attributions that we find in the medieval manuscripts are conjectured by later scribes and commentators, and we may be able to correct them by reference to the text itself.[5]) It is Peisetairos, not Euelpides, who becomes the leader of the new city and remains on-stage in the second half of the play; and from this fact (and from the form of his name, if we have got it right) it may be inferred that he takes the lead in the first half too, so that new ideas and proposals should be attributed to him, whereas comic or vulgar comments may be assigned to Euelpides. Marzullo has assigned the lines on this basis;[6]

[4] Murray *Aristophanes* 143.
[5] Cf. J. C. B. Lowe *BICS* 9 (1962) 27–42, Russo *Aristophanes* 37–43.
[6] B. Marzullo *Philologus* 114 (1970) 181–94.

subsequent editors have accepted his assignments with only minor variations, and they are likely to be generally correct, although doubt remains about many individual lines.

TEREUS

The two fugitives from Athens are not wandering at random in their search for a new home. They are looking for Tereus the hoopoe, who should be able to advise them, and are supposedly being guided by two other birds, a jackdaw and a crow, to the place where he lives. (In the original performance these two birds, unlike the others in the play, may have been real birds, allowed to fly away at line 61.)

The story of Tereus must have been familiar to many in Aristophanes' audience. It is one of the more horrific Greek myths. King Pandion of Athens had two daughters, Prokne and Philomela, and gave Prokne in marriage to King Tereus of Thrace. Prokne was lonely without her sister, and so Tereus went to fetch Philomela to stay with her. On the journey north from Athens he became enamoured with Philomela and raped her; then, to prevent her revealing this to Prokne, he cut out her tongue, but she succeeded in conveying the facts to her sister by embroidering them on a cloth (in a picture or, anachronistically, in letters). To take revenge on Tereus, Prokne killed their son Itys, cooked his flesh, and served it to Tereus for dinner, but when Tereus discovered what he had eaten he gave chase to the two sisters, who fled. Zeus then transformed them all into birds: Prokne became the nightingale, Philomela the swallow,[7] and Tereus the hoopoe. The myth is an explanation of the cries of these birds: the nightingale mourns her son (Greek *Itu Itu*), the swallow exclaims at her oppressor (*Tereu*), and the hoopoe searches for them (*pou pou*, meaning 'Where? Where?').

This myth had been brought to the attention of the Athenian audience by two tragedies now lost, the first by Sophocles and the second by Philokles, both entitled *Tereus* and both presumably fairly

---

[7] The transposition of these two, making Philomela the nightingale and Prokne the swallow, is found only in later versions of the myth, including Ovid's *Metamorphoses*.

recent, though their exact dates are not known.[8] So Aristophanes uses it in his play by making Tereus, now transformed into a hoopoe, the leader of the birds. The comic logic is that, having been a human being, Tereus knows what human beings want; being now a bird, he has flown around everywhere and seen all parts of the world. Thus he is uniquely qualified to identify the best place for men to live.

PEISETAIROS. And then you were transformed into a bird
   And flew around all over land and sea;
   You know what men know, and what birds know too.
   That's why we've come to you, as suppliants,
   To see if you can tell us of some city
   Soft as a woollen fleece to lie down in.

(*Birds* 117–22)

This explanation is not given fully until after Tereus has already appeared. But there is a hint of it earlier (46–8), and before his appearance it is made clear that he combines human and avian features. First Peisetairos knocks at the rock, as if it were the door of a house in Athens. (This is the play's door-knocking scene; cf. p. 18.) A servant answers; he is a bird, but played by an actor, and therefore man-sized.

PEISETAIROS. My god, what kind of animal are you?
SERVANT. A slave bird.
PEISETAIROS.   Were you beaten in a cock-fight?
SERVANT. No; when my master turned into a hoopoe,
   He prayed that I should turn into a bird,
   So as to have a servant to attend him.
PEISETAIROS. What, does a bird require a servant too?
SERVANT. *He* does, because he used to be a man.
   Sometimes he longs to eat Phaleric sprats:
   I take the bowl and buzz off for some sprats.
   He wants pea-soup; tureen and spoon are needed:
   I buzz off for a spoon.

---

[8] For recent discussion of Sophocles' *Tereus* see A. Kiso *The Lost Sophocles* (New York 1984) 57–84. For Philokles' *Tereus* see *Birds* 281–2 with scholia. Bowie *Aristophanes* 167 suggests a reference to cult, but in fact there is virtually no evidence for an Athenian cult involving Tereus, and *Birds* 100–1 and 281–2 show that Aristophanes expects the audience to think rather of the tragedies.

PEISETAIROS.   This bird's a buzzard![9]
  Here, buzzard—know what? Call your master for us.
SERVANT. But I assure you he's asleep just now,
  After a meal of myrtle-berries and gnats.
PEISETAIROS. Still, wake him up!

(Birds 69–83)

The hoopoe has a mixed diet. He eats myrtle-berries and gnats,
as other birds do. But he also eats sprats from Phaeron, like any
urban Athenian, and soup, for which he needs a spoon; and he has
a servant to run and fetch them for him. Thus he is still partly
human. One wonders what he looked like in the original performance. There are some clues in 93–106: a triple crest is mentioned, and a funny-looking beak, but his feathers have moulted.

  I, Tereus, am disfigured in this way
  By Sophocles, when I'm in tragedies.

(Birds 100–1)

The basis of this joke must be that in Sophocles' play the costume
of Tereus, when transformed into a hoopoe, was rather unconvincing, with a strange beak and no feathers; and now, some years
later, Aristophanes reproduces the same costume.[10] There seems to
be no resemblance in the characterization, however. Sophocles'
Tereus must have been tyrannical. Aristophanes' Tereus, as the play
proceeds, turns out to be genial and conciliatory. In fact, once the
character has been introduced, Aristophanes makes no further use
of the original myth, except in one respect: the piper who as usual
accompanies the songs is regarded as being Tereus' wife Prokne,
the nightingale, who still laments their son Itys (212). She too
is evidently half-human, and there is some comic business when

---

  [9] In translating I have changed the species of bird ($\tau\rho o\chi\iota\lambda o\varsigma$, probably meaning
a plover) in order to preserve the pun.
  [10] There is no evidence that Tereus did not appear as a hoopoe at the end of
Sophocles' play, and *Birds* 100–1 implies that he did. Probably Sophocles gave the
actor only a special mask or head-dress to symbolize the transformation, not a
bird-costume for his whole body; that would explain the Aristophanic complaint
that there were no feathers.

Euelpides tries to kiss her (671–4);[11] but there is nothing to suggest any lack of conjugal affection between her and Tereus. Nor can any line of *Birds* be identified as a quotation or parody of a line of *Tereus*. Aristophanes does not use *Tereus* here, as he had used *Telephos* in *Akharnians*, to illuminate the theme of his own play, and he does not require his audience to remember anything of it but the transformation of Tereus and Prokne into a hoopoe and a nightingale.[12]

THE BIRDS

Tereus' suggestions about where they might live do not appeal to Peisetairos and Euelpides. But then Peisetairos has a brilliant idea, that the Birds should establish a new city in the sky, between heaven and earth, where they will be able to control communication between gods and men and so rule over both. The plan is fantastic and impossible; but in Aristophanic comedy impossible things are frequently done, and all the rest of the play is devoted to carrying out Peisetairos' scheme.

First, though, the Birds have to be persuaded to adopt it. Tereus and Prokne sing (that is, the actor playing Tereus sings with pipe accompaniment) to call them together. This song probably had unusual music. We have only the words, but even from them we can see how various bird-cries such as *tio tio tio* and *kikkabau kikkabau* are incorporated, and different metres are used to summon different classes of bird: marsh-birds, sea-birds, and so on.[13] Soon they begin to arrive: first four individuals, and then a whole lot in a rush. Twenty-four species are named (297–304), and since a comedy had twenty-four choristers we can guess that each chorister was dressed

[11] F. E. Romer *TAPA* 113 (1983) 135–42 convincingly argues that the nightingale's 'beak' is actually the double pipe, which gets in the way of a kiss. If that is correct, we should assume (*pace* Romer) that the piper himself appeared here as the nightingale in a comic female costume, and did not merely play an accompaniment from off-stage. Cf. O. Taplin *Comic Angels* (Oxford 1993) 106–7.

[12] Possible connections between *Tereus* and *Birds* have been much discussed, but those suggested are generally unconvincing. See especially Hofmann *Mythos* 72–8, Zannini Quirini *Nephelokokkygia* 39–44, G. Dobrov *AJP* 114 (1993) 189–234.

[13] For metrical analysis see Zimmermann *Untersuchungen* 1.74–82.

as a different bird, forming an exceptionally colourful and spectacular chorus.

At first the Birds are hostile to Peisetairos and Euelpides, and threaten to attack them. If this hostility surprises us, that is because of our peculiar attitude to birds. In Britain in the twentieth century there has been an unprecedented surge of affection for 'our feathered friends', and birds enjoy the protection of a Royal Society which is one of our most popular charities. But this sympathy for birds did not exist in the past, and indeed does not exist today in many parts of the world. In ancient Greece birds were considered primarily as a source of food. So it is quite natural that the Servant-bird, on seeing two men, immediately jumps to the conclusion that they are bird-catchers (62); and the Birds of the chorus, on discovering that Tereus has admitted two men, are appalled that he has betrayed them to the enemy (327–35).

The two speeches in which Peisetairos wins over the Birds (462–538, 550–626) have the formal structure of an agon, although there is no individual opponent and Peisetairos delivers both speeches. In the first he uses comic logic to argue that birds are older than gods and were once kings over gods and everything else. The farmyard cock, for example, ruled Persia; that is why he is called 'the Persian bird' and wears a tiara on his head, and even now, when he crows in the morning, everyone obediently jumps out of bed and goes to work. Similar comic arguments 'prove' that the kite ruled Greece and the cuckoo Phoenicia, while human rulers and gods were under the surveillance of birds. That was in the old days; now the Birds have lost their former power, and in the second speech Peisetairos expounds his plan for getting it back. They must first construct walls around their territory, namely the air, to make it a fortified city. They must then demand that Zeus restore the kingship to them; if he refuses, the Birds will prevent gods from travelling through the air from heaven to earth to conduct love affairs with women in their customary manner. As for human beings, they will be required to give the Birds priority over gods when sacrificing; if they disobey, the Birds will eat up the seeds on their farms, but if they obey, the Birds will gobble up the insect pests and give them good signs. (Soothsayers predicted the future from observing the flight of birds.)

The Birds are delighted with the plan, and make Peisetairos their leader to carry it out. The individual characters then go off-stage, making way for the chorus to perform the parabasis; but the parabasis in this play, unlike earlier plays, does not digress into other topics, but makes further points about birds rather similar to those already made by Peisetairos. First comes a grandiose account of the origins of the universe, making birds out to be older than gods.

> There was Space, there was Night, there was Erebos black, and broad Tartaros,[14] in the beginning,
> But no Earth and no Air and no Heaven. And then, within Erebos' infinite bosom,
> The first birth that occurred was when black-winged Night brought forth an unfertilized wind-egg,
> Out of which, as the seasons came round in their turn, Love the ever-desirable sprouted
> With a glitter of gold from the wings on his back and resembling the wind's rapid eddies.
> And then Love was conjoined with winged Space down below in broad Tartaros, hidden in darkness,
> And so hatched out our race, and in this way we Birds were the first race brought up to the daylight.
> The race of immortals did not yet exist, until Love mated all things together.
> But when one mating after another occurred, Heaven came into being, and Ocean,
> And Earth, and then all the unperishing race of the blessed gods. Thus we are clearly
> Far older than all of those blessed ones are.

> (*Birds* 693–703)

Aristophanes is making fun of myths about the origin of the universe. The one which was probably the most widely known in his time was that recounted in Hesiod's *Theogony* 116–36. According to Hesiod the first thing to exist was Space (*khaos*); then came Earth, Tartaros, and Love; from Space were born Erebos and Night, and from Erebos and Night were born Sky (*aither*) and Day; Earth produced Heaven and Mountains and Sea (*pontos*), and then Earth and Heaven produced Ocean and the Titans. Aristophanes' comic cosmogony is similar to this, and his minor changes in the sequence of creation (putting Earth later, for example) are generally of no significance, but the comic point is that he has inserted the Birds in

---

[14] Erebos and Tartaros are two areas of underworld darkness, not very clearly distinguished from each other.

the middle of it, and has made some of the other entities birdlike
by giving them wings (Night, Love, and most ridiculously Space)
and making one of them lay an egg. The notion that some supernatural beings are winged is familiar, and Aristophanes naturally
makes the most of it here. The egg may at first sight seem to be his
own comic invention. However, an egg appeared in two other Greek
cosmogonies, in poems which are now lost and cannot be dated
with confidence but were probably composed before Aristophanes'
time. In one, attributed to Epimenides (fr. 5), two Titans mated
and produced an egg, from which other beings came forth. In the
other, attributed to Orpheus, the creation of other things was due
to Time, which fashioned a silvery egg in or from Sky; this probably
means not that Time or Sky laid an egg but rather that the whole
cosmos was at first oval, and is a notion of oriental origin.[15] Evidently
these myths struck Aristophanes as ludicrous, and he seized on
the egg as a suitable motif for inclusion in the comic cosmogony
propounded by the Birds.

The style becomes less high-flown as the chorus goes on to list
ways in which the Birds assist men. Birds, being children of Love,
help lovers to win over their loved ones—by giving them birds as
presents. The migrations of the Birds mark the changes of the
seasons, showing when to plough, when to shear the sheep—and
when a thief will need a warm cloak to wear as he goes out to steal
a cloak. Birds are also used for prophecy and divination. This passage
may also be regarded as a comic variation on themes of Hesiod, but
based this time on *Works and Days*; for that poem too refers to the
departure of the crane and the arrival of the swallow as signals to
perform the tasks of autumn and of spring, and at the end of it there
was once a passage, now lost, about divination by birds.[16] The whole
anapaestic part of the parabasis leads to the conclusion that, if men
honour the Birds as gods, the Birds will bring them health, wealth,
happiness and success of every kind, and of course the proverbial
ultimate Greek luxury—birds' milk! The second half of the parabasis includes jokes in a broader comic style about the advantages
of being a bird, with some cracks about individual Athenians who

---

[15] *Orphica* 54, 57, 60, 70 Kern, Plutarch *Ethika* 636d; cf. M. L. West *The Orphic Poems* (Oxford 1983) 103–4, 111–12, 198–202.

[16] Hesiod *Works and Days* 448–52, 568–70, and the scholium on 828; cf. M. L. West's commentary (Oxford 1978) on 828.

would be better off as birds, and also the passage about flying away from the theatre (see p. 10).

CLOUDCUCKOOLAND

After the parabasis Peisetairos and Euelpides reappear with wings. They have now become birds, and are ready to begin establishing the new city. First a name is selected for it. The chorus acclaims Peisetairos' suggestion *Nephelokokkygia*, a marvellous compound of the words for 'cloud' and 'cuckoo', thus combining sky, birds, and vapidity. It is traditionally translated into English as Cloud-cuckooland, although '-land' is a misleading termination, for the new foundation is not an area of countryside but an independent fortified city.[17] They select the farmyard cock to be the city's patron god, because of his pugnacity; and then Peisetairos sends Euelpides off to assist with the building of the walls, and to dispatch one herald to the gods above and another to human beings below. Euelpides now leaves the scene and never reappears. Thus Peisetairos alone is henceforth the organizer and leader of the Birds, and the actor who was playing Euelpides becomes free to take other roles.

There are certainly plenty of roles for him to take. *Birds* has more characters than any other play of Aristophanes, and many of them are what the modern cinema calls cameo roles, characters who make their mark in a single appearance lasting only a few minutes. They include a number of men who arrive from Athens wanting to participate in the affairs of the new city, each according to his own bent. The effect is that of a cavalcade of typical Athenian characters, satirically presented.

First, a Priest. Peisetairos brings him on to conduct a religious ceremony inaugurating the new city. He begins delivering a lengthy prayer, appropriately invoking birds instead of gods, but he invokes so many that Peisetairos interrupts and sends him away, for fear that the puny goat to be sacrificed will not be enough to feed them all.

[17] Cf. Sommerstein *Birds* 1 n. 2: ' "Cloudcuckooland" is perhaps the only Aristophanic expression which has become part and parcel of modern English, without the vast majority of its users being in the least aware of its origin.' Sommerstein prefers 'Cloudcuckooville', but '-ville' suggests a provincial town rather than a city-state.

The joke here is the parody of long-winded prayers to numerous gods, and it may have been enhanced in the performance by imitation of priestly mannerisms or a 'churchy' tone of voice.

Second, a Poet. He claims to have written many beautiful songs in honour of Cloudcuckooland, and wants to be rewarded for them. He sings snatches of several; they are a farrago of high-flown lyric phrases, including some from Pindar, sounding absurd out of context. None of them refers to Cloudcuckooland, and since Peisetairos has not yet even completed the ceremony of inauguration it is obvious that the Poet has not really had time to write songs especially for it but has just brought out some material from his stock. Peisetairos gives him a present to get rid of him. Evidently there were in fact poets in Athens at this time who offered for sale songs for special events, like Pindar's odes at an earlier date, and Aristophanes is mocking them here.

Third, an Oracle-collector. He claims to have an oracle of Bakis referring to Cloudcuckooland, and quotes some of it; an important part is to the effect that the first man to reveal this oracle must be given sundry gifts. Peisetairos produces another oracle, that any intruding charlatan must be beaten; and he immediately carries out this instruction. This passage bears a strong resemblance to *Peace* 1043–1126 (see pp. 194–6). Probably the scene in *Peace* was a success and Aristophanes decided to use the same joke again.

The fourth of these characters, on the other hand, is a new one, and the only one of them who is a real named individual, not just a type. He is Meton the mathematician. In later times Meton was remembered as the man who devised an improved calendar, bringing the lunar months into a correct relationship with the solar year in a nineteen-year cycle (although the Athenians did not adopt it). But that is not mentioned in *Birds*. Here he appears as a town-planner, offering to design a street-plan in the air for Cloudcuckooland. He reels off a pseudo-scientific rigmarole, beginning with the statement that the air is like a baking-cover (cf. p. 120), and proceeding to draw a diagram with a curved ruler and a straight ruler 'so that the circle may become square' (1004–5), and straight streets lead to an agora in the middle like the rays of a star. Ingenious modern scholars have made sense of this, more or less, and reconstructed the diagram.[18] This is misguided. Even if Meton did draw a diagram in

---

[18] Cf. R. E. Wycherley *CQ* 31 (1937) 22–31, Sommerstein *Birds* 266.

the dust on the ground, most of the audience was too far away to see its details. Aristophanes has strung together a number of phrases which the real Meton may well have used, but which would have sounded absurd to ordinary people, notably 'the circle may become square'. Peisetairos does not understand them (1003), and the Athenian spectator is here expected to identify himself with Peisetairos, who chases Meton away as another charlatan. We may infer, though there is no other evidence, that not long before 414 the real Meton had produced a town-planning scheme which many Athenians regarded as unintelligible rubbish.[19]

Fifth, an Inspector (*episkopos*). There is not much other evidence about this type of official, but evidently inspectors were sent from Athens to supervise affairs in the cities of the Empire.[20] They did not reside in those cities permanently; the Inspector in our scene has been appointed by lot and sent out in accordance with a recent decree (1022–5), and indeed is annoyed at being made to come, because he is a politician and would rather be at a meeting of the Assembly back in Athens. He has brought a pair of voting-urns (1032, 1053), which probably means that he has come to establish lawcourts on the Athenian model. The joke is that Cloud-cuckooland, which has barely been founded yet, is already being treated as part of the Athenian Empire and compelled to adopt Athenian institutions—including the very courts which Peisetairos and Euelpides left Athens in order to get away from.

The same thing is implied by the next intrusion. This sixth character is a Decree-seller. Like the Oracle-collector, he hopes to sell to Peisetairos copies of documents referring to Cloud-cuckooland, but in this case the documents are Athenian laws and decrees. Athenian laws and decrees were inscribed on stone and set up in a public place for all to read, but anyone wishing to have the text for reference had either to copy it from the stone himself or buy a copy made by someone else. In *Birds* the Decree-seller has made such copies and is offering them for sale.[21] But when he

---

[19] But there is an alternative possibility, suggested by B. Zimmermann in *Ar. Hardt* 274: just as in *Clouds* Aristophanes uses Socrates as 'the sophist' and assigns to him various activities and beliefs not held by the real Socrates, in *Birds* he may be using Meton as 'the mathematician' and assigning to him a type of scheme which really emanated from some other mathematician.

[20] Cf. R. Meiggs *The Athenian Empire* (Oxford 1972) 212–13, 583–6.

[21] They are copies of laws and decrees already passed, not drafts for Cloud-

reads out some samples, they turn out to be very unfavourable to Cloudcuckooland. One lays down penalties for any Cloud-cuckoolander who wrongs an Athenian (but not, presumably, vice versa). Another orders the Cloudcuckoolanders to use Athenian weights and measures—and decrees. A third lays down penalties for expelling Athenian officials. So again it appears that the Athenians are already treating Cloudcuckooland as a city under their control.[22]

Pcisctairos chases away both the Inspector and the Decree-seller in a nice variation of the usual hitting scene: they come from opposite directions, and each time he beats away one of them to one side the other reappears behind him. The spectators will enjoy this slapstick, identifying themselves with Peisetairos.[23] Does this mean that they identify themselves with a city in the Empire downtrodden by the imperialist power? Surely not. The Athenians generally thought it right and proper that they should rule over others. If Aristophanes had wanted them to change their minds about that, the opposite point of view would have needed much fuller and more tactful presentation (comparable to Dikaiopolis' plea for peace in *Akharnians*). No, the point is rather that, whereas it is reasonable that other peoples like the Olophyxians (1042) should be kept under control, Peisetairos and Cloudcuckooland are quite different. They are independent and free. They are not to be bothered by these tiresome officials and profiteers. The six characters introduced in this part of the play (862–1057) are not merely a random collection of Athenian types; they are men who try to exploit others for their own advantage. That is why Peisetairos wants to be rid of them.

THE DESIRE FOR WINGS

Once Cloudcuckooland is established, many men wish to join it. A herald reports to Peisetairos that people on earth are already imit-ating birds, and thousands will soon be arriving here wanting wings. Peisetairos hastens to get a supply of wings ready, and immediately

cuckooland to consider passing. Sommerstein *Birds* 269 (on lines 1035–6) mis-leads slightly when he writes of Cloudcuckooland's 'own versions'.

[22] For parallels in real Athenian laws about cities in the Empire see Meiggs *The Athenian Empire* 586–7.

[23] Cf. MacDowell *Themes in Drama* 10 (1988) 7–8.

some would-be immigrants appear. The first arrival is a Young Man.

YOUNG MAN. I'm bird-mad, and I'm flying, and I want
　To live with you! I'm longing for your laws!
PEISETAIROS. Which laws are those? The birds have many laws.
YOUNG MAN. All; specially the law of birds that says
　It's good to throttle and to peck one's father!

(*Birds* 1344–8)

He is a rebellious youth who wants to beat up and murder his father, a proverbially wicked crime (cf. p. 126), and he has heard that young cocks fight their fathers and oust them from control. But this is not the kind of immigrant Peisetairos wants. Indeed one might have expected him simply to drive the Young Man away with a thrashing, as he has already driven away other intruders. But instead he gives some advice. First he says that there is also a different law among the birds: storks feed their fathers in old age. This damps the Young Man's keenness to be a bird. Peisetairos then proceeds to arm him.

PEISETAIROS. No, since you've come to wish us well, my friend,
　I'll give you wings, just like an orphan bird,
　And good advice, young man, 'such as I learned
　When I was a boy'.[24] Don't beat your father up.
　Take this wing; in the other hand, this spur;
　Imagine this is a cock's crest that you have;
　Serve in a garrison; go on a campaign;
　Support yourself by earning service pay,
　And let your father live. You are a fighter;
　So fly off to the Thracian coast, fight there!
YOUNG MAN. By Dionysos, your advice seems good.
　I'll take it.
PEISETAIROS. You'll be sensible, by Zeus!

(*Birds* 1360–71)

The reason for mentioning an orphan is that every year at the town Dionysia (the festival at which *Birds* was performed) the young sons of Athenians killed in war, who had been brought up at the city's expense and had just reached adulthood, were given a full set of armour and paraded in the theatre wearing it before the

---

[24] The quotation is adapted from Theognis 27–8.

performance of the tragedies.[25] In our scene, when the Young Man wants to imitate a pugnacious cock, Peisetairos gives him weapons under the names of parts of a cock. When he says 'Take this wing' and 'this spur', he gives him a shield and a spear, and the 'cock's crest' (which in English we call the comb) is a helmet with a crest.[26] Thus the Young Man now has the essential equipment of a hoplite and is ready to go off to war as a volunteer.[27] Peisetairos has found an ingenious way to get rid of him.[28]

The next arrival is (like Meton) a real person, Kinesias. Later in life Kinesias was a politician, but there is nothing in *Birds* about his political activity, which perhaps had not yet begun. Here he is simply a dithyrambic poet, rather like the Poet who appears earlier. He sings snatches of songs about flying, wings, birds, air, and wind, and wants to become a bird, but it is likely that the main comic point here is musical. Kinesias was an avant-garde composer, and another comic dramatist, Pherekrates, made Music, as a character, criticize him on this account.[29] So probably that is Aristophanes' target too: he makes his character Kinesias sing in a manner which somehow mocks or parodies the music of the real Kinesias, and the joke is lost to us because we do not have the music. It is also hard to make out from the text how Peisetairos responds to Kinesias' request for wings. Kinesias first expresses pleasure (1401) and then is suddenly indignant (1403), and it seems that Peisetairos brings him a pair of wings but then, instead of attaching them to his shoulders, uses them to beat him and chase him away.[30]

After him comes a Sycophant. We have already met in *Akharnians* sycophants who make profits for themselves by accusing traders of offences in Athens. This Sycophant likewise makes money by

[25] Aiskhines 3.154.

[26] The words 'in the other hand' show that the Young Man is not being given an actual wing and spur (which would go on the shoulder and heel), and 'imagine' shows that he does not get an actual cock's crest.

[27] He is evidently below the age at which men became liable to compulsory military service. Cf. H. D. Westlake *CR* 4 (1954) 90–4.

[28] Sommerstein *Birds* 288–9 (on lines 1360–1) discusses why Peisetairos 'would agree to give the young man wings', but his difficulty seems to arise from a misunderstanding. Peisetairos does not give the Young Man wings and does not admit him to Cloudcuckooland.

[29] Pherekrates 155.8–13. Cf. B. Zimmermann *Giornale Filologico Ferrarese* 12 (1989) 8–9.

[30] Cf. Zanetto *Uccelli* 292–3 (on lines 1401–2).

prosecuting, but he has a different sphere of operation: he prosecutes citizens of cities in the Empire overseas. For some types of case, when an Athenian prosecuted a citizen of a subject-ally, the trial was held in Athens.[31] Peisetairos regards this as a poor way for an able-bodied man to make a living (1430–5), but the Sycophant insists that sycophancy is a tradition in his family, and he will be able to carry it on much better if he has wings.

SYCOPHANT.   I won't disgrace my ancestry.
  I'm a hereditary sycophant.
  So fit me out with swift, light wings, a hawk's
  Or kestrel's, so that I can serve a summons
  On foreigners, then prosecute them here,
  Then fly back there again.
PEISETAIROS.   I understand.
  You mean the foreigner will lose his case
  Before he gets here.
SYCOPHANT.   Yes, you understand.
PEISETAIROS. Then, while he's sailing here, you fly back there
  To seize his property.
SYCOPHANT.   You've got the point.
  I need to spin round like a top.
PEISETAIROS.   A top!
  I understand. In fact I've just the thing,
  By Zeus: some splendid Kerkyraian—wings!
SYCOPHANT. Oh help, you've got a whip!
PEISETAIROS.   No, these are wings
    With which I'm going to make you spin today!

                          (*Birds* 1451–65)

A Kerkyraian whip was a large ivory-handled whip with a double thong. A whip is needed to make a top spin, and Peisetairos calls it 'wings' because it makes the Sycophant fly.

Although Peisetairos was ready to give wings to a large number of men and admit them to Cloudcuckooland (1308–36), the only ones seen on-stage are unwelcome characters who are turned away. But that does not mean that, after all, no one is to be admitted. The reason why we do not see anyone being admitted is simply that Aristophanes thought that routine admissions would make a dull

[31] Cf. MacDowell *Law* 224–8.

scene, whereas chasing people away would be more entertaining for the audience.

THE GODS

The climax of *Birds* is the confrontation with the gods. From the start it was an essential part of Peisetairos' plan that the Birds would vanquish the gods by intercepting sacrifices and so cutting off their food supply (186–93). A herald was to be sent up to the gods to declare war unless Zeus surrendered his power to the Birds (554–6, 843). But that herald seems not yet to have been sent, and the Birds have only just finished building the walls to protect the air, which is their territory, when a messenger-bird rushes up in alarm.

MESSENGER. A god has flown in through the gates just now
   Into the air! It's one of Zeus's gods,
   Slipped past the jackdaws on day sentry-duty!
                                          (*Birds* 1172–4)

The Birds' army is called out and they prepare to resist the invader. But by a delightful comic bathos the invader turns out to be a most ladylike goddess, Iris the rainbow, who has never heard of Cloudcuckooland and has no idea why men have ceased sacrificing to the gods. Peisetairos informs her forcefully that the Birds have replaced the gods, and she flies away. The next visitor from above is Prometheus. In myth Prometheus was punished by Zeus for his friendly assistance to mankind, and so Aristophanes has chosen this god as the one to give away the gods' plan to the Birds. His arrival is comical: he is so anxious that Zeus, looking down from the sky, shall not see him that he has his head covered by a cloak, he wonders whether there are clouds overhead (Zeus could not see through a cloud!), and eventually he converses with Peisetairos under an umbrella. He explains that the gods are getting hungry for lack of sacrifices. The barbarian gods, who live in the inland part of heaven (1522), are threatening to march against Zeus unless he gets the trading ports opened up. Peisetairos is surprised to hear that barbarian gods exist, as well he may be: Aristophanes has just invented them, describing heaven as if it were an area like Thrace, with Greek settlements along the coast and savage tribes inland. Indeed Prometheus says that the barbarian gods are called Triballians. The

Triballians were a real non-Greek people living in what is now western Bulgaria. In Aristophanes' time the Athenians can have known little about them, but possibly there had been some report about them in the Assembly recently, making the joke topical. Prometheus goes on to give Peisetairos some advice.

PROMETHEUS. Envoys for making peace will soon arrive
    From Zeus and the Triballians inland.
    But don't you make a treaty, not unless
    Zeus yields the sceptre to the Birds again
    And gives you Basileia as your wife.
PEISETAIROS. Who's Basileia?
PROMETHEUS.   She's a lovely girl.
    She's the custodian of the thunderbolt
    Of Zeus, and absolutely everything—
    Wise counsel, law and order, good behaviour,
    Dockyards, abuse, paymasters, and three-obols!
PEISETAIROS. So she looks after all he has?
PROMETHEUS.   That's right.
    If you get her from him, you've got it all.

                (*Birds* 1532–43)

    The sceptre and Basileia together represent all the power of Zeus. The sceptre is the symbol of sovereignty over the world, and it is to belong to the whole community of Birds. Basileia represents administrative authority, both in general policy and in organization of details (and once again the joke is that the details are of the same kinds as in Athens: ships, slander, and pay for jurors); this will belong to Peisetairos alone, as the Birds' leader. Scholars have worried about the exact nature of Basileia: is she a person or a personification?[32] It used to be taken for granted that she was a personification of Royalty or Sovereignty, much like the personifications of other abstract notions in other plays (especially those appearing in the form of girls with whom the hero makes merry at the end of a play, such as the Peace-terms in *Horsemen* and Vintage in *Peace*). Against this interpretation it has been objected that the metrical form of the word, with a short final alpha, signifies not an abstraction but a person, 'queen' or 'princess'. Recent writers have

---

[32] Newiger *Metapher* 92–102 discusses this question at length, but his interpretation of Basileia as primarily a divine bride for Peisetairos does not give sufficient weight to 1538–41.

therefore regarded the character as a goddess named Queen or
Princess; either this is an alternative name for a known goddess,
probably Athena or Hera, or Aristophanes has simply invented a
goddess. The identification with Athena or Hera is not very plausible: when Peisetairos demands Basileia as his wife he explicitly
distinguishes her from Hera (1633–4), and also refers to Athena
(1653) without any suggestion that she is the same person, and it is
unlikely that an Athenian audience would have liked to see their
national virgin goddess being married to a comic hero. Inventing a
goddess, on the other hand, was certainly a possibility; compare
Amphitheos in *Akharnians*, who seems to be an invented god (see p.
52). Personification of Royalty need not be absolutely ruled out,
for the metrical argument is not conclusive.[33] But we do not really
have to choose between a personification and a person, because
Greek gods are regularly both. Just as Aphrodite is an individual
goddess who embodies love, and Ares an individual god who embodies war, so Basileia can be an individual goddess invented by Aristophanes to embody government.

Soon after Prometheus' departure the three official envoys from
the gods arrive: Poseidon, Herakles, and a Triballian god. Three
was a normal number for envoys sent to negotiate with another
state, but Aristophanes has cleverly selected three who make a
strong contrast with one another. Poseidon, the brother of Zeus, is
generally thought of as the god of the sea, earthquakes, and horses,
but none of those spheres of activity is mentioned here. Here he is
dignified, conservative, and aristocratic. He is dismayed, for
example, that the Triballian whom the gods have elected to
accompany him does not know the proper (that is, the Athenian
gentleman's) way to wear his cloak: 'Democracy, what will you
bring us to?' (1570). Herakles, the son of Zeus, in myth is the
prototype of the physically strong hero. Comedy therefore presents
him as all brawn and no brain, with a tremendous appetite for food.
This characterization of Herakles was a comic convention, not an

---

[33] In other authors 'royalty' is βασιλεία, with long final alpha, but there is no
passage in which Aristophanes certainly uses that form, and, for all we can prove
to the contrary, he may have regarded βασίλεια, with short final alpha, as a
permissible form for 'royalty' as well as for 'queen'. The possibility that the
length of such alphas was considered variable, at least by Aristophanes, is indicated
by *Birds* 604, where he gives ὑγιεία a long final alpha although other authors
make it short.

innovation by Aristophanes, who claims in earlier plays to have risen above it (*Wasps* 60, *Peace* 741) but nevertheless exploits it not only here in *Birds* but again later in *Frogs* and in the lost *Aiolosikon*. The Triballian god, on the other hand, is purely an Aristophanic invention. He is hardly characterized at all, and his dramatic function is to reduce the negotiation to comic confusion by speaking unintelligibly.

The whole scene is a brilliant display of comic persuasion. Peisetairos has two aims: the sceptre of sovereignty is to be handed over by the gods to the Birds, and Basileia is to be given to him as his wife. His strategy is to divide the enemy: Herakles is stupid, and can be duped more easily than Poseidon. To win over Herakles, Peisetairos arranges to be cooking a delicious meal just as the gods arrive, and invites them to lunch on condition that they hand over the sceptre. On those terms Herakles can hardly wait to agree; Poseidon demurs; and Herakles interprets the Triballian's barbaric babble as supporting himself, so that Poseidon is outvoted by two to one. Only then does Peisetairos produce his second demand, for Basileia. This time he exploits Herakles' stupidity rather than his greed, and bamboozles him with legal argument.

POSEIDON [*to Herakles*]. Fool! Don't you realize you're being cheated?
 And it's yourself you're harming. If Zeus dies
 After he's given the sovereignty to them,
 You'll be a pauper; all of it comes to you,
 The property that Zeus leaves at his death.
PEISETAIROS [*to Herakles*]. You poor chap! How he's trying to outwit
  you!
 Come over here and let me tell you something.
 Your uncle's trying to deceive you, mate.
 By law you don't inherit from your father,
 Since you're a bastard, not legitimate.
HERAKLES. Me? Bastard? What d'you mean?
PEISETAIROS.   That's right, by Zeus!
 Your mother was a foreigner. How could
 Athena, as a daughter, be the heiress
 If she had brothers of legitimate birth?
HERAKLES. What if my father leaves his property
 To me, as bastard's share?
PEISETAIROS.   The law won't let him.
 Poseidon here, who's raising up your hopes,
 Will claim your father's property instead,

As being his brother and legitimate.
I'll tell you what the law of Solon says.
[*He brings out a legal document.*] 'A bastard is not to have right of kinship,
    if there are legitimate children. If there are no legitimate children,
    the next of kin are to share the property.'
HERAKLES. So I don't share my father's property?
PEISETAIROS. You don't, by Zeus! Has he inducted you
    To be a member of his phratry yet?
HERAKLES. Not me, he hasn't. I'd been wondering why.

(*Birds* 1641–70)

The fun here arises from speaking of the gods as if they were
ordinary human beings, and Athenians at that. Really Zeus is immortal, but here that fact (as most Greeks believed it to be) is ignored;
so when he dies, what will become of his property (which happens,
in his case, to include the sovereignty of the world)? It will be
inherited in accordance with law. Aristophanes develops the joke by
introducing one legal rule after another, all of them genuine rules
of the Athenian law of inheritance. The property will be inherited
by the son of the deceased, but only if the son is of legitimate birth;
a law of Perikles forbids marriage between an Athenian and a
foreigner (and Alkmena, mother of Herakles, is comically called a
foreigner because she was human although Zeus is a god); if there
are no legitimate sons, a daughter may be the heiress (*epikleros*), but
the heiress and the property may be claimed by the nearest legitimate
male relative; a phratry (brotherhood or clan) admits only men of
legitimate birth, so that membership is good evidence of legit-
imacy.[34] All these rules will have been familiar to the Athenian
audience, whose hilarity will have increased each time Peisetairos
produces yet another rule of law and applies it to the gods.

Herakles is convinced, the Triballian utters some more gibberish
which is taken to signify his agreement, and so Poseidon finally gives
in. It is agreed that Basileia shall be given in marriage to Peisetairos.
The play concludes with a wedding scene,[35] and thus Peisetairos has
triumphed. He is indeed the most successful of all comic heroes,
since he ends up as the ruler of the world.

The gods in this play, as in others (especially Dionysos and Herak-

[34] For a summary of Athenian marriage and inheritance law see MacDowell
Law 84–108.
[35] On the wedding scene see Hofmann *Mythos* 138–60.

les in *Frogs*, and Hermes in *Peace* and *Wealth*), are used by Aristophanes as comic characters. They are presented ignominiously; they are undignified or unscrupulous, cowardly or greedy. They are not characters to be admired or imitated. Aristophanes' treatment of them seems, by our standards, to be neither religious nor pious. Many modern readers have found this puzzling. One possible explanation is that he did not believe in these gods, and did not expect most of his audience to believe in them either; for him, as for Offenbach, the traditional Greek gods were simply a set of ready-made comic characters. But this explanation is unlikely to be right. The evidence that most ordinary Athenians believed in the gods is strong. We need only point to the general alarm that arose in 415 BC, only a year before the performance of *Birds*, when the images of Hermes in Athenian streets were mutilated and the Eleusinian Mysteries were profaned. Many Athenians believed that the gods, especially Hermes, would be offended at those acts and, if not propitiated, would exact vengeance, perhaps by destroying the great fleet which was setting out for Sicily. Yet evidently they did not believe that Hermes or Poseidon or Dionysos would be offended and exact vengeance if made to look ridiculous in a comic play. Why did they regard the cases as different? The best explanation is that the performances of comedies at the Dionysiac festivals were regarded as occasions when laughter at anyone, even the gods, was appropriate. The gods, like other powerful people, were expected to accept on that occasion mockery which they might not tolerate at other times.[36]

A CASTLE IN THE AIR

Birds more than any of the other plays has suffered from over-interpretation. 'Professor after Professor has advanced some new theory which if satisfactory to its author has proved satisfactory to nobody else.'[37] Not every theory will be mentioned here, but it is worth while to notice a few which are good examples of different approaches.

[36] Cf. Dover *Ar. Comedy* 31–3 on the ordinary man's need for an opportunity to assert himself against the superhuman powers which dominate the world.
[37] Rogers *Birds* xvi–xvii.

In the nineteenth century the play was sometimes interpreted as a political allegory, most notably by Süvern.[38] At the time of its first performance the Athenians had recently dispatched their great expedition against Syracuse, with hopes of conquering the whole of Sicily. Süvern argues that the setting up of Cloudcuckooland is a satirical allegory of that over-ambitious scheme, and that the Birds' device of isolating the gods reflects an Athenian plan to isolate the Peloponnese. He regards the Birds as representing the Athenians and the gods the Peloponnesians: Poseidon the sea-god stands for Corinth, Herakles for Boiotia, and Zeus for Sparta; the character of Peisetairos contains elements drawn both from Alkibiades the instigator of the Sicilian expedition and from Gorgias the clever orator, Euelpides resembles Gorgias' adherent Polos, and Tereus resembles Lamakhos. Critics have found little difficulty in pointing out specific details of the play which conflict with this interpretation. For example, at the start of the play Peisetairos and Euelpides, when they come to the Birds, are not coming to the Athenians as Gorgias did, but abandoning them.[39] But the more fundamental objection to this approach is that Aristophanes does nothing to show the audience that the play is allegorical. How he would have done so, if he had wished, can be seen from the trial of the dog in *Wasps*, where the two dogs are called by names that are nearly the same as the names of Kleon and Lakhes, and references to Sicily, cities, and soldiers are thoroughly mixed in with the references to dogs, cheese, and kitchen utensils. *Birds* has no such clues to an allegory, and it is not good enough to say that the allegory is concealed by 'the mysterious veil which was thrown over the main idea of the whole play'.[40] The intention of an allegory has to be made clear, not veiled.

A more moderate political interpretation has been preferred in recent years by some scholars, of whom the best example is Newiger.[41] He does not identify particular characters in the play

[38] J. W. Süvern *Essay on the Birds of Aristophanes* (trans. W. R. Hamilton, London 1835). This type of interpretation is not yet extinct; for a recent example of identification of Peisetairos with Alkibiades, based largely on far-fetched word-play, see M. Vickers *Historia* 38 (1989) 267–99.

[39] Süvern attempts to answer some of these criticisms in the appendices to the English translation of his *Essay*.

[40] Süvern *Essay* 160.

[41] H.-J. Newiger in Ἀρετῆς μνήμη, ἀφιέρωμα εἰς μνήμην τοῦ Κ. Ι. Βουρβέρη (Athens 1983) 47–57.

with particular historical individuals, but he does consider that the play as a whole refers to the Sicilian expedition and is intended as a criticism of Athenian imperialism. He considers that all Aristophanes' plays are aimed at some political or social or intellectual target, and that the Sicilian expedition was the obvious target for criticism in 414. But there is really no evidence or probability that people in Athens in that year were so preoccupied with the activities of their troops at Syracuse that they would assume every comedy they saw to be about this subject; and if they did not assume it in advance, they could not know that a play was about this subject unless they were told. There is in fact no mention in *Birds* of the Sicilian expedition or of Syracuse. There is one joke about a summons-server arriving by ship, an event that did befall Alkibiades (145–7), and there are two passing jokes about Nikias, neither of which necessarily refers to anything which had happened in Sicily (363, 639); all three jokes are quite incidental and might not bring Sicily to the audience's mind at all. The main enterprise in *Birds* is to abandon Athens and found a new city somewhere else; that is quite different from the Sicilian expedition, which was intended to build up the power of Athens by conquering another powerful city already in existence. In short, the theory that Aristophanes is somehow satirizing the Sicilian expedition is unconvincing, because he does not indicate to the audience that he is doing so. Even Newiger concedes that 'at first sight' the critical and sceptical purpose of the play may have been concealed from the audience by the jubilant ending. I must therefore re-emphasize that for the Athenian audience the first sight of a play was the only sight. With rare exceptions, they neither saw a second performance nor studied a written text. Aristophanes knew that any satirical point he wished to make must be clear and obvious.

Recently Hubbard has presented another variant of the political interpretation, regarding the play as a reaction to the religious scandals of the previous year (the mutilation of the Hermai and the profanation of the Mysteries) and to the political groups which were believed to have planned them.[42] On this view it 'dramatizes not only the abandonment of Athenian democracy, but also the overthrow of the city's traditional religion', and, like *Clouds*, is an attack on the sophists to whom the decline in religious belief is attributed. But

[42] Hubbard *Mask* 158–82.

this too is unconvincing. At the beginning of the play Peisetairos and Euelpides have left Athens to avoid prosecution for debt, not for sacrilege as Hubbard alleges, and there are no clear references at all to either the mutilation or the profanation. Certainly the play contains some jokes about sophists, but it is very far from identifying Peisetairos with them. There is also a fundamental reason why all interpretations of this type must be rejected. The spectators are encouraged to identify themselves with Peisetairos and to side with him against his opponents throughout the play, and at the end he is triumphantly successful. The play therefore cannot be an attack on the kind of thing Peisetairos does. It is rather an encouragement to follow his example—if only it were possible.

This objection may be made also to the interpretation put forward by Ničev, who argues that the basic idea of *Birds* is the degeneration of democracy: Peisetairos begins as a democratic leader but ends as a tyrant.[43] He places much emphasis on the moment when Herakles first notices that Peisetairos is cooking some meat.

HERAKLES. What sort of meat is this?
PEISETAIROS.   These are some birds
Who were condemned for rising up against
The democratic birds.

(Birds 1583–5)

Ničev considers that Peisetairos, under the name of democracy, is really an absolute ruler who condemns his opponents to death. Perhaps he (writing in Sofia) has been too much influenced by the modern history of eastern Europe, and he makes too much of a brief joke. In ancient Athens a normal kind of meat for a first-rate private dinner (as distinct from a religious festival) was small birds.[44] So naturally this is what Peisetairos is preparing in order to tempt Herakles—but how can it be right for birds to be cooked by birds? Aristophanes invents a clever explanation to get out of the difficulty: these particular birds were traitors, and execution was the normal penalty for treason in Athens as elsewhere. There is no reason why this penalty should not have been imposed democratically; nothing in the text supports Ničev's assumption that Peisetairos personally

---

[43] A. Ničev *Euphrosyne* 17 (1989) 9–30. A similar view is held by Bowie *Aristophanes* 168–72.
[44] e.g. *Akharnians* 1007, *Clouds* 339, *Peace* 1149, 1197.

imposed it. But anyway the line is merely a joke which passes immediately. There is no further reference to democracy, whether real or pretended. At the end of the play Peisetairos is hailed as the ruler of the world, such as Zeus had been before. This is not a degenerate position, but an admirable and enviable one.

Another approach to the play gives it a basis which is not political but literary. This view was already current in antiquity.

Some say that the poet confuted the fantastic tales in tragedies in other works, and in the present work, to show that the compilation of the Gigantomachy was stale, gave to birds a dispute with gods about sovereignty.

(*Birds hyp.* ii)

The suggestion is that, just as *Akharnians* mocks Euripides' *Telephos*, so *Birds* mocks the Gigantomachy. The Gigantomachy was a myth recounting the attempt of the Giants to overthrow the gods. There must have been an epic poem on this theme, although nothing survives of it now. Recently this interpretation of *Birds* has been taken up and developed by Hofmann,[45] who points out that the gods' defeat of the Giants is mentioned in the play (824–5) and two individual Giants, Porphyrion and Kebriones, are also named (553, 1252); in one of those places (553) a scholiast remarks 'He deliberately mentioned the fighters of the gods, because they themselves will also fight the gods'. Actually the Birds resemble the Titans rather than the Giants. Both the Titans and the Giants were children of the Earth; but the Titans, including Kronos, were themselves gods, who were attacked and deposed by Zeus and other gods of the younger generation, whereas the Giants were merely uncouth mortals who attacked the gods. The Birds, like the Titans but unlike the Giants, are represented as having ruled before Zeus and the other gods. But here the distinction between the Giants and the Titans may be unimportant. The two myths were so similar that they had already become confused by Aristophanes' time. A more serious difficulty is that neither myth is really much like *Birds*. The Giants and the Titans both opposed the gods by brute force, and were defeated. The Birds oppose the gods by clever strategy, under the guidance of Peisetairos, and are victorious. The scholia do not tell us that Aristophanes quotes or parodies any words of a poem

---

[45] Hofmann *Mythos* 79–90. Cf. also Zannini Quirini *Nephelokokkygia* 47–87.

about the Gigantomachy. Although he may well have had the Gigantomachy at the back of his mind, there is no strong evidence that
any part of *Birds* copies it at all closely, still less that parody or
mockery of it was the main point of the play.

Another popular interpretation, well expounded by Ehrenberg,[46]
sees the play not so much as an allegory of the real Athens and its
activities but rather as a presentation of the ideal city. Cloudcuckooland, on this view, is Athens as Aristophanes would like it to
be. An opposite interpretation has also been proposed: Cloudcuckooland is Athens as Aristophanes hopes it will not be, but fears
it soon will be if present trends continue unchecked.[47] Why can the
play be read in two ways so contradictory? The reason is that
Aristophanes gives so little information about what Cloudcuckooland, when established, is actually like, and readers tend to
fill in the picture with their own ideas. Consider the evidence. At
the start Peisetairos and Euelpides are seeking a carefree place with
no lawcourts. When they are asked what they want to do there,
their answers mention a wedding-feast and sex (128–42). The
attractions of the life of birds are that they do not use money and
that their meals are like wedding-feasts (155–61). Later there are
passages about the usefulness of wings, which enable you to get
around quickly to do whatever you want to do, and the Birds'
situation in the air enables them to attain power over both gods and
men; but those are means, not ends. Nothing substantial is said
about the organization of society in Cloudcuckooland; the brief
reference to democracy is, as we have seen, a momentary joke, not
a description of the constitution. At the end Peisetairos prepares
food for a wedding-feast and marries Basileia. Thus, if we ask what
the inhabitants of Cloudcuckooland actually do with their time, the
only answers provided are feasting and sex. These are just the same
activities as at the end of several other Aristophanic plays, and they
are not enough to be regarded as a blueprint for the ideal city, still
less as a depiction of the deteriorating city. Cloudcuckooland turns
out to be much the same as Dikaiopolis' peacetime Athens; but

---

[46] Ehrenberg *People* 57–60. Cf. also E.-R. Schwinge *Würzburger Jahrbücher für
die Altertumswissenschaft* 3 (1977) 52–6, B. Zimmermann ibid. 9 (1983) 66–72.

[47] This is the main conclusion of Zannini Quirini *Nephelokokkygia*. Cf. also
W. Arrowsmith *Arion* 1 (1973) 119–67, E. Corsini in *Atti del Convegno Nazionale
di Studi su la città ideale nella tradizione classica e biblico-cristiana* (ed. R. Uglione,
Turin 1987) 57–136.

whereas Dikaiopolis attains it by a method which the Athenians collectively could actually have adopted, namely making a peace treaty, Peisetairos attains it by acquiring wings and fortifying the air, which in real life are impossible.

But although positive statements about life in Cloudcuckooland amount to so little, there is more emphasis on what it does not have. When the new city is founded, Peisetairos has first of all to get rid of people who are not wanted: a priest, a poet, an oracle-collector, a town-planner, an inspector, a decree-seller, a rebellious youth, another poet, and a sycophant. The most important thing about life in Cloudcuckooland is not what people do there, but the freedom from obnoxious and interfering persons. This lends attraction to Murray's interpretation of *Birds* as a play of escape: 'It seems to be just an "escape" from worry and the sordidness of life, away into the land of sky and clouds and poetry.'[48] But Murray goes too far. For one thing, it will not do to call Cloudcuckooland the land of poetry; poetry is the only profession of which Peisetairos expels not just one but two practitioners. Murray attempts to explain the play as a reaction to 'the shadow of an awful apprehension' arising from the religious scandals and accusations of the previous year—not (like Hubbard) as an allegory or parody of them, but simply as an escape from them.[49] But there is no evidence that the Athenians were still worried about that topic in particular in the spring of 414. What the play shows is not an escape from a specific religious or political or military situation,[50] but the escape of an ordinary man from the selfish busybodies who get in his way in everyday life. In this sense it is a play of escape.

The spectators in the theatre are expected to sympathize and to identify themselves with Peisetairos and Euelpides from the start, and this attitude is confirmed by the scenes in which Peisetairos disposes of obnoxious intruders. Everyone in the audience (except the few who themselves are oracle-collectors, sycophants, and so on) is naturally on his side in those scenes. Some modern critics have found this part of the play inconsistent with the beginning: at the start Peisetairos is looking for a peaceful place to live, but then

[48] Murray *Aristophanes* 156.
[49] Ibid. 142–3.
[50] Cf. Dover *Ar. Comedy* 145–6.

he becomes aggressive.[51] That is a misunderstanding. He does not seek out his opponents in order to attack them; it is they who intrude upon him.[52] In order to make Cloudcuckooland a peaceful place he has to get rid of the men who are preventing it from being so. He needs power, including power over the gods, to secure peace and prosperity.

The play shows this ordinary Athenian accomplishing what the ordinary Athenians in the audience can only dream of doing: getting control over everyone else, and using it for his own personal pleasure. It enables the spectator to imagine himself doing the same. Peisetairos achieves this by becoming a bird, and the use of wings is a brilliant dramatic stroke by Aristophanes. Many people have at some time dreamed of rising off the ground effortlessly and weightlessly, and flying out of trouble is a constant motif in literature both ancient (for example, Daidalos and Ikaros) and modern (for example, Peter Pan and Wendy). Getting wings is the perfect image for leaving worries behind and doing what one has always longed to do, and the charm of *Birds* is that it is a dramatization of dreams coming true.

[51] See especially G. Paduano *Studi Classici e Orientali* 22 (1973) 115–44.

[52] The Priest is an exception, but hardly a significant one. Peisetairos does take the initiative of inviting him to perform a religious ceremony, but then dismisses him because he performs it in an unsatisfactory way (848–94).

Lysistrata

TWO PLOTS

The title of the play is a woman's name, and women predominate in the cast and in the action. We do not know how much of an innovation this was. There had been many tragedies about women; perhaps there had been comedies about women too. But if so, they are lost; the only women in surviving earlier comedies are minor characters.[1] For us, comedy about women begins with *Lysistrata*.

Lysistrata herself first appears alone, already in the middle of expressing her indignation (her first word is 'But . . .'). She has called a meeting of women, but not one has turned up. They would have come fast enough, she says, if they had been invited to a religious festival of the more excited kind, but they have failed to come for something much more important. Gradually they do arrive: first, a neighbour named Kalonike; then Myrrhine and other Athenian women; and finally some women from other cities, including a Boiotian and a Corinthian, led by a Spartan, Lampito. None knows why Lysistrata has summoned them. Aristophanes builds up the suspense: it is not until line 112 that she says that she wants the women to end the war, and not until 124 that she reveals the first of her two schemes for doing so.

By now, at the beginning of 411 BC,[2] the war against Sparta was going as badly as ever. The Peace of Nikias made in 421 had not lasted. Various infringements of its terms had occurred, and in 413, after the disastrous end of the Athenians' expedition to Sicily, fighting was renewed in the mainland of Greece and in the Aegean. The Athenians still held Pylos in the Peloponnese, but the Spartans

---

[1] Cf. Henderson *Lysistrata* xxviii n. 4, Taaffe *Ar. and Women* 48–9.
[2] On the date of the play see A. H. Sommerstein *JHS* 97 (1977) 112–26, A. Andrewes *HCT* 5.184–93.

in retaliation occupied Dekeleia, from where they could raid the Attic
countryside. Most ominously, many of the cities around the Aegean
which formed the Athenian Empire, such as Khios and Miletos,
revolted. All this keeps the women's husbands away from home.

LYSISTRATA. Don't you desire the fathers of your children
    While they're away at war? I know quite well
    You all have husbands now away from home.
KALONIKE. My husband's been away five months, my dear,
    Up Thrace way, keeping watch on Eukrates.[3]
MYRRHINE. And mine's been seven solid months at Pylos.
LAMPITO. And mine, if ever he gets back from service,
    Fits on his shield-band and flies off again.
KALONIKE.[4] There's not a lover even—not a glimmer!
    Since the Milesians have deserted us,
    There isn't even an eight-fingered dildo
    That might have given us some leather comfort!
LYSISTRATA. Would you be willing, if I find a means,
    To help me end the war?
KALONIKE.   I would for one,
    By the Two Goddesses! I'd even pawn
    This cloak for it, and that day—drink the proceeds!
MYRRHINE. And I would, if I had to cut myself
    In two and give up one half, like a flounder!
LAMPITO. And I would climb up Mount Taygetos,
    If I could get a sight of peace from there!
LYSISTRATA. Well, here's my plan; no need to keep it secret.
    We women, if we really mean to force
    The men to live in peace, we must abstain—
KALONIKE. Abstain from what?
LYSISTRATA.   And will you do it, then?
KALONIKE. We'll do it, if we have to die for it!
LYSISTRATA. The thing we must abstain from is the prick.

                              (*Lysistrata* 99–124)

    The startling obscenity at the end of that passage reflects the
startling nature of her proposal. She plans that the women should
all refuse sexual intercourse with their husbands until the men end

---

[3] The joke is that the Athenian soldiers spend more time looking out for their
own general than for the enemy.

[4] Lines 107–10 have hitherto been assigned to Lysistrata, but I suggest that
their vulgar tone makes it more probable that they are spoken by Kalonike. Cf.
N. G. Wilson *GRBS* 23 (1982) 159.

the war. At first the other women are comically reluctant to agree, but in the end they do swear an oath to dress up in the most enticing manner and then repulse all advances by husbands or lovers. As in *Akharnians*, the genuine problem of the continuing war is solved by a fantastic scheme which in real life would be impossible. Critics point out that in real life the scheme would be open to both logical and practical difficulties: men who were away on campaigns would not be affected by their wives' abstention at home, and anyway other forms of sexual activity (prostitution, pederasty, masturbation) would remain available.[5] Aristophanes naturally ignores those difficulties for the sake of the comic idea of a sex-strike and the comic sight of the men's frustrated priapism in later scenes.

But Lysistrata has another plan too, which she suddenly brings out in response to an objection by Lampito. Lampito thinks that she and the other Spartan women can persuade their husbands to make peace, but that the Athenian democracy (which the Spartans, with their more rigid political structure, look on as a disorganized rabble) will never give up the war as long as there is enough money in the treasury on the Akropolis to maintain the Athenian navy.

LAMPITO. The Athenian rabble, on the other hand—
    How can they be persuaded not to stray?
LYSISTRATA. We'll soon do the persuading here, don't worry.
LAMPITO. Not while those triremes still have ropes and there's
    Abundant silver stored up with the Goddess!
LYSISTRATA. But that's already taken care of too.
    We'll occupy the Akropolis today.
    The oldest women have been given orders:
    While we arrange this business, they're to feign
    A sacrifice and seize the Akropolis.

                (*Lysistrata* 170–9)

The two plans seem at first to be complementary: while the younger women stage the sex-strike, the older women, no longer attractive to men, will control the treasury. But it does not work out quite like that; for, when the Akropolis is taken, Lysistrata and her Athenian comrades go to occupy it themselves.

LAMPITO. What cry was that?
LYSISTRATA.   Exactly what I said.

[5] Cf. Dover *Ar. Comedy* 160.

The Goddess's Akropolis has now
Been taken by the women. Lampito,
You go off home and make arrangements there,
But leave these women here as hostages.
We'll go inside and help the other women
To bar the gates of the Akropolis.

(Lysistrata 240–6)

Distinctions among the women seem to become blurred. One
might expect the Corinthian and the Boiotian to return to their own
cities to organize the sex-strike there, but in fact only Lampito
leaves; the other women from enemy cities are retained 'as hostages'
and do not appear again as individuals. The 'oldest women' of
177 have become simply 'the women' in 241; and subsequently
Lysistrata and younger women are holding the Akropolis, whereas
older women, forming half of the chorus, arrive later to support
them. Possibly Aristophanes did not have enough actors available
(even for non-speaking parts) to keep the various groups of women
distinct; anyway he does not seem concerned to do so. The point is
that women—all women together, not particularly young women
or old ones, Athenian women or Peloponnesians—are opposing the
men.[6]

Likewise the two plans become confused. One might expect
women tantalizing their husbands at home and women on the Akropolis withholding funds from men at war to provide the plots for
two separate plays. Aristophanes has combined them, concentrating
now on one and now on the other in different parts of the play.[7] If
he had kept to only one of the two plots throughout, the play might
have been simpler and more logical, but also more monotonous. It
is richer and more entertaining with two comic plots instead of one.

THE AKROPOLIS

The Akropolis is a natural fortress. From prehistoric times possession of it must have implied control of the surrounding area. In
the seventh century Kylon and in the sixth century Peisistratos, in

---

[6] On the women's solidarity cf. D. Konstan in *Tr.Com.Pol.* 431–44.

[7] Cf. A. O. Hulton *G&R* 19 (1972) 32–6, J. Vaio *GRBS* 14 (1973) 369–80,
J. Henderson *YCS* 26 (1980) 153–218.

order to become tyrant of Athens, proceeded to seize the Akropolis. Perhaps the rulers of Athens had at one time resided on it. But by the time of Aristophanes the focus had changed. The town had grown, and most business of the democracy was done elsewhere: major decisions were taken by the Assembly on the Pnyx, and the Council-house and other public buildings were mostly situated in or near the Agora. The main use of the Akropolis now was religious: it belonged to Athena, the patron goddess of Athens. Her temples and statues were located there, and it was the site of the principal rituals in her honour. Yet religion and politics were never wholly separated in Athens, and the Akropolis continued to have one political use of the greatest importance: the safe keeping of funds. The Athenians' treasuries were placed under the protection of the Goddess and located in or beside her temples. Thus, when the women in *Lysistrata* seize the Akropolis, their act means two things. It is a symbol that they are taking control of Athens, and in practical terms it obstructs the men's access to public money.[8] The men react to both of these, the chorus to the former and the Proboulos to the latter.

This play has a chorus of old men and a chorus of old women; presumably each is a semichorus of twelve persons, so as to make the normal total of twenty-four. The old men appear first, labouring up the hill to the gates of the Akropolis, carrying logs of wood and fire in pots, in order to set light to the gates and get the women out. In the course of their song they recollect how they expelled Kleomenes, King of Sparta, when he occupied the Akropolis long ago.

> Demeter! They shall not mock me—
> > Over my dead body!
> Nor did Kleomenes, who was
> > First to occupy it,
> Get out and go away scot-free;
> But, breathing a Lakonic blast,
> He gave his weapons up to me,

[8] Whitman *Aristophanes* 203 suggests that the Akropolis symbolizes chastity, and this idea is elaborated by N. Loraux *The Children of Athena* (trans. C. Levine, Princeton 1993) 147–83. However, the reactions of the men's chorus and the Proboulos do not support it; they are concerned respectively about the national shrine and about the treasury. If chastity were the main point of occupying a temple, one would expect it to be a temple of Artemis rather than Athena.

And went off in his little cloak,
  Unfed, unwashed, and hairy,[9]
  Six years' dirt upon him!

So that's how I besieged that man, that's how I fought him fiercely;
In ranks of seventeen I spent the night before the gateway.
And now these women, hated by Euripides and heaven –
You think that I won't put a stop to such audacious conduct?
In that case may my trophy stand at Marathon no longer!

                                        (*Lysistrata* 271–85)

This is partly a standard joke about the Spartans, a combination of amusement and scorn; the Athenian view of the normal appearance and life-style of Spartans was that their food and clothing were scanty, they let their hair grow long, and they rarely washed. Complementary to this is the Athenians' pride in having defeated them. The year in which Kleomenes seized the Akropolis to support Isagoras against Kleisthenes and the prospective Athenian democracy was 508/7, almost a century before *Lysistrata*. There cannot really have been any men still living who had taken an active part in his expulsion. But the point here is not the involvement of any particular individuals. It is that the seizure of the Akropolis was and is an act against democracy. The men of Athens resisted it successfully before, and now they will resist it again. In 508/7 the enemy was Sparta; in 490 (at Marathon, line 285) it was Persia; and now it is— women. The audience is expected to laugh at this equating of women with the terrible foes of the past. But in the event it is the women who defeat the men quite easily. When they (the other semichorus) arrive, they bring buckets of water to extinguish the fire which the old men are trying to light in order to burn the closed wooden gates of the Akropolis; and they throw the water all over the men, leaving them comically wet.[10]

Attention now shifts from the Akropolis as national symbol to the Akropolis as treasury. An official arrives, one of those having the title Proboulos. Ten men with this title had been appointed in 413 BC, immediately after the failure of the Sicilian expedition, evidently because it was felt that the Assembly and the Council could not administer the war efficiently. The Probouloi were required to be over forty years of age, and in fact the only two whose names are

---

[9] In 279 I read κομήτης. Cf. MacDowell *CQ* 30 (1980) 294–5.
[10] On the slapstick see MacDowell *Themes in Drama* 10 (1988) 10–11.

known, Hagnon and Sophocles, were a good deal older than that. The Proboulos in *Lysistrata* is elderly and fussy. He exclaims in disgust at the indiscipline of the women, to whom he thinks men have been too indulgent, and then comes to his specific problem.

PROBOULOS. This sort of thing ends in this sort of trouble:
  When I'm Proboulos, and I've just secured
  Supplies of oar-spars and I need the money,
  The gates are shut against me by the women!

(*Lysistrata* 420–3)

Lampito pointed out earlier that the money on the Akropolis supported the Athenian navy (173–4, quoted on p. 231). Now the Proboulos has arranged for a supply of timber to be imported to provide oars for the ships, and cannot get at the money to pay for them. The two archer-policemen whom he has brought with him are not enough to arrest all the women,[11] and a debate (agon) ensues, in which Lysistrata easily gets the better of him. She declares that the women will look after the money, just as they always look after housekeeping money for their husbands (493–5). Women can sort out the whole tangle of the war, just as they untangle wool at home (567–70). The Proboulos is ignominiously dressed up, first as a woman and then as a corpse, and he runs away, leaving the women still in control of the Akropolis.

LYSISTRATA'S ADVICE TO THE CITY

The defeat of the Proboulos is not due to the strength of Lysistrata's arguments. He is simply overpowered by the number of women, and the agon ends in slapstick comedy. Yet it contains one passage in which the comic element fades and the tone becomes more serious than anywhere else in this play. Lysistrata's boast that the women will untangle war as easily as wool, sending envoys hither and thither (567–70), is merely a vague simile, of no help at all to any real-life negotiator; but she then goes on to say that, if men had any sense, *they* (not, it should be noticed, the women) would conduct the city in the same way as the women deal with wool

[11] On the number of characters in this scene see MacDowell *CQ* 44 (1994) 331–2.

(572–3). This leads to an extended metaphor, describing politics in terms of wool-work.[12] The shift from what the women will do to what the men ought to do is significant. It is a shift, for a few lines, from the comic story of the play to advice about real life; for in real life it is the men, not the women, who take political decisions.

The sentence introducing this passage uses a verb (*politeuesthai*) which means being a citizen (*polites*) and doing the business of the city (*polis*). As the passage proceeds, it becomes clear that it is the former sense (the earlier and stricter one) which is relevant here; the advice is about membership of the body of citizens. First the city must be cleansed, like a fleece, by having the bad men removed from it, like dirt and burrs. Then, just as good wool is collected in a basket for spinning and weaving, the worthy should all be gathered in.

Who, in Aristophanes' view, are the men who ought to be expelled from the citizen body? 'Those men who combine, and the men who mat themselves together for offices' (577–8). The verbs 'combine' and 'mat together' (meaning the compression of wool to make felt) are literal and metaphorical words for the same thing, not for two distinct activities;[13] Aristophanes is attacking politicians who collaborate to get one another elected to office. We may compare a sentence in Thucydides' account of the events which led to the oligarchic revolution in this same year.

Peisandros went to all the conspiratorial groups[14] which already existed in the city for trials and offices, and urged them to draw together and make common plans for subversion of the democracy.

(Thucydides 8.54.4)

Thucydides seems to imply that all such groups were, or could easily be persuaded to be, opposed to democracy and supporters of the forthcoming oligarchic revolution. Politicians not favouring oligarchy certainly had their groups of supporters too, and these had been a target in Aristophanes' earlier plays; Lamakhos, for example, was elected by 'three cuckoos', and Kleon had 'a hundred

---

[12] The poetic rhetoric of this passage is analysed by Moulton *Ar. Poetry* 49–58.

[13] Cf. Sommerstein *Lysistrata* ad loc.

[14] ξυνωμοσίαι: groups of men who have sworn an oath to collaborate. In *Horsemen* and *Wasps* this word, used by Kleon and his supporters, refers to plotting with a foreign enemy (cf. p. 159), but here it refers to Athenians plotting not with foreigners but with one another.

heads of flatterers' around him.[15] It is possible that here Aristophanes is attacking those who were planning an oligarchic coup,[16] but his words are not so precise, and it is more likely that when he wrote this play he did not yet realize that a revolution was imminent.[17] But he clearly implies that democratic elections ought to be more open than they are, and if the Athenians had been able to act immediately on his advice perhaps the revolution might have been averted.

After these bad men have been removed, the rest of the wool is to be carded, mixing everyone into a basket of common goodwill. Who are the men who ought now to be given citizenship?

1. Metics (580). These are non-citizens who have permission to reside in Athens permanently. Some metic families had been there for several generations. They paid taxes and did military service, and Aristophanes considers that there is no good reason to exclude them from the status and rights of citizens.

2. 'Any alien who is friendly to you' (580). This means foreigners who do not yet have permission to reside in Athens but would like to.

3. Those owing money to the public treasury (581). A man was a debtor to the state if he had failed to make some payment by the due date, such as a tax, or rent for leasing property from the state, or a fine imposed for an offence. As long as he owed it he was disfranchised: he forfeited most of the rights of a citizen until he paid up. If he could not pay he remained disfranchised, and on his death his heir inherited the debt and so was disfranchised too. It is impossible for us to know how many Athenians were in this position, but Aristophanes evidently thinks it worthwhile to reincorporate them in the citizen body; their poverty does not mean that they are not patriotic. But he does not mention men disfranchised permanently for reasons other than debt.[18]

4. 'All the cities which are colonies of this land' (582). 'Colonies'

---

[15] *Akharnians* 598, *Wasps* 1033.

[16] For that interpretation see Hugill *Panhellenism* 40–9.

[17] Cf. Henderson *Lysistrata* xv–xxv. Lines 489–91, mentioning Peisandros, refer not to the oligarchic plot but to earlier events, perhaps especially those following the mutilation of the Hermai and the profanation of the Mysteries in the summer of 415; cf. Sommerstein *Lysistrata* 178 (on line 489).

[18] For a fuller summary of disfranchisement (*atimia*) see MacDowell *Law* 74–5; for detailed discussion, M. H. Hansen *Apagoge, Endeixis and Ephegesis against Kakourgoi, Atimoi and Pheugontes* (Odense 1976) 55–90.

(*apoikoi*) means settlements, founded by Athenians, which have become autonomous cities. (Cleruchies are not meant here, because their inhabitants were Athenian citizens already.) Not many autonomous Athenian colonies had been founded in recent times, but it has been plausibly suggested that Aristophanes means all the Ionian cities, because in myth they were all founded by descendants of the Athenian hero Ion, as Euripides had recently recounted (*Ion* 1575–88).[19] However, this does not mean that Athenian citizenship should be given to all the citizens of all the Ionian cities in the Aegean and along the coast of Asia Minor. Such a drastic measure would have submerged Athens itself, because the new citizens would have far outnumbered the existing ones, and it is not credible that Aristophanes is suggesting that. What the Athenians are being urged to do is, rather, 'taking the strand [of carded wool] from all these, bring them together here and unite them into one' (584–5). 'From' indicates a part or selection, not the entire population of the cities concerned. 'Here' means 'to Athens'. Many cities of the Empire are now in revolt, and individuals loyal to Athens are few and isolated in each city. Such individuals should be brought to Athens and incorporated in the Athenian citizen body. Thus, by spinning all loyalists into one big ball of wool, there will be enough to weave a warm cloak to protect the Athenian people (585–6).[20]

So Aristophanes, through the mouth of Lysistrata, is urging changes in the roll of citizens to exclude individuals whose loyalty is only to a small group, and whose aim is to obtain offices for themselves, and to include all who are loyal to Athens, whatever their origins. To a modern reader two omissions are obvious. There is no mention of slaves; the possibility that slaves could become Athenian citizens is not considered. And there is no mention of women. In the present context this is the more striking omission, because only a few lines earlier Lysistrata was maintaining that women were capable of giving men good advice (507–28). But the notion of female participation in politics is merely comic fantasy. In

[19] Hugill *Panhellenism* 67–71, Henderson *Lysistrata* 144 (on lines 582–6), Sommerstein *Lysistrata* 183–4 (on line 582).

[20] My interpretation of this passage is similar to the one briefly indicated by Wilamowitz *Lysistrate* 51–2. Other interpretations are reviewed by Hugill *Panhellenism* 72–95, but his conclusion, that Aristophanes is advocating a revival of the council of the maritime confederacy, is unacceptable because it does not fit the context, which concerns Athenian citizenship.

572–86 Aristophanes is making a serious practical proposal; that is the reason why women are not mentioned here.

The serious tone extends a little further. When the Proboulos declares that women have no share in the war, Lysistrata retorts that it weighs more than twice as heavily on them as on the men. They give birth to sons and send them out as soldiers, and they have to sleep alone because the men are away on campaigns. In particular, girls lose the chance of getting husbands because they grow too old before the war ends (588–97). The Proboulos is not allowed by Aristophanes to make any effective reply to these complaints (by saying, for example, that giving birth to a son who becomes a soldier and gets killed is not as bad as actually being a soldier who gets killed). But the lines are obviously not comic. For these few moments Aristophanes is seriously inviting his male audience to view a situation from a woman's rather than a man's viewpoint.[21]

RELIGIOUS TRADITION

Lysistrata has no parabasis in the usual form. Instead it has at this point, halfway through the play, a sequence of songs and speeches in which the two semichoruses threaten or mock each other. The old men take a patriotic standpoint: they will defend Athens against this new enemy, the women, just as against other enemies in the past (614–35, 658–81). The old women defy them and claim the right to advise on Athenian policy, not only because they contribute men to the city (651, the same point as Lysistrata makes in 589–90) but also because of their participation in Athens' religious rituals.

> Now hearken, all citizens! This is where
> We start to give Athens some good advice.
> Quite right too: the city nurtured me in splendid luxury.
> When I reached the age of seven, I was an *arrephoros*;
> Then I was a grinder for the foundress at the age of ten,

[21] M. S. Silk *BICS* 34 (1987) 95–6 rightly sees the passage as presenting 'a sympathetic argument', but is surely not right in saying that it is so 'only in so far as woman's condition is defined, after all, with reference to men's old age'.

And I shed my saffron gown as bear at the Brauronia;[22]
And I was a basket-bearer once—I was a lovely girl
    With a necklace of figs!

                                    (*Lysistrata* 638–47)

The passage is important evidence about ceremonies involving girls, about which there is not much other information.[23] The exact meaning of *arrephoros* is not known, but the position was held each year by two girls between the ages of seven and eleven, who lived on the Akropolis and performed various duties under the supervision of the priestess of Athena Polias. The position of grinder (*aletris*) is said by a scholiast here to have been held by girls who prepared sacrificial cakes for the Goddess, probably meaning Athena, the foundress of Athens.[24] At the festival of the Brauronia, held in honour of Artemis, girls between the ages of five and ten were called 'bears' (*arktoi*); they wore saffron-coloured dresses, which they discarded at some point in the ritual. A basket-bearer was a girl given the honour of carrying at a public festival the basket containing the implements required for the sacrifice; no other evidence tells us anything about the necklace of figs. Many details of these rites remain obscure, but at any rate it is clear that the women of the chorus are associating themselves with the religious traditions of Athens.

That might be regarded as a matter of little significance for the theme of the play as a whole, if it were not for a comparatively recent suggestion that Lysistrata herself is a representative of traditional religion. This theory was originated by Papademetriou and developed by Lewis.[25] Its basis is as follows. The most important priestess in Athens was the priestess of Athena Polias (Athena as represented by the ancient olive-wood statue on the Akropolis). This office was confined to the aristocratic family of Eteoboutadai, and there is good evidence that its holder in the late fifth century

---

[22] The text of 643–5 is disputed. I follow T. C. W. Stinton *CQ* 26 (1976) 11–13 and Henderson *Lysistrata* ad loc., in preference to C. Sourvinou *CQ* 21 (1971) 339–42, M. B. Walbank *CQ* 31 (1981) 276–81, and Sommerstein *Lysistrata* ad loc. With Stinton's reading καὶ χέουσα it is not necessary to assume that the various honours are listed in exact chronological order.

[23] Cf. C. Sourvinou-Inwood *Studies in Girls' Transitions* (Athens 1988), but her reconstructions go rather beyond what is justified by the scanty evidence.

[24] Cf. *IG* 2² 674.16–17, Plutarch *Alkibiades* 2.6.

[25] D. M. Lewis *ABSA* 50 (1955) 1–12. See also Sommerstein *Lysistrata* 5–6.

was a woman named Lysimakhe, who held it for sixty-four years.[26] The name Lysimakhe ('dissolving battles') is virtually synonymous with Lysistrata ('dissolving armies'). Furthermore, a woman named Myrrhine served the temple of Athena Nike (Athena as goddess of victory, also on the Akropolis) in the second half of the fifth century, probably as the first priestess after the new temple was completed in the 420s.[27] This evidence points towards identification of Lysistrata and Myrrhine in the play with two real-life priestesses. One might wonder then whether Kalonike and Lampito were priestesses too; but there is no evidence for that, although Lampito was a name used in one of the royal families in Sparta[28] and would certainly have been suitable for a Spartan priestess of high birth.

When considering this theory, it is important not to misunderstand the nature of ancient priestesses. They were not women who devoted their whole lives to religion like Christian nuns. A priestess had the duty and honour of performing certain rituals for a goddess, but that was not a full-time activity; a particular ritual would be due only on certain days, in some cases on only one day each year. For the rest of the time she would live the same kind of life as other women, probably with a husband and children.[29] Thus the fact that the women in the play have domestic lives and an interest in sex[30] is in no way incompatible with the view that they are priestesses.

Several features of the play support this view. At the beginning, how would an ordinary woman be able to summon the rest to a meeting and expect them to follow her lead? This is more natural if Lysistrata is the priestess of Athena Polias, whom the other women respect because she holds the most distinguished position open to a woman in Athens. When Lampito arrives and the Athenian women admire her physique, she complains that they are prodding her like

---

[26] Pliny *Natural History* 34.76 reports that the sculptor Demetrios made a statue of Lysimakhe, and *IG* 2² 3453, although it does not preserve the name, is convincingly identified as the base of that statue and belongs to the first half of the fourth century.

[27] *IG* 1³ 1330. Her epitaph and a memorial lekythos depicting her are discussed and illustrated by P. J. Rahn *ABSA* 81 (1986) 195–207.

[28] Herodotos 6.71.2.

[29] *IG* 2² 776.26–30 mentions the husband of a priestess of Athena Polias, named Lysistrata as it happens, in the third century.

[30] It is sometimes assumed (e.g. by Wilamowitz *Lysistrate* 54) that Lysistrata herself has no husband, but that is refuted by lines 507–20.

a sacrificial victim (84); naturally they do, if they are priestesses accustomed to conducting sacrifices. Then Lysistrata leads the women to the Akropolis, which becomes their headquarters; that is the place where the priestess of Athena has authority. Later in the play symbols of Athena (helmet, snake, owl) are prominent in a scene in which some of the women are seeking excuses for going home and Lysistrata overrules them (742–61).[31] Then Myrrhine meets her husband at the gates of the Akropolis, the Propylaia, and is able to fetch a light bed and other equipment from somewhere close by (916–47); the nearest building to the Propylaia is the temple of Athena Nike, and who would have belongings there but the priestess of that temple?[32]

We should therefore accept that Lysistrata and Myrrhine are the priestesses of Athena Polias and Athena Nike respectively. They are prominent women, not just ordinary ones. However, we do not have here satirical caricatures of real personalities, like those of Kleon in *Horsemen* and Socrates in *Clouds*. Whereas prominent men were heard making speeches in the Assembly or conversing in the Agora, respectable women were never so well known. Even priestesses would merely be seen performing rituals; their personalities would not be familiar to the general public. So Aristophanes is not depicting the real Lysimakhe and Myrrhine. Perhaps indeed his reason for making the almost insignificant change of name from Lysimakhe to Lysistrata is to suggest that the character is a typical priestess of Athena Polias, rather than the individual who happens to hold the office at present.

So Lysistrata and her supporters represent not just a feminine attitude to war and politics, but also Athenian religious tradition. This tradition is contrasted with newer religious rituals which had recently become popular. They were mostly of foreign origin, and involved emotional songs or cries and ecstatic dancing to the accompaniment of drums or tambourines. At the very beginning of the play, when Lysistrata complains that no other women have yet arrived, she comments sarcastically that they would have been only

[31] Cf. L. Bodson *L'Antiquité Classique* 42 (1973) 5–27.
[32] A priestess would not reside permanently in her temple, but might sometimes need to spend a night there for the purpose of some ritual. Recent editors (Henderson *Lysistrata* 180, Sommerstein *Lysistrata* 111) think that Myrrhine fetches the bed and other items from Pan's grotto, a cave on the north-west side of the Akropolis; but why should Myrrhine have such equipment there?

too keen to go to a celebration of one of the newer or less solemn cults.

LYSISTRATA. But if one asked them to a Bakkhic revel,
Pan's shrine, Kolias, or Genetyllis's,
You couldn't have got through there for the drums!
But now there's not a single woman here.

(*Lysistrata* 1–4)

Later the Proboulos assumes that the women have been led astray by enthusiasm for Sabazios (a Phrygian god of wine) or Adonis (a mythical hero of probably Semitic origin).

PROBOULOS. Has women's self-indulgence, then, flared up—
Their constant drumming and Sabazios cries
And that Adonis ritual on the roofs?

(*Lysistrata* 387–9)

Both suppositions are false. The women in this play do not in fact indulge in celebrations of Bakkhos or Genetyllis, Sabazios or Adonis. Instead they are upholders of the traditional religion of Athens, and in particular Lysistrata may be thought to have the authority of Athena herself. She speaks not just for women, but for Athens.

RECONCILIATION

In the second half of the play the sex-strike takes effect. Some of the women begin to weaken and make various excuses for going home, but Lysistrata sternly persuades them to stay (726–80). Then there is a famous scene in which one of them, Myrrhine, tantalizes her husband in the manner which the women planned earlier (829–953). Her husband is Kinesias, the gangling and cadaverous poet who is also mocked in *Birds*. This identification is denied by most recent editors, who think that Myrrhine's husband is a fictional character. But Kinesias is a rare name, and the audience on hearing it would certainly think of its only well-known bearer, the poet, who was a constant butt of comic dramatists; indeed one dramatist, Strattis, wrote a whole play about him.[33] From his role in *Lysistrata* it is probably right to conclude that Kinesias the poet was in historical

[33] Lysias fr. 53 Thalheim, Athenaios 551d.

fact the husband of Myrrhine the priestess of Athena Nike.

After leading him on, like a cat playing with a mouse,[34] Myrrhine suddenly leaves Kinesias in an agony of sexual frustration, and it soon transpires that all the men in both Athens and Sparta are in the same plight. Their wives will not satisfy them until they make a peace treaty. So envoys from both cities arrive, all sporting comically huge erections, for Lysistrata to reconcile them.

If we now expect Aristophanes, through the mouth of Lysistrata, to explain to the audience the way in which peace may be attained in real life, we are in for a disappointment. The serious elements in this part of the play are overwhelmed by sexual puns and farce. At first Lysistrata does seem to have a serious point to make. Appropriately for a priestess, she remarks that the Athenians and the Spartans participate together in religious rituals at Olympia, Thermopylai, Delphi, and elsewhere, and they ought not then to be destroying each other (1128–34). She goes on to give an example of how the Athenians did assist the Spartans some fifty years ago, at the time of an earthquake and a revolt by the helots of Messene.

> Next, Spartans—since I now shall turn to you—
> Remember Perikleidas came here once,
> A Spartan, as a suppliant to Athens;
> He sat at altars, pale in scarlet cloak
> And begging for an army. That was when
> Messene and the god of quakes as well
> Attacked you, both at once; and Kimon with
> Four thousand hoplites saved the whole of Sparta.
> And when the Athenians did that for you,
> Do you lay waste the land that gave you aid?
>
> (*Lysistrata* 1137–46)

And then she gives an example of how the Spartans, nearly a hundred years ago, liberated Athens from the tyrant Hippias and the Thessalian horsemen who supported him.

> And do you think I'll let the Athenians off?
> Remember when the Spartans in their turn
> Came armed here, in the days when you wore smocks,[35]

---

[34] Cf. Albini *Interpretazioni* 3.88–9.

[35] 'Smock' here is an imprecise translation of *katonake*, a rough woollen garment commonly worn by slaves. It is unlikely that all Athenians actually wore such clothes; Lysistrata is expressing metaphorically their subjection to Hippias.

And slaughtered many men of Thessaly
And many friends and troops of Hippias'.
Alone they helped to drive him out that day
And set you free; they took away the smock
And clothed your people in a cloak once more.

(*Lysistrata* 1149–56)

Both examples are misleading.[36] Kimon did not 'save the whole of Sparta'. On the contrary, the Spartans suspected the Athenians of sympathizing with the helots and ignominiously dismissed Kimon and his force, and 'it was as a result of this expedition that disagreement between the Spartans and the Athenians first became evident'.[37] On the other occasion Kleomenes and the Spartan army did expel Hippias, but they also returned to Athens two or three years later to prevent the establishment of democracy, and were forcibly driven out by the Athenian people. Thus neither case is a good instance of Athenian and Spartan co-operation. No doubt many in Aristophanes' audience were unfamiliar with the details of historical events which had occurred fifty or a hundred years before. Yet the Spartans' insulting treatment of Kimon was notorious; and as for Kleomenes, Aristophanes has already reminded the audience of his ejection from the Akropolis earlier in this very play (271–80; see pp. 233–4).

To believe that these examples are meant to be taken seriously becomes even harder when we consider their context.[38] Lysistrata opens the negotiations by calling out Reconciliation (*diallage*). Like the Peace-terms in *Horsemen*, Reconciliation is represented as a pretty girl. She is invited by Lysistrata to lead the Spartan and Athenian envoys together by the hand—or by the phallus if necessary (1119–21). The envoys stand with rampant erections on either side of Lysistrata while she makes her speech about co-operation, and make comments which show that they are hardly listening to it because they are preoccupied with the girl's physique (1136, 1148, 1157–8). Eventually Lysistrata gets them to negotiate, but the places in Greece which are the objects of the bargaining (Pylos, Ekhinous, the Malian gulf, and 'the Megarian legs') are ones selected by

---

[36] Cf. N. G. Wilson *GRBS* 23 (1982) 161.
[37] Thucydides 1.102.3.
[38] Cf. Heath *Political Comedy* 14–16.

Aristophanes because they give scope for sexual puns,[39] and probably the envoys at the same time perform some comic business around the person of Reconciliation. The audience therefore will be laughing during this passage, and will not take it as a serious basis for a real-life treaty.

Nor does any serious proposal follow. The rest of the play is taken up with feasting, singing, and dancing. However, it includes two sentimental or nostalgic songs, sung by a Spartan, about Spartan religious dancing and about the days when the Athenians and the Spartans fought against the Persians at Artemision and Thermopylai (1247–72, 1296–1321). The audience is left with more favourable thoughts about Sparta than are to be found in any other play of Aristophanes. There can be no doubt that he wishes that the hostilities would come to an end, but he has no practical suggestion for bringing that about.

WOMEN AND PEACE

Is *Lysistrata* a satirical attack on women?[40] Some critics have thought so, and they can point to many parts of the play where a woman, or the female sex in general, is the butt of a joke. Obviously the audience is expected to laugh at the women's keenness on sexual intercourse and their reluctance to give it up, especially when Lysistrata first propounds her plan. They are also mocked for being wine-bibbers, for example when they use wine to confirm the oath which Lysistrata administers to them; Kalonike and Myrrhine, after regarding the plan with reluctance, suddenly become enthusiastic when they see what form the oath is going to take (207–8). More generally, Aristophanes seems to mock their naïvety, their preoccupation with trivialities, and their use of weak excuses, which comes to the fore when several of them want to leave the Akropolis and go home to their husbands.

[39] The puns are explained in detail by Henderson and Sommerstein in their commentaries on 1162–74.

[40] For discussion of the presentation of women in this play see especially T. M. de Wit-Tak *Lysistrata* (in Dutch with English summary, Groningen 1967), E. Lévy *Ktema* 1 (1976) 99–112, M. Rosellini in *Ar. Femmes* 11–32, H. P. Foley *CP* 77 (1982) 6–13, J. Henderson *TAPA* 117 (1987) 105–29, Taaffe *Ar. and Women* 48–73.

WOMAN. O Ileithya,[41] hold my baby back
   Until I've got outside the sacred place!
LYSISTRATA. What's all this nonsense?
WOMAN.   I'm just giving birth.
LYSISTRATA. What, you? But you weren't pregnant yesterday.
WOMAN. I am today. Quick, send me home at once
   To the midwife!

                              (*Lysistrata* 742–7)

Thus Aristophanes seems to be laughing at women from an external viewpoint, which is what one might expect in a play written by a male author and performed by male actors for a male audience.[42] But this is not the whole story. There is at least one passage in which he invites the men's sympathy for women: because of the war young women miss their chance of getting husbands, while those already married lose their husbands or sons (588–97; see p. 239). Throughout the debate between Lysistrata and the Proboulos it is the woman who appears sensible and the man who does not, and it therefore seems quite reasonable for Lysistrata to complain at the men's refusal to listen when the women offer good advice (507–28). Lysistrata is indeed a dignified figure who commands respect throughout the play, and her dignity is not undermined when she occasionally makes a humorous or cynical remark.[43] In the choral passages too the women come off better than the men: early in the play it is the men who are made to look foolish by being drenched, and in subsequent songs it is always the old men who first deliver some blustering threat and the old women who then cap it and have the last word, never the other way round. More generally, there is a persistent implication that domestic tasks, performed by women, are carried on more efficiently than political affairs, for which the men are responsible. This becomes explicit when Lysistrata maintains that the men ought to handle the citizens in the same way as the women

---

[41] Goddess of childbirth. Birth, like sexual intercourse, was forbidden in a sacred precinct.

[42] Taaffe *Ar. and Women* 72 maintains that the play is 'a celebration of masculinity'.

[43] Nearly all critics have found Lysistrata serious-minded. An exception is N. G. Wilson *GRBS* 23 (1982) 157–61. One of his arguments is invalid, that the audience will not have taken her seriously because the part was played by a man; on that basis none of the heroines of Greek tragedy could be taken seriously either.

handle wool (572–86; see pp. 235–6). Furthermore, if we accept that the women represent the traditional religion of Athens (see pp. 239–43), that is another feature likely to attract the audience's sympathy.

So Aristophanes sometimes laughs at women and sometimes supports them. As a whole the play is neither a feminist manifesto nor a misogynistic jeer. Even if this is the first play in which he makes extensive use of women for his comic and dramatic purpose, that purpose is not to make a point about women. He is certainly not advocating that women should be given political responsibility or power. In fact in this play (unlike *Women at the Assembly* some twenty years later) the women do not take political power or action. The object of the sex-strike and of the seizure of the Akropolis is, rather, to induce the men to take action. Even Lysistrata's comparison of politics to wool-work advocates a programme which she says men, not women, ought to carry out (572–3). At the end of the play she does not impose a peace-treaty; she merely persuades the men on both sides to make one. After that, we assume, the women will return home to the same domestic lives which they lived before the war began. They will not be enfranchised, and there is nothing in this play to suggest that it had ever occurred to Aristophanes that women might be enfranchised. His proposal about citizen-rights is a different one: that all men loyal to Athens should be citizens, and the disloyal men excluded (572–86; see pp. 236–8). That is a serious suggestion, but it appears only in this one passage of fifteen lines and is not a main point of the play.

The main theme of the play, then, is not women, and not citizenship. It is peace—once again. Fourteen years after *Akharnians* Aristophanes is still upholding peace as the goal at which the Athenians ought to be aiming. Not that he has any practical proposal for bringing it about: the women's sex-strike and their seizure of the Akropolis are comic fantasies, and the detailed peace-terms are merely a series of verbal jokes (1162–74). In real life the approach to negotiations will be difficult; Aristophanes must realize that Athens, now weakened by the disaster of the Sicilian expedition, cannot hope for terms as favourable as those of the Peace of Nikias ten years earlier.[44] But negotiations will be possible, one way or another, if the Athenians will just make up their minds that peace is

---

[44] Cf. de Ste. Croix *Origins* 368, H. D. Westlake *Phoenix* 34 (1980) 38–54.

what they want. As in *Akharnians*, Aristophanes is trying to prod them into opening negotiations. The new element in *Lysistrata* is the broadening of the range of people concerned. Peace is what is needed not only for countrymen like Dikaiopolis,[45] but for all the women of Athens, and thus for the domestic life of everyone.

This is reinforced by Aristophanes' skilful blending of the political and domestic themes.[46] In the first half of the play, when Athens is at war with Sparta, the women are at odds with the men. Just as Athens makes no headway against Sparta, so too the men's pugnacity is ineffective against the women. In the second half of the play the men, represented by Kinesias, try persuasion instead. Kinesias' main motive is of course sexual desire, but he has a few lines which seem to reflect more widely on the pain of marital separation: he takes no pleasure in life since his wife left the house, 'and everything seems empty to me now' (865–8). His attempt to win over Myrrhine fails; but as soon as the first steps are taken towards reconciliation on the political level, there is also a reconciliation between the old men and women of the chorus. The lines here are attributed to the two semichoruses, but probably only one woman and one man speak on behalf of them all. The woman takes the initiative and gradually overcomes the man's surly grumpiness. First she comes and puts back on to him the tunic which he had taken off to prepare for a fight, and then:

WOMAN. If you hadn't so upset me, I'd do something else for you:
   I'd have caught this little creature in your eye, and got it out.
MAN. Oh, so that's the thing that's killing me! Look, take this ring of
      mine;
   Poke it out with that, and when you've got it, show me what it is.
   It's been there for ages now, by Zeus, and biting at my eye!
WOMAN. Well, I will, although you don't deserve it, you bad-tempered
      man!
   Look at that! Zeus, what a monstrous gnat it is you've got in there!
   There! You see it? Don't you think this gnat's a Trikorysian?[47]

---

[45] M. Dillon *TAPA* 117 (1987) 97–104 correctly notes that agriculture is less prominent in *Lysistrata* than in *Akharnians* and *Peace*, but I doubt whether he is right to see the women in terms of a 'fertility theme'.

[46] Cf. R. Harriott *Themes in Drama* 7 (1985) 11–22.

[47] Trikorynthos was a marshy place near Marathon, where the insects were presumably large.

MAN. That's a real good turn you've done me. It's been digging wells in me

    All this time, and now it's out my eyes are watering so much!

WOMAN. Let me wipe them; I'll soon dry them, though you *are* a naughty man,

    And I'll kiss you—

MAN.   No, don't kiss me!

WOMAN.   —if you want me to or not!

MAN. Well, I hope you have bad luck, then! What a coaxing lot you are!

    That old saying's right, the poet understood it very well:

    'Deadly pests are they to live with, deadly pests to live without'.[48]

    Still, I make my peace with you now, and for all the time to come

    I shan't do you any harm, and you will do no harm to me.

                                  (*Lysistrata* 1025–41)

This is a sentimental passage, but very effective in conveying the give-and-take needed for a happy marriage. It is followed by the scene of political reconciliation and finally by the songs about Sparta and Athens as allies in the past, with men and women dancing together. So the theme of personal and domestic harmony between women and men enhances the theme of ending the war, which is the principal focus of the play.

[48] A sardonic proverb about women.

Women at the Thesmophoria

THE ABSENCE OF POLITICS

Women at the Thesmophoria, in Greek Thesmophoriazousai, is one of the least political plays, even though it was produced at a time of political upheaval and uncertainty. In the summer of 411 unrest and dissatisfaction with the conduct of the war against Sparta led to a revolution in which democracy was abandoned. For a few months it was replaced by the oppressive regime of the Four Hundred, and then by the more moderate one of Five Thousand; the traditional democratic constitution was restored in 410. It is not absolutely certain at what date in this period Women at the Thesmophoria was performed. No hypothesis or scholium gives the date. Some scholars have assigned it to 410, in the time of the Five Thousand, but it is now generally agreed that it belongs to the Dionysia of 411.[1] It refers (804) to the defeat of an Athenian naval force commanded by Kharminos, which occurred in the winter of 412/11, but not to anything which can certainly be dated later; a comment about Councillors handing over their function (808–9) probably refers not to the establishment of the Four Hundred in the summer of 411, but simply to the Council's annual change of membership.[2] It also refers (1060) to Euripides' Andromeda as having been performed 'last year', and a scholiast (on Frogs 53) says that Andromeda was produced in the eighth year before Frogs; reckoned inclusively, the eighth year before 406/5 is 413/12.

So it seems that Women at the Thesmophoria was performed just two or three months before the Four Hundred took power. According to

---

[1] Cf. A. H. Sommerstein JHS 97 (1977) 112–26, A. Andrewes HCT 5.184–93, Hubbard Mask 187–99, 243–5, Sommerstein Thesm. 1–3.
[2] Cf. Croiset Ar. and Pol. Parties 146, Hubbard Mask 198 n. 112. For an alternative explanation of 808–9 see Sommerstein Thesm. ad loc.

Thucydides (8.65–6) the coup was preceded by a period of suspicion and fear, with some political assassinations. Yet the play makes little or no reference to this. There are two passages which have been thought to hint at it.[3] One is the opening of the meeting of the women's assembly. A woman delivers a curse which is a comic parody of the curse delivered at the beginning of meetings of the real Assembly, and the chorus then adds a song which repeats some of the same points in lyric form. Those cursed include anyone who plans to set up a tyranny (338–9) and any who seek to change around decrees and laws (361–2). If revolution was already expected, those phrases could have been taken to refer to the conspirators; yet it is much more likely that they are simply comic distortions of a traditional formula about tyranny and subversion which Aristophanes is mocking (just as he mocks a proclamation about tyranny in *Birds* 1074–5). The other passage occurs in a hymn to Athena: 'Appear, thou who hatest tyrants as is right' (1143–4). This could possibly have been taken as a call to protect Athens against the conspirators; yet it may be nothing more than routine praise of Athena as the goddess of democratic Athens. So it is not likely that Aristophanes intends any reference in this play to the difficult and dangerous political situation in the spring of 411. Possibly he thought it would be too risky to mention it, and avoided it deliberately. Yet that is not certain either, for he may have planned the play and written most of it before revolution was suspected. Perhaps the best conclusion is simply that on this occasion he did not want to write a political play.

The main theme is a clash between Euripides and the women of Athens. It was a standing joke that Euripides was hostile to women. This joke was probably not yet current in 425, since Aristophanes does not use it in the Euripides scene of *Akharnians*; but in 411 the audience is expected to be already familiar with it, for it occurs without explanation in *Lysistrata* 368–9. There is no reason to think that Euripides was a misogynist in real life. (He is said to have married twice.) Nor do his plays systematically attack women; they contain many sympathetic presentations of female characters. But it is a fact that he often gives a more penetrating analysis of their motives than the earlier tragedians had done, and shows women being led by love or other emotions into wrong conduct: for

---

[3] Cf. Dover *Ar. Comedy* 170–2, Sommerstein *Thesm.* 231–2 (on lines 1143–4).

example Medea, whose jealousy and anger at being deserted by Jason causes her to kill Jason's new wife and her own children, and Phaidra, who falls in love with her own stepson Hippolytos. So it is not altogether untrue that Euripides reveals some murky aspects of female psychology which had previously received little attention. This is a good enough reason for Aristophanes in a comedy to make the women regard Euripides as their enemy.

The play shows the women at their festival of the Thesmophoria plotting against Euripides, who gets an old relative to dress up as a woman and attend the festival to discover their plans. The old man, the 'hero' of the play, is a buffoonish character similar in some ways to Strepsiades or Philokleon. He is never named in the dialogue; he is just called a *kedestes* of Euripides. This word means a relative by marriage: brother-in-law, father-in-law, or son-in-law. He is called Mnesilokhos in the scholia, and sometimes also in the abbreviations of speakers' names in the margins of the only manuscript of the play; Mnesilokhos is said by late authorities to have been the name of Euripides' father-in-law.[4] It is possible that this information is true, and that Aristophanes did mean the character in his play to be Euripides' father-in-law named Mnesilokhos. But, if so, it is hard to see how the audience can have known that. It is safer to leave the character unnamed, and I shall call him simply the Relative.

SEXUAL AMBIGUITY

In the prologue Euripides, accompanied by his old Relative, goes to the house of Agathon the tragedian to ask for help.[5] In some ways this scene resembles the scene of *Akharnians* in which Dikaiopolis goes to the house of Euripides the tragedian to ask for help. In each case a slave appears first and then the tragedian himself; both speak or sing in a style which parodies the style of the real tragedian.

Agathon was over thirty years younger than Euripides, and had begun competing in the contests of tragedies only a few years ago; his first victory had been in 416. Thus he belonged to a new

---

[4] *Souda* ε 3695 and the anonymous *Life of Euripides*.
[5] For recent discussions of Aristophanes' presentation of Agathon see F. Muecke *CQ* 32 (1982) 41–55, M. L. Chirico *Parola del Passato* 45 (1990) 95–115, G. Stohn *Hermes* 121 (1993) 196–205.

generation of tragedians, but the surviving evidence does not really make clear what was novel about his plays.[6] In Aristophanes his music is mocked as 'soft' (fr. 178) and is compared to 'the paths of an ant' (*Thesm.* 100), whatever that means; no doubt the point was brought out in the music of the parodies of his songs (39–62, 101–29). The quotations which we have from his actual work are all very short, but some of them display a fondness for symmetrical verbal patterns (antithesis and chiasmus) such as:

Success attracts skill, skill attracts success.

(Agathon fr. 6)

Now if I speak the truth I shall not please,
And if I please I shall not speak the truth.

(Agathon fr. 12)

That this sort of thing was characteristic of Agathon is confirmed by Plato's *Symposium*, in which he appears and delivers a speech (194e–197e) containing many instances of parallel phrasing and rhyme, in the manner of Gorgias the rhetorician. So we can safely assume that in lines 198–9 we have a parody of this feature of Agathon's style, or perhaps even an actual quotation from one of his tragedies, which Aristophanes then mocks by adding some vulgar derision by the Relative.

AGATHON. It is not right by ingenuity
To bear mischance, but by passivity.
RELATIVE. And so, you bugger, you've become wide-arsed
Not just by speech, but by passivity!

(*Women at the Thesmophoria* 198–201)

This conjunction of rhyme and sex confronts us with the question: is Aristophanes mocking Agathon's poetry or his personality? The answer is complex. It is known from other sources that Agathon as a boy was loved by a man named Pausanias and that this erotic relationship continued after he had grown up.[7] In classical Athens the active partner in a homosexual relationship was not particularly

---

[6] The extant fragments and other evidence are in *Tragicorum Graecorum Fragmenta* 1 (ed. B. Snell, 1971) 155–68. For extended discussion see P. Lévêque *Agathon* (Paris 1955). On Aristophanes' parody of Agathon see Rau *Paratragodia* 98–114.

[7] Plato *Protagoras* 315e, *Symposium* 193c, Xenophon *Symposium* 8.32.

frowned on, but the younger or passive partner tended to be regarded with contempt, especially if already adult.[8] Aristophanes' jokes imply that Agathon has a naturally pretty and effeminate appearance, with a high-pitched voice (191–2); that he cultivates such an appearance deliberately (172), notably by shaving his beard, which was not the normal practice of Athenian men;[9] and that he enjoys passive homosexual intercourse (200, 206). In the play he is wearing woman's clothes, so that the Relative at first sight thinks he actually is a woman (97–8) but then comments on his strange mixture of masculine and feminine garments and attributes (134–43). Agathon's answer, however, is not that he has a natural desire to look like a woman (as an instinctive transvestite), but that his attire has a practical purpose.

AGATHON. The clothes I wear are suited to my thought.
    A man who is a poet must adapt
    His manners to the plays he needs to write.
    So if the plays one writes are feminine,
    Those are the ways the body must adopt.
RELATIVE. And ride on top, if you're composing *Phaidra*?[10]
AGATHON. But if the plays are masculine, one has
    That quality already in the body.
    What we don't have, we chase and imitate.[11]
RELATIVE. Well, when you write a satyr-play, call me;
    I'll stand erect behind you to assist!
AGATHON. Besides, it isn't in good taste, to see
    A poet rough and hairy. Just consider
    Anakreon of Teos, Ibykos,
    Alkaios, who gave seasoning to music:
    They wore snoods in Ionian luxury.
    And Phrynikhos[12]—you've heard him, I suppose—
    Himself was lovely and wore lovely clothes,

[8] Cf. K. J. Dover *Greek Homosexuality* (London 1978) in general, and especially p. 144 on Agathon.

[9] Line 191 does refer to shaving of the beard, not of bodily hair, because it draws a contrast with the bearded Euripides (190); cf. also 33.

[10] Phaidra is regarded as the most notorious adulteress in tragedy; cf. *Thesm.* 497, 547–50, *Frogs* 1043, 1052.

[11] 'Imitation' ($\mu i\mu\eta\sigma\iota\varsigma$) refers to dress and behaviour ($\tau\rho\delta\pi\sigma\iota$). It does not here have its Aristotelian sense of poetic representation.

[12] The early tragic dramatist, not the comic dramatist contemporary with Aristophanes.

And so that's why his plays were lovely too.
One's compositions must be like one's nature.
RELATIVE. So Philokles is foul and writes foul plays,
And Xenokles is bad and writes bad plays;
Theognis, too, is cold and writes cold plays!

(*Women at the Thesmophoria* 148–70)

Here Agathon offers three different justifications for his feminine dress, sliding almost imperceptibly from one to another. First he claims that he needs it in order to write a female role in a play. He must mean that adopting a woman's clothes and manners helps him to know what a woman would do and say. This is virtually the same idea as in *Akharnians* 410–13, where Euripides wears rags and lies on a couch when writing roles of cripples and beggars. Probably Aristophanes is mocking a theory that someone had actually propounded, arguing that a dramatist by physical imitation could feel his way into a character's natural speech and behaviour; there is, however, no other evidence for this theory in Aristophanes' time. Secondly Agathon points out that he is following a poets' tradition, because Ionian poets of the previous century customarily wore dress which looked effeminate and luxurious. Vase-paintings prove that Anakreon did wear clothes similar to those worn by Agathon in this scene.[13] It may be true that Agathon in real life affected this kind of attire in emulation of his Ionian predecessors, and that Aristophanes is mocking this.[14] But thirdly, after linking beauty of person, beauty of clothes, and beauty of plays in the case of Phrynikhos, Agathon refers to 'nature' (167); the feminine dress reflects his own nature, which is what makes his style of composition effeminate, just as, the Relative rudely remarks, the foul, bad, and frigid compositions of other poets match their respective natures. In strict logic these three explanations of Agathon's attire are incompatible. If he is trying to look like Anakreon, he is not trying to look like a woman; and if he is imitating feminine qualities which he does not possess (155–6), it is not true that those qualities are in his own nature (167). But Aristophanes blends the different explanations in such a way as to give a general impression of Agathon's effemi-

---

[13] Cf. J. M. Snyder *Hermes* 102 (1974) 244–6.

[14] Compare W. S. Gilbert's mockery in *Patience* of the effeminate dress of 'aesthetes' in the late nineteenth century, who claimed to be imitating medieval predecessors.

nacy, both in personality and in poetic style. Probably there was some factual basis for the satire, but it is not possible for us to know just how effeminate the real Agathon and his poetry actually were.

The true facts are even more uncertain concerning the other 'womanish' man who appears in this play. Kleisthenes is the butt of jokes in many of Aristophanes' plays, but it is only in this one that he appears on-stage,[15] as the women's friend and representative among the men (574–6). From several of the jokes it is clear that he looked like a woman because he had no beard: when the Relative is shaved and sees himself in a mirror, he thinks he sees Kleisthenes (235). But there is no suggestion that Kleisthenes, like Agathon, shaved his beard deliberately, and it is more likely that it just did not grow naturally. Some of the jokes imply that his conduct is effeminate: he is engaged in weaving (*Birds* 831) and is available as a passive sexual partner (*Lysistrata* 1092, *Frogs* 57). We cannot tell whether these have any basis in fact. They may be simply comic inferences from his beardless face.[16]

Besides the womanish characters of Agathon and Kleisthenes, the Relative is dressed as a woman for much of the play, and so is Euripides briefly at the end. Thus sexual ambivalence and disguise are an important element of the play. Some critics have looked for a wider significance in this,[17] but its main purpose is surely to make the audience laugh at the characters' odd appearance. We have to visualize what they look like in the theatre. In the modern theatre a male actor playing a woman is generally funny. The traditional pantomime dame is the most obvious case: 'she' looks and sounds comic because a deep voice, long strides, and other male characteristics are incongruous in a female character. Modern readers sometimes assume that female characters in Aristophanes must have been funny likewise because they were played by male actors, but that is an error. In Athens men playing women were not exceptional, like the pantomime dame, but normal, in tragedy as well as comedy. Antigone, Elektra, Phaidra, Iphigeneia—they all spoke with male

[15] Kleisthenes does not appear on-stage at *Akharnians* 118. The character appearing there is a Persian eunuch, and the joke is that he looks just like Kleisthenes.

[16] Cf. Dover *Greek Homosexuality* 144–5.

[17] G. Paduano *Quaderni Urbinati di Cultura Classica* 40 (1982) 103–27, Taaffe *Ar. and Women* 74–102.

voices and had a male physique. So, when male actors appeared as
women in *Lysistrata* and *Women at the Thesmophoria*, that was not in
itself funny; it was perfectly normal. But a male actor playing a man
dressed as a woman was funny, as is clear from Agathon and the
Relative in this play. He did not look the same as a male actor playing
a woman.

The difference lay in the mask. An actor wore a white mask
to play a woman, a darker mask to play a man.[18] This reflected,
or rather exaggerated, the normal conditions of ancient life, in
which men were generally sunburnt because they spent much
time out-of-doors whereas women lived mainly indoors. Normally
a male mask would also have a beard. In *Women at the Thesmophoria*
the actor playing Kleisthenes must wear a mask with no beard;
but it is a dark mask, and he wears man's clothes, so that he is
easily seen to be a man, and it is only the absence of a beard that
looks incongruous. The actor playing Agathon, besides having no
beard, wears woman's clothes. Does he also wear a white mask?
He is called 'white' (191, cf. 31–2), but if he wore a white
female mask the audience would be left with no visible indication
that the character is really a man. Thus it seems more likely that
his mask is simply pale, intermediate in colour between normal
male and female masks.[19] When the Relative is dressed up as a
woman, the beard is removed from his mask by some stage
business (218–35), but he undoubtedly continues to wear the
dark mask, and the combination of a dark face and feminine
clothes give him an absurd appearance for all the rest of the play,
becoming even more ludicrous when the feminine clothes are
found to have a phallus underneath (643–8). At the end, when
Euripides appears disguised as an old woman, there is no mention
of shaving; perhaps he wears a cloth wrapped all round his head
and chin, concealing the beard but leaving the forehead, eyes,
and nose of the dark mask visible. Whatever the exact details, in
all these characters it is the combination of male and female
indicators which is grotesque and laughable.

[18] Cf. Stone *Costume* 22–7.
[19] Masks of this colour were probably used also for other male characters
mocked for their pallor, such as the students in *Clouds* and Khairephon in *Wasps*
1412–14.

THE THESMOPHORIA

The Thesmophoria were an annual festival in honour of Demeter and her daughter (Kore or Pherephatta or Persephone), who on this occasion had the title *thesmophoros*. In antiquity this title was believed to mean 'bringing law', implying that the two goddesses were givers of civilization;[20] there is no strong reason to reject this interpretation, although modern scholars have proposed various others. The festival was held in the autumn, on 11, 12, and 13 Pyanopsion. The middle day was apparently the most important, and that is the day on which the action of the play takes place.[21] Many women probably attended on that day only; the Relative remarks on the crowd which can be seen going up to the temple on that day (280–1). But huts or tents are also mentioned (658, cf. 624), in which those attending the whole festival may have stayed at night.

The place of celebration was called the Thesmophorion, but there is doubt about its location. There are two main views. One is based on 657–8, where the women say they must search the whole Pnyx to see if a man has got in. From this it is inferred that the Thesmophorion was situated on the Pnyx hill, close to the normal meeting-place of the Assembly.[22] However, since the women in the play have been holding their own assembly, which Aristophanes has presented partly as a comic reflection of the real Assembly of men, it is possible that they are merely calling their meeting-place Pnyx in imitation of the real Assembly. If so, there is no evidence that the Thesmophorion was on the actual Pnyx, and Broneer has argued that it is more likely to have been in the precinct of the Eleusinion, which was the main centre for worship of Demeter and Kore in Athens, situated where the south-east corner of the Agora slopes up towards the Akropolis; or it may even be simply an alternative name for the whole Eleusinion, used on the occasion of the Thes-

[20] Kallimakhos *Hymn to Demeter* 18, Virgil *Aeneid* 4.58 with Servius ad loc.

[21] Lines 80 and 375 call it the middle day; 80 also calls it the third day. A scholiast explains that the Thesmophoria were celebrated on 10 Pyanopsion in the deme Halimous, so that the middle day of the celebration in Athens was the third day if the celebration at Halimous was counted in; cf. C. Austin *Dodone* 19 (1990) 15.

[22] This, the more widely held view, is best expounded by H. A. Thompson *Hesperia* 5 (1936) 151–200.

mophoria.[23] No archaeological evidence gives substantial support to either view.

The question is not unimportant for our understanding of the play. If the Thesmophorion was on the Pnyx hill, it must have been very small (for a large temple would have left archaeological traces) and the women cannot have met inside it but must have gathered in the meeting-place of the men's Assembly.[24] There will have been room there for thousands of women, and their proceedings, influenced by the formal setting of tiered seats, may have resembled an Assembly meeting in real life and not merely in Aristophanes' comic imagination. If, on the other hand, the Thesmophoria were celebrated at the Eleusinion, that precinct cannot have held more than a few hundred women. We know that each deme chose two women to be *arkhousai*, 'leaders', who (or some of whom, selected by lot) assisted in the ritual of the Thesmophoria; to be so chosen was an honour and a mark of respectability.[25] Perhaps only these women (about three hundred) customarily attended. If so, we should imagine the gathering at the festival not as an indiscriminate crowd of women of all classes, but as a relatively small and sedate meeting of respectable ladies, justifying the phrase 'well-born women' (330). In that case the notion of their holding an assembly meeting at the festival is not modelled on real life, but is a comic flight of fancy by Aristophanes. I am inclined to think this latter interpretation preferable, but I see no way of deciding the question for certain.

The plot of the play clearly implies that no men were allowed to attend the festival, and that the proceedings were secret from men. It is a joke that the beardless Kleisthenes is allowed in because he is the women's representative among the men, and even he is told to stand aside when the women become suspicious of the Relative and question 'her' about the secret rituals to check 'her' claim to have attended the festival every year.

---

[23] O. Broneer *Hesperia* 11 (1942) 250–74.

[24] This view is possibly supported by the fact that, on the only known occasion when the Assembly met on 11 Pyanopsion, the men met in the theatre, not on the Pnyx (*IG* 2² 1006.50–1). Was that because the Pnyx was occupied by the women on that day? The force of this evidence is doubtful, because it belongs to a later era (122 BC).

[25] Isaios 8.19–20, *IG* 2² 1184.

WOMAN [*to Kleisthenes*]. Let me; I'll question her on last year's rites.
    But you must move away, please; you're a man
    And mustn't overhear. [*To the Relative*] Now tell me, you,
    Which of our rituals was first performed?
RELATIVE. Well now, which one was first? We had a drink.
WOMAN. And after that, what next?
RELATIVE.   We drank a toast.
WOMAN. Well, someone's told you that. And what was third?
RELATIVE. Xenylla was caught short, and used a bowl.
WOMAN. What rubbish! Here, come back here, Kleisthenes!
    This is the man.

                      (*Women at the Thesmophoria* 626–35)

Here, as in *Lysistrata*, we have the conventional joke that women drink whenever they get a chance; the Relative guesses that their main activity at the festival was drinking, and hilariously his guess turns out to be right. This is not evidence for the proceedings at the festival in real life. Although it was known that the women fasted (948–9, 984), it is not clear that Aristophanes otherwise knew what the proceedings really were. Modern scholars have tried to reconstruct the rituals of the Thesmophoria, using mainly evidence from later periods, much of it not Athenian, and to establish their 'meaning'.[26] Such investigation is not relevant here. Aristophanes is not trying to portray or interpret the real rituals. He has simply picked on the Thesmophoria as being a festival well known to be attended only by women and thus a good setting for his comic story of women protesting about Euripides.

He stages a feminized version of the proceedings in the real Assembly of men. First come prayers to various gods for the success of the meeting, and curses on those regarded as traitors to the community.[27] Some details of the joke elude us because we do not possess the wording of the prayers and curses in the real Assembly, but the main points seem to be two. The first is to mock the verbose rigmarole of the traditional wording, which evidently included a long list of gods and also some prohibitions which seemed to Ari-

[26] For two recent discussions see W. Burkert *Greek Religion* (trans. J. Raffan, Oxford 1985) 242–6, H. S. Versnel *Inconsistencies in Greek and Roman Religion* 2 (Leiden 1993) 228–88. An attempt to link the myth and rituals of the Thesmophoria to the play is made by Bowie *Aristophanes* 205–17.

[27] This passage (295–371) is analysed by J. A. Haldane *Philologus* 109 (1965) 39–46.

stophanes to be absurdly out-of-date, including curses on anyone who tried to make peace with Persia (hostilities with the Persians had ended around 449 BC) or to restore the tyrant (who was expelled in 510 BC). The second is to include feminine references throughout. In our era of sensitivity to gender in language this may seem to some readers to be perfectly proper, but to the Athenians it will have sounded ridiculous. This part of the joke involves changing 'the people of Athens' (the supreme authority in the democracy) into 'the people of women', and treating Euripides as an enemy alongside Persia. In these lines notice how the feminine words are mostly reserved for the beginning of a new line where, following a slight pause, they come with greater impact.

> Pray to the gods, to the Olympians
> And Olympianesses, to the Pythians
> And Pythianesses, to the Delians
> And Delianesses, and the other gods.[28]
> Whoever makes a plot against the people
> Of women, or sends out a herald to
> Euripides and Persia to the harm
> Of women, or aspires to tyranny
> Or to restore the tyrant . . .

> (*Women at the Thesmophoria* 331–9)

The curse goes on to list various kinds of traitor to women; I shall return to them in a moment. Next a resolution of the council of women is read out; its prescript is like that of a resolution of the real Council, but the proposer and officials mentioned in it have women's names, not men's. The resolution orders the holding of an assembly to discuss how Euripides should be punished, and the heraldess then opens the debate with the words traditional in the real Assembly, 'Who wishes to speak?' One woman steps forward, puts on a crown as speakers in the Assembly did, makes a speech which, at least at the start, parodies real politicians' speeches, and ends with an undertaking to draw up a written proposal in consultation with the secretaryess (432). Another woman delivers a shorter speech, and then the Relative makes his contribution. But at this stage the joke about the procedure of the Assembly gets forgotten. Instead there are jokes about women.

[28] The Pythian and Delian gods are those worshipped at Pytho (Delphi) and Delos.

WOMEN

Jokes about women are more fully developed in *Women at the Thesmophoria* than in either of the other two plays in which women are prominent, but they are mostly on the same two themes: wine and sex. Essentially they are men's jokes about women.[29]

Wine appears in the women's curse against their enemies at the start of their meeting: their enemies include wine-sellers who give short measure (347–8). The woman who makes the first speech complains that nowadays husbands, taught by Euripides to distrust their wives, lock up their stores of food and drink with keys and seals difficult to copy (418–28). The climax of the jokes about wine comes when the Relative, caught by the women, seizes the baby of one of them as a hostage and threatens to kill it if he is not released; the 'baby', when unwrapped from its clothes, turns out to be a wineskin full of wine, and as he plunges his knife into it the mother is desperate to catch its 'blood' in a bowl (689–762). Clearly it was a standing joke among men that women were constantly having drinks in secret. Perhaps some women did, but there is no evidence that alcoholism among women was actually commoner in ancient Athens than at any other time or place.

The sex jokes are not about marital intercourse between wives and husbands, but about wives having secret affairs with other men. Husbands bar and seal the women's rooms and keep dogs to scare lovers away (414–17). When they come home they look suspiciously at their wives and search the house for a hidden lover (395–406). Yet, says the Relative when disguised as a woman, 'we' are cunning enough to have lovers all the same.

> RELATIVE. Well, not to mention anybody else,
>   I know the cunning things I've done myself.
>   The worst was three days after I was married.
>   My husband was in bed with me, and then
>   A friend who'd screwed me at the age of seven
>   Came scratching at the door for love of me.
>   I knew him straightaway, and crept downstairs.
>   My husband asked 'Where are you going?' 'Where?
>   I've such a colic pain, dear, in my stomach.
>   I'm going to the loo.' 'All right, go on.'

[29] On the women in this play see especially Taaffe *Ar. and Women* 74–102.

Then he mixed juniper and dill and sage,[30]
While I poured water on the hinge[31] and went
To meet my lover. That's when I was bonked
Beside Agyieus,[32] clinging to the bay-tree!

(*Women at the Thesmophoria* 476–89)

This story is an outrageous invention, told by a character who is not actually a woman at all. Of course the notion that wives are always having it off with lovers is comic overstatement. Yet Athens was a place where most marriages were arranged by a girl's father with a man who was often considerably older than she was. It may often have been the case that a young wife had no romantic feeling towards her husband, who therefore had some cause to suspect her. One real-life instance is well known: Euphiletos kept a careful eye on his wife until their child was born, and his trust in her even after that turned out to be unjustified.[33] So Aristophanes is humorously exaggerating what may have been a real problem in Athenian life.

The traitors cursed by the women include the woman-servant who introduces a lover to the wife and then tells the husband or who takes false messages between the wife and the lover, the deceitful lover who does not keep his promises, the old lady who pays a lover, and the courtesan who takes money and cheats a lover (340–6). They also include anyone who betrays a wife who smuggles a baby into the house (339–40). The first woman speaking at the meeting also complains at the difficulty of doing that (407–9); and the Relative, still disguised, tells another outrageous story about how it was once done.

RELATIVE. Another woman claimed to be in labour
    For ten days, while she tried to buy a baby;
    Her husband went round buying birth-inducers.
    A woman brought the baby in a pot,
    Its mouth stopped with a piece of honeycomb.
    Then, when she tipped the wink, the wife called out
    'Now leave me, husband, for the baby's coming!'
    Because it kicked the belly—of the pot.

---

[30] Remedies for the gripes which he thinks his wife has.
[31] To prevent creaking, which would make the husband aware that his wife was going out.
[32] The altar and pillar of Apollo standing outside the house.
[33] Lysias 1.6–8.

He joyfully ran out, she pulled the comb
Out of the baby's mouth, and then it yelled.
The wicked hag that brought the baby in
Ran smiling to the husband and declared
'You've got a lion for a son, a lion!
Your spitting image—specially his cock!
It's just the same as yours, a pinecone shape!'

(*Women at the Thesmophoria* 502–16)

A modern reader naturally wonders why a wife might want to bring in a baby secretly and pass it off as her own. We get a clue from another assertion by the Relative, that a woman exchanged her own baby girl for a slave's baby boy (564–5). The explanation is that a husband generally wanted a son to be his heir, and if his wife failed to give birth to a son he might divorce her and marry someone else for this purpose. So a wife who had not produced a boy, and was desperate to avoid being discarded, might procure an unwanted male baby from a poor woman and pretend that it was hers.[34]

All these jokes about women are men's jokes. They are tales about the mischief that women get up to if one doesn't keep an eye on them: they are *always* trying to filch a drink, get off with a lover, or pretend they have done their job of producing a boy. None of these situations is presented with any real sympathy for the woman. The audience is not encouraged to think that women should be free to drink wine when they wish, or that it is hard on them to be thrust into an arranged marriage with an unloved husband, or that they should not feel threatened if no male baby is born. It is simply assumed that it is their duty in real life to conform to their husbands' requirements, but it is laughable in a comedy if they try to wriggle out of them. To a modern reader, especially a modern female reader, it all seems exceedingly patronizing.

There is just one passage in this play which at first sight appears to be a defence of women. But this impression is misleading, for Aristophanes here is sarcastic. It is the parabasis, in which the chorus, as often, speaks about its own character (785–829).[35] The women purport to praise themselves and show that they are superior

---

[34] Cf. J. F. Gardner *G&R* 36 (1989) 55–7.

[35] For different views of this parabasis see Moulton *Ar. Poetry* 127–35, Hubbard *Mask* 195–9, Taaffe *Ar. and Women* 76–8.

to men. If (they say) women are an evil, as you allege, why do you marry us? Why are you so keen to keep us in your houses? Why does every man gaze at a girl who shows herself at a window? Women's names imply that they are better than men; for example, Nausimakhe (meaning 'fighting with ships' and apparently a common woman's name)[36] is obviously better than Kharminos, who recently lost a naval battle! *These* people (the spectators in the theatre) are more often criminals than we are; and some of them throw away their weapons (spear and shield) whereas we preserve ours (loom and wool-basket). The whole passage is a sequence of comic paradoxes, mocking the Athenian audience, in much the same way as the chorus of *Clouds* boasts of its services to the Athenians (575–94) and the chorus of *Birds* tells them that they would be better off with wings (785–800). Just as in those plays Aristophanes is not saying seriously that clouds and birds are better than men, so also in the parabasis of *Women at the Thesmophoria* the argument that women are superior to men is intended to be laughable; every Athenian man knew perfectly well that women were inferior. There could hardly be plainer evidence that Aristophanes was addressing his play to a male audience.

EURIPIDES

The second half of the play consists almost entirely of the Relative's attempts to escape from the women. The ideas for escape come from plays of Euripides.

First, *Telephos*. The Relative seizes the baby of one of the women, runs to the altar with this hostage, and threatens to kill it if he is not released. Aristophanes must have in mind the seizure of the baby Orestes by Telephos, which he had already put to comic use in *Akharnians* (see pp. 56–7).[37] However, by now it was twenty-seven years since Euripides' *Telephos* was performed. Presumably many (say half) of the audience at *Women at the Thesmophoria* had not seen it, and those who had seen it might well have forgotten it. Aristophanes cannot assume that they will recognize the Euripidean

---

[36] If this seems to us a strange name for a woman, perhaps we should recall the lady named Trafalgar in Pinero's *Trelawny of the 'Wells'*.

[37] Cf. Rau *Paratragodia* 42–50.

origin of the device, and does not remind them of it; neither Euripides nor Telephos is named in this passage (689–762). Instead he makes it comic in itself: the 'baby' turns out to be a wineskin, so that the main point of the incident is mockery not of tragedy but of women's bibulousness.[38]

Second, *Palamedes*.[39] This was a more recent play of Euripides, performed in 415 BC. Thus many in the audience would remember it, and for the benefit of those who do not Aristophanes takes care to make the Relative say 'I know a device from *Palamedes*' (769–70). In that tragedy, the scholiast tells us, Oiax, brother of Palamedes, wanted to inform their father in Greece of the treacherous manner in which Palamedes had been put to death at Troy, and to keep the message secret he carved it on oars and cast them into the sea, hoping that one or other of them would be washed up on the Greek shore. We do not know why Euripides made Oiax employ this strange method of communication; presumably it was done off-stage and described in a speech. Aristophanes evidently thought it ludicrous. So the Relative looks around for oars on which to send a message to Euripides; at a temple he naturally fails to find any, and instead writes his message on votive tablets and casts them in all directions. The point of this is simply to mock a rather absurd passage in a tragedy.

Euripides does not respond to *Palamedes* ('He must be ashamed of it', 848), and the Relative wonders which other play will draw him. 'I know! I'll imitate his recent[40] *Helen*' (850). This makes clear to the audience that the next passage will be based on *Helen*, performed last year.[41] Many would have a general recollection of that play, but of course would not know the lines by heart. *Helen* is a play we still have; so in this case we can compare the two texts and see exactly how Aristophanes uses Euripides. He keeps some

---

[38] Aristophanes may have had *Telephos* in mind also in the Relative's speech in defence of Euripides (466–519), which at some points resembles Dikaiopolis' speech about the origin of the war (*Akharnians* 497–556); cf. p. 61 and Rau *Paratragodia* 38–40. But in this speech too he does not name *Telephos* and does not expect the audience necessarily to think of it.

[39] Cf. Rau *Paratragodia* 51–3.

[40] This word (καινήν) may imply 'newfangled'. For discussion of the novelties in *Helen*, which may have encouraged Aristophanes to make fun of it, see W. G. Arnott *Antichthon* 24 (1990) 1–18.

[41] On this parody see Rau *Paratragodia* 53–65.

lines verbatim, but he selects, abridges, simplifies, and adapts so as to make a brief but effective reminiscence of the tragedy. The Relative, who is still dressed as a woman, plays the role of Helen marooned in Egypt after the Trojan War, and Euripides arrives to play her husband Menelaos. The most hilarious feature of the scene is the incomprehension of the woman left by the others to guard the Relative, for example:

EURIPIDES. Who holdest sway within these mighty halls
   To welcome strangers from the ocean swell,
   Exhausted by the storm and wreck of ships?
RELATIVE. This Proteus' palace is.
WOMAN.   What! Proteus's,
   You utter wretch? By the Two Goddesses,
   He's lying! Proteas died ten years ago.[42]
EURIPIDES. What country makes the landfall of our bark?
RELATIVE. Egypt.
EURIPIDES.   Ah me, to what a place we've voyaged!
WOMAN. Do you believe the trash this scoundrel talks?
   This place here is the Thesmophorion.

(*Women at the Thesmophoria* 871–80)

In *Helen* Menelaos succeeds in rescuing Helen from Egypt, but in *Women at the Thesmophoria* the scheme to emulate him fails when it is interrupted by one of the Prytaneis with a Skythian archer-policeman. Euripides flees, the Relative is tied up with his back to a board, and the Archer is left to guard him. But when the Archer leaves his post for a few minutes to fetch a mat to sit on, the Relative and Euripides launch into yet another Euripidean parody.

Andromeda had been performed in the previous year at the same festival as *Helen*, and so will have been equally fresh in the audience's mind. The text is not preserved, but a central feature of it was Andromeda chained to a rock on the shore and liable to be devoured by a sea-monster; Perseus then flew down with his winged sandals to rescue her.[43] The Relative fastened to a board (and still wearing

---

[42] Proteus was a mythical king of Egypt, but Proteas was an Athenian general at the beginning of the Peloponnesian War.

[43] For the fragments and reconstruction of this play see F. Bubel *Euripides: Andromeda* (Stuttgart 1991), R. Klimek-Winter *Andromedatragödien* (Stuttgart 1993) 55–315. On the parody see Rau *Paratragodia* 65–89.

woman's clothes) represents Andromeda fastened to a rock, and Euripides plays Perseus effecting a rescue. Although in this case we cannot compare the parody with the original, it seems to be more ambitious and varied than the previous one. The parody of *Helen* is based on the spoken lines only. The parody of *Andromeda* is partly musical. The Relative first sings an elaborate lament, which presumably guys the music as well as the words of a lament by Andromeda. Then follows a passage with Echo. Euripides' play must have had the nymph Echo heard from off-stage repeating words sung by Andromeda among the rocks. The device struck Aristophanes as ludicrous; so now he makes Euripides play Echo, first irritating the Relative by repeating whatever he says, and then creating utter bewilderment in the Archer, who rushes around trying to find the person who is flinging his own words back at him.[44] Only then does Euripides appear as Perseus, but the Archer is too stupid to appreciate the tragic references and chases him away, so that this rescue attempt fails too.

Finally Euripides abandons the idea of re-enacting his own plays, and offers to make peace with the women. If his Relative is released, he will not criticize them in future; but if they do not accept these terms, he will reveal their surreptitious activities to their husbands. They agree immediately, but point out that they do not control the Archer, whom Euripides himself must persuade. Euripides, now dressed as an old woman, produces a glamorous dancing-girl who absorbs the Archer's attention.[45] While the Archer is off-stage enjoying the girl, Euripides and the Relative make their escape, and the play ends with the chorus sending the Archer off in pursuit in the wrong direction.

The comic logic underlying these scenes of parody is as follows. The Relative, having been captured by the women, wants to get

[44] Heath *Political Comedy* 51 n. 106 and Sommerstein *Thesm.* 226–7 (on lines 1056–97) think that Echo is not played by Euripides; but who else would be participating in this parody of *Andromeda*? Their error arises from their belief that Echo appears on-stage. She does not; in 1083–97 the Archer becomes frantic because he cannot see her. Aristophanes is making fun of the use of an invisible character in *Andromeda*, but Heath's and Sommerstein's interpretation destroys the joke.

[45] The suggestion of E. Bobrick *Arethusa* 24 (1991) 67–76, that this device is inspired by Euripides' *Iphigeneia in Tauris*, seems to me far-fetched. Sexual temptation is a comic method of influencing a man; cf. *Frogs* 513–20, and of course the main theme of *Lysistrata*.

Euripides to come and rescue him, as he promised he would if necessary (269–76). So he wants to communicate to Euripides the fact that he is a prisoner, and he thinks that the way to attract Euripides' attention is by imitating a Euripidean character. The imitation of *Palamedes* fails, but the imitation of *Helen* succeeds in getting Euripides to come. But then there is the second problem of how Euripides is to rescue the Relative from his guards (first the Woman, afterwards the Archer). The comic idea is that he will use the same methods as he used last year, in this same theatre, for the rescue of Helen and Andromeda. But these methods fail, because the successive guards are too hostile or too stupid to join in the dramatic illusion as the audience at a tragedy should. When the devices of tragedy fail, Euripides resorts in the end to a phallic scheme more appropriate to comedy.

Critics have wondered whether all this is intended to be a satirical attack on Euripides or not. Hansen, for example, writes of 'the supposed failure of Agathon and Euripides as tragic poets',[46] whereas Murray says 'it is difficult to see how Euripides can have regarded the *Thesmophoriazusae* as anything but a tremendous compliment'.[47] Murray is surely right to distinguish the treatment of Euripides in this play from the treatment of Agathon; Agathon is ridiculed for his effeminacy, but there is no suggestion that Euripides is effeminate. Nor is there really any implication that his tragedies are failures, as tragedies. What they fail to do is to resolve a comic problem; for that a comic solution is required. The humour of these scenes arises from the incongruity of the tragic language and actions in the comic context; this need not imply that there was anything wrong with them in their original tragic context.

THE SKYTHIAN ARCHER

The Archer is the largest barbarian role in any of Aristophanes' plays. He is one of the force of Skythians who were established in Athens earlier in the fifth century as public slaves to assist magistrates

---

[46]   H. Hansen *Philologus* 120 (1976) 184.
[47]   Murray *Aristophanes* 117.

in keeping order.[48] They were armed with bows and arrows, the traditional weapon of Skythians. In some ways they resembled modern police constables, but there was one very important difference: they could not take action on their own initiative, but only under the orders of a magistrate. They appear three times in Aristophanes. In *Akharnians* 54–8 the Herald, on behalf of the Prytaneis, orders archers to arrest Amphitheos who is impeding the business of the Assembly (and similar action is mentioned in *Horsemen* 665); in *Lysistrata* 433–62 the Proboulos orders archers to arrest Lysistrata and other women; and in *Women at the Thesmophoria* 930–4 the Prytanis orders the Archer to bind and guard the Relative, and to strike with a whip anyone who approaches him. These instances show adequately the kinds of function which the Skythian archers performed.

In *Akharnians* and *Lysistrata* the archers are non-speaking characters, but in *Women at the Thesmophoria* the Archer, though silent on his first appearance when given his orders by the Prytanis, becomes a speaking character when he reappears with the bound Relative. He speaks bad Greek, full of mistakes but still intelligible. Aristophanes is ridiculing the way Skythians talked, to make the Athenian audience laugh; he may be caricaturing it, but it has been plausibly argued that the character's speech is likely to be a realistic, though exaggerated, representation of the manner in which Skythians actually did try to speak Greek.[49] Many Athenians probably thought patronizingly that a man must be stupid if he could not speak Greek properly, and the Archer is presented as stupid in other ways too. He knows nothing about tragedy, and does not understand what Euripides and the Relative are doing when they perform passages of *Andromeda*. He is very easily taken in by Euripides' device of getting a pretty girl to distract his attention, and again by the women who send him off in the wrong direction at the end.

So the main comic effect in this part of the play is the simple one of the stupid character who gets things wrong; the spectators laugh because they feel superior. However, two recent critics have seen

---

[48] Andokides 3.5 dates the establishment of this force after the Thirty Years Peace (446/5 BC), but some scholars have suggested that it could have been as early as the 470s. Cf. U. Albini *Andocide: De Pace* (Florence 1964) 60–1, E. M. Hall *Philologus* 133 (1989) 44, V. J. Hunter *Policing Athens* (Princeton 1994) 145–9.

[49] Hall *Philologus* 133 (1989) 38–40.

more than this in the character of the Archer. Long argues that he combines cruelty with stupidity, and considers this depiction of a barbarian to be 'unforgiving'.[50] The chief evidence for this interpretation is 1002–6, where the Relative asks him to slacken his bonds, and he tightens them instead. This might be deliberate cruelty, or it might just be stupidity, if the Archer moves the nail or peg the wrong way by mistake; but it is much more likely that Aristophanes has inserted these lines because the Relative's squeals will amuse the audience, rather than to make any particular point about the character of the Archer.

Hall, agreeing that the Archer is cruel, sees further subtleties.[51] She suggests that he contributes to the paratragedy because he resembles the barbaric rulers who appear near the end of certain Euripidean plays, especially Thoas in *Iphigeneia in Tauris*, Theoklymenos in *Helen*, and probably Kepheus in *Andromeda*. It is certainly possible that those characters were at the back of Aristophanes' mind; he had obviously been thinking about *Helen* and *Andromeda* recently and must have had access to copies of the texts. But it is not the case that he expected the audience to make this connection. When he wants the audience to understand that someone is imitating a particular tragic character, he makes the identification explicit; thus in the previous scene, parodying *Helen*, the Relative calls himself Helen, Euripides Menelaos, and the woman guarding him Theonoe (862, 897, 910), and in this scene he tells us that he himself is becoming Andromeda and Euripides Perseus (1011–12). But he does not call the Archer Theoklymenos or Kepheus. More generally, Hall sees the ridicule of the Archer as an expression of the resentment of Athenian citizens at the humiliation of being arrested by slaves, and she links this with the repression imposed by the oligarchic regime in 411 BC. But here also she goes too far. There is no evidence that the force of Skythian archers in Athens was viewed as inimical to democracy and the rights of citizens. It had already been in existence for at least thirty years, and the democratic Assembly could have abolished it at any time in that period if it had wished to do so. It did not, because these Skythians were merely instruments of the Athenian magistrates; if a citizen felt humiliated by being arrested, it was the magistrate whom he blamed, not the

---

[50] T. Long *Barbarians in Greek Comedy* (Carbondale, Ill. 1986) 106–7.
[51] Hall *Philologus* 133 (1989) 40–54.

archers. When Amphitheos is arrested by archers, Dikaiopolis cries 'You're wronging the Assembly, Prytaneis!' (*Akharnians* 56). So also in *Women at the Thesmophoria* it is a Prytanis, a citizen selected by lot, executing the orders of the Council (943), who gives instructions for the Relative to be bound to a board.

Thus I doubt whether the last part of this play is intended as a serious criticism of barbarians in general or of the Skythian archers in particular. It is a scene of farce, in which the Relative and the Archer are both absurd. Indeed *Women at the Thesmophoria* as a whole contains hardly anything which has a serious intent. It does include three hymns to various gods, which may have been impressive musically as well as poetically (312–30, 953–1000, 1136–59); but the rest of the play is for laughs, making fun in turn of Agathon, women, Euripides, and the Skythian archers, with a comic old man as the connecting thread. This play has a stronger claim than any of the others to be regarded as pure entertainment.

Frogs

DIONYSOS

Euripides died in 406 BC, and in *Frogs*, performed at the Lenaia in 405, Dionysos, the god of drama, has come to the conclusion that there are no good tragedians left alive. So he decides to go down to the underworld and fetch Euripides back. Naturally he has never made the journey to Hades before, and he knows that most people who make it never come back.[1] One of the few who have successfully made the return journey is Herakles, who as one of his famous labours stole away Kerberos, the terrible three-headed hound which guarded the entrance to Hades. So Dionysos has disguised himself as Herakles (his own brother, since both are sons of Zeus), and begins the journey by calling at Herakles' house to ask his advice about the route. With him goes his slave Xanthias, who is riding on a donkey and carrying the luggage.

The opening lines include verbal jokes about overloaded slaves in comedy, but much of the comic effect must be visual. Xanthias grumbles loudly about a bundle of luggage which is visibly very small, and his steed is a 'pantomime' one, either one or (more likely) two actors dressed as a donkey.[2] Such a creature inevitably

[1] Actually a descent to Hades was not a new theme for a comedy. Aristophanes himself had already used it in the lost *Gerytades* (fr. 156), if that play is rightly dated before the departure of Agathon from Athens (fr. 178).

[2] Although real animals were probably used in Greek plays sometimes, the donkey in *Frogs* (like that in *Wasps*) is unlikely to have been a real one, because it makes its exit on its own some time before 165, and a real donkey could not be relied on to do that. If the donkey was real, it must have been led off by a slave of Herakles, as suggested by Dover *Frogs* 194 (on line 35); that seems less probable, because no slave, but Herakles himself, responded to Dionysos' call for a slave (37), and because it would not be as funny. A 'pantomime' donkey is both practicable and entertaining, as I have found when playing Xanthias myself with a donkey of this sort in an amateur production of *Frogs*.

looks funny and walks funnily. Dionysos looks funny too. To disguise
himself as Herakles he has adopted Herakles' traditional attributes,
a lion-skin and a club, but has failed to discard his own usual clothes.
Herakles of course is wearing his normal garb, so that when he
opens his door two lion-skin-clad and club-bearing figures confront
each other.

HERAKLES. Who's that knocked at the door? He jumped at it
    Just like a centaur, who—I say, what's this? [*He guffaws.*]
DIONYSOS. Here, boy!
XANTHIAS.   What is it?
DIONYSOS.   Didn't you notice?
XANTHIAS.   What?
DIONYSOS. How afraid of me he was.
XANTHIAS.   Yes—afraid you're mad.
HERAKLES. I really can't help laughing, by Demeter!
    I'm trying to bite my lip, but still I laugh!
DIONYSOS. Come here, old boy. I want to ask you something.
HERAKLES. But I can't shoo away my laughter when
    I see a lion-skin over a saffron robe!
    What for? Why a buskin and a club together?
    Where have you been?
DIONYSOS.   I served on Kleisthenes' ship.
HERAKLES. And were you in the battle?
DIONYSOS.   Yes, we sank
    Some enemy ships, about twelve or thirteen.
HERAKLES. The two of you?
DIONYSOS.   That's right.
XANTHIAS.   —Then I woke up!

                                        (*Frogs* 38–51)

A saffron-coloured robe (*krokotos*) and buskins (*kothornoi*, a kind
of high boots) were generally women's rather than men's attire, but
they were also the traditional dress of Dionysos.[3] Dionysos is
wearing them because they are his normal clothes (and in the theatre
this is what enables the audience to recognize him as soon as he
appears), but because they look rather effeminate they make a
ridiculous contrast with the exceedingly virile lion-skin and club.
The incongruity of softness and toughness is developed and varied
in the next lines: Dionysos boasts that he served in the navy and

---

[3] The *krokotos* and *kothornoi* are named as characteristic of Dionysos in Kratinos
40, Athenaios 198c, Pausanias 8.31.4; cf. Stone *Costume* 230–1.

fought in the recent battle, but the commander of the ship was Kleisthenes, a man of notoriously womanish appearance (see p. 257), and the claim to have sunk about a dozen enemy ships, so many that he cannot even remember the exact number, is obviously absurd. Dionysos is an effeminate character pretending to be manly and bold.

As the play goes on, this characterization is emphasized and elaborated. Dionysos boasts about his bravery as long as there is no danger (68–70, 279–84), but as soon as he thinks danger is imminent he is terrified (286–310, 479–93), and after his arrival in the underworld there is a splendid series of farcical scenes in which he twice gets Xanthias to take over the lion-skin and club and assume the role of Herakles to face some peril or unpleasantness. He is fat and physically unfit (128, 200). Despite his earlier boast about serving on Kleisthenes' ship, it turns out that, when he has to row Kharon's boat across a lake to reach Hades, he has no idea how to do it (197–205); this would seem contemptible and ridiculous especially to Athenian spectators, many of whom would have been oarsmen in the navy. Later in the play, when as god of drama he is invited to judge between Aeschylus and Euripides, surely he will be in his element? No; some of his comments on tragedy are uncomprehending and silly (e.g. 916–21, 930–4), while others reflect the standpoint of an ordinary spectator rather than an expert (e.g. 1028–9). Thus the audience is encouraged to laugh sometimes with him, sometimes at him.[4]

It is not possible for us to know for sure how far this characterization was new. Dionysos appears in no other extant comedy, but he did appear in some now lost, including Aristophanes' own *Babylonians* (see p. 30) and *Dionysos Shipwrecked*. Since all the plays were performed at his festivals, it was perfectly reasonable that both tragedies and comedies should include him; indeed, according to some accounts, the earliest plays were always about him, and people complained when this custom ceased to be kept and some plays were presented which were 'nothing to do with Dionysos'.[5] The fragments of other comedies in which he appeared amount to very little, but they are at least not incompatible with the assumption that it was traditional in comedy for him to be an effeminate,

[4] Cf. Dover *Frogs* 38–9.
[5] Cf. Pickard-Cambridge *Dithyramb* 124–6.

cowardly, incompetent buffoon. So perhaps Aristophanes has simply continued this existing tradition in *Frogs*.

The characterization of Herakles is certainly the traditional one in comedy, and we have seen it already in *Birds*. He is brawny and well-meaning, but completely unintellectual, and quite unable to understand why his little brother wants a poet. The one thing that really interests him is food.

DIONYSOS. Don't mock me, brother. I'm really in bad shape.
　　It's such a longing that's afflicting me.
HERAKLES. What sort of longing, kid?
DIONYSOS.　　　　　　　　　　　I can't explain.
　　But still, I'll tell you by analogies.
　　Have you ever felt a craving for pea soup?
HERAKLES. Pea soup? Oo yes, yum yum! Thousands of times!
DIONYSOS. Is it clear, or shall I explain another way?
HERAKLES. No, not about pea soup; I understand!

(*Frogs* 58–65)

As in *Birds* (see pp. 220–1), Aristophanes is using the gods as comic characters and wants the audience to laugh at them, but this does not necessarily mean that he and the audience do not believe in their real existence. Rather, the performance of a comedy was the right time and place for making fun of everyone, and the gods were assumed to be sensible enough to take a joke.

SLAVES AND THE NAVY

Dionysos, like an Athenian gentleman on a journey, is accompanied by his slave. Xanthias is a common name for a slave, borne by slaves in other plays too; but this Xanthias is a particularly prominent character. He cracks jokes, argues with his master, grumbles at the orders given to him and especially at having to carry luggage, pulls his master's leg by scaring him[6] and comments sarcastically on his terror, and twice takes over the role of Herakles.

His smartest trick is to get Dionysos whipped. When Dionysos has, for the second time, persuaded him to take over the lion-skin

---

[6] In 285–311 probably Xanthias is only pretending to hear and see a monster. This is not quite clear from the text, but the stage action would make it so.

and club to face whatever peril arises next, he is confronted by the doorkeeper of Hades (called Aiakos in most of the manuscripts) who arrests him for stealing the dog Kerberos. Xanthias then does just what an Athenian gentleman accused of theft might do: he offers his own slave as a witness to his innocence. (A personal slave would know more than anyone else about his master's activities.) A slave was expected to be generally ready to lie for his master, and so under Athenian law his testimony was not admissible unless he stuck to it even when subjected to torture by the opponent who wanted him to give evidence on the other side.[7] So Xanthias in a lordly manner gives the doorkeeper permission to torture his slave— Dionysos. Dionysos indignantly objects that he must not be tortured because he is a god, but Xanthias retorts that if he's a god he won't feel the pain, and the upshot is a slapstick passage in which both get beaten. Aristophanes here (as in *Birds*; cf. p. 220) is exploiting the logical absurdities that result from assuming that gods are subject to Athenian law.

Later Xanthias has a conversation with a slave of Plouton (possibly the doorkeeper or Aiakos again) in which they find that they both enjoy the same pleasures: cursing the master behind his back, grumbling after a beating, poking one's nose into the master's business and telling it to other people (743–53). These are jokes put in by Aristophanes to amuse an audience of slave-owners, who would think that naughty slaves did those things and would feel complacent if their own slaves did not. The other slave also tells Xanthias about the forthcoming contest between Aeschylus and Euripides, and then both exit and never reappear—probably because Aristophanes wants these two actors to play other parts in subsequent scenes.

Xanthias never openly defies his master. Even when he gets Dionysos whipped, he is ostensibly just pretending to be Herakles, which is what Dionysos told him to do. But he is certainly cheeky, not as respectful as we might have expected a slave to be. Dover, in an important discussion of this character, has pointed out that he sometimes dominates Dionysos, and communicates with the audience about his master in asides; 'so far as our extant evidence goes, Xanthias plays a new kind of slave-role', comparable only with (but not quite the same as) Karion in *Wealth*.[8] Dover

---

[7] Cf. MacDowell *Law* 245–7.
[8] Dover *Frogs* 43–50.

somewhat overstates the case because he fails to compare Xanthias in *Wasps*, who speaks more lines than Xanthias in *Frogs*, and who also confides in the audience about his old master and tells Philokleon to his face that he is mad (*Wasps* 1476–96, quoted on pp. 20–1). Nevertheless we may agree that Xanthias in *Frogs* has greater strength of character than any earlier slave in Greek literature.

Dover connects this with a recent development in the war. In the summer of 406, when the Peloponnesians had built up a fleet with assistance from Persia, the Athenians were desperate to find enough men to man their ships, and they offered Athenian citizenship to anyone who volunteered to serve in the navy. Some slaves did volunteer, served in the battle of Arginousai, and 'straightaway became Plataians,'[9] masters now instead of slaves' (694). Xanthias wishes he had volunteered, so that he would no longer need to obey a master's orders (33–4); because he failed to serve in the battle, he is still a slave, and that is why Kharon refuses to let him on to his boat (190–3).[10] The Athenians' willingness at this time to trust slaves to fight alongside them, and to make them citizens, must mean that they were gradually coming to accept that slaves could be as good as free men; and the creation by Aristophanes of more capable and confident slave characters is another sign of this change in public attitudes to slaves.

The battle of Arginousai was an Athenian victory, but it had an unfortunate aftermath. Twenty-five Athenian ships had been sunk, and because of bad weather no attempt was made to rescue the men on them, who consequently drowned. Recriminations followed in Athens, and eventually six of the generals who had been in command were executed for incompetence. Even though the battle had been won, these events must have cast a gloom over Athens around the time when *Frogs* was performed.

[9] At this period Plataians had almost the same status in Athens as Athenians. They were excluded only from holding office as an Arkhon or as a priest (Demosthenes 59.104–6; cf. MacDowell *Law* 71), and *Frogs* 694 means that the enfranchised slaves were subject to the same limitation as Plataians.

[10] I. Worthington *Hermes* 117 (1989) 359–63 questions this interpretation of the three passages of *Frogs*, but his alternative explanations seem to me much less plausible.

CHORUSES AND FESTIVALS

The chorus of this play, unusually, has two distinct roles. First, when Dionysos is rowing Kharon's boat across the lake to reach Hades, a chorus of Frogs appears.[11] Later, after arriving in Hades, he and Xanthias meet a chorus of Initiates, which remains on-stage for the rest of the play. Presumably the same choristers appeared in both roles.

The scene with the boat and the Frogs is a comic one. It probably involves some farcical business, with the Frogs clumsily hopping around and getting in the way of Dionysos' oars. It includes the famous refrain 'brekekekex koax koax', which is said to be a fair representation of the croak of the Marsh Frog,[12] and this leads to some kind of contest between the Frogs and Dionysos, although we cannot know exactly how the scene was staged. But it begins with references to the festival of Anthesteria.

This festival[13] was held over three days in early spring (approximately February) in celebration of Dionysos as god of wine, and its centre was the precinct of Dionysos in the Marshes. This was a separate precinct from the one which contained the theatre of Dionysos; its exact location is uncertain, but it was also near the Akropolis and so not far away from the other. On the first day, called Pithoigia, meaning 'cask-opening', the casks of grape juice from the previous autumn were opened and the new wine was tasted for the first time, with libations in honour of Dionysos. The second day was called Khoes, meaning 'jars' or 'jugs', presumably because on this day it was traditional to transfer the new wine from casks to smaller containers. Ceremonies included a public procession and a secret ritual inside the temple. For ordinary men it was a day for drinking, and there was a drinking contest, with a prize for the competitor who was the first to drain his jar or jug (the standard size of which was about five pints); this is the competition that Dikaiopolis wins

---

[11] The chorus of Frogs does, I believe, appear on-stage, visible to the audience, because otherwise the words of its song would not be clearly heard; cf. MacDowell *CR* 22 (1972) 3–5, Sifakis *Parabasis* 94–5, Dover *Frogs* 56–7. For the opposite view, that it is merely heard from off-stage, see R. H. Allison *G&R* 30 (1983) 8–20, Zimmermann *Untersuchungen* 1.164–7.

[12] Cf. Rogers *Frogs* 35, Dover *Frogs* 219.

[13] For details of the Anthesteria see W. Burkert *Homo Necans* (trans. P. Bing, Berkeley 1983) 213–47, *Greek Religion* (trans. J. Raffan, Oxford 1985) 237–42.

in *Akharnians*. In the evening the revellers trooped down to the
precinct of Dionysos in the Marshes to dedicate the garlands they
had been wearing; since sunset (not midnight) was regarded as the
end of a day, it was now the third day of the festival, named Khytroi,
which means 'pots' or 'pans' for cooking. (On this day a meal of
various grains was cooked in pots.) So the Frogs sing of the drinkers
coming to the precinct on Pots day.

> Brekekekex koax koax!
> Brekekekex koax koax!
> Marshy children of the streams,
> Let us join the pipe and raise
> Sounds of hymns, my lovely tune
>   Koax koax!
> Which we sing[14] for Zeus's son
>   Nysan[15] Dionysos in the Marshes,
> When the tipsy-revelling crowd
> On the holy day of Pots
>   Comes down to my precinct.
> Brekekekex koax koax!

> (*Frogs* 209–20)

This shows that these Frogs are the ones who dwell in the marshes
around the precinct of Dionysos in Athens. People who go down
there after the drinking on Jugs day hear them croaking in the dark.
Just as the Frogs 'sing' for Dionysos on that occasion, now they have
come to sing for him on his journey to Hades. That does not mean
that they are dead. Dionysos is not in Hades yet; the lake is at an
intermediate point on the route. (If we wish, we can assume that
the Frogs have travelled along a stream linking their marshy home
with Kharon's lake, but Aristophanes does not bother with such
details.) The whole passage (209–68) is a stroke of Aristophanes'
genius. In these few verses he combines the tradition of comic
hymns, the tradition of animal choruses, a joyful celebration familiar
to the audience, and the character of Dionysos with (one assumes)
effective music and amusing action.

After Dionysos has disembarked, the scene in which Xanthias

[14] *Pace* Dover *Frogs* ad loc., I take ἰαχήσαμεν to refer to a regular event
('gnomic aorist') because the next clause (ἡνίχ' ... χωρεῖ) synchronizes it with
a present tense; cf. the tenses in 229–34.

[15] Nysa was the name of a mountain associated with Dionysos.

scares him by pretending to see a monster gives the choristers a few minutes to change into their second role as people who have been initiated into the Mysteries. Various places in Greece had secret rituals known as mysteries, but for the Athenians 'the Mysteries' meant the ones held at Eleusis, a few miles west of Athens. Many believed that initiation would secure for them a happy existence after death. So, for a comedy set in Hades, what chorus could be more appropriate than one composed of people who have now actually reached that joyful state?

The secret rituals at Eleusis, including the initiation of new members, were the culmination of an annual festival held at the end of the summer in honour of Demeter and her daughter (Kore or Persephone or Pherrephatta).[16] Demeter is a goddess of the earth, who makes plants grow out of it, and her daughter is the seed, disappearing beneath the earth in autumn and re-emerging in spring; she is regarded as married to the god of the underworld, spending the winter with him and the summer with her mother. Thus the mother and daughter have it in their power to give life after death; hence their connection with the Mysteries. The festival also honoured another deity named Iakkhos. Little is known of him; when mentioned elsewhere, he is sometimes identified with Dionysos, but Aristophanes seems not to make this identification, for in *Frogs*, when the chorus invokes Iakkhos, Dionysos shows no sign of thinking that he himself is being addressed.

The entrance-song (parodos) of the chorus of Initiates is an elaborate sequence of songs and speeches, in which several parts of the Eleusinian festival are imitated or parodied; Aristophanes assumes that the Initiates' happy existence in the underworld consists, at least in part, of the same kinds of activity as the festival on earth.[17] The festival began with a proclamation by a herald in the Agora of Athens, inviting people to attend and be initiated: anyone might come who had clean hands (that is, was not guilty of bloodshed) and intelligible speech (that is, Greek), and who had lived righteously; all others were excluded. Aristophanes parodies

[16] For details of the Eleusinian Mysteries see especially G. E. Mylonas *Eleusis and the Eleusinian Mysteries* (Princeton 1961), Burkert *Homo Necans* (trans. Bing) 248–97, *Greek Religion* (trans. Raffan) 285–90. Bowie *Aristophanes* 228–53 seeks echoes of the Eleusinian festival throughout *Frogs*, but those which he finds in and after the parabasis are not very convincing.

[17] Cf. Dover *Frogs* 61–3.

this by having the chorus-leader deliver a speech excluding all not acquainted with——comedy, of which Kratinos is taken as representative.

> Keep holy silence and stand aside, give our choruses room for their
>   dances,
> All ye who are not clean in thought and are still unacquainted with this
>   kind of speeches,
> Who never have witnessed the rites of the generous Muses nor joined
>   in the dances,
> And were not introduced to the Bakkhic tongue-rites that belong to
>   bull-eating Kratinos!

(*Frogs* 354–7)

Pigs were the customary sacrifice at the Eleusinian festival, and that is why Xanthias smells pork cooking (338).[18] After preliminary proceedings in Athens anyone could join in the great procession to Eleusis, led by the priest and image of Iakkhos. It was a long walk of about fourteen miles. People would sing as they walked, and some of the songs which Aristophanes provides for this scene probably echo those which were customary in the procession.

> Iakkhos, full of honour, the inventor
> Of lovely festal song, come hither with us
>   To see the Goddess,
> And show us how you painlessly
>   Complete a lengthy journey.
> Iakkhos, lover of dancing, join in my procession!

(*Frogs* 398–403)

It seems to have been a custom that, where the road to Eleusis crossed a bridge over the river Kephisos, men waited with heads covered and hurled insults at important people in the procession as they passed, perhaps for an apotropaic purpose, in the belief that men humbled in this way were less likely to be humiliated by misfortunes sent by the gods; and Aristophanes echoes this in an abusive song about some well-known men (416–30).[19] When the

---

[18] The mention of pork makes a comic anticlimax. There is no good reason to seek in addition 'a very coarse joke' (Dover *Frogs* ad loc.).

[19] Dover *Frogs* 247–8 refers to the evidence of this custom, but expresses some doubt about its relevance to the play.

procession reached Eleusis, dancing continued in the fields all night by torchlight, and Aristophanes' songs make reference to that too (340–53, 371, etc.). But there is no allusion at all to the secret rituals inside the temple. Thus Aristophanes avoids any accusation of the kind made against Alkibiades and others ten years earlier, that he is profaning the Mysteries by revealing their secrets.

The whole scene is one in which we miss a great deal by not having the music. We may also miss echoes of other features of the Eleusinian festival which are not known to us. But it is clear that the scene has two main functions: it is an elaborate musical entertainment, and it presents an important part of Athenian religious life in a manner suitable for comedy.

POLITICIANS AND CITIZENS

Political topics are notably absent from the early part of *Frogs* but become more prominent towards the middle of the play, where jokes are made about three individual politicians.

Theramenes was notorious for changing sides. In 411 BC he was a member of the oligarchic regime of Four Hundred, but a few months later he was one of those who overthrew the Four Hundred and set up the broader oligarchy of Five Thousand. After that government in turn was overthrown in 410, he continued to live in Athens under the restored democracy, although other leaders of the Four Hundred had been executed or banished. He was in command of an Athenian ship at the battle of Arginousai in 406, and afterwards was blamed for the failure to rescue the shipwrecked sailors (see p. 279), but managed to avoid punishment. His political nimbleness and side-changing caused him to be nicknamed 'buskin' (*kothornos*) because that type of footwear fitted either foot. In *Frogs*, when Dionysos repeatedly swaps roles and dress with Xanthias, the chorus call him 'a natural Theramenes' (541), and later Dionysos himself makes Theramenes the object of a sarcastic joke about his cleverness whenever he is on the point of getting into trouble (968–70).

Kleophon had become the leading politician in Athens after the restoration of democracy in 410, and between then and his death in 404 he strongly and successfully resisted proposals that Athens should enter into peace negotiations with Sparta. That being so, it is surprising that Aristophanes pays so little attention to him; he is mentioned only three times. 'Let Kleophon fight,' says the chorus at the very end (1532), implying that the rest of us don't want to, but otherwise there is nothing in this play about the desirability of making peace. Near the end Kleophon is just one in a list of men whom Plouton would like to see in Hades (1504), and in the ode of the parabasis, he is merely mocked for having a Thracian accent: 'Kleophon, on whose bilingual lips a Thracian swallow utters a terrible roar' (678–81). It seems to have been a regular joke to say that Kleophon's mother was Thracian; whether she really was is not clear.[20] The antode of the parabasis mocks Kleigenes, the keeper of a public bath, who is said to be 'not peaceful' (714–15); that possibly, but not certainly, means that he made a speech in the Assembly supporting Kleophon's opposition to peace negotiations.

These jokes about individuals do not give much political content to the play. More significant are the two speeches of the parabasis. The first (the epirrhema) begins with the statement that it is a duty of the chorus to offer good advice and instruction—a clear indication that something serious is coming (cf. pp. 4–5).

We, the sacred chorus, have a duty to the citizens:
We should offer good advice and teaching. First, then, we believe
Citizens should all be equal and should not be under threat.
Those who came a cropper, tripped by Phrynikhos's[21] wrestling-
          tricks—
Well, they did slip up that time, but now they ought to be allowed
Pardon for their past offences, and atonement for mistakes.
I say no one in the city should incur disfranchisement.
It's disgraceful that, whereas the men who fought at sea just once
Straightaway became Plataians, masters now instead of slaves—
And I don't say that they shouldn't; that's a good thing, I agree;
It's the one thing that you've done that really showed some common
          sense—
But, besides, there are the men who've fought so often by your side
In the navy, and their fathers also; they're your kith and kin:
Surely you should let them off this one misfortune, when they ask.
You Athenians are clever: let your anger take a rest.
Let's make everyone our kinsfolk, let's be willing to accept

[20] Cf. MacDowell in *Tr.Com.Pol.* 369–70.
[21] Phrynikhos was one of the leaders of the Four Hundred. He is not to be confused with either the early tragic dramatist or the contemporary comic dramatist of the same name, both mentioned elsewhere in *Frogs*.

All who fight in naval battles as enfranchised citizens.
If we get all high-and-mighty, standing on our dignity
Even when the city's storm-tossed, sinking in the troughs of waves,
People in the future will look back and think that we were fools.

(*Frogs* 686–705)

The first part of the advice given here concerns men who supported the oligarchic government of the Four Hundred. They had not all suffered the same fate when it fell. Phrynikhos himself was murdered. Other ringleaders, including Peisandros and Antiphon, were either condemned to death by a court or fled into exile to avoid execution. Some, notably Theramenes, were exonerated because they had turned against the oligarchy, or at least had not misused their power. Other members of the regime continued to live in Athens but suffered disfranchisement (*atimia*),[22] while those who were not actual members of the Four Hundred but supported them by military service suffered partial disfranchisement, losing only the right to speak in the Assembly or be members of the Council.[23] Now, says Aristophanes, more than five years later, it is time to forgive them. He does not distinguish the different categories, and presumably means that pardon should be extended to the worst offenders who are now in exile as well as to the others who are merely disfranchised. Any opposition to democracy is a serious offence, but he tries to minimize it by the language he uses here, suggesting that they were led astray by Phrynikhos, and were unfortunate rather than criminal.

But then he goes further. Not only those who supported the oligarchy, but all citizens who have been disfranchised, for debt to the state or for any other offence, should have their rights restored (692). They are, after all, Athenians; they and their ancestors have fought for Athens for centuries—unlike the slaves who have been enfranchised with Plataian status after volunteering for service in the battle of Arginousai (cf. p. 279). Yet he does not object to the enfranchisement of the slaves. He emphasizes his approval of that step, and then goes further still: this policy should be continued, and everyone who is willing to serve in the navy in future should be enfranchised likewise (701–2). All men, whether citizens, for-

---

[22] Andokides 1.78; cf. Lysias 20.19, 20.35.
[23] Andokides 1.75.

eigners, or slaves, should be equal, provided that they fight for Athens in its time of need.

This is, for fifth-century Greece, an astounding proposal. It echoes the proposal made six years before in *Lysistrata* (see pp. 235–9), but goes beyond it; for in the *Lysistrata* passage there is no mention of slaves, nor of citizens disfranchised for offences other than debt. The enfranchisement of all slaves volunteering for naval service, if it had been made a permanent arrangement, not just for the one occasion in 406, would have produced a big drop in the number of slaves, and it is not surprising that the Athenians did not adopt this suggestion. They did, however, follow the advice to restore the rights of disfranchised citizens (see p. 298).

There is more advice in the speech which concludes the parabasis (the antepirrhema). This is not about ordinary citizens, but about political leaders, and it is introduced by a famous comparison with Athenian coinage. The same thing has happened to the best men, says the chorus, as to the old silver coins and the new gold ones. At this time the Athenians had three kinds of coinage. For nearly two centuries they had used silver coins, but in the latter part of the Peloponnesian War, when the Spartans occupied Dekeleia, they could no longer get regular access to their silver mines at Laureion. So in 407/6 they melted down some gold dedications on the Akropolis to make gold coins; but even a small gold coin has a high value, and these were not much use for everyday shopping. A few months before the performance of *Frogs*, therefore, they produced some bronze coins plated with silver. These were, like most modern coins, tokens, representing a higher amount than the intrinsic value of the metal they contained. Consequently they were unpopular, and Gresham's law operated: the bronze coins were constantly in circulation, while the silver and gold disappeared.[24]

That is just how it is, says the chorus, with our citizens. We treat insultingly those who are well-born, well-behaved, upright, fine, good men, with the traditional education in music and athletics, and instead we use for every purpose the bronze, foreign, red-haired ones, bad sons of bad fathers, the latest arrivals (727–33).

[24] I follow the usual view here, but there is some disagreement about the numismatic details. Cf. W. E. Thompson *Mnemosyne* 19 (1966) 337–43, A. Giovannini *GRBS* 16 (1975) 185–90, J. H. Kroll *GRBS* 17 (1976) 329–41, W. Weiser *ZPE* 76 (1989) 275.

'We use' must mean that they are elected to be generals and to hold other important offices. The passage seems to mean that such offices are now given to recent immigrants and not to the members of old-established Athenian families. But no names are mentioned.

Whom has Aristophanes in mind? Since the chorus has recently been singing about Kleophon's Thracian accent, and he was the most prominent politician at this time, we can be sure that he is supposed to be one of the 'bronze' leaders who ought to be discarded. But the identity of the man or men whom Aristophanes would like to lead Athens instead is less clear; for this we have to await an indication later in the play (see pp. 293–7). Meanwhile we may note a significant difference between the two speeches. The epirrhema welcomes foreigners and slaves for rowing and fighting in the navy, but the antepirrhema makes clear that such men are not welcome as leaders. A position of command needs a real Athenian.

EURIPIDES AND AESCHYLUS

At the start of the play Dionysos declares his intention of bringing Euripides back to life. But down in Hades it turns out that Euripides has challenged Aeschylus for the throne of tragedy. A contest is to be held to decide between them, and Dionysos is appointed judge; who could be more appropriate to judge such a contest than the god of drama? Sophocles is not competing; the reason given is that he is content to accept Aeschylus' tenure of the throne (786–94). Modern scholars have speculated that Sophocles may in fact not have been dead when Aristophanes planned the play, and that the three references to him (the other two are 76–82 and 1515–19) were added when he died after much of the script was written but before it was performed. (It is known that Euripides and Sophocles both died in 406 BC, and that Sophocles died after Euripides, but it is not known how long after.) That may be true; but in any case a contest with two sides is more effective dramatically than one with three, and it is easier to draw striking contrasts between Aeschylus and Euripides than between either one of them and Sophocles. So Aristophanes may well have preferred to exclude Sophocles even if Sophocles was already dead when he began the play.[25]

[25] Cf. Dover *Frogs* 7–9, giving references to many earlier discussions.

The prayers preceding the contest (885–94), in which Aeschylus prays to Demeter, but Euripides prays to Sky, Tongue, Intelligence, and Nose, are a joke mocking Euripides for adherence to the irreligious ideas of some sophists. It is much the same joke as the one made about Socrates' religion in *Clouds*; but, to judge from the plays of Euripides which we have, it is no more accurate in his case than in Socrates', and it is not used again in the ensuing contest.

The contest itself is long and elaborate, and goes through several stages or rounds. The first round is the one which uses the traditional structure of the agon, and it offers some substantial comments on the two tragedians. It can be regarded as the earliest work of genuine literary criticism. Euripides speaks first, and draws several good contrasts between Aeschylus and himself, which are partly borne out by their surviving tragedies.

1. Euripides says that Aeschylus customarily begins a play with choral singing, keeping the characters silent for some time (911–20), whereas he himself begins with a character explaining the nature of the play (945–7). It is indeed true that Euripides' plays often start with an explanatory prologue telling the audience 'the story so far', while two of Aeschylus' extant plays (*Persians* and *Suppliants*) start with a chorus, and evidently it was a notorious feature of his now lost *Niobe* that Niobe sat silent on-stage for a long time while the chorus sang. Aristophanes (as a joke) makes Euripides say (accusingly) that Aeschylus in this way was cheating the audience and getting away with fewer speeches—as if songs were not at least equally difficult to write!

2. When they do speak, says Euripides, Aeschylus' characters use long words and obscure expressions (923–35), whereas Euripides has slimmed tragedy down (936–43). Every student of Greek will confirm that Euripides' vocabulary is simpler than Aeschylus'.

3. It is taken for granted that many tragic characters are heroes or kings, but Euripides claims that he makes every kind of person speak, including women and slaves, and this is 'democratic' (948–52). Here the implied criticism of Aeschylus seems less convincing. His extant plays have some women who are major characters, notably Klytaimestra and Elektra, and various slaves who speak, such as the Nurse in *Libation-bearers*.

4. Euripides claims that he introduced rhetorical skill and clever argumentation on subjects familiar to all; those who have learned from him are such men as Kleitophon and Theramenes (954–79).

Here there is some irony: the boast will not impress favourably those who regard Theramenes as a slippery turncoat (cf. p. 284). But it is true that Euripides' plays contain more rhetorical argument than Aeschylus'.

So on the whole, although we may not agree at every point, Euripides' speech offers a reasonably accurate comparison between his and Aeschylus' plays with regard to dramatic technique and style. Aeschylus in reply does not go over the same ground again (which would be boring for the audience) but opens up a different line of enquiry: what is the function of a tragedy?

AESCHYLUS. First answer this question: what quality found in a poet
    deserves admiration?
EURIPIDES. He deserves it for skill, and for giving advice, and also
    because we make people
Become better in all of the cities.
AESCHYLUS.   All right, I agree; and if *you* haven't done that,
    But starting with worthy magnanimous men have converted them all
    into villains,
What penalty will you admit you deserve?
DIONYSOS.   To die; no need to ask *him* that.

                         (*Frogs* 1008—12)

Skill is mentioned, but it is overshadowed by the instructive purpose of tragedy. Poetry ought, above all, to be improving; and it is striking that this is one point on which Aristophanes makes Aeschylus, Euripides, and Dionysos all agree. Perhaps he thought everyone in Athens would agree with it; or, if not, at any rate he did not wish the alternative view to be heard. The question which concerns him is: are Aeschylus' or Euripides' plays more effective for making people better?

Aeschylus claims that he made people better by putting great warriors on-stage. Plays like *Seven against Thebes* and *Persians*, and heroes like Patroklos and Teukros, inspired men to fight bravely against their enemies. Euripides, on the other hand, showed characters like Phaidra and Stheneboia, each of whom was a married woman who fell in love with a man other than her husband (Hippolytos and Bellerophon respectively). Aeschylus scornfully calls them 'tarts' (1043), and a highly significant exchange follows.

EURIPIDES. What's wrong, then, with my Stheneboias, you wretch?
What harm do they do to the city?

AESCHYLUS. Your characters had an effect on respectable wives of
respectable husbands:
You persuaded the wives to drink hemlock for shame; that's what your
Bellerophons led to.

EURIPIDES. And was it untrue, this story I told in composing my play
about Phaidra?

AESCHYLUS. Not at all, by Zeus; it was perfectly true. But a poet must
hide what is wicked,
And not bring it forth or produce it on-stage. In just the same way as
the children
Have a teacher to tell them the things they should know, so the men
growing up have the poets.

(*Frogs* 1049–55)

It is not quite clear whether Aeschylus means that wives who
saw or heard about Euripides' *Stheneboia* were encouraged by it to
commit adultery and afterwards repented and committed suicide,
or simply that the realization that a woman could behave as Stheneboia did made them commit suicide for shame at being women;
whichever he means, it must be a comic exaggeration, but perhaps
in real life there had been a recent case of a woman's suicide which
was attributed to the influence of a tragedy. Euripides defends
himself by declaring that he was revealing facts, but Aeschylus
maintains that facts should be concealed if they would have a bad
influence on those who hear or see them. The dilemma is a serious
one, unsolved to this day. Undoubtedly many people tend to imitate
behaviour which they see. Is it then the duty of an educator to show
good behaviour and conceal bad behaviour? Or ought he to show
the facts, both good and bad, to make people think for themselves?
In recent years the main focus of the discussion has been violence
shown on television and videos. Some people who see violence try
to imitate it; ought we then to hide it, or is it hypocritical to pretend
that it does not exist? The view attributed to Aeschylus in *Frogs* is
essentially the same as that taken by Mrs Mary Whitehouse and
others in modern times.

This opening round of the contest, concerning the general nature
of the tragedies, is followed by rounds concerning specific features.
First Euripides and Aeschylus criticize each other's prologues for

inaccuracy of wording and for repetitiousness. Next there is criticism of the songs; here parody of the music of the respective tragedians must have been an important part of the fun. And then there is the notorious weighing scene: Euripides and Aeschylus each speak lines of verse into the scales, and every time Aeschylus' line is found to be the heavier.

It is not easy to decide how far this part of the play is intended to be taken as serious criticism of the tragedies. The weighing seems to be entirely absurd. Modern critics have wondered whether it is supposed to mean that Aeschylus' poetry is weightier in a stylistic sense, but in fact the lines with which he wins this round are not stylistically heavy; he wins simply because he mentions heavy things—a river, chariots, and (metaphorically heavy) death. Some serious points may be implied in the rounds concerning prologues and songs. But on the whole the contest seems, until the intervention of Plouton, to have been getting progressively less substantial and more frivolous.

So far Dionysos, as judge, has been unable to award the prize. The weighing round is won unequivocally by Aeschylus, but in the other rounds neither poet has emerged as clearly superior. It is doubtful whether the spectators at this stage could predict the result of the contest. It has been suggested that they could guess that Euripides would lose because they heard before it started that bad people support him and good people support Aeschylus (771–83).[26] But that is not so, because in Aristophanic comedy the bad sometimes win contests, for comic effect: in *Horsemen* the Sausage-seller defeats Paphlagon by badness; in the first agon of *Clouds* Worse Argument defeats Better Argument, and in the second agon Pheidippides wins when maintaining that it is right for a son to beat his father. An expert student of Aristophanes might make a more reliable prediction by observing that the second speaker in an agon usually defeats the first speaker, and it is Euripides who goes first in every round of the contest in *Frogs*. However, most of the Athenian audience probably did not realize this fact about Aristophanes' technique, and anyway it is not acceptable as a dramatic motive for Dionysos' decision in favour of Aeschylus. Dionysos therefore must seek another basis for his verdict.

[26] Dover *Frogs* 11.

ALKIBIADES AND THE SAVING OF ATHENS

In 1411 Plouton, the ruler of the underworld, has appeared.[27] He presses Dionysos to make up his mind and concedes that, if he does so, he will be allowed to take back to the upper world whichever of the two poets he prefers. Dionysos' original plan was to take back Euripides, who had died recently; presumably the possibility of recovering Aeschylus, who had been dead for half a century, had not occurred to him. So now Plouton's offer gives him a chance not only to fulfil his plan, but to fulfil an alternative plan if he decides it would be better; and he tries more urgently than before to reach a judgement.

Earlier in the play the only motive he revealed for his scheme was his own enjoyment of Euripides' poetic style (71–2, 96–103). But now he states a different object: he wants the city to be saved and to continue putting on choral performances (1418–19). 'Saved' in 405 BC inevitably means being saved from defeat and destruction by Sparta. Thus Dionysos' personal concern, the continuation of his own festivals, is identified with the worry uppermost in the minds of all Athenians; and the tie-breaker for the tragedians' contest is now to be not a matter of poetic style or dramatic technique, but a political one. Poets ought to give instruction and advice, as was agreed earlier; so which of the two poets can give the best advice for saving Athens?

Dionysos poses two questions. First he asks what advice the poets can offer about Alkibiades, and afterwards what salvation they have for the city. These are two approaches to a single problem. Since 411 BC Alkibiades had been Athens' most successful general, and had won the battle of Kyzikos in 410. But many Athenians always regarded him with distrust and jealousy because of his flamboyant life-style and his suspected complicity in the profanation of the Mysteries and the mutilation of the Hermai. So in 407/6, when the battle of Notion was lost, even though Alkibiades had not been present at it, he was blamed for the defeat and removed from office, and at the time of *Frogs* he had withdrawn into exile. Although

---

[27] I think two or three lines marking his arrival have probably been lost from the text at this point; cf. *CQ* 9 (1959) 261–2. However, Dover *Frogs* 295 prefers the view that he appears at 830 and remains silent until 1414. Cf. R. Kassel *Rh.Mus.* 137 (1994) 52–3.

Athens did win the battle of Arginousai without him, most of the commanders there had subsequently been put to death. So now the issue of the moment was: is recall of Alkibiades the best, or only, way to save Athens?

DIONYSOS. First, then, what view of Alkibiades
    Do you each have? That gives the city pangs.
AESCHYLUS. What view does Athens have of him?
DIONYSOS.   What view?
    She loves him, hates him, and yet wants to have him.
    But tell me your opinion, both of you.
EURIPIDES. I hate a citizen who will be found
    Slow to assist his country, quick to harm it,
    Resourceful for himself, not for the city.
DIONYSOS. Good, by Poseidon! What do *you* think now?
AESCHYLUS. Best not to rear a lion in the city;
    But if it *is* reared, tolerate its ways.
DIONYSOS. By Zeus the Saviour, still I can't decide:
    One answered cleverly, the other clearly.

(Frogs 1422–34)

Here Dionysos indicates that the Athenians in general have mixed feelings about Alkibiades, Euripides gives a clear rejection of him as selfish and unpatriotic, and Aeschylus uses a less clear but impressive poetic metaphor (probably inspired by the real Aeschylus' famous passage about rearing a lion-cub in *Agamemnon* 717–36) to advise the Athenians to accept Alkibiades even if they do dislike his life-style. There is nothing comic in either the question or the answers. The question is a serious one of the utmost urgency, and each of the answers expresses a view which undoubtedly was fervently held by many Athenians. It is important to notice too that they are answers propounded here by Aristophanes, not really by Euripides and Aeschylus; whereas the earlier part of the agon sets out opinions and beliefs which may, by and large, have been held by those two tragedians in real life, the real Aeschylus certainly did not hold any opinion about Alkibiades, who was not yet born when Aeschylus died.

Dionysos cannot decide which answer is better, and puts his other question about saving the city. Unfortunately at this point we run into difficulties with the text. As it appears in the manuscripts it contains three distinct answers to the question and also one refusal to answer, but they do not seem to proceed in a logical or sensible sequence, and at some points it is uncertain which character speaks which lines. Various solutions have been proposed: perhaps the lines are in the wrong order, or some lines are missing, or some lines from another play have been inserted, or Aristophanes revised the play and the preserved text wrongly combines lines from both versions.[28] However, if we leave aside the problems of sequence and simply observe what items there are, these are the four responses which are given to Dionysos' question, how the city can be saved.

1. One answer must be given by Euripides, because the speaker concedes that Kephisophon (the well-known friend of Euripides) devised part of it (1437–41, with 1451–3). It is an absurd proposal: a man named Kleokritos should fly through the air, using Kinesias (the flighty poet; cf. p. 214) as wings, and squirt vinegar into the enemy's eyes. This answer is obviously intended by Aristophanes simply to raise a laugh.

2. Probably next comes a refusal to answer, attributed by most recent critics to Aeschylus.

DIONYSOS. And what do *you* say?
AESCHYLUS.   What men does the city
   Employ now? Does she use the good men?
DIONYSOS.   What!
   She loathes them.
AESCHYLUS.   Does she like the wicked men?
DIONYSOS. She doesn't, but she can't help using them.
AESCHYLUS. Well, how could anyone save such a city,
   Which neither cloak nor fleece will satisfy?

(*Frogs* 1454–9)

The last line here is probably a proverbial expression for a man who has only two alternatives and rejects both. It does not look like a joke; this response, though refusing to make any positive suggestion, is a serious comment on the political situation in 405.

3. Another answer begins with a paradoxical antithesis which Dionysos finds unintelligible, and the tragedian (whichever it is) then clarifies it as follows.

[28] Dover *Frogs* 373–6 adopts this last solution, but also refers to earlier suggestions. I would no longer defend every detail of my discussion in *CQ* 9 (1959) 263–8.

If we distrust those citizens whom now
We trust, and we employ instead the ones
We don't employ, perhaps we might be saved.

(*Frogs* 1446–8)

This too is hardly a joke. It is recommending a change of political leadership; it says nearly the same thing as the last part of the parabasis (718–37), but more briefly.

4. The final answer, generally attributed to Aeschylus, is also in antithetical form.

When they believe the enemy's land their own,
Their own the enemy's, and they regard
Their ships as wealth, their wealth as poverty.

(*Frogs* 1463–5)

This is serious strategic advice.[29] The Athenians should not worry about the fact that the Spartans, based at Dekeleia, have occupied much of Attica, but instead should themselves invade enemy territory; they should spend money on ships, because money which is never spent serves no useful purpose. In part this is a revival of Perikles' policy at the very beginning of the Peloponnesian War; he advised the Athenians not to defend their countryside but to rely on their navy (cf. p. 46). The invasion of enemy territory was a strategy put into effect with great success by Demosthenes when he occupied Pylos (cf. pp. 82–3). Whether such a strategy was practicable in 405 may be doubted, but there is no sign that the suggestion is a joke.

On the whole this is a serious part of the play. The passage about Kleokritos and vinegar is an exception (and indeed that is why some critics have excised it); all the other responses to both of Dionysos' questions concern policies which may well have been under earnest consideration at the time. The problem which gets most attention is the choice of political or military leaders. At present Athens uses bad leaders and not good ones, but would do better to use the good ones instead (1446–8, 1454–9); and Alkibiades is the principal example of a man whose recall is being considered (1422–34). All this chimes with the part of the parabasis urging the Athenians to discard bad leaders who are recent arrivals and to use instead those

[29] Cf. A. H. Sommerstein *CQ* 24 (1974) 24–7.

who are well-born and traditionally educated (718–37). Alkibiades was of aristocratic birth; through his mother he was descended from the Alkmeonids, one of the most famous families in Athens. Although he is not named there, I think it is impossible to avoid the conclusion that Aristophanes in the parabasis is urging the Athenians to recall Alkibiades.[30]

That is also the advice which he puts into the mouth of Aeschylus (at least in 1431–2, and it is possible that Aeschylus speaks 1446–8 too), and one might then expect that he would make Dionysos declare Aeschylus the winner of the contest on this ground. In fact Dionysos does not give this, or any, reason; he simply chooses Aeschylus as 'the one whom my soul wishes' (1468). After all, it would have been silly for Aristophanes to declare that Aeschylus was the better poet simply because he has put into Aeschylus' mouth some advice with which Aristophanes himself agrees, although the real Aeschylus never gave it and could not have given it. Aristophanes, through Dionysos, just declares his own preference for Aeschylus and leaves us to consider for ourselves whether we share that preference.

THE SECOND PERFORMANCE

Frogs conveys the air of a city hoping to avoid disaster, but in the event disaster was not avoided. Alkibiades was not recalled to take command. In the late summer of 405 the Athenian navy confronted an enlarged Spartan fleet in the Hellespont; the Spartan commander (nominally 'secretary') was Lysander. The Athenians occupied a position on the open beach at Aigospotamoi, and Alkibiades, who at this time was living nearby in exile from Athens, advised them to move to a better position at Sestos; but the Athenian generals would not listen to him, and then Lysander caught them out by a surprise attack and destroyed most of their ships on the beach. So much for Aristophanes' advice that they should make use of Alkibiades.

Their navy gone, the Athenians could not prevent the Spartans closing in on Athens both by sea and by land. A siege lasted most of the winter, and at last they were forced into abject surrender, the

[30] There have been many discussions of this topic. The best, in my opinion, is that of R. F. Moorton *GRBS* 29 (1988) 345–59.

demolition of their city walls, the abolition of democracy, and the establishment of the oppressive oligarchic regime of the Thirty. It was when the siege began in the autumn of 405 that they carried out one part of Aristophanes' advice: they passed a decree, proposed by a man named Patrokleides, restoring the rights of disfranchised citizens.[31] And it was probably in connection with this decree that they also authorized a second performance of *Frogs*.

> The play was so much admired because of the parabasis in it that it was also performed again, according to Dikaiarkhos.
>
> (*Frogs hyp.* i)

> He was commended and crowned with a garland of sacred olive (which is regarded as an honour equivalent to a gold crown) after speaking those words in *Frogs* about the disfranchised: 'The sacred chorus has a duty to the citizens, to offer much good advice'.
>
> (*Life of Aristophanes*)[32]

These are late, not contemporary, sources, and at first sight one may wonder whether they can be trusted. A second performance of this sort is unparalleled; Aeschylus' plays were revived after his death, and plays performed in town may perhaps have been repeated at rural festivals, but there is no known precedent for an immediate repetition of a play at the festivals in town. And even if the Athenians did like the parabasis, that is a very short part of the play; why call for the whole play to be repeated just for that? Much else in the play is surely more entertaining to see and hear: the comic disguise of Dionysos, the Frogs, the elaborate parodos of the Initiates, the parodies of Aeschylus and Euripides, in fact the whole of Dionysos' visit to Hades. Hence the suggestion that there is an error in the text of the *hypothesis*: only two letters of 'parabasis' need correction to give the word for 'descent to Hades'.[33] This conjecture is attractive; nevertheless we have to reject it, because the *Life of Aristophanes*, presumably referring to the same occasion, quotes the parabasis as the passage which prompted the Athenians to honour Aristophanes.

---

[31] Andokides 1.73, Xenophon *Hellenika* 2.2.11.

[32] *Prolegomena de Comoedia* (ed. Koster) p. 135 = *Poetae Comici Graeci* (ed. Kassel and Austin) vol. 3.2 pp. 2–3. The quotation of *Frogs* 686–7 is slightly inaccurate.

[33] Weil's emendation of παράβασιν to κατάβασιν is adopted in Coulon's edition of the play. Against it see E. Fraenkel *Beobachtungen zu Aristophanes* (Rome 1962) 131, Taillardat *Images* 390–1 n. 4.

The most plausible explanation is that both these late authorities got their information from Dikaiarkhos, and that Dikaiarkhos, a learned follower of Aristotle living around 300 BC, had before him the text of an Athenian decree praising Aristophanes for what he said about the disfranchised in the parabasis and authorizing an olive garland and a second performance. So we should accept that the passage about the disfranchised was the main reason for the honour; and since the Athenians would hardly confer such an extraordinary honour for a particular piece of advice without acting on that advice, the decree honouring Aristophanes must belong to the same time as the decree of Patrokleides, the autumn of 405. The second performance of *Frogs* presumably took place at the next dramatic festival, the Lenaia of 404.[34]

Modern critics also have often praised Aristophanes for his advocacy of mercy to past offenders and unity in a time of peril. But recently Arnott has argued that this piece of advice, however lofty Aristophanes' motives, had a disastrous effect, because the return of exiled oligarchs to Athens led in 404 to the setting up of the Thirty.[35] The effect was perhaps less direct than Arnott suggests. The return of exiles was not authorized by the decree of Patrokleides, but was imposed by the Spartans as one of the peace terms in 404.[36] And anyway neither of the two leading members of the Thirty, Kritias and Theramenes, had been disfranchised or exiled in 411,[37] and so they are not included in Aristophanes' specific plea. Still, the parabasis must have contributed to a current of opinion which led eventually to the establishment of the Thirty.

Sommerstein indeed argues that that was the purpose of the second performance.[38] He points out that it was in the winter of

---

[34] Cf. A. H. Sommerstein in *Tr.Com.Pol.* 461–76.

[35] W. G. Arnott *G&R* 38 (1991) 18–23.

[36] Andokides 1.80, Xenophon *Hellenika* 2.2.20–3.

[37] Kritias was exiled after prosecution by Kleophon (Xenophon *Hellenika* 2.3.15, Aristotle *Rhetoric* 1375b 31–4), but that was at a later date, for he was active in Athenian politics in 410 (Lykourgos *Leokrates* 113), and so it is not covered by *Frogs* 689–91. However, he is of course part of 'everyone' in line 701.

[38] *Tr.Com.Pol.* 466–9. A similar view is taken by F. Salviat in *Architecture et poésie dans le monde grec: hommage à Georges Roux* (ed. R. Étienne, M.-T. Le Dinahet, and M. Yon, Lyon 1989) 171–83. But Salviat's suggestion that much of the parabasis, as we have it, was newly written for the second performance can hardly be right if the parabasis was specifically mentioned, in the decree authorizing repetition of the play, as the part which the Athenians wanted to see and hear again.

405/4, not long before or after the Lenaia, that men hoping to subvert the democracy prosecuted Kleophon for dereliction of some military duty (the precise charge is obscure) and got him condemned to death;[39] and he suggests that they contrived a second performance of *Frogs* because it was a play attacking Kleophon, which would influence public opinion against him. This suggestion too may attach more weight to a small part of the play than it deserves. Kleophon is not really prominent in *Frogs*.[40] There is the short song joking about his alleged Thracian accent (674–85), another joke mocking him along with four other men, one of them being Nikomakhos who, so far from being a supporter of Kleophon, is said to have been an ally of his opponents (1504–14),[41] and the concluding quip 'Let Kleophon fight!' (1532). He is named nowhere else; and the sarcastic treatment of Theramenes, who would soon become one of the Thirty and must have been opposed to Kleophon, is not so very much milder (539–41, 967–70).[42] When one recalls Aristophanes' treatment of Kleon or Lamakhos or Socrates in earlier plays, or even Euripides and Aeschylus in this one, it seems an overstatement to say that he attacked Kleophon 'so viciously', 'in terms very hostile to Kleophon'.[43] If Kleophon's opponents really wanted to see him pilloried in a comedy at the Lenaia of 404, they might have done better to call for a revival of Platon's *Kleophon*, which like *Frogs* had been performed at the Lenaia of 405; or, better still, they might have persuaded one of the dramatists to write a new play on this theme, closer in tone to *Horsemen*. Nevertheless *Frogs*, both at its first and at its second performance, no doubt contributed, to some extent, to Kleophon's unpopularity and to the rehabilitation of some men who favoured oligarchy. We must cautiously agree with Sommerstein and Arnott that the serious political advice given in *Frogs* turned out to be not such good advice as Aristophanes thought.

---

[39] Lysias 13.12, 30.10–13.

[40] Cf. Croiset *Ar. and Pol. Parties* 149: 'he is mentioned only casually.' *Pace* Dover *Frogs* 69, the treatment of Kleophon in *Frogs* is very different from the treatment of Kleon in *Horsemen*.

[41] On Nikomakhos see Lysias 30.11–14.

[42] Cf. Ostwald *Sovereignty* 446: 'Aristophanes is even-handed in his criticism.'

[43] Sommerstein in *Tr.Com.Pol.* 467–8.

Women at the Assembly

THE POLITICAL CIRCUMSTANCES

An interval of more than ten years separates *Frogs* from *Women at the Assembly*, the longest gap among the eleven plays we have. It was one of the hardest and most humiliating periods in the history of Athens.[1] The defeat and loss of the navy; the loss of the Empire and its tribute; the siege and the capitulation to Sparta; the suppression of democracy; the oligarchic regimes of the Thirty and the Ten, followed by counter-revolution and the restoration of democracy, with the executions, exiles, and recriminations that these changes involved: all these events must have had a devastating effect, both materially and psychologically, even on ordinary Athenians who took little part in politics. Then came a slow recovery, with the rebuilding of the town walls and the navy; but from 395 onwards Athens became embroiled in hostilities with Sparta once again, as an ally of Thebes in the Corinthian War.

There was a feeling that the disastrous outcome of the Peloponnesian War had been due to failings in the democratic system of government. Oligarchy was tried instead in 404/3, but was found to be intolerable; so, after democracy was restored, various constitutional changes were introduced in the hope of making democratic rule more effective. One that concerns us here is the institution of pay for attending the Assembly. As long ago as 425 Aristophanes in *Akharnians* had satirized the late and low attendance at meetings, which allowed decisions to be taken by a few politicians in their own interest. Yet in the lawcourts, as we see in *Wasps*, the attendance of citizens as jurors was high, because jurors, up to a limit of 6,000 in any year, were paid three obols for each day's work.

[1] Cf. David *Ar. and Ath. Society* 3–20, A. H. Sommerstein *CQ* 34 (1984) 314–33.

So now it was resolved to try a similar arrangement for the Assembly. It was proposed by a politician named Agyrrhios, and at first the pay was one obol for each meeting. Later it was increased to two obols on the proposal of Herakleides, and afterwards, on the proposal of Agyrrhios again, to three obols. It was given only to the first 6,000 citizens to arrive for a meeting.[2] The exact date when this system was introduced is not known, but it was already operating at the time of *Women at the Assembly*. No doubt it created greater interest in the meetings, and that may have prompted Aristophanes to make the Assembly one of the themes of his play.

The exact date of the play itself is also uncertain. No date is given in the *hypothesis*. In the prologue there are some allusions to political events from which scholars have tried to fix the date.

PRAXAGORA. Next, this alliance: when it was discussed,
They said 'If it's not made, the city's done for!'
But when it *was* made, they were cross; the speaker
Who got it carried ran away at once.

(*Women at the Assembly* 193–6)

The alliance was made between Athens and Thebes in 395. A scholium on this passage says: 'Philokhoros records that two years previously an alliance of the Spartans and the Boiotians was made. "Who got it carried": he means Konon.' The scholiast (or Philokhoros) has made at least two mistakes: the Spartans were the enemy, not the ally, of the Boiotians, and Konon was not in Greece in 395 or 394. So one hesitates to trust the figure of two years, and all that can safely be inferred from this passage is that the play was written after 395. The identity of the speaker who persuaded the Athenians to make the alliance and 'ran away at once' is unknown, but a few lines later Praxagora refers to the politician Thrasyboulos.

Salvation peeped out; Thrasyboulos, though,
Is angry that there's no call for himself.

(*Women at the Assembly* 202–3)

'Salvation' no doubt means peace. There was an opportunity to make peace in 392/1: three Athenian envoys went to Sparta to

---

[2] Aristotle *Ath.Pol.* 41.3; cf. M. H. Hansen *The Athenian Ecclesia* 2 (Copenhagen 1989) 147–53, P. Gauthier in *Aristote et Athènes* (ed. M. Piérart, Paris 1993) 231–50.

conduct negotiations, and brought back proposed terms which one of them, Andokides, recommended to the Assembly in a speech which we still have (*On the Peace*), but the Assembly rejected them. That could be the occasion when 'salvation peeped out'; yet there could also have been some earlier occasion, of which we know nothing, when Aristophanes thought there was a prospect of peace. Praxagora's words seem to imply that Thrasyboulos objected to the making of peace, perhaps because it would deprive him of the opportunity to hold a military command. We know that he was at the battle of Corinth in 394 and that he commanded a fleet of forty ships in 390,[3] but he is not known to have held any command between those dates; so that may be the period when he was angry that he was not called on. It seems, then, that the latest possible date for the performance of *Women at the Assembly* is the Lenaia of 390 (before the election of generals that year). The earliest possible year is 394, but a later date is more likely; the known fact of peace negotiations in 392/1 tilts the balance of probability towards 391 as the year of the play.[4]

WOMEN DISGUISED AS MEN

The opening of *Women at the Assembly* resembles the opening of *Lysistrata*. The women of Athens are dissatisfied with the way the men conduct the city's affairs. One woman, determined to do something about it, has called a meeting of women, but they are late in arriving. Thus both plays begin with a soliloquy by the woman who is the principal character, and the others trickle in during the next few minutes. But one difference is that in *Lysistrata* the meeting is called to enable Lysistrata to reveal her plan to the other women, and the plan comes as a surprise both to them and to the audience. In *Women at the Assembly* the plan has already been laid by the women at an earlier meeting, at the Skira festival (which like the Thes-

[3] Lysias 16.15, Xenophon *Hellenika* 4.8.25.

[4] For various views about the date see R. Seager *JHS* 87 (1967) 107 n. 110, Ussher *Ecclesiazusae* xx–xxv, Carrière *Carnaval* 177–82, P. Funke *Homonoia und Arche* (Wiesbaden 1980) 168–71, David *Ar. and Ath. Society* 2 n. 2, B. S. Strauss *Athens after the Peloponnesian War* (London 1986) 149 n. 85, Vetta *Donne* xxx–xxxii.

mophoria was a festival for women only); they know all about it, and are meeting now to carry it out.

Nor can the plan (the first part of it, at least) be a surprise to the audience. Probably the title of the play was announced in advance, either at the proagon held a few days beforehand or just before the performance itself; if so, the audience knew before it began that it would be about women attending the Assembly. Even if the title were not known, the plan becomes clear as soon as the first character appears, a woman dressed as a man going to the Assembly.[5] She has a woman's pale beardless face, but is wearing a man's cloak and shoes, and is carrying a false beard and a man's stick. The stick was a normal accessory for attendance at the Assembly, not generally carried at other times.[6] Her name, Praxagora, seems to be a comic invention meaning 'a woman active in public',[7] but it is not mentioned until 124 and so does not affect the audience's understanding of the character at the beginning of the play. As well as the stick and beard, she carries a lamp (which shows the audience that the time is before dawn), and she begins her soliloquy by addressing the lamp in tragic style as the sharer of women's secrets. Soon she starts worrying because the other women have not arrived. The meeting of the Assembly will begin shortly, and it is important to arrive early in order to get seats. Can they have had difficulty in making their beards, or in stealing their husbands' cloaks? Gradually they arrive. Their parts are not easy to distinguish in the text, and different editors distribute the lines differently, but there are probably three speaking parts besides Praxagora's, and in addition the twenty-four members of the chorus, some of whom are named individually as they arrive during 41–53. They describe the preparations they have been making to disguise themselves as men. One has been standing in the sun to try to darken her colour. (Presumably she has failed, and the actor is still wearing a pale mask portraying a female character.) Another has thrown away her razor, so as to become hairy all over and not like a woman (65–7, an interesting reminder for us that razors were normal equipment for women, not for men). One silly woman has brought her wool-carding with

[5] Cf. p. 258 on the appearance of a character dressed in the clothes of the opposite sex. The women's disguise as men is discussed by Taaffe *Ar. and Women* 104–23.

[6] Cf. MacDowell *Wasps* 131 (on line 33), Rothwell *Politics* 83 n. 20.

[7] Cf. Rothwell *Politics* 82–3.

her (as a modern woman might bring her knitting) to do while listening to the speeches at the Assembly; it has not occurred to her that this might give her away.

Praxagora decides that they should now practise making speeches. One of them sees no point in that, because all women are good at talking anyway. But it turns out that this woman knows little about the Assembly. She has been looking forward to it because she thinks there will be plenty to drink there; the men, at any rate, must always be drunk at the meetings, to judge by the decrees they pass. So another woman has a go at making a speech. But she soon commits a blunder, which would give her away at once: she uses an oath 'by the Two Goddesses', a form of words which was employed only by women. The previous woman (she who was expecting wine) now tries, but blunders immediately, and her excuse turns out to be a joke against a man in the theatre audience.

SECOND WOMAN. I'm going to speak again.
 I think my speech is well enough prepared.
 'In my opinion, ladies here in session—'
PRAXAGORA. You call men 'ladies', do you, wretched woman?
SECOND WOMAN. It's that Epigonos over there; I looked
 That way and thought I was addressing ladies.

(*Women at the Assembly* 163–8)

So far this is a scene of fairly simple fun, garnished with jokes of familiar Aristophanic types. In particular, there are the same kinds of jokes about women as in *Lysistrata* and *Women at the Thesmophoria*. There are sex jokes: one woman's excuse for lateness is that her husband is an oarsman on the *Salaminia*[8] and has been rowing her in bed all night (37–9). There are drink jokes: the speech which one woman makes for practice is a proposal to make it illegal to have water-tanks in taverns (153–5). There are jokes about effeminate politicians: Agyrrhios was once a woman, but no one notices that, now that he has a beard (102–3). All this, together with the comic dressing-up, is no more than one would expect in a comedy about women going to the Assembly.

---

[8] 'Salaminian' here does not mean that he resides on the island of Salamis, for he lives next door to Praxagora (33–5), nor that he is a veteran of the battle of Salamis, which would make him far too old for this joke.

PRAXAGORA'S SPEECH

But the tone changes when Praxagora, irritated at the other women's
stupidity, makes a speech herself to show them how it should be
done, pretending all the time to be a man addressing men.

PRAXAGORA. Now, as for me, this land belongs to me
As much as you; but I'm annoyed and grieved
At all the city's conduct of affairs.
I see the leaders that it now employs
Are always bad; or if one does become
Good for one day, he's bad for ten days more.
You choose another: he'll do more harm still.
So how can one advise men hard to please?
You are afraid of those who want to serve,
And yet you keep on asking those who don't.
There was a time when we ignored Assemblies
Completely, and we thought Agyrrhios
A rogue. But now, when people do attend,
Whoever gets the money sings his praises;
Whoever's not paid says 'They ought to die,
If they want pay for going to the Assembly!'

(*Women at the Assembly* 173–88)

She complains that the Athenians choose the wrong men as
leaders, which is much the same point, though made more briefly,
as in the parabasis of *Frogs*. (Compare especially *Assembly* 176–7 with
Frogs 731.) Here, as there, names of those likely to make good
leaders are not given, although the Athenian audience may have
been able to identify 'those who want to serve'. The lines about pay
for attendance at the Assembly mean that anyone who arrives in
time to get pay is in favour of it, and anyone who is too late is against
it. That is a cynical joke; but next come the lines about the alliance
and about the failure to make peace (quoted on p. 302), which do not
look like jokes. Rather they seem to be expressions of exasperation at
the Athenians' failure to agree on any consistent policy. They lead
up to an accusation that the citizens themselves are to blame.

You, people, are responsible for this.
The public funds are spent upon your pay,
While each of you looks out for personal gain.

(*Women at the Assembly* 205–7)

So far this speech is mostly serious. It says that the Athenians fail to support a consistent policy to attain peace and prosperity, and just vote for anyone or anything that will enable them to make a little money for themselves; in particular, those who get three obols for doing nothing more than attending a meeting vote for Agyrrhios. Although the passage contains one or two sarcastic jokes (186–8, 208), as a whole it is plainly not jocular. It is clear who is being attacked: Agyrrhios, and those who support him. What is not yet clear is what is being advocated. Which policies, and which politicians, *are* the right ones for attaining peace and prosperity? Now Praxagora goes on to a positive proposal.

> If you take *my* advice, you'll be saved yet.
> What I say is, we ought to hand the city
> Straight over to the women. After all,
> We use them as our housekeepers at home.

> (*Women at the Assembly* 209–12)

Here she implies that the main function of government is to control the use of resources and the spending of money. Since women do that on a small scale for each household, they should be able to do it on a large scale for the whole city. She proceeds to argue that women are more conservative than men.

> They sit to do the cooking, as of old;
> They use their heads for carrying, as of old;
> They hold the Thesmophoria, as of old;
> They make and bake the flat-cakes, as of old;
> They wear away their husbands, as of old;
> They keep their secret lovers, as of old;
> They buy themselves nice titbits, as of old;
> They like wine undiluted, as of old;
> And they enjoy a screwing, as of old.
> So no more talking, men: let's just hand over
> The city to them; let's not wait to ask
> What they intend to do, but let them rule,
> No argument. All that we need consider
> Is, first, that being mothers they'll be keen
> To save the soldiers' lives; and, secondly,
> Who'd be more likely to send extra rations?
> A woman's very shrewd at raising funds,
> And when in power she'll never be deceived:
> Deceiving is what women always do!

I'll say no more. Just do as I propose,
And you'll live happily for ever after.

    (*Women at the Assembly* 221–40)

This last part of Praxagora's speech is very different from the first part. Lines 221–8 are almost like a traditional song with the refrain 'as of old'. The subject is traditional customs which continue unchanged. The implication is that changes which have occurred in other activities have been changes for the worse, and that life was better in the old days. Just when the good old days were is not stated; but since the continuation of old customs is attributed to women, the argument (if you can call it an argument) leads logically to the conclusion that women are better than men at organizing life. The end, about living happily ever after, is as sentimental as could be, but the passage as a whole is not pure sentiment, nor is it straightforward praise of women. The usual men's jokes against women make their appearance once again: fondness for drink in 227, fondness for sex in 225 and 228, trickery in 237–8. The arguments near the end, about saving the lives of soldiers and sending them extra rations, are arguments about benefits to men. Praxagora does not forget that her audience in the Assembly is male; nor does Aristophanes forget that the theatre audience is male too.

What then is the effect of the speech as a whole? It is, of course, a parody of real Assembly speeches: we can identify some phrases as being characteristic of political speeches of the time,[9] and in the performance the actor may have parodied politicians' gestures too. But the content of the speech? The first half is largely serious, it directs criticism at the Athenian people, and the criticism strongly resembles that in the parabasis of *Frogs*. We should therefore take it as expressing Aristophanes' own view of Athenian politics in the late 390s. It does not have a sustained image like the *Frogs* passage comparing politicians to coins, but makes a series of similar points briefly and with little explanation. That makes it rather less effective; there is a faint impression that the author is becoming elderly and peevish, irritated that things he has said before have to be said again because no one has taken any notice.

But the solution proposed in the second half of the speech is neither serious nor practical. It is fantastic. A modern reader is

---

[9] Cf. Vetta *Donne* 158–9, J. Ober and B. Strauss in *Noth.Dion.* 264–5.

liable to misunderstand it. In the twentieth century we have become accustomed to the view that men and women should have equal political rights. That is not what Praxagora proposes. Her plan is that the women should take over and rule the men. Yet that is not to involve any change in the distribution of other functions. Although she does not say in this speech what policies the women will pursue, except that they will take care of the soldiers and send them extra rations (233–5), that exception in itself makes clear that soldiers will continue to be men, not women. This is not the sort of thing that modern feminists advocate. But Aristophanes is not a modern feminist; he is an ancient comedian and fantasist. His basic outlook on life is perfectly traditional; as we have seen, the merit of women most emphasized in Praxagora's speech is that they maintain old traditions better than men. But he adds a characteristic comic fantasy: the problems of Athens, which are real, are once again to be solved by a remedy which is fantastic. Just as in *Birds* the solution is to hand over power to the birds, so in *Women at the Assembly* the solution is to hand over power to the women. To Aristophanes and to the men who formed his audience, government by birds and government by women seemed equally impossible. That was why they were funny.

MEN OUTWITTED BY WOMEN

Praxagora's speech is enthusiastically cheered by the other women, who elect her their general, and soon they don their false beards (that is, each actor attaches a false beard to his female mask, so that the face still looks pale) and go off to the Assembly, expecting more women to join them on the way. As they go, they draw their husbands' cloaks up over their heads, and sing a song in the manner of old countrymen trudging into town from the remote countryside. The song in fact resembles the song of the old jurors on their way to the lawcourt in *Wasps*, playing variations on the themes 'Let's get a move on . . .; we mustn't be late, or we won't get our three obols . . .; it's not like the old days, when . . .'. Most of the time they remember their disguise; at one point they comically forget, refer to their company in the feminine, and hastily correct themselves (299).

The meeting of the Assembly takes place off-stage. It is not

necessary to discuss at length why Aristophanes chose in this play
not to show it on-stage, as in *Akharnians*, but merely to show a
rehearsal and let a character describe the actual meeting later. Two
reasons at least are obvious: it is amusing to see and hear the women
making their preparations and mistakes at the rehearsal, but to show
the actual meeting as well as the rehearsal would be excessive; and
it is difficult to show on-stage the Assembly voting. (In *Akharnians* it
is adjourned without voting, but in *Women at the Assembly* there has
to be a vote in favour of the proposal, without which the rest of the
story could not proceed.)

Instead, while the women are away, we see something of the
men. Blepyros, Praxagora's husband, comes out of their house; and
immediately the audience laughs, because he is wearing his wife's
clothes. Of course, he would be, one realizes at once, because we
saw his wife going off in his own clothes only a few moments ago.
So he is wearing a little yellow dress and a pair of lady's boots. This
is one of the visual high points of the play, and the reasons for its
effectiveness deserve a brief analysis. It is not only a comic surprise.
It is indeed a surprise, for the audience has not been led to expect
the appearance of a man dressed as a woman at this moment. Yet,
as soon as it happens, it seems that it ought to have been expected,
because it is a logical consequence of what has gone before. If the
wife is wearing the husband's clothes, the husband has nothing
to wear but the wife's. Modern critics have wondered about the
plausibility of this. Does Blepyros not possess another cloak to wear?
Evidently not, and some critics have taken this fact as making a
serious point about the poverty of ordinary Athenians at this period.
That is an error; just as a modern man, though comfortably off,
may have only one raincoat, and when it is worn out he buys another,
but sees no point in possessing two at the same time, so an average
Athenian saw no need to possess more than one cloak at a time.[10]
So Praxagora's escapade leaves Blepyros without a cloak. If it were
a warm day, he might go outside in only a tunic (*khiton*)—though
not to the Assembly, where a cloak (*himation* or *tribon*) was *de rigueur*.
But it is not a warm day, it is a cold night (539). So that makes it
logical that he should put on his wife's clothes when he cannot find

---

[10] Cf. 670–1 (even in the ideal city a man will have only one cloak at a time)
and Plato *Phaidon* 87b–d (even a weaver has only one cloak at the time of his
death).

his own. The spectator gets a surprise, and yet at the same time has the feeling that what he sees fits in exactly with what has happened already. It is a good combination of logic and absurdity, and it also supports the theme of the whole play. The first man the audience sees has lost his clothes to his wife; and that, metaphorically, is what the play is about—the men losing their assets to the women. While the audience is laughing at Blepyros bereft of his garments, off-stage the men of Athens are being bereft of their powers in the Assembly. Aristophanes here uses visual means to convey a dramatic point symbolically.

Blepyros explains in a soliloquy that he has come outside in the dark in order to defecate. He is seen by a Neighbour, who calls out from his window or door, and who likewise has found that his wife has taken his clothes away. When the Neighbour has withdrawn, Blepyros continues to try to ease himself, in the longest excremental passage in Greek literature. There are of course other places in Aristophanes where excretion is mentioned,[11] but very few in which it occurs on-stage. In two it is a consequence of a sudden fright (*Birds* 65–8, *Frogs* 479–90). Nowhere else is constipation displayed, and the audience is expected to laugh in surprise at seeing something normally hidden from view. The passage also reinforces the theme of the play, by showing a man preoccupied with a mundane or degrading activity while his wife is concerned with higher things.[12]

A citizen named Khremes then passes by, and tells Blepyros that the meeting of the Assembly has already ended. Blepyros is disappointed at hearing that he has lost his chance of earning three obols, and naturally wants to know why it was over so quickly. Khremes describes it. The Pnyx was crowded, and most of the crowd was made up of a whole lot of very pale men, he says; they looked like cobblers (who worked indoors and were not sunburnt), and they packed the meeting so that a lot of ordinary men could not get in. The debate was about how to secure the salvation of the city. After a couple of other speeches (here Aristophanes ridicules two politicians, Neokleides and Euaion) a pale handsome young man (evidently the disguised Praxagora) stood up and made a speech

[11] Cf. Dover *Ar. Comedy* 40–1.

[12] Cf. Albini *Interpretazioni* 2.141–2. But the suggestion that constipation is 'the perfect symbol for his individualistic hoarding of material possessions' (Rothwell *Politics* 53) is unconvincing. There is no evidence that Blepyros is a hoarder.

proposing that the city should be handed over to the women, who would manage it better than the men. All the rest of the pale crowd cheered and voted in favour, so that the proposal was passed, and the women are now taking control.

Soon Praxagora and the women forming the chorus return and hastily strip off their disguises.[13] Now Praxagora has to face her husband without giving away the fact that she was at the meeting. She spins him a yarn about how she went to help a friend who was having a baby, wearing her husband's cloak because the night was cold. This is a most effective piece of feminine bamboozling. She feels no compunction in telling a lie to trick her slower-witted husband. He is suspicious, but not smart enough to see through the cajolery. This passage, more than any other, shows that Aristophanes is not just trotting out the character of Lysistrata again under a new name.[14] Praxagora has indeed the determination of Lysistrata, but she combines it with the winsomeness of Myrrhine, and the effectiveness of the scene is in some ways similar to that of the *Lysistrata* scene in which Myrrhine tantalizes Kinesias. In both these scenes the husband is honest, and the Athenian audience would consider him essentially reasonable in the kind of control that he wishes to exercise over his wife. But she outwits him because he is not clever enough; and the husbands in the audience laugh at him with the complacent feeling that *they* are not so foolish as to let their wives outwit them in that way.

COMMUNITY OF PROPERTY

Praxagora pretends to know nothing about the meeting of the Assembly, and so her husband tells her that it has been resolved to make the women rulers of Athens. Immediately she predicts great benefits for the city, and with hardly any encouragement from Blepyros she launches into a long exposition of her plan for reform. She then remarks that she has been elected to take command (714–15), and she goes off to carry out the reorganization. Here Aristophanes has compressed the sequence of events. His play has two

---

[13] On the details of this piece of business see S. D. Olson *AJP* 110 (1989) 223–6.

[14] Cf. Rothwell *Politics* 90.

comic subjects: women attending the Assembly in disguise, and the establishment of a communist regime. He has now reached the point at which he wishes to move from the first subject to the second, and he simply does so. He does not think it necessary to provide a realistic link, with an explanation for the benefit of Blepyros of how his wife was elected and arrived at her policies, which would waste time and bore the audience.

Praxagora's plan is that everyone shall be equal. There shall be no more private property or individual families; possessions, including sexual partners, shall be common to all. She makes clear that her purpose is to rectify the present state of affairs in which some men are rich and others poor.

> This will be my proposal: that everyone ought to go shares and hold all
>   things in common
> And live on that basis. It's wrong for one man to be rich and another a
>   pauper,
> For one to have plenty of land for his farm and another no space to be
>   buried,
> For one to have plenty of slaves for his use and another not one to
>   attend him.

> (*Women at the Assembly* 590–3)

It has recently been argued that poverty is the main subject of the play as a whole,[15] but that is an overstatement. It is of course common for Aristophanic characters to be short of funds: Dikaiopolis grudges money for coal, vinegar, and oil (*Akharnians* 33–6), Strepsiades and Peisetairos are debtors (*Clouds passim*, *Birds* 115–16), and so on; that is a usual feature of the comic persona. Blepyros and the other men in *Women at the Assembly* are no exception to this. But in the first half of the play poverty is not particularly emphasized, and evidence which has been adduced to prove that it is does not stand up to examination. The fact that Blepyros possesses only one cloak does not show that he is especially poor (see p. 310); and when one of the women wants to get on with her wool-carding because 'my children are naked' (92), she is no more to be taken literally than the Mayfair lady who is invited to a ball and exclaims 'But I haven't a stitch to wear!' When Khremes has failed to get his

[15] David *Ar. and Ath. Society* 3–20, Sommerstein *CQ* 34 (1984) 314–33.

three obols for attending the Assembly, his shopping-bag is no less
and no more empty than the shopping-bag of the old juror in *Wasps*
who fails to get his three obols for attending the lawcourt (compare
382 with *Wasps* 314). At the off-stage meeting of the Assembly a
politician named Euaion makes a speech from which it appears that
he possesses no cloak to wear by day and to use as a blanket by night,
and so is afraid of catching pleurisy (408–21). Since we know
nothing else about Euaion, the exact point of the joke escapes us;
but it is certainly a joke about Euaion as an individual, implying that
he is peculiarly cloakless, and it ought not to be used, as it has been,
as evidence that many Athenians lacked cloaks and were liable to
take pleurisy. Nevertheless, at the start of the second half of the
play, the passage just quoted (590–3) does indicate Praxagora's
concern that some men are poor. Hence her plan for communism.

Modern readers have been struck by the resemblance between
this plan, especially the part of it concerning sexual relations, and
Book 5 of Plato's *Republic* (although in Plato the plan is one for the
guardian class only); and the question whether Aristophanes got the
idea from Plato or Plato from Aristophanes has been copiously
discussed.[16] Probably Plato's *Republic* was written later than *Women
at the Assembly*, although the possibility that some parts of it were
written earlier, or that Plato expounded some of his ideas orally
before writing them down, cannot be definitely excluded. However,
neither text contains any explicit reference to the other, and in
recent years it has become generally accepted that neither is derived
from the other. Communism was not a new idea in the time of
Aristophanes and Plato. It was known that the holding of women in
common for sexual intercourse, instead of having a single wife, was
the practice of some non-Greek peoples, specifically the Agathyrsoi
and the Ausees (who lived in the countries now called Transylvania
and Tunisia respectively).[17] Aristophanes and Plato may both have
heard communism being discussed by sophists and others, but it is
not possible for us to say who was the first person to talk about it
in Athens. There is no reason to think that anyone in Athens had
already drawn up a serious theory or proposal, which Aristophanes

[16] For recent discussions see Ussher *Ecclesiazusae* xv–xx, David *Ar. and Ath.
Society* 20–9, D. Dawson *Cities of the Gods* (New York 1992) 37–40, S. Halliwell
Plato: Republic 5 (Warminster 1993) 224–5.
[17] Herodotos 4.104, 4.180.5.

was satirizing. For him, communism was just a fantastic and funny idea. Plato was the first to develop it seriously.[18]

As far as property is concerned, Praxagora's plan is that all that each man has at present, including money, is to be handed in to the common store. In return everyone will be given free meals and free clothes. This will all be arranged by the women, who will set up dining-halls for the men in the buildings which have previously been used as lawcourts; those buildings will not be needed for trials any more, because when no one has any property there will not be any thieves. So instead of drawing lots to decide which court each man is to sit in as a juror, the men will now draw lots to discover which dining-hall they are each to have dinner in. The slaves will do the farming, the women will make the clothes and cook the meals, and the men will have a marvellous easy life.

It hardly needs saying that this is a plan thought up by a man. Modern feminists, who begin reading *Women at the Assembly* in the expectation that it will show women becoming equal or superior to men, are liable to be outraged when they reach this point. Alternatively they try to defend Aristophanes by making out that the scheme is really intended to degrade men. Thus one distinguished female scholar has written: 'In Praxagora's household utopia, men are *reduced* to leading a drone-like life of pleasure in a world run by others' (my italics).[19] That is a complete misunderstanding of the play. Perhaps a modern woman is bound to see it that way. But Aristophanes did not write his play for modern women. He wrote it for ancient men who would be only too delighted to have 'a drone-like life of pleasure'. If he had shown the men doing the domestic tasks, that would have seemed to his male Athenian audience to be unpleasant rather than comic. Praxagora's plan will not have succeeded, in their eyes, unless it establishes a life of blissful ease; and an important part of utopia is having women to provide you with food and clothes, so that you do not have to provide them yourself.

What happens when they try to carry out this part of the project? In the next scene there is a conversation between two men. Their identity is uncertain in the text: if Aristophanes preferred to economize in characters and masks, they are probably the two men who

---

[18] Aristotle *Politics* 1266a 34–6. [19] H. P. Foley *CP* 77 (1982) 18.

appeared earlier, one named Khremes and the other an unnamed Neighbour; I shall assume that this is so, although the possibility remains open that they are two different men. Khremes is busily bringing all his possessions out of his house and lining them up ready to be handed in: sieve, saucepan, water-jar, and so on. But the Neighbour is reluctant to follow suit.

NEIGHBOUR. Me, hand in my possessions? I shall be
    Quite crazy then, with not a bit of sense.
    No, by Poseidon, never! First of all
    I'll take a thorough look and see what's what.
    Well, all my sweat, all my good housekeeping—
    I'm not a fool; I won't throw them away
    Just for a word, till I see how things go.

(*Women at the Assembly* 746–52)

When a herald comes along with a proclamation that dinner is ready and all citizens should go at once to draw lots for their dining-halls, he changes his tune.

NEIGHBOUR. I'd better go, then. Why keep standing here,
    When that's the state's decree?
KHREMES.   Where are you off to,
    If you've not handed in your property?
NEIGHBOUR. To dinner.
KHREMES.   Not if those women have some sense,
    Until you take it in.
NEIGHBOUR.   I will do.
KHREMES.   When?
NEIGHBOUR. I shan't make any difficulty.
KHREMES.   What?
NEIGHBOUR. I shan't be last to take it in, I tell you.
KHREMES. And still you'll go and dine?
NEIGHBOUR.   What can I do?
    We ought to give the city our support,
    We patriotic men.

(*Women at the Assembly* 853–62)

And so the Neighbour offers to help Khremes carry *his* property to the Agora. Khremes won't have that, and finally the Neighbour goes off thinking up some other ruse to avoid handing over his possessions. We never learn whether he does hand them over in the end.

COMMUNITY OF SEX

The other part of Praxagora's plan concerns community of sexual relations. A man will not be allowed to have his own personal wife, but all women are to be available to all men for sexual intercourse free of charge. Blepyros objects that in that case all the men will want the prettiest girl, but Praxagora has thought of a solution for that: the ugly girls and the old women will sit beside the pretty ones, and any man who wants a pretty girl will have to satisfy an ugly one first. The converse arrangement will also operate: any woman who fancies a handsome man will have to satisfy an ugly man before she may receive the good-looking one. So there will be equal sexual opportunities for all, and no unfair disadvantage for those who happen to have big noses. One consequence of the system is that children will not know who their fathers are; so the rule will be that a boy must treat respectfully as his father every man who is old enough to be so.

Later in the play we see the attempt to make this arrangement work. A Young Woman is at the window of her house, on the look-out for her Young Man who will soon be returning from the public dinner. But at the window or the door of the next house[20] there is an ugly Old Woman, determined to exercise her rights by having the boy for herself before he is allowed to go on to the pretty girl next door, because that is what the new law lays down. She claims that her lover is on the way to her, but the girl does not believe it; so they both agree to go indoors, each in her own house, to see which door the Young Man knocks at when he arrives. They go inside, and then the boy comes along, sings a serenade, and knocks loudly at the girl's door. Immediately the Old Woman rushes out of her own door and cries 'Hey! Why are you knocking? Are you looking for me?' (976). He denies it, but she tries to persuade him to come into her house, and when he refuses she catches hold of him and starts pulling him in. But just in time the girl runs out and challenges the old hag by saying that the hag is old enough to be the boy's mother.

YOUNG WOMAN. He isn't old enough to sleep with you;

---

[20] The number and use of doors and windows in this scene have been much discussed. See especially Dover *Greek and the Greeks* 263–6, Ussher *Ecclesiazusae* xxx–xxxii, Vetta *Donne* 233–4.

You'd be his mother rather than his wife.
If you establish this to be the rule,
You'll fill the country up with Oedipuses.

(*Women at the Assembly* 1039–42)

This argument defeats the Old Woman, and in baffled rage she relinquishes the Young Man and goes back into her house. Why does she give in so easily? The girl's argument is really quite illogical. It is all very well to say that with community of sexual relations no one will know who is the father of which child, but it does not follow that no one will know who is the mother of which child. The new system will make it no harder than before to identify mothers. (Praxagora, unlike Plato in *Republic* 5, has no plan to take infants away from their mothers at birth.) And anyway this is the first day of the new system, and the Young Man was born years ago. So he and the Old Woman both know perfectly well that she is not his mother and there is no possibility of incest between them. But this is one of those places where Aristophanes simply does not care about exact logic or probability. His concern is to entertain the audience. This old hag has been on-stage long enough; if she stays any longer the audience will be getting bored with her. So a joke is made to get her off, and at first hearing the joke sounds appropriate enough; it is only when you stop to think about it that you realize that it does not really work out logically. But the audience is not given time to think about it. No sooner is the joke cracked than the hag is bundled off-stage and a Second Old Woman is arriving from another direction, even older and uglier than the first one.

SECOND OLD WOMAN. Hey, you, girl! That's against this law! Where
     are
You taking him to? Look, it's written down
That he's to sleep with me first.

(*Women at the Assembly* 1049–51)

This time the girl is so terrified that she runs away, leaving the boy by himself to argue with the Second Old Woman, who catches hold of him and starts dragging him away towards her house. It looks as if she has really got him when yet another hag pops out, still more ancient and still more hideous, to claim that she has a prior right. And so a tug-of-war develops, with the unfortunate

Young Man in the middle and the two Old Women pulling at him in opposite directions.

YOUNG MAN. Are you a monkey plastered with white lead,
Or an old woman risen from the grave?
THIRD OLD WOMAN. No joking now, but come this way.
SECOND OLD WOMAN.   No, this way.
THIRD OLD WOMAN. I'll never let you go.
SECOND OLD WOMAN.   Neither shall I.
YOUNG MAN. You're tearing me in half, you wretched women!
SECOND OLD WOMAN. You've got to come with me. The law says so.
THIRD OLD WOMAN. No, not if a still uglier hag shows up.
YOUNG MAN. Well, tell me this: if you two kill me first,
How shall I ever reach that pretty girl?
THIRD OLD WOMAN. That's your look-out, but this is what's required.
YOUNG MAN. Well, which am I to get stuck into first?
SECOND OLD WOMAN. I've told you: this way.
YOUNG MAN.   *She* must let me go, then.
THIRD OLD WOMAN. No, come this way to me.
YOUNG MAN.   If *she* lets go.
SECOND OLD WOMAN. I shan't let go, by Zeus!
THIRD OLD WOMAN.   Neither shall I.

(*Women at the Assembly* 1072–85)

Eventually the Young Man is hauled away by both Old Women together. The scene is knockabout farce, but at the same time it presents an important part of the story of the play, the putting into practice of the plan to communize sex. Critics have had much difficulty in interpreting the scene: does it show the success of the plan, or its failure?[21] A modern reader may feel inclined to sympathize with the Young Man, whose love affair is so violently interrupted; but that is a misreading of the scene. Aristophanes seldom, perhaps never, invites sympathy for strong young men; 'it appears to be one of the functions of comedy to take them down a peg'.[22] This particular Young Man is not a deserving case. On the contrary,

---

[21] The best analysis is that of Sommerstein *CQ* 34 (1984) 320–1. He gives references to earlier discussions; for more recent ones see J. Henderson *TAPA* 117 (1987) 118–19, Taaffe *Ar. and Women* 123–8, Bowie *Aristophanes* 264–7.
[22] Sommerstein *CQ* 34 (1984) 321.

he is trying to seduce a girl of citizen birth (not a prostitute or courtesan). By real Athenian law that was a grave offence, which might be punished even by death.[23] By Praxagora's new law it is allowed, but only if he satisfies an ugly old woman first. Thus he is trying to cheat, just like the Neighbour in the previous scene, by conforming to the new law when it suits him and not when it does not; and when his attempt fails, that means that the law has prevailed.

PRAXAGORA'S SUCCESS

Women at the Assembly has two main subjects: women attending the Assembly to take control of the state, and the communistic organization of property and sex. These two subjects have no necessary connection with each other. Aristophanes could have used the first subject without the second: the women, on taking control, might have introduced some quite different form of organization instead of communism. Or he could have used the second subject without the first: a communist regime might have been imposed by quite different characters—sophists, for example, or ants (Kantharos and Platon are each said to have written a comedy called *Ants*)—and not by women. Furthermore, he has taken remarkably little trouble to blend the two. The first subject runs from the beginning of the play to line 557. Up to that point there is not the slightest hint of the communism to come. On the contrary, it is plainly stated by Praxagora that women are conservative and will not introduce innovations (cf. pp. 307–9). At line 558 she suddenly begins to predict a happy future for Athens based on innovations of the most drastic kind; her only worry is that her proposals may be too novel for the Athenians to accept (583–5). Although we cannot know for certain how Aristophanes went about writing this play, an obvious hypothesis is that he originally planned a play about women attending the Assembly, but after writing 557 lines found that he had exhausted that subject; he therefore thought up a second subject, communism, in order to complete a comedy of normal length, but did not bother to alter anything in the first half of the play to prepare the way for the second half. This feature of the play must be accounted a fault, but it is a fault that is not likely to have troubled the

[23] Demosthenes 23.53.

audience much, since both subjects in themselves are entertaining.

The entertainment in the first half of the play arises primarily from the incongruity of the women pretending to be men, and of a man appearing in woman's clothes. There are the usual types of jokes about women, especially their fondness for drink and sex, and one passage which shows more originality and is the most amusing in the first half, in which Praxagora bamboozles her husband. Praxagora's long speech includes some criticism of those Athenians, especially Agyrrhios, who give individual profit priority over consistent policy, and this probably does represent Aristophanes' own opinion (cf. p. 308). But nothing else in the first half conveys a serious view or message to the audience. In particular, the notion of handing over the government to the women is absurd. Apart from Praxagora, all the women in the play are more or less ignorant or incompetent, and are obviously not capable of governing sensibly. When they get to the Assembly, they dominate the meeting not because Praxagora's arguments are convincing but simply because, having packed the meeting early, they outnumber the men (434); and the reason why the men eventually acquiesce in the proposal to let the women govern is merely that this is the only expedient that has not yet been tried (456–7). To modern readers Aristophanes' view of women's abilities may seem patronizing. But his original male audience undoubtedly considered it right, natural, and inevitable that men should control women, because 'the male is by nature more of a leader than the female',[24] and the notion that this control might be reversed was simply an amusing fantasy.

When we turn to the second half of the play, we face the much-discussed question whether Aristophanes was really in favour of communism or against it.[25] The fact that Plato proposed a rather similar scheme shows at least that it was possible for a fourth-century Athenian to be seriously in favour of it, and this interpretation of Aristophanes' intention might be supported by the way in which he makes Praxagora introduce it. Along with the chorus, she is addressing Blepyros and another man, probably Khremes.[26] But she is not addressing them only.

[24] Aristotle *Politics* 1259b 1–2.

[25] For a convenient summary of different interpretations see Rothwell *Politics* 5–10.

[26] Vetta *Donne* 198–9 and S. D. Olson *CQ* 41 (1991) 36–40 argue for the Neighbour rather than Khremes.

CHORUS. But you mustn't delay; it is time, as you see, to take up what
    you are intending.
    Quick action's the thing that wins the applause and approval of all the
    spectators.
PRAXAGORA. Yes, indeed, and I'm sure that what I have to teach them
    is good. But will the spectators
    Be willing to make a fresh start, and not be too devoted to old-fashioned
    habits
    And the old way of life that they've formerly lived? That's the thing
    that I'm mainly afraid of.
BLEPYROS. You certainly needn't be frightened of that. A fresh start is
    just what we like making.
    Rather that than exerting executive power: all that's 'ex' is much better
    forgotten!

                                    (*Women at the Assembly* 581–7)

So Praxagora is going to expound her plans to the audience in
the theatre, and Blepyros, by his use of 'we', makes himself a
member of that audience. She is addressing all the men in Athens;
she is going to teach them good things, and she expects them not
merely to listen, but to change their whole way of life in accordance
with her instructions. We remember other plays in which the leading
character or the chorus claims to give good advice to the Athenians;
the phrase about teaching them good things is especially reminiscent
of *Akharnians* 658 and *Frogs* 686–7. So the wording of 581–7 looks
like a signal that what comes next will deserve serious attention.

After the exposition of the communist plan we have the scenes
in which it is put into effect. As with the plans in earlier plays, there
turn out to be some difficulties. Just as Dikaiopolis' new market
and Peisetairos' new city attract sycophants and other characters
who at first prevent the schemes from succeeding in the manner
intended, so Praxagora's scheme does not run smoothly from the
start. It is hard to get every man to give up his personal possessions,
or to secure the same sexual opportunities for the ugly as for the
beautiful. Some men try to take advantage of the new arrangements
without making their proper contribution. Modern critics who
argue that the scheme is a failure generally concentrate their attention on these scenes.[27] But in order to see whether it fails or succeeds

---

[27] See especially S. Saïd in *Ar. Femmes* 49–60. The view of J. Ober and B.
Strauss in *Noth. Dion.* 264–9 is slightly different: they consider that Aristophanes
is pointing out the difficulties of egalitarianism, but avoids showing whether the
scheme is a success or not.

we must look at the end, and in the end it is triumphantly successful. Blepyros,[28] who more than any other character in this play represents the ordinary man, reappears in the final scene and goes off to a scrumptious feast (described in one monstrous compound word in 1169–75) accompanied by some girls. He thus attains the pleasures of food and sex which regularly constitute the happy ending of an Aristophanic comedy.[29]

Yet the very fact that this festivity resembles the festivities which conclude several of the earlier plays should put us on our guard against taking the communist scheme as a serious proposition. For in each of those plays a real-life problem is solved by a plan which is fantastic and could not be carried out in real life; and it is the impossible plan which leads to the concluding festivity. In *Akharnians* the scheme which leads to the festivity is the making of a personal peace-treaty; in *Peace*, flying to heaven on a beetle; in *Birds*, building a city in the sky; in *Frogs*, fetching a poet from Hades. If the analogy holds, the communist scheme is on a par with those: a funny idea for a comedy, but not possible in practice. The serious tone of Praxagora's introduction of the scheme to the spectators may suggest that Aristophanes genuinely wants the Athenians to adopt it, and that possibility cannot be absolutely disproved. But it seems to me improbable. I think it more likely that in this case the serious introduction is deliberately misleading, and that communism is not meant to be a practical solution to Athens' problems. It is just a delightful dream.

[28] This character is not named in the text, but must be Blepyros because he is the husband of the 'most blessed' woman (1113), who can only be Praxagora. It would anyway be strange if the final triumph of the play were given to an anonymous character whom the audience had never seen before. Some inconsistencies with earlier parts of the play, pointed out by S. D. Olson *GRBS* 28 (1987) 162 and *CQ* 41 (1991) 36–40, are relatively unimportant; cf. Dover *Ar. Comedy* 193 n. 3.

[29] Sommerstein *CQ* 34 (1984) 322–3 convincingly refutes the suggestion that the feast is illusory.

14

Wealth

THE TWO VERSIONS OF THE PLAY

Wealth was first performed in 408 BC. Twenty years later Aristophanes revised it, and it was performed again in 388. A scholiast, who annotated the version which we have, believed that this was the earlier one. At 115 and 119 he comments that these two lines are changed 'in the second', and he quotes the other version of 115, which is a rewording giving the same sense. This shows that he had both versions in front of him when he was writing his note. It also shows that the two versions were very similar, at least in this part of the play; for he was able to identify which line in one version corresponded to which line in the other, and noticed that there was a change of wording without a change of sense. But further on, at 173 and 1146, he is puzzled by references to events which occurred later than 408 BC, and suggests that these two lines have been erroneously transferred from the second version; yet it appears that he did not bother to check the other version to see whether these lines were in it too, or perhaps for some reason the other version was no longer available to him when he came to write these notes. In fact he has missed the obvious explanation, that the version on which he is commenting, and which we have, is in fact the revised version of 388. This is confirmed by other topical references which we can date but the scholiast probably could not, especially in a passage where Karion (addressing Khremylos) and Khremylos (addressing Wealth himself) are listing the advantages that Wealth confers.

KARION. Isn't he the reason the great King preens himself?
  Isn't he the reason the Assembly meets?
KHREMYLOS. And don't you man the triremes? Tell me that!
KARION. He feeds hired troops at Corinth, doesn't he?

Isn't he the reason Pamphilos will wail?
KHREMYLOS. And the needle-seller as well as Pamphilos?
KARION. Isn't he the reason that Agyrrhios flouts us?
KHREMYLOS. Isn't it for you Philepsios tells stories?
Aren't you the reason we're allied to Egypt?
And the reason Laïs loves Philonides?
KARION. Timotheos' tower—
KHREMYLOS [*to Karion*]. —will fall on you, I hope!

(*Wealth* 170–80)

The prominence of Agyrrhios as a politician, his introduction of pay for citizens attending the Assembly, and the use of mercenary soldiers in the Corinthian War all belong to the 390s (see pp. 301–2); Timotheos came to prominence no earlier than the battle of Knidos in 394; and it seems likely that Pamphilos was tried, on a charge of stealing public funds, upon his failure as commander of an expedition against Aigina in 389/8.[1] Even though we cannot date the activities of Philepsios and Philonides, and the references to the needle-seller, the alliance with Egypt, and the tower remain obscure, the datable allusions are enough to show that these lines belong to the revised version of the play. The same period is indicated by jokes about Neokleides (665–6, 716–25), because this politician is mentioned also in *Women at the Assembly* (254–5, 397–407) and in a fragment of the lost and undated *Storks* (fr. 454), but not in any of the earlier plays.

When Aristophanes revised a play for a second performance, one of the main requirements must have been to remove the outdated allusions to personalities and events, and insert new ones. Can we see how this has been done in *Wealth*? Of all the topical allusions in the play as we have it, about half are concentrated in the one passage already quoted (170–80). This looks very much like a package which has been thrust in at a convenient point; the continuity of the dialogue would be perfectly satisfactory without it. The lines about Neokleides (665–6, 716–25) could have been inserted in the revision to replace lines about politicians who were prominent twenty years earlier. Lines 550, referring to Thrasyboulos and

[1] Xenophon *Hellenika* 5.1.2–5, Platon com. 14, and Demosthenes 40.22 can be interpreted with plausibility, though not with certainty, as evidence for a trial of Pamphilos in that year. *Wealth* 385 probably refers to the pleading of Pamphilos at this trial, rather than to an artist named Pamphilos; cf. K. Holzinger *Aristophanes' Plutos* (Vienna 1940) 140–52.

Dionysios, and 1146, referring to the amnesty following the restoration of democracy, could be late additions; neither is essential
to the passage in which it occurs. The reference to Pauson (602),
on the other hand, may have been retained from the earlier version
of the play, since he was already well known as a hungry man before
then (cf. *Women at the Thesmophoria* 949). There are also passing
references to men named Patrokles (84) and Dexinikos (800), which
could have been either added in the revision or retained from the
earlier version, since we do not know when those men first became
prominent.

One other passage contains topical allusions: the song sung by
Karion and the chorus, which includes jokes against Philonides
(303) and Aristyllos (314). But here we come to another problem.
This is the only song in the whole play: why are there no others? In
fact there are several places in the play where *XOPOY*, meaning
'⟨Song⟩ of the chorus', is either written in the manuscripts or added
by editors, just as we also find it in the plays of New Comedy.[2] In
these places presumably the chorus sang songs which were not
composed especially for this play and so were not included in its
text. In the earlier plays the songs are often topical and contain
references to specific individuals; so it is likely that in the first
version of *Wealth* too the songs were topical and all had to be
removed in the revision. The one song now in the play (290–321)
must have been newly written for the second version; for a scholiast
tells us that it, or part of it, parodies a work (probably a dithyrambic
performance) by Philoxenos of Kythera about the Cyclops and
Galateia, which itself was a satire on Dionysios of Syracuse composed after Philoxenos fled from that tyrant's court—and Dionysios
did not come to power until 406 BC.

We may conclude: when Aristophanes decided to revise *Wealth*
for another performance in 388, he excised all the out-of-date
passages in the original play, including all the songs. He wrote one
new song, and he inserted new topical allusions in a few other
places; but he wrote no further songs, and the new topical allusions
are much less numerous than those in the original play probably
were. The fewness of the topical references has generally been
attributed by modern scholars to a change in the taste of Athenian
spectators, who were becoming less interested in politics and more

---

[2] Cf. E. W. Handley *CQ* 3 (1953) 55–61, W. Beare *CQ* 5 (1955) 49–52.

appreciative of dramatic coherence not interrupted by irrelevant jokes.[3] That may be correct; but another possible reason is that Aristophanes in his old age lacked the energy and will to do much new writing for the revival. It may be that much of the play as we have it dates from 408, and we should beware of trying to link its theme closely (as some scholars have wished) to the circumstances of 388.

THE GOD OF WEALTH

The play is opened by an Athenian citizen and his slave. Their names, Khremylos and Karion, are not given until much later, and are mentioned only twice each altogether (336, 1171; 624, 1100); evidently the audience is not expected to pay much attention to the names, but it is convenient for us to use them. Khremylos is an honest old citizen with a strong resemblance to Dikaiopolis in *Akharnians* and Trygaios in *Peace*. Karion is also a prominent character, something like Xanthias in *Frogs* (see pp. 277–9). He likes food better than work, and is not afraid to make cheeky comments on what is going on, but he is essentially loyal to his master.[4]

They are just arriving home from a visit to the oracle at Delphi; this is probably clear to the audience at once, even before it is mentioned in the dialogue, from the wreaths which they are wearing on their heads.[5] They are following a blind old man in dirty clothes; Karion does not know why, and after grumbling to the audience that his master must be mad, he insists on being told the reason. Khremylos explains, in a passage put in to make the situation clear to the audience.

KHREMYLOS. I've been an honest and god-fearing man,
    But poor and unsuccessful.

[3] Cf. M. Dillon *CA* 6 (1987) on the *second* run of pages numbered 155–83.
[4] Cf. Dover *Ar. Comedy* 204–8. However, Dover somewhat overstates the importance of Karion, who is entirely absent during the central part of the play (322–624) and at other times is often acting on his master's orders (for example, when he goes to fetch the chorus of farmers) or as a traditional type of messenger reporting events off-stage (627–770, 802–22). S. D. Olson *TAPA* 119 (1989) 193–9 goes too far in a different direction when he describes Karion as aggressive and rebellious.
[5] The various functions of wreaths in this play are studied by A. H. Groton *Classical Journal* 86 (1990) 16–22.

KARION.   Yes, I know.
KHREMYLOS. While temple-robbers, politicians, rogues,
  And sycophants got rich.
KARION.   You're telling me!
KHREMYLOS. I went to put a question to the god:
  Although the quiver of my own poor life
  Has shot out nearly all its arrows now,
  I went to ask about my only son,
  Whether he ought to change the way he lives
  And be dishonest, villainous, no good,
  Because that's what would pay in his career.
KARION. 'And what quoth Phoebus from his laurel wreaths'?[6]
KHREMYLOS. I'll tell you. His reply to me was plain:
  Whoever I met first on going out,
  He told me not to let him get away
  But urge him to come with me to my home.
KARION. And who did you meet first, then?
KHREMYLOS.   This man here.

(Wealth 28–44)

It may have been a traditional folklore motif that, after one
consults a god, the first person one meets has a special significance.[7]
The significance of this blind old man is soon revealed: he is Wealth
(Ploutos). But how has it come about that Wealth is reduced to such
a pitiful condition? He tells Khremylos that Zeus is to blame. When
Wealth was young he declared his intention of going only to good
men; so Zeus made him blind, to prevent him from distinguishing
the good from the bad. That explains why bad men now get rich. If
he could see again, of course he would leave the bad men and go to
the good; but when Khremylos says he thinks he will be able to
restore Wealth's sight, Wealth becomes frightened that Zeus may
destroy him in some other way. So Khremylos, with Karion's
support, proceeds to argue at length that Wealth is more powerful
than Zeus and controls everything in the world. If he wishes he
can stop providing money for sacrifices, and so starve Zeus into
submission (an echo of the device by which Peisetairos and the Birds
defeat the gods). People do everything for money.

---

[6] Line 39, or part of it, is said by a scholiast to be quoted from Euripides.
[7] Compare Euripides *Ion* 534–6, where Xouthos receives an oracle from
Apollo saying that when he goes out of the temple the first person he meets will
prove to be his own son. Cf. Bowie *Aristophanes* 278 n. 44.

KHREMYLOS. And it's because of you that every skill
And clever artifice has been invented.
One man sits working as a shoemaker,
One is a blacksmith, one's a carpenter,
And one's a goldsmith, getting gold from you—
KARION. And one's a cloak-stealer, and one's a burglar—
KHREMYLOS. And one cleans clothes—
KARION.   One washes woollen fleeces[8]—
KHREMYLOS. And one tans leather hides, and one sells onions—
KARION. And one's a plucked seducer,[9] all for you!
WEALTH. Oh dear! I never realized all this.

(*Wealth* 160–9)

Eventually Wealth is convinced, but is still doubtful how he can regain control of all this power. Only if he recovers his sight will he be able to make good men wealthy,[10] but Khremylos is sure that he can somehow bring that about, with all honest poor men as his allies, and sends Karion off to call his fellow-farmers in from the fields while he himself takes Wealth indoors. The farmers form the chorus of the play; and when they arrive and are told by Karion that Wealth will make them all rich, they are naturally overjoyed.

This representation of wealth is one of the most complex allegories in any of Aristophanes' plays,[11] second only to the allegory

[8] Fleeces were sold by weight, and so wetting a fleece to make it heavier was a way of cheating the customer; cf. *Frogs* 1386–7.

[9] Plucking out the pubic hair seems to have been a traditional punishment for seduction: cf. *Clouds* 1083. (This is disputed by D. Cohen *Zeitschrift der Savigny-Stiftung für Rechtsgeschichte, Rom. Abt.* 102 (1985) 385–7; but he is wrong to say that there is no corroborative evidence, since the references in *Clouds* and *Wealth* support each other. They were written some years apart and cannot both refer to a single recent case: they make no sense unless the practice was well known. Cf. C. Carey *Liverpool Classical Monthly* 18 (1993) 53–5.) Here the reference is to a man who makes himself liable to this punishment by providing sexual service to a woman for money. Such a man appears later in the play (959–1096).

[10] Just why the entry of Wealth into Khremylos' house while still blind does not make Khremylos wealthy is never explained, but the whole play is written on the assumption that it is the restoration of his sight which brings prosperity. Cf. S. D. Olson *HSCP* 93 (1990) 230–1 n. 29.

[11] Cf. Newiger *Metaphor* 167–73.

of democracy in *Horsemen*. Not that it is a new idea to personify wealth; that tradition begins at least three centuries previously. In early poetry Wealth is a son of the goddess Demeter, whom she sends to the houses of men she loves, and he is sometimes depicted in art as a child with a cornucopia.[12] The reason for the association with Demeter must be that wealth was originally thought of as being simply an abundance of grain and other agricultural produce. Wealth thus came to be regarded as a god, and Aristophanes in another play makes the women of Athens pray to him among other gods (*Women at the Thesmophoria* 297). The notion that Wealth is blind, so that he cannot tell good men from bad ones and often goes to the wrong person, occurs first in a sardonic piece by the sixth-century poet Hipponax.

> For me, Wealth never—he's so very blind!—
> Came to my house and stated 'Hipponax,
> I hereby give you thirty silver mnai
> And much else too'—he's not intelligent!
>
> (Hipponax 36 West)

But Aristophanes' personification of wealth is much more thoroughgoing than any previous one now known. He makes Wealth not only blind but old and decrepit, as Karion says when he patronizingly tells the chorus what his master has done.

> KARION. A poor lot you are! He's come home and brought an old man with him,
> A filthy, hunchbacked, wretched man, with wrinkles, hairless, toothless;
> And if he's foreskinless as well, I really shouldn't wonder!
>
> (*Wealth* 265–7)

If Wealth is a god, it seems strange that he has not only grown old but is apparently unable to rescue himself from his miserable condition. There is in fact some uncertainty about his status: usually he is called a god (327, 392, etc.), but sometimes he is called a man, especially in the scene in which he is taken to another god for a cure (654, 658, etc.). Sometimes he is simply the substance of money and affluence—wealth rather than Wealth (as we may write

---

[12] *Hymn to Demeter* 488–9, Hesiod *Theogony* 969–74; cf. N. J. Richardson *The Homeric Hymn to Demeter* (Oxford 1974) 316–20.

it although Aristophanes, lacking the distinction between capital and small letters, could not), as when Khremylos says to him 'No one ever has his fill of you' (188) and each of Khremylos' friends is to receive a part of him (226). On other occasions he is a rich man, living in his own house: a burglar called him a coward because he was prudent enough to lock up his valuable possessions (203–7). And these different kinds of personification can be blended in a single passage.

> WEALTH. I really do dislike it, every time
> I go into another person's house.
> I've never yet got any good from it.
> For if the man I visit is a miser,
> He buries me beneath the ground at once,
> And when a friend, some good man, comes and asks
> To borrow just a little spot of cash,
> He says he's never seen me in his life.
> But if I visit some young madcap's house,
> I'm thrown away on prostitutes and dice,
> And stripped and pushed outside in half a tick.
>
> (*Wealth* 234–44)

Here, within a single speech, Wealth is first a god, whose entrance into a house makes the house's owner rich; then he is the actual money, buried underground or spent; and then he is a rich man, robbed of his clothes and pushed out. Similar blending can occur even within one line: 'if Wealth distributed himself equally' (510) means 'if the god distributed money equally'. This allegory is hard to analyse logically, but it is very effective as a poetic method of conveying the various aspects of wealth.

POVERTY

Khremylos greets the chorus, and then is joined by another friend. His name is Blepsidemos, and for the next part of the play (during which Karion does not appear) he is the character who serves as a foil to Khremylos, asking questions and making comic comments. When he arrives, he has already heard, from talk in the barbers' shops, that Khremylos has suddenly become rich. At first he is surprised that Khremylos is then sending for his friends—not typical behaviour for an Athenian!——and he is suspicious that Khremylos has stolen a lot of money in some way. He affects a disapproving attitude, though it is clear that he really hopes Khremylos will give him a share of the loot to get his support. Eventually Khremylos reveals that he has Wealth in his house, but he has to assert it in various ways nine times before Blepsidemos will believe it. The passage displays Aristophanes' skill at writing rapid iambic dialogue.

BLEPSIDEMOS. Have you thieved that much?
KHREMYLOS.   Bah! You'll be the death
   Of me!
BLEPSIDEMOS. You'll be your own, it seems to me.
KHREMYLOS. Oh no I shan't, because, you scoundrel, I
   Have Wealth.
BLEPSIDEMOS. You, wealth? What sort?
KHREMYLOS.   The god himself.
BLEPSIDEMOS. Where is he?
KHREMYLOS.   Inside.
BLEPSIDEMOS.   Where?
KHREMYLOS.   My house.
BLEPSIDEMOS.   Yours?
KHREMYLOS.   Yes.
BLEPSIDEMOS. The hell he is! Wealth in your house?
KHREMYLOS.   That's right.
BLEPSIDEMOS. Is that true?
KHREMYLOS.   Yes.
BLEPSIDEMOS.   By Hestia, please tell me!
KHREMYLOS. Yes, by Poseidon!
BLEPSIDEMOS.   You mean the sea-god, do you?
KHREMYLOS. And any other Poseidon that there is!

(*Wealth* 389–97)

So now they must restore Wealth's sight. Khremylos reveals his plan. They are to take Wealth to the temple of Asklepios to spend the night, in the hope of a miraculous cure. But suddenly they are interrupted by a mad-looking female figure with a white face, who denounces them in tragic language for trying to expel her. She turns out to be Poverty.
   Poverty (Penia) with her sister or daughter Resourcelessness (Amekhania), like Wealth, had already been personified in earlier

literature, but not strongly characterized.[13] That she is female, whereas Wealth is male, is probably due only to the accidental fact that the Greek nouns for wealth and poverty are masculine and feminine respectively. Aristophanes makes her a termagant, who can be comically mistaken for a tragic Fury, a landlady, or a gruel-seller (423–8). At first Blepsidemos wants to run away, but Khremylos is determined to stand firm, and soon the argument becomes a formal debate. It is like the agon of earlier plays, though it is shorter and does not have the usual symmetrical form. One might have expected Aristophanes to make it a debate between Poverty and Wealth, but actually Wealth is not present in this scene; indeed throughout the play Wealth is a remarkably passive character. Instead Khremylos is Poverty's antagonist in the debate.

The basis of Khremylos' argument is moral. Justice requires that the good should prosper and the bad should not, but at present many bad people are rich and many good people are poor. Khremylos and Blepsidemos therefore intend to restore Wealth's sight so that he will go to the good and avoid the bad. The effect will be that the bad will take care to become good, and so they will become rich too. What greater blessing could befall mankind? In this argument we see a new development in the theme of the play. Previously it was said that the restoration of Wealth's sight would make the good rich instead of the bad (95–8). Only now is it explained that that eventuality will prompt the bad to become good, so that in the end everyone will be rich. This makes clear, in retrospect, why Poverty complained that she was being banished from Greece, and now she seizes on this point as the basis of her reply. If everyone is rich, no one will want to do any work.

POVERTY. But if knowledge and skill are abolished by you, who then will be ready and willing
  To work as a blacksmith or builder of ships, or else as a tailor or wheelwright,
  Or a maker of shoes, or a tanner of hides, or to labour at bricks or at laundry,
  Or 'to break up the surface of earth with the plough and to harvest the fruits of Demeter'?

(*Wealth* 512–15)

[13] Alkaios 364 (Lobel and Page), Theognis 351–4, 384–5, 649–52, Herodotos 8.111.3. Cf. Newiger *Metapher* 160–4.

Nor, she says, will there be any slaves to do the work, because no one will be willing to work as a slave-merchant to procure them. Thus universal wealth will provide neither the necessities nor the luxuries of life; but Poverty does provide these, because she makes people work for a living. It is striking that Poverty here lists among her gifts to mankind some of the same benefits as Khremylos earlier (160–9, quoted on p. 329) attributed to Wealth. In a sense, of course, it is true that poverty and wealth both cause work to be done: people work because they are poor enough to want to be paid and other people are rich enough to pay them. But the weakness of Poverty's argument is that she has not shown that poverty is an advantage to the poor men themselves. Consequently Khremylos is able to riposte with a vivid description of the unpleasantness of being poor, with starving and wailing children, buzzing insects, ragged clothes, a mattress full of bugs, a stone for a pillow, makeshift furniture, and bad food (535–47).

So Poverty still needs to find a way of arguing that it is a good thing to be poor. She maintains that she was not talking about utter destitution, and she draws a distinction between being poor and being a pauper or beggar. A pauper has nothing, but a poor man is just an ordinary person who has to work for his living; he never has more than he needs of anything, but he never runs short either (548–54). Being poor, in this sense, is good for the body, because it prevents one from eating too much, and it is also good for the character: rich men become insolent and antidemocratic. Khremylos concedes one of these points, that politicians get rich on public money and then become enemies of the people (567–71; Aristophanes is always ready to make a cynical joke against politicians). He rejects the other points, but does not really refute them; he just dismisses them contemptuously. After a squabble about whether Zeus is rich or poor (which displays Aristophanes' skill at devising comically sophistic arguments) he tells Poverty that she will never convince him, and with the support of Blepsidemos he chases her away.

Some critics have doubted whether Khremylos can be regarded as the true winner of this debate. He does not disprove all that Poverty says, but simply refuses to go on listening. It has therefore been supposed that Aristophanes intends the audience to conclude that Khremylos has a bad case and wealth is not a good thing; the view expressed by Poverty, that it is good for people to be moderately poor, is the one with which Aristophanes really agrees.[14] But that interpretation is certainly wrong, and has been effectively refuted by Sommerstein.[15] Khremylos is the hero of the play, who triumphs in the end, whereas Poverty is presented from the start as an unpleasant character; with this presentation Aristophanes could not have expected the audience to side with Poverty against Khremylos. The reason why he has not bothered to refute her case in every detail is that the conclusion is already obvious. No one in the Athenian audience could possibly think seriously that poverty was a good thing.

ASKLEPIOS

Khremylos, with Blepsidemos and Karion, takes Wealth off to spend the night in the precinct of Asklepios, the god of medicine and healing. Shrines of Asklepios in ancient times were something like the modern Lourdes, and many sick people visited them in the hope of a cure. A great deal of evidence shows beyond doubt that many did in fact recover from various illnesses and attributed their recovery to Asklepios. The actual causes of their recovery are uncertain. Some may have recovered naturally after a disease had taken its course, some cures may have been effected by medicines provided at the shrine, and some by the patients' own faith. But that question is beyond the scope of this book.[16] Here we are concerned with the way in which Aristophanes presents the episode to his audience.

The particular temple of Asklepios to which Wealth is taken, though not named in the play, is probably the one at Zea near Peiraieus, not far from Athens and beside the sea (cf. 656).[17] He is first led out of Khremylos' house 'as is customary' (625); this probably means that he is dressed in the manner customary for

[14] This view has been held mainly by German scholars. For recent presentations in English see David *Ar. and Ath. Society* 38–43, Bowie *Aristophanes* 284–91.

[15] A. H. Sommerstein *CQ* 34 (1984) 314–33.

[16] See E. J. and L. Edelstein *Asclepius* (Baltimore 1945), especially vol. 2 ch. 3.

[17] Cf. S. B. Aleshire *The Athenian Asklepieion* (Amsterdam 1989) 13.

patients going to Asklepios, perhaps in white.[18] Karion is told to bring bedding for the overnight stay 'and everything in there that's been got ready' (626); that must include items of food for dedication to Asklepios and for their own meals.

The events at the shrine are not shown on-stage but narrated by Karion in a comic messenger-speech addressed to Khremylos' wife, who has stayed at home. They are given in considerable detail; Aristophanes himself must have seen the procedure, either as a patient or accompanying a patient, and some but not all of the Athenian audience must have been familiar with it too. First, says Karion, they took Wealth to the sea and bathed him; this was a normal kind of purification before a religious act. Then they took him to the precinct of Asklepios, and as a preliminary sacrifice burned some cakes of the round type called *popanon*, the standard preliminary offering at Zea.[19] They put Wealth to bed, and went to bed themselves. Khremylos' wife asks if there were other patients; Karion replies that one was Neokleides, the blind (perhaps really just short-sighted) politician, and there were many others. It is surprising that only one name is given. One might have expected Aristophanes to take the opportunity to attribute comic illnesses to some other politicians; possibly he did so in the original version of the play (see p. 325). Karion then goes on with his narrative.

WIFE. And had the god some other suppliants?
KARION. Yes, one was Neokleides, who is blind
But beats the sighted when it comes to thieving,
And many others, having every kind
Of ailment. When the sacristan had doused
The lamps and had instructed us to sleep,
Saying that anyone who heard a noise
Must remain silent, all lay quietly.
And yet I couldn't sleep, because I was
Distracted by a pot of frumenty
Which an old woman had beside her head,
And I'd a marvellous wish to ambush it!
But then I looked up, and I saw the priest
Snatching away the cheese-cakes and dried figs

---

[18] There is no other evidence for special dress at the shrine at Zea, but white dress seems to have been the rule at the shrine of Asklepios at Pergamon in later times. Cf. Edelstein *Asclepius* vol. 1 T513 line 5.

[19] Cf. *IG* 2² 4962.2–10.

From off the holy table. After that
He went round all the altars one by one
To see if there were any round-cakes left,
And then he blessed them all—into a bag!
And so I thought my action sanctified,
And went to get the pot of frumenty.
WIFE. You wretch! And weren't you frightened of the god?
KARION. I damn well was—frightened he'd get there first
And beat me to the pot, him and his wreaths!
You see, his priest had taught me what to do.
But the old woman heard the noise I made
And put her hand out. So I hissed and bit her,
Pretending that I was a sacred snake.
She pulled her hand back in a hurry then,
Wrapped herself up, and lay there quietly
Farting in terror, worse than any weasel!
So I got stuck into the frumenty
Till I was full, and then went back to bed.

(*Wealth* 664–95)

I quote this at length because it is the best messenger-speech in the whole of Aristophanes, so vivid that it is difficult for a reader to remember that the actions were not seen by the audience in the theatre. First there was the sacristan giving instructions and putting out the lights, and the patients and their companions lying in the dark; but the darkness was not total, for they were out-of-doors in the precinct, or perhaps under a portico, but not inside the temple.[20] So Karion, who was hungry (because comic slaves always like food and drink; this is not evidence of starvation), could see that an old woman had a pot of frumenty beside her. Frumenty is a sort of porridge made from wheatmeal rather than oatmeal, and the woman had brought it presumably for her own breakfast in the morning.

Meanwhile the priest was gathering up the offerings from the holy table. The cheese-cakes (tastier than the round-cakes which were burned as sacrifices) and the dried figs would be the priest's meal, an honorarium for his services. Formally they were dedicated to Asklepios, but no doubt everyone knew that Asklepios would

[20] They must have been outside, because later the god and the snakes disappeared into the temple (741). The contrary argument of Aleshire *The Athenian Asklepieion* 29 n. 7, that the incubation was inside the temple because there was a table (678), is not cogent.

not really eat them.[21] We may compare the offertory in a modern church, where money contributed by the worshippers is dedicated to God, but they all know that, after the congregation has left, it will be taken away and spent on the church or given to charity, and a modern comedian or satirist can represent the minister as being out for his own profit. In the same way Aristophanes manages to suggest that the priest of Asklepios was a hypocrite. Not only was he 'snatching away' the cheese-cakes and figs when he thought no one was watching, but he also went round the altars to see whether any round-cakes had escaped being burned (cf. 660–1); and 'he blessed them all—into a bag!' is a brilliant phrase for implying that the priest's intention was less holy than he liked people to suppose.

So Karion drew the comic conclusion that, if it was a holy act for the priest to lay hold of any food he could see, it would be equally holy for Karion himself to do likewise. The old woman heard him coming, but did not see him, although he could see her; like Wealth and Neokleides she suffered from blindness or defective sight. So Karion pretended to be a snake. This is an excellent comic idea: snakes of the non-venomous variety known as *pareias* were regarded as servants of Asklepios, so that the old woman would naturally expect them at his shrine.[22] Karion hissed and bit her, she shrank back under her blanket, and he was able to enjoy his meal.

Up to this point the narrative of events is perfectly realistic and contains nothing supernatural. But then the god Asklepios himself appeared, with his daughters Healing and Allcure (Iaso and Panakeia) and a slave carrying his medicine chest and his small mortar and pestle for compounding ingredients. He inspected all the patients, and first treated Neokleides by applying to his eyes a stinging vinegar poultice, which made him yell and left his blindness uncured. Wealth received much gentler treatment, culminating in the appearance of two huge snakes which licked his eyes, and in a trice he could see. Karion clapped his hands for joy and woke Khremylos, and the god and his snakes forthwith disappeared into the temple.

How are we to interpret this divine apparition? In real life the worshippers of Asklepios slept during the night. They saw the god only in their dreams, if at all. Karion, however, was not dreaming.

---

[21] Cf. E. Roos *Opuscula Atheniensia* 3 (1960) 80–7.
[22] Cf. Aelian *Nature of Animals* 8.12.

He had been told to go to sleep (669) but, being a naughty slave, he stayed awake to steal some food; when the god arrived, he pulled his cloak over his head and pretended to be asleep, but watched what was going on through the holes (713–15). Thus he saw what he ought not to have seen. By putting the narrative into the mouth of a slave, whom the Athenian audience would expect to have a lower standard of morality, Aristophanes has contrived to provide an eyewitness account of events which the respectable Khremylos could not see, because he was quite properly sleeping. Despite the comic incidents, including one particularly vulgar one (697–706), there is nothing in this scene to disturb conventional religious belief. Asklepios is described doing what religious Athenians believed him to do, even though they had never seen it: he made a round of his patients during the night, giving appropriate treatment to each. He is here presented with complete respect, as a true healer.[23]

THE REDISTRIBUTION OF WEALTH

Wealth, his sight restored, returns in triumph with Khremylos. On the way he has been greeted by throngs of poor but honest men, who now look forward to being rich. He is welcomed into Khremylos' house, which immediately becomes hugely wealthy. Karion's next speech, addressed to the audience, is interesting because it shows what form an ordinary Athenian's dreams of riches might have taken.

KARION. How pleasant to be prosperous, gentlemen,
   Especially when you haven't paid for it!
   A heap of goods has burst into our house,
   Although we've done no wrong to anyone—
   This is the way it's pleasant to get rich!
   The bin is full of good white barley-meal,
   The jars are full of dark and fragrant wine,
   And everything is crammed with gold and silver,
   All our utensils, marvellous to see!
   The well is full of olive-oil, the flasks

[23] In this conclusion I agree with E. Roos *Opuscula Atheniensia* 3 (1960) 55–97. However, I do not accept his suggestion (on p. 95) that after 696 Karion is recounting a dream.

Brimming with perfume, and the loft with figs,
While every cruet, casserole, and pot
Has turned to bronze, and all the wooden plates
Rotted by fish are gleaming silver now.
Our oven suddenly is ivory.
We slaves can use gold stater coins to play
At odd-and-even. We don't wipe ourselves
With stones, but garlic bulbs—such luxury!

(*Wealth* 802–18)

While preparations for a feast are in progress, several visitors arrive. First comes a Good Man, who had become poor by helping out needy friends but now is suddenly rich. He has come to dedicate his old cloak and shoes, symbolic of the poverty from which he has escaped, to the god who has performed this miracle for him. Then, by way of contrast, comes a bad man who is suddenly poor. The particular type of bad man that Aristophanes chooses to bring in as an example is once again a Sycophant, as in some earlier plays (cf. pp. 74–5). This one attempts to give a reasoned defence of his activities: because he prosecutes offenders, he claims to be an upholder of law, a defender of democracy, and a benefactor of Athens. His argument is not refuted, any more than Poverty's argument is refuted, and it is perhaps strange that Aristophanes includes a defence which might evoke sympathy for the Sycophant,[24] for at the conclusion of this passage it is simply taken for granted that the Sycophant is a bad man; he is brusquely stripped of his cloak and sent packing.

So far we have a clear contrast between a good man who has become rich and a bad man who has become poor. But the next visitors do not fit into the same pattern. A rich Old Woman arrives, pretending by her manner of speech, dress, and make-up to be young. She complains that ever since the god began to see he has made her life unbearable, because her boy-friend has deserted her. As she goes on, it becomes clear that he is a gigolo who has been giving her sexual satisfaction in return for payment, but now his attitude has changed completely. A few moments later he appears, wearing a garland and carrying a torch. The Old Woman surmises

---

[24] D. Konstan and M. Dillon *AJP* 102 (1981) 374–8 interpret the Sycophant as 'an ideologically complex figure'. Cf. Bowie *Aristophanes* 277–8.

that he is going to a party, but in fact he has come from one and is already drunk.

YOUNG MAN. I greet you!

OLD WOMAN. What's he saying?

YOUNG MAN. Ancient friend,
You have gone quickly grey, by heaven you have!

OLD WOMAN. Oh my, the insolence! I'm being insulted!

KHREMYLOS. It seems he hasn't seen you for some time.

OLD WOMAN. For some time! He was with me yesterday.

KHREMYLOS. His sight is different, then, from other people's:
He sees more accurately when he's drunk.

OLD WOMAN. No, it's his way: he can't resist a joke.

YOUNG MAN. Ocean-Poseidon and ye elder gods!
She has so many wrinkles in her face!

OLD WOMAN. Hey, hey!
Don't wave that torch near me!

KHREMYLOS. Yes, she's quite right;
For if a single spark should touch her, she'll
Go up in flames, like an old harvest-branch.

YOUNG MAN. You'd like to play a game now with me?

OLD WOMAN. Where?

YOUNG MAN. Here. Take some nuts.

OLD WOMAN. And what's the game to be?

YOUNG MAN. To see how many teeth you've got.

KHREMYLOS. Oh, I
Can guess that. She's got three, perhaps, or four.

YOUNG MAN. Pay up! She has *one* grinder in her head.

(*Wealth* 1042–59)

The Young Man has now become rich, so that he no longer needs to flatter and serve the Old Woman. But why has he become rich? Unlike the Good Man in the previous scene, he is not presented by Aristophanes as one who has earned Wealth's favour by virtuous conduct.[25] True, the Old Woman says he was good (976–7), but it is made obvious that the conduct she is praising was really disreputable. He was making money by disgraceful means, and now that he no longer needs to do so he is drunken and boorish. The Old Woman is not a good character either; she is prurient, hypocritical, and ridiculous. Yet she has not been deprived of her

---

[25] Sommerstein *CQ* 34 (1984) 324–5 makes a gallant attempt to defend the Young Man, but it seems to me a hopeless case. Cf. Bowie *Aristophanes* 276–7.

wealth, but is still able to offer the Young Man presents (995–7). Thus both these characters are more or less bad, and both are now rich. This state of affairs is inconsistent with the earlier plot of the play, and particularly with the immediately preceding scene with the Good Man and the Sycophant. Aristophanes has suddenly and without explanation changed the plot to one in which wealth has come to everyone, good or bad. Nor does Khremylos find any fault with this state of affairs. He tries to reconcile them, and later he reassures the Old Woman that the Young Man will come to her tonight after all (1200–1). This presages a happy ending not just for good people but for everyone.

THE DEFEAT OF ZEUS

Early in the play Khremylos assures Wealth that he has more power than Zeus, if he only chose to exercise it, and could get the better of Zeus by stopping people making sacrifices to him. The success of this scheme forms the climax of the play. Now that all men are wealthy, no one needs to sacrifice to the gods to obtain their favour. Consequently the gods are starving. This is almost the same comic idea as the one at the end of *Birds*, though in *Wealth* the resulting scene is briefer and perhaps less effective. The only god who actually appears is Hermes, who surreptitiously comes and says that Zeus plans to destroy Khremylos and his whole household.

KARION. But why is it he's planning to do that
    To us?
HERMES. Because you've done most dreadful deeds.
    For ever since Wealth first began to see,
    No one makes sacrifices any more—
    No incense, bay, cake, victim, anything—
    To us gods.
KARION.   I should think not, and they won't.
    You didn't take good care of us before.
HERMES. It's not the other gods I care about;
    It's me! I'm dead, I'm famished!
KARION.   Glad to hear it.

                 (*Wealth* 1111–19)

Hermes wants to come and live in Khremylos' house, but none of his traditional capacities—as a sentinel at the door, as a patron of trade and craftiness, as a guide—seems to be any use now. Finally he is admitted as being a patron of musical and athletic contests, which are appropriate to wealth. But then comes a Priest, who makes a very similar complaint.

PRIEST. For ever since that Wealth began to see,
  I'm dead with hunger. I've no food to eat,
  And that though I'm the priest of Zeus the Saviour!
KHREMYLOS. My goodness, tell me, what's the cause of that?
PRIEST. No one thinks fit to sacrifice now.
KHREMYLOS.   Why?
PRIEST. Because they're all rich now. Before, you see,
  When they had nothing, a man who came home safe
  From sea, or got acquitted in a trial,
  Would give a victim; one who got good omens
  Would ask the priest to dinner, whereas now
  No one makes any sacrifice at all.

(*Wealth* 1173–83)

The joke is that people perform religious rituals for purely practical and selfish purposes, and give them up as soon as they think they will gain nothing by them; the gods and priests alike then go hungry. But it is virtually the same joke in both passages, and even the wording is similar. It is surprising that Aristophanes included them both in the play; and, if they are both included, there is a sense of anticlimax in the arrival of a god first and a priest afterwards. It seems possible that one of the two passages was written for the earlier version of the play and the other for the later version, and then somehow both have been included in the text as we have it.

The Priest, like all priests in Aristophanes, regards religious observances as means of procuring benefits for himself, especially food. He is a bad character, and it seems that Aristophanes has reverted to the plot by which the good have become rich and the bad have become poor. However, unlike the Sycophant, the Priest is then permitted to join in the new prosperity, in which it turns out that even the most unexpected person of all is included.

PRIEST. So I've decided that I'll say goodbye
  To Zeus the Saviour too, and settle here.

KHREMYLOS. Don't worry; it will turn out well, God willing.
  For Zeus the Saviour has already come
  Here of his own accord.
PRIEST.   That's splendid news!

(*Wealth* 1186–90)

Even Zeus himself, who was the ruler of the universe and the
oppressor of Wealth, has now given in, and like Hermes has left
Olympos to become a follower of Wealth.[26] Khremylos has won,
but prosperity and happiness now belong to everyone, not to him
alone. Consequently he does not keep Wealth in his house permanently: it might be thought an unacceptable conclusion if one
man were to monopolize the god for ever.[27] So the characters and
chorus make their final exit in a procession to restore Wealth to his
old home, the state treasury in the back room (*opisthodomos*) of the
Parthenon. Thus Athena—and that means Athens—will enjoy the
prosperity which she enjoyed in the good old days.

THE UNFAIRNESS OF LIFE

Wealth is more like a fable than the other plays. It is a tale of an
ordinary man who gets hold of Wealth and so achieves happiness.
The attainment of an ideal world or paradise, or the restoration of
a Golden Age, was a common theme of Old Comedy. Athenaios
(267e–270a) quotes from several plays on this subject. The earliest
apparently was Kratinos' *Wealths*, in which the plural title indicates
a chorus of personifications of wealth. There were also Krates'
Beasts, Telekleides' *Amphiktyons*, Pherekrates' *Miners* and *Persians*,
and others. But all those plays, to judge from the quotations,
described life in paradise as a kind of idler's or gourmand's dream,
with rivers of soup or wine, sausages growing on trees, self-laying
tables and self-frying fish. Aristophanes' play is different. His

---

[26] The scholiasts, followed by some modern scholars, most recently S. D.
Olson *HSCP* 93 (1990) 237–8 n. 50, think that when Khremylos says 'Zeus the
Saviour' he means Wealth. But that interpretation is rightly rejected by Rogers
Plutus ad loc., followed by others. Not only is there nothing in the text to indicate
to the audience that 'Zeus' does not mean Zeus, but a reference to Zeus here is
essential to complete the comic story, because there is nothing else to tell us that
Zeus has capitulated to Wealth.

[27] Cf. Albini *Interpretazioni* 1. 169.

description of prosperity contains only abundance, not impossibilities, and occupies only thirteen lines (806–18, quoted on pp. 339–40). Most of the play is rather about the means by which prosperity is attained and the difficulties which are encountered on the way. Above all, he has introduced a moral element: the notion that Wealth, when his sight is restored, will go to good men instead of bad men was a new idea, as far as we know, not used in previous comedies.

This innovation has led him into some inconsistency, as we have already seen.[28] The earlier part of the play keeps fairly well to the principle that only the good will become wealthy, but towards the end he seems to be overcome by his instinctive feeling that everyone should be happy at the end of a comedy, so that some characters— the Old Woman, the Young Man, and the Priest—are allowed to participate in the general prosperity without showing themselves to be reformed. It would of course be possible to devise an explanation of this inconsistency by reference to the rewriting of the play. We could suppose that the play as originally written in 408 BC kept strictly to the principle that the good become rich and the bad become poor, but twenty years later Aristophanes decided that he wanted a happier ending and altered the later scenes accordingly without adjusting the earlier ones. But such a hypothesis is not really necessary. There are other examples of inconsistencies of plot in plays for which there is otherwise no evidence of rewriting. *Akharnians* in particular is very similar to *Wealth* in this respect. In both these plays the good men (peace-lovers in *Akharnians*, honest men in *Wealth*) are very few at the beginning, and only they are to receive the desired benefit (peace, wealth), but later on more people are allowed to join in (cf. p. 76), so that the play ends with an impression of universal rejoicing.

A more serious criticism which has been made is that Khremylos is not really a good man but a selfish one.[29] At the start of the play he seriously entertains the possibility that it would be preferable for his son (and himself too, if only he were younger) to be dishonest (28–38, quoted on pp. 327–8). Later he says he wants to get rich

---

[28] D. Konstan and M. Dillon *AJP* 102 (1981) 371–94 discuss in greater detail the combination of different themes within this play.

[29] H. Flashar *Poetica* 1 (1967) 159–60, reprinted in *Aristophanes und die Alte Komödie* (*Wege der Forschung* 265, ed. H.-J. Newiger, 1975) 412–13.

'by fair means or foul' (233) and that he loves Wealth even more than he loves his wife and son (250–1). There are also lines remarking that good men are non-existent (99, 111, 362–3). These are cynical jokes, not to be taken literally. Some scholars, however, have taken them as proof that Aristophanes does not approve of Khremylos and does not want the audience to approve of him either. It follows that the conclusion of the play, in which Khremylos triumphs, is 'ironic': the audience is intended to realize that universal wealth would not be a good thing, and that the arguments of Poverty against it are correct. A recent variant of this view is that Aristophanes, while not actually disapproving of universal wealth, regards it as an illusion or an escapist dream, whereas the argument of Poverty that everyone must work for a living is realistic.[30] But, as we have already seen, such interpretations are refuted by the fact that Poverty is presented as an unpleasant character, who is put to flight by the hero, and nothing is said later to suggest that the hero was mistaken. If Aristophanes had wanted his audience to think that Poverty was right, he would have had to show Khremylos' plan failing in the end, just as in *Clouds* he shows Strepsiades' plan failing in the end. He could, for example, have concluded the play with Khremylos chasing Wealth away as a fraud. Since he does not, it is clear that he expects the audience to side with Khremylos and Wealth, not with Poverty.

Sommerstein, whose article is the best discussion of *Wealth* yet published, effectively demolishes the 'ironic' interpretation.[31] His own view is that the main purpose of the play is to criticize selfishness and the unjust distribution of wealth, and to champion the poor, and that this is a remarkable change from the earlier plays in which Aristophanes had written from the standpoint of the well-to-do. Certainly this interpretation is more in accord with the evidence of the text, though the contrast with earlier plays is perhaps overstated. We should recall that Dikaiopolis lives in wretched conditions while idle officials enjoy high pay and luxuries (*Akharnians* 65–72), that Kleon has made his pile while keeping the people in poverty (*Horsemen* 792–804), and that the jurors are far poorer than the peculators whom they try (*Wasps* 240–58, 291–316, 664–95). It is

---

[30] J. H. Barkhuizen *Acta Classica* 24 (1981) 17–22, S. D. Olson *HSCP* 93 (1990) 223–42.

[31] Sommerstein *CQ* 34 (1984) 314–33. See also Konstan and Dillon *AJP* 102 (1981) 378–9 n. 10.

true that poverty and wealth get more attention in *Wealth* than in any other play, but that is only to be expected in a play which has wealth as its subject. Had Aristophanes himself become poorer by the time he wrote it? It is possible; there is no evidence one way or the other. It is probably not true that Athenians generally were worse off economically in 388 than they had been in the 420s; during the Peloponnesian War they were impoverished by repeated Spartan invasions and destruction of their crops, whereas by 388 agriculture must largely have recovered.[32] Poverty in Athens may have been approaching its worst level in 408 when Aristophanes wrote the first version of the play. But even if that is so, it hardly affects the interpretation. *Wealth* is the least topical of all the plays of Aristophanes that we have.

Aristophanes is writing for ordinary average citizens, and he looks at life from their viewpoint. The hero of the play, Khremylos, is just such an average citizen. He is not rich, but he is not destitute either: he owns other slaves besides Karion (26, 816), and he is as moderate in means as in character, saving sometimes and spending sometimes (245–8). Yet he regards himself as poor (29). That is normal. Most ordinary people consider that they are poorer than they deserve to be. He also regards himself as honest (28). That is normal too. Most ordinary people believe that what they do is justified; otherwise they would not do it. Thus far, nearly everyone in the Athenian audience will have considered that Khremylos was a man just like himself.

Khremylos also claims to be god-fearing (28), and that brings us to the religious aspect of the play. The religious beliefs of ordinary Athenians were complex, and not entirely logical. In Aristophanes' time there still survives the primitive concept of a god as being a natural force beyond human control: Zeus causing rain, Demeter causing plants to grow, Aphrodite causing sexual attraction, and so on. Such a force is not in itself good or bad, but it may be propitiated by sacrifice and other rituals, and thus be won over to help rather than harm human beings. But in addition the gods are believed to be the source of human morality: they have laid down rules of justice and other good conduct, and require men to obey them. Thus one honours the gods in two ways, by rituals and by virtuous behaviour, and in return one expects the gods' favour. The trouble

---

[32] Cf. A. French *G&R* 38 (1991) 24–40.

is that the gods often seem to fail to keep their side of the bargain.

That is the situation of Khremylos, and it is a situation which many in the Athenian audience would feel to be their own. He honours the gods, yet remains poor, while he can see that others who dishonour the gods by being dishonest have become rich. Does that cause him to become an atheist and cease to believe in the gods? Not a bit of it: what he does is to ask the advice of a god, Apollo at Delphi. Apollo is extremely helpful, for he tells Khremylos how to find Wealth; and Wealth reveals that it is the malice of Zeus that blinded him and so kept Khremylos and other good men poor.

WEALTH. Zeus did this to me, out of spite to men.
    You see, when I was young, I made a threat
    That I would only go to honest, wise,
    And well-behaved men; and he blinded me
    So that I wouldn't know which ones those were.
    He is so very spiteful to the good.
KHREMYLOS. And yet it's only from the good and honest
    That he gets worship!
WEALTH.   That's right.
KHREMYLOS.   Well, what now?
    If you could get your sight back, as of old,
    Would you begin avoiding bad men?
WEALTH.   Yes.
KHREMYLOS. You'd go to honest men then?
WEALTH.   Certainly.
    I haven't seen them for a long time now.
KARION. No wonder; nor have I, and I'm not blind!

(Wealth 87–99)

So the reason why the few good men are poor is only that one god is spiteful to them, but unfortunately he is the god who rules the others. Wealth himself is well-disposed towards honest men, and Khremylos' brilliant idea is to circumvent Zeus by supporting Wealth against him. He proves, by a comic type of proof, that Wealth can be more powerful than Zeus. Wealth after some misgivings agrees, Asklepios also co-operates by restoring Wealth's sight, and so Zeus is defeated and enrols himself as a follower of Wealth (1189–90).

When the story is summarized thus, it appears that there is no opposition between Khremylos and the gods in general. Only Zeus is the enemy (until he changes sides at the end), whereas Apollo and Asklepios assist Khremylos. On this basis it is perfectly logical that Khremylos and other good men continue to honour the gods and make sacrifices, as we are told in two places that they do (497, 819–20), although naturally they cease making sacrifices to Zeus (1173–83, quoted on p. 343). Yet one passage remains inconsistent with this: the scene with Hermes, in which we are told that no one any longer makes sacrifices to any of the gods because they failed to take good care of men (1111–19, quoted on p. 342). That seems grossly unfair to Apollo and Asklepios at least, and we have to acknowledge that in this matter also different parts of the play do not fit together very well.

Despite a certain amount of disjointedness in its moral and religious themes, and a certain lack of energy in its humour,[33] *Wealth* is a play that would obviously be attractive to the ordinary Athenian spectator because of its sympathy with his own circumstances. Farmers could identify themselves with Dikaiopolis or Trygaios, but townsmen as well as countrymen could identify themselves with Khremylos. All would enjoy his complaints about poverty and his efforts to overcome the apparent unfairness of life. But the unfairness of life is attributed simply to the malice of Zeus, with no analysis of political or social or economic causes of the maldistribution of wealth; and the remedy which is found is a fantastic one, getting the better of Zeus, not a solution that can be adopted in real life.

---

[33] I do not know what Olson *HSCP* 93 (1990) 224 means by 'the typically Aristophanic slapstick humor'. Karion's antics at the shrine of Asklepios are merely narrated, not presented on-stage. Possibly the Young Man chases the Old Woman with his torch (1052), but otherwise it is hard to detect any slapstick in this play.

I 5

Aristophanes and Athens

Each play of Aristophanes has its own subject and its own comic aims, which have been outlined in the preceding chapters. They were not the same from first to last. Times changed; no doubt his personal character and opinions changed too in the course of forty years. But there are at least a few respects in which we can see that he maintained a particular opinion or attitude over a long period. One policy or social class or individual is regularly treated with more favour or sympathy than another.

One such preference is for old men as against young men.[1] Old age begins in the forties (Greek has no word corresponding to the modern English use of 'middle-aged'), and in this sense the chief character, with whom the audience is expected to have some kind of sympathy, is often old: Dikaiopolis, Strepsiades, Philokleon, Trygaios, Peisetairos, Euripides' Relative, Khremylos. These characters are not all alike in other ways; for example Strepsiades is stupid but Peisetairos is clever. Nor are they necessarily in the right. In *Wasps* Philokleon is quite wrong in his mad enthusiasm for the lawcourts, while his son Bdelykleon presents the sensible view. Yet all spectators and readers like Philokleon and find Bdelykleon comparatively dull. The choruses of old men in *Akharnians* and *Wasps* are wrong-headed in the early scenes, but they are patriotic, and as the play goes on they see the error of their ways; their hearts are in the right place. In the parabasis they present pleas for more favourable treatment of old men and complaints about the selfish young: the old men fought for Athens in the days gone by, but now degenerate young men harass them in the courts and deprive them of their livelihood (*Akharnians* 676–718, *Wasps* 1060–1121). Both passages

---

[1] For a more detailed study of this topic, laying perhaps too much emphasis on 'rejuvenation', see T. K. Hubbard in *Old Age in Greek and Latin Literature* (ed. T. M. Falkner and J. de Luce, Albany 1989) 90–113.

invite sympathy for the old men, not laughter at them. It is possible, though not certain, that the lost *Old Age* also had a chorus of old men sympathetically presented. Even in the latest extant play the honest men are old (*Wealth* 759, 787); but on the whole, interestingly, the favourable treatment of old men is most prominent in the earlier plays, written when Aristophanes himself was young. There are no comparable passages of sympathy for young men in any of the plays, early or late.

Another preference is for the countryside as against the town. Several of the characters intended to attract the audience's sympathy are countrymen. In *Akharnians* Dikaiopolis hates living in the town and makes peace in order to get back to his rural home, and Democracy likewise returns to the country when he obtains peace (*Horsemen* 805–7, 1394–5). In both *Banqueters* and *Clouds* the naïve countryman discovers the degenerate trickery of the sophists in town, and the contrast between Strepsiades' rustic life and his wife's urban habits is written so as to imply that the former is preferable (*Clouds* 43–55). *Peace* ends in a celebration of agricultural prosperity, and the same motif recurs in the extant fragments of the lost *Farmers* and *Islands*.

> You fool, you fool! In peace there is all this:
> A country life, down on his little farm,
> Free from all business in the Agora,
> Possessing a pair of oxen of his own;
> Next, listening to the bleating of the sheep
> And to new wine being strained into a bowl;
> And then, for dinner, eating finch and thrush,
> Not waiting in the Agora for fish
> That's three days old, and costs the earth, and has
> Been weighed up by a cheating fishmonger!
>
> (*Islands* fr. 402)

All this has been interpreted as showing that Aristophanes was a countryman himself,[2] but it does not really do so. If he could sympathize with old men when he was young, he could also sympathize with countrymen while living in the town. His deme was Kydathenaion, which proves that his family resided in central Athens when the demes were organized in the late sixth century; we may assume that he still lived there, in the absence of evidence to the

---

[2] Croiset *Ar. and Pol. Parties* 9.

contrary. Yet he does reveal an affection for country people and country life.

This sympathy for countrymen is related to his obvious desire for peace, because countrymen, through the destruction of their farms, suffered more than townsmen from the war. The longing for peace is prominent especially in three plays: in *Akharnians* Dikaiopolis argues that it was a mistake to make war on Sparta and triumphantly secures his own treaty; in *Peace* Trygaios rescues Peace and enjoys the prosperity she brings; in *Lysistrata* the women carry out an ingenious scheme to obtain peace. The lost *Farmers* seems also to have had a similar theme. This does not mean that Aristophanes is a pacifist. His old men are proud of their fighting in the Persian Wars (*Wasps* 1071–90). It is only the war against Sparta that he dislikes, and his jokes about Sparta are on the whole less hostile to that city than might have been expected.[3] This has led to the suggestion that he was a 'Cimonian', supporting the policy of Greek collaboration against the Persians which was championed by the mid-fifth-century general Kimon.[4] The name is not a good one: Kimon died around 450 BC, and we cannot know what his policy would have been if he had lived in the time of Aristophanes. But it is true that a few passages imply approval of co-operation among the Greek states. Trygaios and Hermes urge on different nationalities to help haul Peace out of her prison (*Peace* 464–507). Lysistrata, in lines which are to some extent but perhaps not wholly undermined by their farcical context (cf. pp. 244–6), emphasizes the religious kinship of Greeks, who would do better to fight the Persians than one another.

> And now I've got you here, I'll reprimand you
> Together, as is right. You share the sprinkling
> Of holy water, like one family,
> At Pytho, Pylai, and Olympia—
> How many other altars I could name!—
> And yet, with foreign enemy forces near,
> You are demolishing Greek men and cities!

(Lysistrata 1128–34)

What other preferences in politics can be discerned? It has some-

---

[3] Cf. D. Harvey in *The Shadow of Sparta* (ed. A. Powell and S. Hodkinson, London 1994) 35–58.

[4] De Ste. Croix *Origins* 358; cf. E. Lévy *Athènes devant la défaite de 404* (Paris 1976) 158–60.

times been supposed that Aristophanes is against democracy and supports those who established an oligarchy in 411 BC, on the grounds that he satirizes the democratic Assembly (*Akharnians, Horsemen, Women at the Assembly*), Council (*Horsemen*), and lawcourts (*Wasps*), and supports the re-enfranchisement of disfranchised supporters of the oligarchy (*Frogs*). But that is a mistake. The plea in *Frogs* 688 is to make all citizens equal, not to give a privileged position to a few. In the other plays it is not his purpose to attack the democratic institutions as such. He never suggests that the Assembly, Council, or juries should be abolished. In *Women at the Assembly* the conversion of the courts into dining halls is a comic consequence of the abolition of crime; there is no suggestion that crime, while it exists, should be judged by anyone other than the existing juries. His complaint is rather that the citizens are not at present making good use of their power. They are taken in by clever speeches, which they ought to treat more critically, and they vote as the politicians tell them to. When Aristophanes describes the Councillors scrambling out of a meeting to buy sprats (*Horsemen* 640–82) and the jurors acquitting defendants who entertain them (*Wasps* 566–82), he is satirizing their tendency to think only of immediate gratification and not of long-term advantage. They ought to take their power more seriously. What he wants is more democracy, not less.[5]

When it comes to individual politicians, although any prominent man is good for a joke, it is obvious that he attacks some much more than others. In the early plays Kleon is the main target. Aristophanes' campaign against Kleon has been expounded in earlier chapters; here I summarize it. *Babylonians* in 426 BC criticized Kleon in some way, perhaps in connection with policy towards the cities of the Athenian Empire. Kleon angrily denounced Kallistratos, the director, in a speech to the Council, but no formal punishment followed; probably the Council resolved to take no action. But resentment smouldered. In 425 *Akharnians* alluded to the dispute, and expressed defiance of Kleon (659–64); and in 424 Aristophanes, now presenting a play on his own account for the first time, launched against

---

[5] Although Croiset's book *Aristophanes and the Political Parties at Athens* uses a more rigid concept of political parties than is properly applicable to classical Athens, he is certainly right in his main conclusion that Aristophanes never supports any opposition to democracy.

Kleon in *Horsemen* the fiercest onslaught to which he ever subjected any individual. Kleon retaliated by a speech and possibly a prosecution, and Aristophanes in some way withdrew or apologized (see p. 176). In 423, in the first version of *Clouds*, Kleon seems to have been mentioned only briefly; but in 422 Aristophanes assailed him again in *Wasps* with an exposure of his influence over the juries. It was later in that year that Kleon was killed at Amphipolis, and so Aristophanes' campaign against him ended.

Aristophanes' hostility to Kleon is related to his belief that the war against Sparta is unnecessary and should be stopped, for one of his complaints about Kleon is that he obstructs efforts to make peace. But the criticisms range far beyond this. (For a list see pp. 108–11.) And they are not merely jokes, but are intended to damage Kleon's reputation and deter the Athenians from supporting him in the Assembly and courts; that is clear enough from Kleon's reactions. Aristophanes regarded his campaign against Kleon as one of his greatest services to Athens.

> And at once, from the very beginning, he boldly faced up to the jagged-
> toothed monster . . .
> But he still carries on the campaign even now to defend you.

(Wasps 1031, 1037)

He never assailed any one other politician to the same extent— not even Kleophon, although Kleophon towards the end of the Peloponnesian War opposed peace at least as firmly as Kleon had done in the earlier years. By that time Aristophanes seems to have given up hope that a negotiated peace was a practical proposition. *Lysistrata* is a fantasy about making peace rather than a serious proposal, while in *Frogs* a peace treaty is never mentioned. The question at the end of that play is whether Athens can be saved from military or naval defeat; and the answer suggested, hesitantly but seriously, is that it might be saved by recalling Alkibiades (see pp. 293–7).

It would, however, be wrong to see Aristophanes as a consistent supporter of Alkibiades. In the early plays there are only brief references to him, just enough to show that in the 420s he was already familiar as a speaker in the Assembly and courts;[6] and the

---

[6] *Banqueters* fr. 205 (quoted on p. 28), *Akharnians* 716, *Wasps* 44–6.

fact that he was an established orator by then refutes the modern suggestion that young Pheidippides in *Clouds* somehow represents him.[7] After *Wasps* 44–6 he is never named in the extant plays until *Frogs* seventeen years later.[8] Evidently Aristophanes never saw Alkibiades as being, like Kleon, a serious threat to Athens and its democracy, but it was only at a late stage that he came round to the view that the city's salvation might lie in him.

Thus we can infer from the plays, with more or less confidence, Aristophanes' opinions and preferences on several aspects of Athenian politics and society. I return finally to the problem raised in Chapter 1: did he intend his plays to influence public opinion and lead to political or social action? Anyone who holds an opinion on a subject is likely to be pleased if other people come to share it. Not all changes of opinion lead to action, but some naturally do. In several plays Aristophanes does assert plainly that he is teaching the Athenians what is right, and is doing them good; see the quotations on pp. 4–5. Although in theory many of those passages could be interpreted as elaborate irony, there is really no good reason for adopting this contorted interpretation. It is much more likely that they mean what they say.

I conclude that Aristophanes did sometimes want to influence the Athenians. In particular, he hoped that *Akharnians* would make them seriously consider opening negotiations for peace, that *Horsemen* would make them more critical of Kleon's speeches in the Assembly and Council, that *Clouds* would make them more sceptical about science and rhetoric, that *Wasps* would make the jurors take their responsibilities more seriously, and that *Frogs* would encourage the setting aside of past quarrels in order to save Athens from defeat in the war. *Banqueters* and *Babylonians* too, as far as we can tell from the scanty evidence we have, made serious points, and altogether it is noticeable that such points are more prominent in the plays of the

---

[7] D. Ambrosino *MC* 21–2 (1986–7) 101–5 points out the differences between Pheidippides and Alkibiades. Cf. R. F. Moorton *GRBS* 29 (1988) 346–7, I. C. Storey *AJP* 114 (1993) 81–2.

[8] *Birds* 145–7 is a joke about the *Salaminia* which would bring Alkibiades to mind, though it does not name him. It is wrong to see implied allusions to him in *Lysistrata*; cf. Henderson *Lysistrata* xxiv, Sommerstein *Lysistrata* 2 n. 14. The attempts of M. Vickers *Historia* 38 (1989) 41–65, 267–99 to show that the heroes of *Birds* and *Women at the Thesmophoria* represent Alkibiades are unconvincing and have found few supporters.

420s than later. The political pleas in *Frogs* are confined to the parabasis and the last part of the play, and in the other late plays the serious elements are briefer or non-existent. Aristophanes may indeed have been quite an earnest young man, who as he became older gradually realized that he would never be able to set the world to rights. Such a psychological development is common. And yet that is not adequate as a final verdict, for the early plays are fun too. The unique achievement of Aristophanes was to give good advice to the Athenians while never ceasing to entertain them.

INDEX

Adonis 243
advocates 162–5
Aeschylus 288–97
  Niobe 289
Agathon 253–7
Agora 63–5, 93, 110
Agyrrhios 302, 305–7, 321, 325
Aigina 33 n. 11, 39 n. 23
Aigospotamoi, battle of 297
air 121–3
Akestor 199
Akharnai 48
Akropolis 232–5
Alkibiades 159–60, 222–3, 293–7, 354–5
ambassadors, *see* envoys
Anakreon 255–6
Anaxagoras 119–24
Andokides 303
animals on-stage 166, 274, 280
Anthesteria 280–1
Antiphon 129–30, 173, 286
Araros 35
Arginousai, battle of 279, 284, 286, 294
Argos 99, 180, 184
Aristophanes:
  Aiolosikon 35
  Akharnians 34–79
    5–8: 57, 95–7
    19–27: 49
    32–6: 47
    54–8: 271
    65–76: 50
    118: 257 n. 15
    358–67: 57
    377–82: 30, 42–4
    440–4: 77
    497–556: 4, 16, 31, 42–4, 59–67, 78, 186–92
    558–62: 67
    593–614: 68–70

626–7: 67
628–33: 4, 38–42
630–58: 4, 31–4
659–64: 44
729–30: 71–2
734–9: 72
753–63: 72–3
1018–36: 47, 76
1051–3: 76
1073–83: 68
schol. 6: 96
schol. 67: 25
schol. 378: 31, 43–4
schol. 446: 56 n. 16
Amphiaraos 34
Babylonians 30–44
Banqueters 27–9, 34–40
Birds 199–228
  9–11: 199
  30–45: 199–200
  69–83: 203–4
  100–1: 204
  108–16: 200
  117–22: 203
  693–703: 207
  785–9: 10
  793–6: 15
  1172–4: 216
  1344–8: 213
  1360–71: 213
  1451–65: 215
  1470–81: 24
  1532–43: 217
  1583–5: 224
  hyp. ii: 225
  schol. 553: 225
  schol. 1297: 25
Clouds 113–49
  7: 89
  16–18: 114
  88–118: 115–16, 120

Aristophanes (*cont.*):
  Clouds (*cont.*):
    144–66: 117
    222–34: 118–21
    346–54: 23–5
    366–81: 122
    439–56: 125
    518–26: 134
    528–33: 27, 40
    547: 3
    549–50: 112
    731–4: 22
    882–5: 126, 143
    973–8: 138
    1002–4: 140
    1107–12: 143
    1043–54: 140
    1076–82: 141
    1085–1104: 142
    1113–14: 148
    1303–20: 147
    1409–32: 127
    1452–66: 149
    1508–9: 124
    hyp. i: 135–6, 143–4
    schol. 520: 134 n. 41
    schol. 543: 144
    schol. 889: 137
    schol. 1115: 148
  Farmers 351–2
  Frogs 274–300
    38–51: 275
    58–65: 277
    209–20: 281
    354–7: 283
    398–403: 283
    686–7: 4–5
    686–705: 285–6
    734: 4
    1008–12: 5, 290
    1036–8: 22–3
    1049–55: 291
    1422–34: 294
    1446–8: 296
    1454–9: 295
    1463–5: 296
    hyp. i: 298
  Gerytades 274 n. 1
  Horsemen 35–41, 80–112
    40–68: 84–6

    125–44: 89–90
    178–219: 92–3
    225–9: 94
    230–3: 88
    284–99: 98
    417–26: 98
    509–10: 4
    512–16: 35–6, 41
    541–4: 35–6, 38
    551–64: 17–18
    580: 94 n. 29
    667–82: 100–1
    919: 86
    1111–30: 106
    1192–206: 102–3
    1369–72: 23
    schol. 44: 81
    schol. 226: 95
  Islands 351
  Knights see Horsemen
  Kokalos 35
  Lysistrata 229–50
    1–4: 243
    99–124: 230
    170–9: 231
    240–6: 231–2
    271–85: 233–4
    387–9: 243
    420–3: 235
    433–62: 271
    567–97: 235–9
    638–47: 239–40
    742–7: 247
    1025–41: 249–50
    1050–3: 14–15
    1128–34: 352
    1137–56: 244–5
  Merchant-ships 75
  Old Age 351
  Peace 180–98
    50–3: 15
    173–6: 181
    203–20: 182
    601–56: 186–92
    966: 14
    1075–6: 196
    1111–12: 196
    hyp. iii: 9
  Ploutos see Wealth
  Proagon 34 n. 12

Storks 325
Wasps 150–79
  54–66: 4, 112, 176–7
  67–73: 150
  87–110: 152–3
  291–311: 154–5
  488–92: 160
  552–8: 164–5
  592: 24
  650–1: 161
  665–711: 161–2
  736–40: 22
  907–30: 169
  950–9: 166
  968–72: 168
  1015–22: 4, 37–8
  1018: 35 n. 13
  1029–31: 170, 354
  1037: 354
  1043–50: 145
  1102–21: 155–6
  1284–91: 176
  1450–61: 175
  1476–96: 20–1
Wealth 324–49
  28–44: 327–8
  87–99: 348
  160–9: 329
  170–80: 324–5
  234–44: 331
  265–7: 330
  389–97: 332
  512–15: 333
  664–95: 336–7
  802–18: 339–40
  1042–59: 341
  1111–19: 342–3
  1173–83: 343
  1186–90: 343–4
Women at the Assembly 301–23
  163–8: 305
  173–88: 306
  193–6: 302
  202–3: 302
  205–7: 306
  209–12: 307
  221–40: 307–8
  581–7: 322
  590–3: 313
  746–52: 316

  853–62: 316
  1039–42: 317–18
  1049–51: 318
  1072–85: 319
  1154–62: 11–12
Women at the Thesmophoria 251–73
  148–70: 255–6
  198–201: 254
  331–9: 262
  395–7: 15
  466–519: 61
  476–89: 263–4
  502–16: 264–5
  626–35: 261
  785–829: 265–6
  789–807: 15
  871–80: 268
  930–4: 271
Aristotle _Ath. Pol._ 28: 82
  Poetics 1449a 11–13: 21
  Rhetoric 1402a 22–8: 128
Arkhon 9, 11, 40, 151
arrephoros 239–40
Artemis 240
Asklepios 335–9
Aspasia 65–6, 187–8
Assembly 48–52, 70, 84–6, 106, 260–2,
    301–3, 306–9
atheism 124–5, 146
Athena 218, 233, 240–3, 252, 344
Athenaios 494d–e: 30
audience 7–26
aulos 20, 205 n. 1

babies 264–5
baking 120
Bakis 195–6, 210
Basileus 9, 40
'bears' (girls) 240
birds 202–9
Boiotia 74, 302
Boule, _see_ Council
boys: in audience 14
    on-stage 154, 166, 197
Brasidas 180, 183
Brauronia 240

cavalry, _see_ Horsemen
charcoal 48
charge, for admission 13–14

citizenship 236–9, 279
clothes, *see* costume
Cloudcuckooland 209, 226–7
coinage 287
colonies 237–8
communism 312–23
competitors, number of 8–10
conspiracy, accusations of 158–9
constipation 311
Corinthian War 301–3
cosmogony 207–8
costume 21, 155, 171, 204, 304, 310–11
Council 12, 31, 42–4, 100–1, 194, 262
countrymen 351–2
crane, *see* mekhane

dance 19–21, 174
deme-judges 114 n. 5
Demeter 259, 282, 330
Demosthenes:
  18.28: 13
  21.10: 10
Demosthenes (general): 82–3, 87–8,
  107–8
Derketes 76
Dikaiarkhos 298–9
Diogenes of Apollonia 120–2
Dionysia:
  at Peiraieus: 7, 10
  rural: 7, 13
  town 7–11, 15–16, 213
Dionysios 326
Dionysos 18, 30, 274–7, 280–2
  in the Marshes 8, 280
Diopeithes 124
director 36–42
disfranchisement 237, 286, 298–9

education 28–9, 125–33, 138–9
egg 208
Ekklesia, *see* Assembly
ekkyklema 1
Eleusinian Mysteries, *see* Mysteries
Eleusinion 259–60
Empire, Athenian 16, 31–2, 63–6, 109,
  161–3, 189–90, 211–12, 215, 230,
  238
envoys 32–3, 49–52, 69–70
Epikharmos 136 n. 49
Euaion 311, 314

Euegoros, law of 10–11
Eukrates 90–1
Euphiletos 264
Eupolis 41, 42 n. 30, 134
Euripides 53, 177, 252–3, 266–70, 288–
  97
  Andromeda 268–9, 272
  Bellerophon 181
  Helen 267–8, 272
  Iphigeneia in Tauris 269 n. 45, 272
  Palamedes 267
  Stheneboia 291
  Telephos 53–62, 266–7
Eurykles 37 n. 18
euthyna (examination of officials) 164,
  167–8
Exekestides 199

festivals, dramatic 7–11
Four Hundred (411 BC) 251, 284–6

Giants 225
gods 17–18, 216–21, 277, 347–9
Gorgias 222
Gryttos (or Grypos) 109

hair, long 94, 159, 234
helots 244–5
Hera 218
Herakleides 302
Herakles 18, 29, 169–70, 177, 218–22,
  274–7
Hermai, mutilation of 25 n. 57, 221, 223
Hermes 182, 221, 342–3
Herodotos 62–3
Hesiod 207–8
Hierokles 194–8
Hippias 244–5
Hippon 120–1
Hipponax 330
homosexuality 139, 254–7
Horsemen 94–7
hybris 173–4

Iakkhos 282–3
Iris 216
Isokrates 7.52: 13 n. 23

judges (of plays) 11–12
jurors 151–65, 175

Kallistratos 34–43
Karkinos' sons 21, 174
Kephisophon 295
Kephisos, river 283
Kharminos 266
Kimon 244–5, 352
Kinesias 214, 243–4, 295
King's Eye 51
Kleainetos 81
Kleigenes 285
Kleisthenes 257, 276
Kleokritos 295
Kleomenes 233–4, 245
Kleon 30–3, 42–5, 80–112, 124, 135,
     159–80, 183, 191–2, 353–5
Kleonymos 23–5, 197
Kleophon 284–5, 288, 300, 354
Konon 302
Kore 259, 282
kottabos 64 n. 31
Krates 35, 344
Kratinos 35, 283, 344
Kritias 299
Kydathenaion 81, 97, 351

Lakhes 167–9
Lamakhos 67–71, 184, 197–8
lawcourts 151–67
laws 211, 220, 278
leather 81, 110
Lenaia 7–11, 15–16
Life of Aristophanes 298
Lykon 173
Lysander 297
Lysikles 90–1
Lysimakhe 241
Lysistratos 173

Magnes 35
masks 87–8, 104 n. 43, 258, 304, 309
Megakles 69 n. 44
Megara 60–6, 71–3, 177, 184
Megarian decree 63–6, 186–7
mekhane 1, 118 n. 13, 181
metics 14, 237
Meton 210–11
Mnesilokhos 253
music 19–21, 205, 214, 284
Myrrhine 241–4
Mysteries, Eleusinian 282–4

profanation of 25 n. 57, 223, 284

naval service 104–5, 279, 286–7
Neokleides 311, 325, 336
Nikias 83, 87–8, 107, 180, 223
     Peace of 180, 197, 229
Nikomakhos 300

obscenity 21–2
old age 350–1
Old and New day 114, 126
oracles 89–90, 194–6, 210
orphans 213

Pamphilos 325
Pantakles 22, 24
Paphlagonia 86
Patrokleides, decree of 298–9
Pauson 326
peace, personified 105, 192–3
Peisandros 236–7, 286
Peloponnesian War:
     causes 59–67, 186–92
     course 46–8, 72–3, 82–3, 229–30,
          279
     negotiations for peace 108, 180, 197,
          284–5
Perikles:
     foreign policy 46–8, 65–7, 186–90,
          296
     law on marriage 220
     personality and friends 65, 124, 187–
          9
     theoric payments 13–14
Persia 50–1, 262, 352
personal ridicule 22–6
phallus 21–2
Pheidias 186–9
Pherekrates 11 n. 19, 214, 344
Philokles 202–3
Philokhoros 302
Philomela 202
Philonides 34–41
Philoxenos of Kythera 326
Phrynikhos (politician) 173, 285–6
Phrynikhos (tragic dramatist) 20, 255–
     6
Pindar 32 n. 10, 210
pipe, see aulos
Plataians 279

Plato 130–3
  Apology 18b–d: 131
  Laws 659a: 12 n. 22
  Republic 5: 314–15
Platon (comic dramatist) 9, 25 n. 57, 41, 300
Plutarch:
  Nikias 8: 82
  Perikles 9: 13–14
Pnyx 49, 84, 259–60
'poet' as 'maker' 39–41
Poseidon 17, 218–22
poverty 313–14, 332–5, 346–7
priestesses 240–2
priests 209–10, 337–8, 343–4
Probouloi:
  in Athens 234–5
  in Megara 72–3
Prokne 202–5
Prometheus 216–18
Protagoras 123–4, 128
Proteas 268
Prytaneis 49, 271
Pylos 82–3, 86–7, 229–30

reading 89 n. 16
religion 17–18, 121–5, 146, 223, 239–43, 342–4, 347–9
  see also gods
rhetoric 29, 125–30

Sabazios 243
Sakas 199
Salaminia 305, 355 n. 8
sausages 91
science 117–21
Sicilian expedition 222–3
Simon 97
Skira 303
Skythian archers 270–3
slander, law of 25–6
slaves 277–9, 286–7
  in audience 14
snakes 338
Socrates 130–3
sophists, see education
Sophocles 288
  Tereus 202–5
Sparta 159, 231, 234, 244–6, 352
  see also Peloponnesian War

Strattis 25 n. 57, 243
sycophants 74–5, 214–15, 340
symposium 171–4
Syracuse 222–3
Syrakosios, decree of 25–6

Telekleides 344
Tereus 202–5
Thargelia 10
theatre 7–8
Thebes 302
Themistokles 89, 105
Theophrastos, On Perception 44: 121
Theopompos 95–6
theoric payments 13–14
Theoros 50–1
Theramenes 284, 286, 289–90, 299–300
Thesmophoria 259–61
Thespis 20
Thirty (404 BC) 298–301
Thrace 50–1
Thrasyboulos 302–3, 325
Thucydides 1.67: 63–6
  1.139: 63–6
  2.14: 46
  3.36: 82
  4.27–39: 83
  8.54: 236
thunder 120
Timotheos 325
Titans 225
Triballians 216–17
tyranny, accusations of 158–60, 252

vines 47, 193

war, personified 183
wealth, personified 329–31
wine 52, 246, 263
women:
  in audience 14–15
  in plays 229, 246–50, 252–3, 257–66, 303–23

Xenophon 130–1

young men 319, 350–1

Zea 335–6
Zeus 121–3, 216–22, 328, 342–9